# Christianity In India: An Historical Narrative

## Sir John William Kaye

E. Augusta Hardcastle.
May 1859.

316

13

# CHRISTIANITY IN INDIA:

## AN HISTORICAL NARRATIVE.

BY

## JOHN WILLIAM KAYE,

AUTHOR OF "THE LIFE OF LORD METCALFE," "THE LIFE OF SIR JOHN
MALCOLM," "THE HISTORY OF THE WAR IN AFGHANISTAN," ETC.

LONDON:

SMITH, ELDER AND CO., 65, CORNHILL.

1859.

[*The right of translation is reserved.*]

BY DEDICATING THIS VOLUME MOST AFFECTIONATELY TO

ALEXANDER DUFF,

I SEEK ONLY TO EXPRESS MY ADMIRATION OF HIS CHARACTER

AND MY GRATITUDE FOR HIS KINDNESS,

NOT TO ASSOCIATE HIS HONOURED NAME WITH OPINIONS

WHICH HE MAY NOT WHOLLY APPROVE.

# CONTENTS.

---

## CHAPTER I.

## CHAPTER II.

## CHAPTER III.

## CHAPTER IV.

## CHAPTER V.

# CHAPTER VI.

# CHAPTER VII.

# CHAPTER VIII.

# CHAPTER IX.

# CHAPTER X.

# CHAPTER XI.

# CHAPTER XII.

# CONCLUSION.

# ERRATA.

Page 41, line 16, *for* " heathen's minds," *read* " heathens' minds."

Page 65, head line, *for* " FRENCH," *read* " FIRST."

Page 228, line 3 from bottom, *for* "fraudulent banker and low swindler,"
*read* " fraudulent *debtor* and low swindler."

Page 432, line 9, *for* " other agency from that," *read* " other agency *for* that."

In some places, in the earlier part of this work, the name " Udny " is mis-
printed " Udney."

# PREFACE.

I HAVE been thinking, for many years, of such a work as this—or of one, perhaps, of greater pretensions. But for circumstances affecting my daily life, and limiting my powers of literary labour, I might have indented more largely upon the patience of the reader. As it is, I give this volume to the world, with some confidence that the interest of the subject will atone for any inefficiency in its treatment.

When the great rebellion of 1857 was at its height, and every mail was bringing from India fresh tidings of disasters suffered or retrieved, I often found in society that men would turn away from the consideration of the most important political events, or the most touching personal incidents, to discuss the great subject of the future place of India among the Christian nations of the world. The missionary seemed, even then, to overlay the military element in men's minds; and now the Indian question has become so largely a religious question, that many have ceased to regard it in any other light. A profound interest, indeed, has been awakened, and I trust that it is an enduring

one.  But, with this interest, it has appeared to me
that there has been mingled much error.  A tendency
to run into extremes has been observable generally
in the controversies which have grown out of the
question, both in private society and in the public
press.  At one time, indeed, the disputants were
divided into two great classes—those who regarded
the mutiny of 1857 as the natural result of our
religious and social innovations, and who, therefore,
suggested the discontinuance of all efforts for the
civilization and evangelization of the people of
India ; and those who, looking upon it as a
chastisement inflicted upon us for the neglect of
our Christian duties, were, therefore, eager to
atone for the remissness of the past by the
activity of the future, and who counselled a course of
vigorous iconoclasm — an unhesitating and undis-
criminating crusade against Error, as something to
be swept away by the strong hand of the dominant
race.  I found, too, that coupled with this extravagance of sentiment there was much ignorance regarding antecedent events ; and I thought, therefore,
that any contribution towards the available means of
forming a more correct judgment with respect to the
Past and the Future of Christianity in India might
be serviceable to the Public.

In  this  belief,  collecting  the  materials  already
within my reach and going in search of others—

exhuming what I had written upon the subject in bygone years, and selecting therefrom whatever appeared to be most worthy of preservation—I set about the preparation of this work. I felt, as it proceeded, that the very moderate views which it enunciated would be palatable to no party—that I might be accused of blowing hot and cold, of halting between two opinions, and giving an uncertain sound. But now that I have brought it to a close, I am surprised to find how much, during the year which has elapsed since I commenced it, public opinion, whether in one extreme or the other, has moderated, and how many people have, so to speak, closed in upon the pivot where I once found myself almost alone.

I have spoken of this volume as merely a contribution to the literature of Christianity in India. I desire that it may be regarded and judged as nothing more. It does not pretend to be a complete history of the efforts which have been made by Christians of various denominations to diffuse the light of the Gospel among the heathen nations of the East. Many very worthy efforts may be found unrecorded, and many very worthy labourers may be found unnoticed in this volume. Anything like a sufficient record of all that has been done would demand not one but many volumes. I have aimed at the production not of an exhaustive, but of a suggestive work; and I hope that it will be judged fairly—not by what it does not, but by what it does contain. No one knows better than I do myself how much more I might have said in every chapter of this work to give completeness to this record.

It will be observed that the subject has been treated biographically in the earlier part of the work. I believe that this mode of treatment, whilst imparting a living interest to the narrative better calculated than anything else to enchain the attention of the reader, is at the same time the most truthful form in which the progress of Christianity in India can be represented. It is to the "advance of individual minds"—to the energy of individual efforts—that we owe the much or the little that has been done; and it is in the thoughts that were taking shape in the minds of these pioneers of the Gospel that we must trace the dawning of Christianity in the East. The first difficulties fairly overcome—the thicket cleared, the road made, the first step taken—the rest depends comparatively little upon individual character and individual exertion. There may at later periods have been many Xaviers and Ziegenbalgs—many Careys and Martyns, but their individuality is lost in the crowd. The history, therefore, as it advances, naturally tends towards diffusion and generalisation. The personal landmarks disappear altogether, and we look only at results in the gross.

This much with regard to the method of the work. A few words now with respect to the materials of which it is composed. The reader will see at once that these are of various kinds, printed, manuscript, and traditional. The published works to which I am indebted are generally named in the foot-notes. They are too numerous for me to indicate them here. Mr. Hough's elaborate "History of Christianity in India" deserves, however, prominent mention by all later writers on the subject. I must also especially acknowledge my obligations to Mr. Marshman, who kindly placed the first volume of his "History of the Serampore Mission" at my disposal many months before its publication, and to which I am indebted for nearly all the information contained in the Seventh Chapter of this book. I have consulted manuscript documents, public and private, whenever I have thought that there was anything to be found in them; but I make no boast of the exclusiveness of my materials. The biographers of the last half century have well nigh exhausted the private correspondence of the Christian worthies of the time; and the zeal of such good men as Sir Robert Inglis and Mr. Arthur Kinnaird, with the consenting voice of Parliament, has made nearly all the official papers illustrative of the subject accessible to the public.

Partly in justice to the public, partly in justice to

myself, I should mention, in conclusion, that, although the greater portion of this volume was written last year, and is now, for the first time, offered to the public, some parts of it were written many years ago, and published, in the shape of review-essays, but with a view to future collection. It is right that this should be stated, in order that the reader may know what is offered to him; and that the writer may not be supposed to have borrowed from others what probably they have borrowed from him.

J. W. K.

*London, February,* 1859.

# CHRISTIANITY IN INDIA.

## CHAPTER I.

The Ante-Protestant Era—Legend of St. Thomas—Pantænus—Frumentius —The Syrian Churches—Francis Xavier—Inroads of the Papacy— Menezes—The Jesuit Missions.

IT is my design that this volume shall contain a popular sketch of the progress of Christianity in India; more especially as it has been affected by the efforts of the Protestant Church and the measures of the British Government. Glancing at the legendary history of the earliest Christian ministrations in the East, I shall touch upon the establishment of the Syrian Churches, upon the first efforts of the Papacy, and upon those great and important facts the Jesuits' missions in the East; until, arriving at the period of British connection with India, I come to speak of the doings of our own countrymen at home and abroad, aided by the efforts of their Danish and American fellow-labourers in the same vineyard. I shall dwell upon the progress of the Anglican Church in India; upon the advancement of practical Chris-

B

tianity as exhibited in the lives of our Anglo-Indian brethren; and upon what is called the "traditionary policy" of the British Government in the East. I shall endeavour to show in what manner Christianity and Heathenism have severally received support or discouragement from that Government; and shall conclude the sketch with some observations on the manner in which the great question has been affected by the calamities which have recently filled so many hearts with fear and so many homes with mourning.

At the outset of his journey the historical inquirer finds himself groping in the dim regions which lie between fact and fable. He cannot clearly discover who were the first apostles who carried to the shores of the Indian ocean the truth of the new religion which Christ had bequeathed to the world. He knows that from the very commencement of the Christian æra there was constant interchange of worldly goods between the shores of the Red Sea and the southern and western coasts of the great Peninsula of India. It was by the enterprise and the ambition of the Macedonian Alexander that a knowledge of the countries of the East had first been opened out to the empires of the West, that the gates of commerce had been unlocked, and the people of India and the colonists of Egypt brought into frequent intercourse with each other. The great city which he founded became in time the mart of the commerce of the East and the stronghold of the new religion of the West. But the glory of the Greek empire had passed away. The advent of the Redeemer found the Romans masters of the world; and Alexandria a Roman city.

With the increased demand for foreign luxuries, there grew new incentives to commercial enterprise. Every year, at the time of the summer solstice, a fleet of more than a hundred merchant ships sailed, under the Roman flag, out of the port of Myos Hormus on the Red Sea, and steered for the rich pearl-fisheries of Ceylon and the spicy coasts of Malabar. In exchange for the rich silks, the costly jewels, and the aromatic treasures of India and Arabia, the Romans gave their precious metals and something more precious still. They carried out tidings of the birth and sufferings of the Redeemer, and of the new faith that he had bequeathed to the world.

Of the first Indian missionaries we have no account. There is a legend which attributes to the apostle Thomas the establishment of the Christian Church in India. Slowly does reason reject a tradition which imagination is so eager to embrace. It would be pleasant to accord the fullest faith to the legend of the apostolic origin of Christianity in India; but there is really no authority in its favour to divest it of all the attributes of fable. A very exciting account of the life and death of the apostle in India is to be found in the pages of a Portuguese historian. With apparent good faith Maffeus relates the miracles that Thomas wrought in India; how he converted certain Magi; how he built a temple at Meliapore; how he brought the dead to life; how he delivered himself of certain wonderful prophecies : and, finally, how he became a martyr for the faith.* The Portuguese, at all events, believed these traditions, and invoked the miraculous aid of the saint when they went into battle.    Marco Polo, who visited India before the time of the Portuguese, relates that St. Thomas was accidentally killed when at prayer in a wood, by a low-caste man, who was shooting at peacocks ; and that, as a consequence of this mischance, none of the poor man's tribe could ever enter the place where the saint lay buried—" Nor," adds the Venetian, " could twenty men force them in, nor ten hold them there, on account of the virtue of that sacred body."† Every one who has visited Madras, knows " St. Thomas's Mount."    It has for centuries been held, both by the Syrian and the Romish churches, to be the burial place of the apostle ; but the more the legend is investigated, the more fabulous it appears. I do not know a modern writer of any note who has the least faith in the story.

That the gospel was ever preached in India during the first century, there is no credible evidence to show ; but this much history may assert, that towards the close of the second century, when the Emperor Commodus, one of the worst and weakest of the many tyrants and idiots who hastened the downfall

* Gibbon says that " Marco Polo was told on the spot that he (St. Thomas) suffered martyrdom in the city of Meliapore." This, however, is clearly an erroneous statement.

† Dr. Fryer, who visited India about 1680, says that "about this mount live a cast of people, one of whose legs are as big as an elephant's, which gives occasion for the divulging it to be a judgment on them, as the generation of the assassins and murtherers of the blessed apostle St. Thomas, one of whom I saw at Fort St. George." Such the miraculous origin of Elephantiasis !

of the Roman empire, exercised bloody dominion in the eternal city and throughout its marvellous dependencies in three quarters of the globe, the glad tidings of the Gospel had reached the ears of the dwellers on the Southern Indian coast. From whosesoever lips the great message fell, it had not fallen on ungrateful soil. Among the pearl-fishers of Ceylon and the rude cultivators on the coasts of Malabar and Coromandel were men who sighed after better teaching and a purer faith than those of the priests of their idol temples.

From those distant Indian shores the Egyptian mariners brought back intelligence which spread joyfully among the Christians of Alexandria. Demetrius held the episcopate of the Alexandrian see. Pantænus presided over the celebrated school which was among the glories of that famous city. He had forsaken the philosophy of the Portico to embrace the faith as it is in Jesus; and now the intelligence brought home by the Egyptian mariners stirred his heart among his pupils and his books. The longings of the heathen were after Gospel teaching. Their prayers for the help of instructed Christian guides did not find utterance in vain. Pondering, perhaps praying over, these strange tidings, the philosopher formed a great resolution, and girded himself up for a great enterprise. He determined to leave his disciples—to abandon the honours and rewards of the academy—and to go forth to preach the Gospel to the heathen upon heathen ground. What he did, and what he taught, it is hard to say. Doubts of the soundness of his doctrines have been freely expressed. It is said, that the taint of the old Stoic philosophy clung to the Christian teacher. But we may at least believe the sincerity and devotedness of the man, who exchanged the learned quiet of the schools, and the amenities of civilization, for the hardships and sufferings of missionary life, beneath a burning sun, and among a barbarous people; and though there be no record of his exploits, or even of the precise scene of his labours,* and it is known that he returned after a time to Alexandria, to take his old place among his disciples, we may cherish the pleasing belief, that the first Indian missionary of whom we have any authentic account, did not labour wholly in vain.

But it is not easy to say what he left behind him, or who succeeded him in the great work. The history of the Christian Church in the East here sinks into a cloud of obscurity. Little is known of the progress of the Gospel on Indian soil throughout the whole of the third century. It was at the commencement of the fourth, that the Emperor Constantine, " seated Christianity on the throne of the Roman world." At the Council of Nice, held under his authority, at the close of the first quarter of that century, one of the

---

* It is even doubted by some writers whether he visited India Proper at all; and it is suggested that the scene of his labours was more probably the coast of Arabia. But the balance of evidence collected by Mr. Hough, in his " History of Christianity in India," is against the latter hypothesis. There is no reason, indeed, to doubt that Pantænus visited India; in all probability the island of Ceylon and the Malabar coast. It is certain, however, that there is something extremely vague and indefinite in the geographical nomenclature of ancient writers, who are too apt to describe Arabia, Abyssinia, Persia, and Central Asia, indifferently, under the comprehensive name of India,—a word, indeed, often made to represent all the countries of the East.

assembled prelates, named Johannes, subscribed his name, as "Metropolitan of Persia and the Great India," a fact which seems to indicate that there was at that time a Christian Church of some bulk and significance planted on the Indian coast. Thirty years later, one Frumentius, a Tyrian by birth, sailed for India, invested by Athanasius with Episcopal authority, and gathered together the scattered Christian flocks which were then dispersed over the southern peninsula.

The story of this man is worth telling. He was the kinsman of a Christian philosopher named Meropius, who had heard from others such accounts of the wonders of the "Great India," as filled him with a strong desire to visit the utmost isles and shores of the East. Taking two young kinsmen with him as companions of his voyage, he sailed for India, satisfied his longings, and was about to turn the prow of his vessel towards home, when the natives of the country seized him and the mariners who had worked his ship, and barbarously murdered them. The young kinsmen of the philosopher alone escaped. Their names were Frumentius and Ædesius. The natives carried the youths to their king, who made the one his secretary and the other his cup-bearer; and when he died, leaving a son in his minority, the queen-mother entreated the strangers to undertake the guardianship of the boy, and to direct the administration of the country. They consented; and Frumentius became the chief ruler of the state. The precise locality in which the Christian tutor and regent of a heathen prince and a heathen country exercised dominion is not on record; but it is narrated by many credible authorities, that in this trying and responsible position Frumentius remembered the lessons of his youth, and turned to good account his influence and authority. He found on inquiry from the merchants that there were many Christians on the coast; he gathered them together; erected a church; exhorted them to the constant worship of the true God, and promised to protect their temporal interests. Many were thus added to the Christian Church; but in due course the prince, attaining to years of discretion, took the reins of government into his own hands, and Frumentius and Ædesius, in spite of the remonstrances of the young sovereign and his mother, prepared to return to the country of their birth. Ædesius repaired at once to the home of his kindred in Tyre, but Frumentius made his way to Alexandria, sought an interview with Athanasius, and urged him to provide for the spiritual wants of the native converts on the Indian coast. The Patriarch besought him to undertake the mission himself, and Frumentius returned to India. It is said that the new bishop made many converts and erected many churches. It is only in accordance with the general character of the traditions of the age, that it should be added that he wrought many miracles.

Of the progress of Christianity in the East during the fifth century there are few, if any, authentic records. Early in the sixth century, a merchant of Alexandria named Cosmas visited India, and wrote an account of the places he had seen. "There is," he said, "in the Island of Taprobane (Ceylon) in the furthermost India, in the Indian sea, a Christian Church, with clergymen and believers. I know not whether there are any Christians beyond this island. In the Malabar country also, where pepper grows, there are Christians, and in Calliana, as they call it, there is a bishop who comes from Persia where he was consecrated."\* The Gospel had indeed been making its way towards India by the northern route, through Central Asia; and was preached, with success, in Persia, in Media, in Armenia, in Bactria, and in the Tartar countries lying to the north of the great Caucasian range. "The Barbaric Churches," says Gibbon, "from the Gulf of Persia to the Caspian Sea, were almost infinite; and their recent faith was conspicuous in the number and sanctity of their monks and martyrs." "In a subsequent age," to borrow the language of the same historian, "the zeal of the Nestorians† overleaped the limits which had confined the ambition and curiosity both of the Greeks and Persians. The missionaries of Balkh and Samarcand pursued without fear the footsteps of the roving Tartar, and insinuated themselves into the camps

---

\* There has been a good deal of learned discussion relative to the identity of this place, but I see no reason to disbelieve that the Greek Καλλιανα represents the modern Callianee, near Bombay. Cosmas evidently knew nothing of the eastern coast of the Indian peninsula; and yet Mr. Hugh Murray, in his "Historical Account of Discoveries and Travels in Asia," a very able and interesting compilation, suggests that the Pudifetania on the Coromandel coast, mentioned by Nicolo Conti, is identical with the Poodabatan of Cosmas, which was on the Malabar coast.

† The Nestorians were the followers of Nestorius, who was consecrated Bishop of Constantinople in 429. For an interesting account of his career, and of his peculiar doctrines, see Mr. Hough's "History," vol. i. chap. 11.

of the valleys of Imaus and the banks of the Selinga."

But as the seventh century dawned upon Asia, the great imposture of Mahomed arose and checked for a time the growth of Christianity in the Eastern world. The faith of the Arabian enthusiast, supported by seductive appeals to the passions of men, began to roll its irresistible tide over the vast extent of country that lies between the banks of the Mediterranean and the confines of the Chinese Empire. The followers of the new creed were men of earnestness and enterprise; they monopolised the trade and navigation of the East; and for a time the Christian churches languished. Commerce had been, hitherto, the great agent of proselytism, and now that agency was suspended. Receiving no new strength from without, and within abject and corrupt, presenting a feeble contrast to the gigantic ascendancy of the new faith, the churches of India visibly declined in power as the mosques of the Mahomedans cast their shadows over the parched ground, and the stillness of the evening was broken by the Muezhin's call to prayer.

Two noticeable events, though not altogether unobscured by that mist of uncertainty which hangs over the early history of the Christian Church in India, distinguished the eighth and ninth centuries. Towards the close of the former, when it appears that the Indian bishoprics were under the authority of the Nestorian Patriarch of Seleucia, an Armenian merchant, named Thomas Cana, took up his abode in Malabar. Before this time the Christian brother-

hood, both on that and the Coromandel coast, persecuted by the native princes, had been driven into the
interior of the country, to seek refuge on the hills.
The influence of Mar Thomas, who whether formally
appointed or not to the episcopal office, appears to
have performed its functions and borne its title, was
great throughout Southern India. Under his protection the native Christians enjoyed security and peace.
It has been conjectured that this man, who married
and died in India, and left behind him a numerous
progeny, is the Christian worthy who has been con-
founded with the Apostolic saint. The chronological
question simply involves a discrepancy of a small
matter of eight centuries; and all we now know about
it, or are likely to know, is that the St. Thomas,
who is venerated by the Christian Churches of
Southern India, and whose name they bear, was
either " an apostle, a Manichæan, or an Armenian
merchant," and that he died in the first century or
the ninth.

The noticeable event of the ninth century, to which
I have alluded, is connected with this history of St.
Thomas. It is on record that Alfred the Great
despatched from Great Britain an embassy, under
Sighelm, Bishop of Shireburn, to the shrine of the
saint at Madras.* Having paid their devotions, the

---

* This was in 883. It seems little
likely that if the legend of the death
and burial of St. Thomas in the
neighbourhood of Madras really arose
out of the fact of the death and burial
of Mar Thomas—an event which took
place only about half a century before
Alfred's embassage — there should
have been at that time, either in
Egypt or Great Britain, any confu-
sion of an incident which occurred
fifty years before with one that was
at least eight centuries old.

holy men returned home, bringing with them a costly recompense in the shape of a rich cargo of pearls and spices. The fame of these precious commodities had reached the monarch of the Western Isle, and the substance now rewarded his zeal. This story is related on such good authority that I am slow to pronounce it apocryphal. It would seem to be at least partly true. It is surmised by Gibbon and other writers, that the pilgrims were despatched from Great Britain, but never proceeded farther than Alexandria, where they "collected their cargo and legend." However imperfectly we may understand the motives of the British monarch, or grope our way through the haze of doubt that besets the tradition, it would be pleasant to accept, without misgivings, this history of the dawn of Saxon enterprise in the East.

From this time, over a large surface of years, lie few and scattered the incidents which mark the progress of the Christian churches in the East. In the tenth century the cause of the pure faith had greatly recovered from the blighting effects of Mahomedan ascendancy, and new efforts were made to support and to recruit the churches. It is said that about this time the Christians of St. Thomas were so many and so powerful in Southern India, that they asserted their independence as a people, and erected a sovereignty of their own. For some time they prospered under their Christian Rajahs, until one of them dying without issue, adopted a heathen prince as his heir, and from that time the race of Christian rulers was extinct—a remarkable instance of the advantages of that system of adoption which now, after the lapse of nearly a thousand years, is debated with as much warmth, and advocated with as much earnestness, as though the welfare of India were dependent upon the issue of the contest.

Hitherto, with but a dim uncertain light to guide us, we have groped through a country of much doubt and perplexity, a desert on which, few and far between, stand up shadowy landmarks of history, scarcely better than the merest fables. Out of the regions of the indistinct and conjectural, we are now about to emerge, by sensible degrees, into the light of substantial history. We have seen the tide of Christianity setting in from Egypt and Syria, through Arabia and Persia, towards the western coast of Hindostan, and thence up the southern peninsula. For a time the ascendancy of Mahomedanism cut off the growing intercourse between Christianity and Heathenism, and kept down the growth of the Nestorian churches. It was but for a time. The growing civilization of the West went out to meet the stern enthusiasm of the East, and the traders of Arabia yielded the commerce of the Indian seas to the merchants of Genoa and Venice. But the enmity of Mahomedanism was not extinguished, and its power was not suppressed. By the victorious arms of Mahomed II., the crescent was planted in the capital of the Greek empire, and the mart of Constantinople closed against the European world. By such hostility as this, the spirit of Christian enterprise was excited rather than depressed. The nations of the West had hitherto known no other sea route than those through the Red Sea and the Persian Gulf, along the Arabian coast to Ceylon; but the aggressiveness and exclusiveness of the Mahomedans stimulated them to seek another channel by which to import into Europe the wealth of the Oriental marts, and on the common road of the great ocean they tried, for the first time, towards the close of the fifteenth century, the great experiment of a western passage to India, around the stormy promontory of Southern Africa. It was in the year 1497, that Vasco de Gama, a subject of the King of Portugal, doubled the Cape of Storms, and steered for the western coast of India. After a voyage of ten months from the port of Lisbon, he cast anchor before the town of Calicut in the month of May in the following year; and from that time we date a new epoch in the history of the Christian churches in the Indian world.

Long before this the Papacy had been established; but the Syrian churches knew nothing about the Papacy—nothing about Rome. They had flourished on the Indian coast long before the days of Papal domination, and when the Romish Church erected its proud front, and overawed the empires of the West, the Christian churches in India had been defended against the inroads of its propagandism, and the tyranny of its intolerance, by the barriers which Mahomedanism had raised up between the

people of Europe and the dwellers on the coasts
of Malabar and Coromandel. But no sooner were
the Portuguese vessels anchored off the shores of
Southern India than the independence of the primitive churches was threatened, and in a little time
was grievously assailed. When Vasco de Gama
appeared a second time on the Indian coast, with
the title of Admiral of the Eastern Seas, the
Christians of Malabar welcomed him with cordiality, and invited him to become the ruler of their
tribe. The deputation which crossed the surf and
ascended the sides of De Gama's vessel presented to
the great navigator the sceptre of the last of their
Christian kings. It was a wooden staff dyed with
vermilion, silver-mounted, and ornamented with bells.
With childlike confidence they placed themselves
under his protection, and besought him to become
their chief. From that time the progress of that
great buccaneering expedition, which subjected many
fair provinces of the Indian continent to the rule of
a tyrannous, lustful, and unscrupulous band of tyrants
and marauders, was, beyond example, rapid and eventful. The success of the Portuguese over the Moorish
power in the East was not without its uses; and it
would be hard to withhold our admiration from the
surprising energy with which it was achieved. But
it is a painful and a terrible chapter of history.
The first Christian settlers in India were the most
unchristian of men; * and it has taken more than

* Maffeus candidly acknowledges
that the unholy lives of the Portuguese formed one of the main obstacles to the conversion of the natives.

three centuries to wipe away the stain cast upon Christianity by the lives of its European professors.

Intent upon worldly conquest, and the acquisition of earthly wealth, the first Lusitanian invaders appear to have troubled themselves little about the propagation of Christianity; and it may be doubted whether the Franciscan Friars who accompanied the Portuguese mariners to India did not, for the most part, suffer the missionary character to subside into the monastic. They established monasteries; they built churches; but they made few genuine converts. Proselytism, in the time of Albuquerque, was a matter of State policy, not of Christian zeal and devotion. The Viceroy, we are told, " in order to breed up soldiers, very wisely *got the Indian maids made Christians*, and married them to the Portuguese, that they might not always stand in need of fresh supplies of men from Portugal." But whilst Albuquerque and his successors were prosecuting their conquests in the East, and the Portuguese power was extending itself from the Arabian gulf to the very confines of China, a greater than Albuquerque was achieving that greater conquest of self, and a mightier power than that of the arms of Portugal in the East was rising among the peaceful colleges of the West. Ignatius Loyola bowed himself to God; and the reign of the Jesuits commenced.

After setting forth other difficulties, he says: " Verum nihil plane majori est impedimento quam nostratium Christianorum (quos Ethnicis præluc ere ad omnem justitiam et castitatem oportuerat) tanto nomini ac professioni minimè consentanea quotidianæ vitæ documenta, neque enim tantam spectata paucorum innocentia et virtus adstruit Evangelio fidem; quantam insignis multorum et notissimi fere cujusque avaritia et improbitas adimit."

It was in the spring of the year 1541 that the first
missionary of the new Society of Jesus turned his
clear, blue eyes, for the last time, upon the orange-
groves of Spain, and set his face towards the shining
Orient. A Portuguese vessel, destined to carry out
to Goa a new Indian viceroy, and a reinforcement of
a thousand men, suffered the great-hearted enthusiast
to slink silently on board, and to mingle with the
noisy crowd of soldiers and mariners on her deck.
No pleasant well-fitted cabin was there for him—no
well-supplied " cuddy-table "—no outfit that he did
not carry on his back. He pillowed his head upon a
coil of ropes, and ate what the sailors discarded.
But there was not a seaman in that labouring vessel,
there was not a soldier in that crowded troop-ship,
who did not inwardly recognise the great soul that
glowed beneath those squalid garments. No outward
humiliation could conceal that knightly spirit; no
sickness and suffering could quench the fire of that
ardent genius. The highest and the lowest held
converse with him; and, abject, prostrate as he was,
he towered above them all, alike as a gentleman and a
scholar. And when, thirteen months after the vessel
sailed out of the port of Lisbon, its rent sails were
furled, and its strained cables coiled before the seaport
of Goa, there was not one of the many enthusiasts
who now, as they dropped down her weather-stained
and shattered side, shaped for themselves in imagination so brilliant a career in the great Indies, or heaped
up such piles of visionary wealth, as stirred the heart
of Francis Xavier. But his career was only that of

c

the Christian missionary, and the riches he was to
gain were countless thousands of human souls.

It was Xavier's will to suffer. The King of
Portugal had ordered, that on his passage to India a
cabin should be placed at his disposal, and furnished
with everything that could render tolerable the dis-
comforts of a sea life. But he had rejected these
kingly offers, and contented himself with the bare
deck as his home; a single cloak to shelter him in
the foul weather, and a few books to solace him in
the fair. And now that he had reached the point at
which were to commence his apostolic ministrations,
the same spirit of self-denial and self-dependence
animated him in all that he did. He had prayed
before his departure for more stripes; he had asked
the Divine goodness to grant him in India the pains
that had been faintly foreshadowed in his Italian
career. He had carried out all sorts of briefs and
credentials from regal and pontifical hands; and the
bishop now eagerly tendered him assistance and
pressed upon him pecuniary support. But he refused
all these episcopal offers, and sought no aid but that
of God. The more dangers seemed to thicken—the
more appalling the difficulties that beset his path—
the more agonizing the trials he endured—the louder,
the more earnest was his cry, "Yet more—O my
God!—yet more!"

Protestant zeal is only contemptible when it denies
that Francis Xavier was a great man. Delusions he
may have had, strong as ever yet wrought upon the
human soul; but the true nobility of his nature is

not to be gainsaid. He faced the most tremendous trials with a courage and a constancy of the highest order, and prosecuted the most arduous and astounding labours with an energy and a perseverance scarcely exampled in the history of mankind. He found himself suddenly thrown into the midst of a mingled community of natives and Europeans, of which it was hard to say whether the one or the other were sunk in the deeper and more debasing idolatry. It was a privilege to him to endure hardship and to be beset with difficulty in the prosecution of his great work. His courage rose as the objects in his path loomed larger and larger, and he waded through the sea of pollution that lay before him as one who never feared to sink. He began his course by endeavouring to entice his countrymen at Goa into a purer way of life; and, as none since the days of the apostle Paul have known better how to abound and how to be abased, he became as weak unto the weak, all things to all men, that by all means he might save some. The knightly spirit was never extinct within him; with the chivalry and the courtesy of the old noble, he united the fulness and readiness of the scholar; and whether among the gay and gallant officers who surrounded the Viceroy of Portugal, or among the degraded fishermen on the coast of Malabar, the gentle blood which flowed in his veins imparted dignity to his presence, softness to his speech, and the most winning generosity to his actions. Whether, placing himself at the head of a band of oppressed Christians, he charged down, crucifix in hand, upon a marauding

enemy, or whether he braved death in fever hospitals
and lazar-houses, performing readily the most sicken-
ing offices for their tainted inmates, the same noble
courage and self-devotion shone out in everything
that he did.

That the doctrines he taught may not have been
the soundest—that his means of teaching were insufficient—that he knew little of the native languages—
—that he made converts who were in reality no converts—that he had an overweening faith, not peculiar
to the sixteenth century, in the efficacy of infant
baptism, are facts which all history records, but no
true history in a grudging spirit.  The more insufficient his means, the greater the faith that sustained
him.  When Francis Xavier went about the streets
of Goa, or traversed the villages on the western coast,
bell in hand, its clear sounds inviting all who heard
to gather round him and accept from his lips the first
rudiments of Christian truth; and when, with inalienable European accent, he enunciated a rude translation of the Apostles' creed, and then of the Lord's
Prayer and the Ten Commandments, he did not
believe that he, so unworthy an agent, so weak a
vessel, could convert thousands of wondering heathens
to the faith as it is in Christ; but he believed that
even a weaker vessel, even a more unworthy agent,
might, in God's hands, become a human medium for
the conversion of tens of thousands, and he did his
best, knowing how little it was in itself, but how
great it might become, if the Holy Ghost descended
upon him as a dove, and birdlike accompanied him in

his wanderings. How far the Divine Spirit may have worked in him, and for him, it is not for us in these days to determine. It was said that a miraculous gift of tongues was vouchsafed to him, that he raised the dead, and performed other prodigies; but he was too truthful, too real a man, to favour the growth of errors which the whole Catholic world was only too willing to accept; and it would be the vilest injustice to fix upon the first Jesuit missionary the charge of dishonesty and insincerity, because among his followers have been liars and hypocrites of the worst class.

The proselytes of Francis Xavier are numbered by his followers, not by tens, but by hundreds of thousands. He is said to have converted seven hundred thousand unbelievers to the Christian faith. His converts were drawn from all classes, from princes to pariahs. That the dishonesty or credulity of his biographers has greatly magnified his successes is not to be denied; but, making large deductions on this score, there still remains a formidable balance of nominal Christianity to be carried to the account of the apostle. His superhuman energies seem to have been attended with almost miraculous results. Idols fell at his approach; churches rose at his bidding; and the sign of the cross became the recognised symbol of fellowship among the inmates of entire villages. From Goa he travelled southward to the pearl-fisheries of Cape Comorin, and after succouring the poor people who had been driven thence to the shores of the Straits of Manaar, returned to the

western coast and commenced his labours, with extraordinary energy and success, in Travancore.  According to his own account he baptized ten thousand
heathens in a single month; carrying on the holy
work till he could no longer articulate the words of
the formula, or raise his hand to perform the office.
Then he took ship for the Eastern isles, visited
Malacca, Amboyna, Ternate, Java; and, after a
while, returned to visit his churches in Southern
India, and to prepare himself for a great crusade
against the Bonzes of Japan.  More than two years
were spent in this holy war; many strange adventures
he encountered, many converts he made, and many
churches he established; but his career was now
drawing to a close.  He returned to Goa, and there
in council with one Iago Pereira, captain of the vessel
which had carried the apostle on his strange and
perilous voyage from Japan, formed the magnificent
design of converting the Chinese Empire.  But he
never reached the flowery land.  Difficulties beset the
enterprise.  The apostle of the Jesuits was landed at
the Island of Sancian; and there as he was about to
join, full of heart and hope, a Siamese embassy of
which he had gained tidings, and thus aided to penetrate into the interior of the Celestial Empire, the
hand of God was put forth to stay his triumphant
career; the Divine mandate, " thus far shalt thou
go, and no further," was issued to that lowly, well-
prepared servant of God; he met the summons with
rapture, and on the bare beach, or beneath a miserable
shed, which sheltered him neither from the heat by

day nor from the cold by night, he closed a life of agony and bliss, of humiliation and of triumph, with scarcely a parallel in the history of the world.

Such briefly told in a few paragraphs was the career of Francis Xavier. He died on the 2nd day of December, 1552, at the portals of the Chinese empire. His mantle descended upon none worthy to be associated with the memory of such a man. In the history of the Jesuits' missions in India, Francis Xavier stands out in solitary grandeur, as the one apostolic man. Beside him all his successors were but mountebanks and impostors. He was too earnest, too assiduous in his ministrations to busy himself about the doctrines of other Christian teachers, and too large-hearted and charitable to sink into a bigot, or to be goaded into persecution. He went about his own work, and the Syrian priests tended their flocks in security and peace. Before his death the Franciscan friars had endeavoured silently and secretly to undermine the Malabar churches; but had resorted to no acts of violence. Soon, however, the overbearing policy of Rome began openly to assert itself; and the Christians of St. Thomas saw their independence threatened by men whom they regarded as little better than idolators in religion and buccaneers in active life.

Then began that great struggle, to the history of which Gibbon has devoted two pregnant pages, and Hough more than a volume of his work. The Christians, long seated on the coast of Malabar, traced their paternity to the Apostle Paul, who

" went through Syria and Cilicia confirming the churches." They looked to Syria as their spiritual home. They owned the supremacy of the Patriarch of Babylon. Of Rome and the Pope they knew nothing. During the rise of the Papacy, the Mahomedan power, which had overrun the intervening countries, had closed the gates of India against the nations of the West.* This had saved the Syrian churches from Roman supremacy and Roman corruption. As to the great question, whether the churchmen of Spain and Portugal or the Christian priests of Southern India entertained purer ideas and practised more orthodox forms of Christianity, authorities may widely differ. The Portuguese were scandalized at the appearance of the Syrian houses of worship, which they declared to be heathen temples scarcely disguised. The Syrian Christians shrank with dismay from the defiling touch of the Roman Catholics of Portugal, and proclaimed themselves Christians and not idolators, when the image of the Virgin Mary was placed before their offended eyes. But it is certain that the Malabar Christians had never been subject to Roman supremacy, and never subscribed to Roman doctrine. The inquisitors of Goa discovered that they were heretics; but they were quietly living in the enjoyment of a faith which had been vouchsafed to them a thousand years before —vouchsafed to them when Rome owned a heathen Emperor, and knew not the sterner, more capacious

* The Abbé Raynal, whose views Robertson adopts not without acknowledgment, has enlarged upon the effect of this exclusion in a very sensible and candid manner.

tyranny of a sovereign Pontiff of the Christian Church.

But like a wolf on the fold, down came the delegates of the pontifical tyrant upon these doomed Indian churches. Their own shepherds, unworthy of such a charge, deserted their flock in the hour of need, scrambled for power, and played a game of dissimulation, that was not even justified by temporary success. The first Syrian prelate who was brought into antagonism with Rome, expiated his want of courage and sincerity in the dungeons of the Inquisition. The second shared the same fate. A third, whose sufferings are more worthy of commiseration, died after much trial and tribulation in his diocese, denying the Pope's supremacy to the last. The churches were now without a Bishop, at a time when they more than ever needed prelatical countenance and support; for Rome was about to put forth a mighty hand and a stretched-out arm. Don Alexis de Menezes was appointed Archbishop of Goa. It was his mission less to make new converts than to reduce old ones to subjection; and he flung himself into the work of persecution with an amount of zeal and heroism that must have greatly endeared him to Rome. Impatient of the slow success of his agents, he determined to take the staff into his own hand. Moving down to the South, with an imposing military force,* he summoned the Syrian Churches to submit

---

* There was other work to be done by this expedition than the reduction of the Syrian Churches; but the authorities of Goa saw the advantage of imparting to the movements of the Archbishop all the circumstance of official pomp and the persuasiveness of military strength.

themselves to his authority. The Churches were under an Archdeacon, who, sensible of the danger that impended over them, determined to temporize, but at the same time to show that he was prepared to resist. He waited on the Archbishop. An escort of three thousand resolute men who accompanied him on his visit to Menezes, were with difficulty restrained, on the first slight and delusive sign of violence, from rushing on their opponents and proving their burning zeal in defence of their religion. It was not a time for Menezes to push the claims of the Romish Church. But no fear of resistance could divert him from his purpose; and he openly denounced the Patriarch of Babylon as a pestilent schismatic, and declared it a heresy to acknowledge his supremacy. He then issued a decree forbidding all persons to acknowledge any other supremacy than that of the Roman Pontiff, or to make any mention of the Syrian Patriarch in the services of their Church; and, this done, he publicly excommunicated the acknowledged head of the Syrian Churches, and called upon the startled Archdeacon to sign the writ of excommunication. Frightened and confused, the wretched man put his name to the apostate document; and it was publicly affixed to the gates of the church.

This intolerable insult on the one hand—this wretched compromise on the other—roused the fury of the people against the Archbishop, and against their own ecclesiastical chief. Hard was the task before him, when the latter went forth to appease the excited multitude. They would have made one desperate effort to sweep the Portuguese intruders from their polluted shores; but the Archdeacon pleaded with them for forbearance; apologised for his own weakness; urged that dissimulation would be more serviceable than revenge; promised, in spite of what he had done, to defend their religion; and exhorted them to be firm in their resistance of Papal aggression. With a shout of assent, they swore that they would never bow their necks to the yoke, and prepared themselves for the continuance of the struggle.

But Menezes was a man of too many resources to be worsted in such a conflict. His energy and perseverance were irresistible; his craft was too deep to fathom. When one weapon of attack failed, he tried another. Fraud took the place of violence; money took the place of arms. He bribed those whom he could not bully, and appealed to the imaginations of men when he could not work upon their fears. And, little by little, he succeeded. First one Church fell, and then another. Dangers and difficulties beset him. Often had he to encounter violent resistance, and often did he beat it down. When the strength of the Syrian Christians was too great for him, he called in the aid of the native princes. The unhappy Archdeacon, weary of resistance, and threatened with excommunication, at last made submission to the Roman Prelate. Menezes issued a decree for a synod; and, on the 20th of June, 1599, the Churches assembled at Diamper. The first session passed quietly over, but not without much secret murmuring.

The second, at which the decrees were read, was interrupted at that trying point of the ceremony where, having enunciated the Confession of Faith, the Archbishop renounced and anathematized the Patriarch of Babylon. The discontent of the Syrians here broke out openly; they protested against the necessity of a Confession of Faith, and urged that such a confession would imply that they were not Christians before the assembling of the Synod. But Menezes allayed their apprehensions, and removed their doubts, by publicly making the confession in the name of himself and the Eastern Churches. One of the Syrian priests, who acted as interpreter, then read the confession in the Malabar language, and the assembled multitude repeated it after him, word for word, on their knees. And so the Syrian Christians bowed their necks to the yoke of Rome.

Resolute to improve the advantages he had gained, Menezes did not suffer himself to subside into inactivity, and to bask in the sunshine of his past triumphs. Whether it was religious zeal or temporal ambition that moved him, he did not relax from his labours; but feeling that it was not enough to place the yoke upon the neck of the Syrian Christians, he endeavoured, by all means, to keep it there. The Churches yielded sullen submission; but there were quick-witted, keen-sighted men among them, who, as the seventeenth century began to dawn upon the world, looked hopefully into the future, feeling assured that they could discern even then unmistakable evidences of the waning glories of the Portuguese in the East.

There was hope then for the Syrian Churches. The persecutions of Menezes were very grievous—for he separated priests from their wives; excommunicated, on trifling grounds, members of the churches; and destroyed all the old Syriac records which contained proofs of the early purity of their faith. The irreparable barbarism of this last act was not to be forgotten or forgiven; but, in the midst of all other sufferings, there was consolation in the thought, that this tyranny was but for a time. "Sixty years of servitude and hypocrisy," writes Gibbon, "were patiently endured; but as soon as the Portuguese empire was shaken by the courage and industry of the Dutch, the Nestorians asserted with vigour and effect the religion of their fathers. The Jesuits were incapable of defending the power they had abused. The arms of forty thousand Christians were pointed against their falling tyrants; and the Indian Archdeacon assumed the character of Bishop till a fresh supply of Episcopal gifts and Syriac missionaries could be obtained from the Patriarch of Babylon." Such, briefly narrated, were the results of the oppression of Menezes. In the course of six months that ambitious and unscrupulous prelate reduced the Syrian churches to bondage, and for sixty years they wore the galling chains of Rome. But Menezes trusted in his own strength; he came as an earthly conqueror, and his reliance was on the arm of temporal authority. "His example," writes Mr. Hough, "should be regarded as a beacon to warn future Christian missionaries from the rock on which he foundered. Without faith and godliness nothing can ensure a church's prosperity. Failing in these, the prelate's designs, magnificent as they were deemed, soon came to nothing; and it deserves special remark, as an instructive interposition of Divine Providence, that the decline of the Portuguese interest in India commenced at the very period when he flattered himself that he had laid the foundation of its permanency."

Leaving the Malabar churches groaning under the weight of papal tyranny, we may now cross the southern peninsula, to track the movements of the Jesuits on the eastern coast. It was at the commencement of the seventeenth century that Robert de Nobilibus, a nephew of Cardinal Bellarmine, and a near relative of Pope Marcellus II., laid the foundation of the Madura Mission. The Jesuits were, by this time, rapidly supplanting the Franciscans in all parts of the southern provinces of India. As the seventeenth century advanced, the glory of the Jesuit missions ascended higher and higher, till it reached its culminating point. From Goa went forth a stream of missionaries to evangelize the whole continent of India; but in the regions watered by the Ganges, they were disheartened and repulsed, and soon abandoned their work in despair. Not so in the Southern Peninsula. There they laboured with marvellous assiduity, and, according to their own accounts, with marvellous success. Rejecting the example of Xavier, whose warm heart had expanded towards the poor and the oppressed, and whose ready limbs had ever borne him amongst them, Robert de Nobilibus, his

associates, and his successors, addressed themselves
to the dominant class, and sought their converts
among the Brahmans. In one respect they went
forth to their work better prepared than the great
Jesuit apostle. They had studied, and they understood the native languages; they had made themselves familiar with, and were ready to adopt, the
habits and customs of the natives. They shrank
from no amount of labour—from no suffering—from
no humiliation. They turned aside from the practice
of no deceit; from the exercise of no hypocrisy. They
lied in word, and they lied in action. They called
themselves western Brahmans; and in the disguise of
Brahmans they mixed themselves with the people,
talking their language, following their customs, and
countenancing their superstitions. Clothed in the
sacerdotal yellow cloth, with the mark of sandal wood
on their foreheads, their long hair streaming down
their backs, their copper vessels in their hands, their
wooden sandals on their feet, these "new Brahmans"
found acceptance among the people, and were welcomed
by the princes of southern India. They performed
their ablutions with scrupulous regularity; they ate
no animal food; they drank no intoxicating liquors;
but found in the simple fare of vegetables and milk
at once a disguise and a protection. The Christians
had hitherto appeared upon the scene, eating and
drinking—gluttonous and wine-bibbers—and they had
paid the penalty of an addiction to these feverish
stimulants under the burning copper skies of the
East. The holy men who now wandered half-naked

among the natives of southern India, and sitting on
their haunches ate the common fare of the country,
braved the climate with comparative immunity, and
were not suspected of fellowship with the sensual
Europeans who had turned Goa into a stye of corruption. Whether it was necessary to the due simu-
lation of the Brahmanical character to preserve in all
other respects very great purity of life, may be left to
all who are acquainted with the habits of that priestly
class to conjecture for themselves.

That these Jesuits made a surprising number of
converts in the South, is confidently asserted on the
testimony of their order ; and inasmuch as they
baptised many thousands of people, the record is
doubtless true. If the sprinkling of water and the
utterance of a certain formula be enough to make a
Christian, as many professing Protestants seem to
believe, even in the middle of the nineteenth century,
these Jesuit missionaries in the seventeenth, doubtless
made multitudes of Christians. According, however,
to their own showing, their success among the
Brahmans was very small, and they soon began to
see the necessity of flying at lower game. They went
among the villagers—condescended to pariahs, and
achieved great triumphs over babes and sucklings.
Under the pretext of administering medicine to them,
they baptized all the dying children. They did their
best to render conversion as easy as possible, by
heathenizing Christianity to the utmost possible
extent. Indeed it may be questioned whether the
Jesuit missionaries were not themselves the only real

converts. It is almost enough to say of the scandalous nature of their proceedings, that they brought a blush to the hard cheek of Menezes. The impiety of the Jesuits in Madura startled even that unscrupulous prelate; and yet the mission was then only in an early stage of progression towards the proficiency which it afterwards attained. The Christianity of Madura under the Jesuits was indeed undisguised idolatry. Except that the image of the Virgin Mary was worshipped in the temples and paraded upon the cars, there was little change in the old ceremonies and processions of Hindooism. There was the same noise of trumpets, and taumtaums, and kettle-drums; there was the same blaze of rockets, and Roman candles, and blue-lights; there were the same dancers, with the same marks of sandal-wood and vermilion on their naked bodies. The new Christianity of Madura disguised itself as adroitly as the priests who taught it. They married children with all the silly observances of Paganism and buried the dead with all its ghastly superstitions. To break down the barriers of Caste were a great achievement; for Caste is the great stumbling-block of the Gospel. The Jesuits did not attempt it. They went among the people with great parade of caste, and declared that they were sprung from the head of Brahma himself. To have made an assault upon Caste would have been to betray their own secret, and utterly to ruin their schemes. They were too wise in their generation so to make shipwreck of their hopes. Among their proselytes they consented to perpetuate

D

the distinctions which it is the ambition of Christianity to destroy. The high-caste Christians and the low-caste Christians were suffered to worship apart. They could not pray in the same temple or dip their fingers in the same holy water. The whole system was one of fraud and dissimulation—of compromise and abnegation. So little of Christianity was there in it, that the English historian of Christian India is compelled to apologise for devoting to it a chapter of his book.

Whilst the Jesuits were thus converting the heathen by becoming heathens themselves, their dominion over the Syrian Churches was rapidly relaxing, and the Christians of Malabar were beginning to look forward with hopefulness to the day of emancipation. The insolence and violence of the Jesuitical prelates roused the churches into resistance. They despatched urgent remonstrances to Rome, and not receiving answers to their prayers, renounced the domination of their Roman bishop, and elected an ecclesiastical chief of their own. Alarmed at these proceedings, the sovereign Pontiff despatched a party of Carmelites on a mission of conciliation. But the breach was too wide for reparation; the gulf which lay between them was not to be bridged over. The temporal power of the Portuguese was declining. The Dutch had established themselves in the Eastern Isles, and were turning their eyes towards the continent of India. The two European principalities were soon in a state of open antagonism. The Dutch appeared on the southern coast, and the Syrian Christians welcomed them as deliverers. Negapatam, Coulan, and Cranganore fell before their arms. They next laid siege to Cochin. Unsuccessful at first, for the setting in of the monsoon compelled them to break off their operations, they renewed the siege at the commencement of the settled weather, and captured the place by assault.* During these operations, the Syrian Christians are said to have taken no active part against their oppressors, but to have awaited quietly the issue of the contest. That their " arms were pointed against their falling tyrants," appears to be a mere figure of speech. That the oppression of the churches, however, was the ruin of Portugal in the East is no rhetorical flourish. The Christians of Malabar, had they put forth their strength, might have turned the tide of conquest against the Dutch, and rescued the strongholds of Portugal from their grasp. Instead of this, they watched the issue of the contest with secret satisfaction, and rejoiced in, if they did not precipitate, the overthrow of their oppressors.

Then followed a season of calm to the Churches. The Dutch did not oppress, but they neglected them. " The trading companies of Holland and England are the friends of toleration; but if oppression be less mortifying than contempt, the Christians of St. Thomas have reason to complain of the cold and silent indifference of their brethren of Europe."† " The Dutch," writes Mr. Hough, " entirely devoted to

* January, 1663. † Gibbon.

D 2

commercial pursuits, are said to have totally neglected them, at least so far as related to their religious improvement." But if they did not encourage the Malabar Christians, they sheltered them against the rapacity of the Jesuits; and the dawn of the eighteenth century found the authority of Rome a mere shadow among the Syrian Churches.

The great field of Madura was still open to these energetic and unscrupulous men. They went about their work with unabated vigour, but their overthrow was now closely at hand. I have not space to speak in detail of the fall of the Jesuits' missions in Southern India, or to write otherwise than generally and incidentally of the further progress of Papacy in the East. It were better, therefore, here to state, that the ruin of the Jesuit missions in Southern India was accomplished, in time, by a natural internal process, rather than by any outward violence. The whole system was based upon a lie; and it fell to pieces. Sentence of death was written down against it from the first; for it was a great fraud—a mighty imposture. The "new Brahmans" were detected at last. They were found to be only Feringhees in disguise; and the natives rejected their ministrations with anger and contempt.* There is no more pregnant chapter in the whole history of human imposture, than that which embraces the astonishing narrative

* The best account of the Jesuits' Missions in India with which I am acquainted, is one written by the Rev. W. S. Mackay, of the Free Scotch Church Mission of Calcutta —originally published in the "Calcutta Review," and since re-issued in London and Edinburgh, as a separate publication. An immense mass of information is here condensed into a small space, and reproduced in a most agreeable manner.

of the Jesuits' Missions in Southern India. For a time the Order "stooped"

"Into a dark tremendous sea of cloud;"

and the Jesuits, under the ban in Europe, disappeared from the Indian coasts. But they are now again overrunning India, and working mightily as of old. Great as is their apparent activity, perhaps the full extent of their efforts is hardly known : for although they may not now simulate Brahmans, it is more than suspected that they have not yet abandoned their old love of disguise.

# CHAPTER II.

Establishment of the East India Company—Immorality of the first English Settlers—Strife at the Presidencies—The first Church Services—Exhortations of the Directors—The first Protestant Church.

THE year which saw the Syrian Churches of Malabar fall before the papal tyranny of Menezes, witnessed also another remarkable event, which was destined to exercise a far greater influence over the progress of Christianity in India. In that year, 1599, a party of merchants, traders, and other capitalists in the City of London, their imaginations inflamed, and their cupidity excited, by the marvellous stories which they had heard of the wealth of the Great Indies, and the profits of the Eastern trade, erected themselves, under Royal sanction, into a corporation; and, in a pure spirit of commercial enterprise, or as they were wont to say, " on a pure mercantile bottom," with no other thought than that of driving a brisk trade and realising good profits, that great fact, the East India Company, was solemnly inaugurated.

There is no great merit to be claimed for them. They sought their own worldly advantage. They had no grand thoughts of the diffusion of civilization and the propagation of Christianity. The conversion of the Moors or the Gentoos was assuredly no part of their design. Indeed, it must be admitted, that they launched into their great commercial enterprise with very obscure ideas of the religions of the people with whom they purposed to trade. But I have no doubt that the members of this corporation were at least as good as their neighbours. There was little or no missionary spirit at that time alive in the country. Our Protestantism was of a homely, home-staying character. It was only striking root in our own soil; the time had not yet come for it to put forth its branches to spread over the remote places of the earth.

There is reason to believe, however, that the infant Company did, according to the circumstances of the times, and the light that was in them, enough to entitle them to the respect of impartial history. They sent out chaplains in their ships; and commonly despatched their ventures with prayer and thanksgiving, sometimes offered up in the presence of the Governor of the Company and his colleagues. A farewell sermon was preached upon these occasions by some respectable divine; and perhaps published for the edification of the outside public. One of these, by Dr. Wood, is prefaced by a dedicatory epistle to Sir James Wood, the Governor, in which the writer thus, eighteen years after the first establishment of the Company, speaks of its charities to the fatherless and the widow, and to poor ministers of the Gospel—
"I must needs set down," wrote Dr. Wood in 1618, "that as God has greatly increased your store, so ye

have not been backward to impart much, and more than any society (that ever I could heare of), to the supply of the wants of its poore members; your daily reliefe of poore ministers of the Gospel; your charitie to prisoners, to widowes, to orphans and all well-minded poore people that you finde to stande in need of your helpe, can not but pleade for you in the eyes of God and of all good men. Goe on, therefore, in God's name in your noble designs, and rest ye still upon His blessing, who (I doubt not) has many more in store for you; and so long as you conscionably seek to honour His name among the heathen, and (under him) to advance the state wherein ye live, will (no doubt) afford you many comfortable assurances of His love and favour, both to your bodies and soules, here in this life, and crowne you with eternal glory with Himself in the life to come."—It is here, at all events, asserted that the Company sought to honour God's name among the heathen; but if, as I am disposed to believe, they did, their will was greater than their power.

Every good Christian is a missionary, though he never seeks to proselytise, except by his holy example. But I am afraid that there were not many missionaries of this class among the first adventurers who voyaged to the East. The first of whom I can find any trace with the pure missionary spirit within him was one Joseph Salbank, a Company's factor at Agra, who was greatly scandalised by the doings of the Jesuits, and the success which attended their efforts in the early part of the seventeenth century; and who, being a devout man himself, wrote home to the Company, that it would be well if they would send out "not only solid and sufficient divines, that may be able to encounter with the arch enemies of our religion, but also godly, zealous, and devout persons, such as may, by their piety and purity of life, give good example to those with whom they live."* That good example was doubtless much needed. Our early settlers were often men of intemperate habits and licentious lives; outraging decency and scandalising Christianity; a terror to the natives of their adopted country and a reproach to their own. It is true that the Portuguese before them had shown how a Christian can live; but they had built churches and imported priests, and the outward observances of their more imposing faith wrought some effect upon the heathen's minds. But it seemed as though the English had no faith and no self-control; and the natives soon began to regard them as little better than fiends. "It is a most sad and horrible thing," wrote one of the first English clergymen who ever visited India,† "to consider what scandal there is brought upon the Christian religion by the looseness and remissness, by the exorbitances of many which come amongst them, who profess themselves Christians, of whom I have often heard the natives, who live near the ports where our ships arrive say thus, in broken English, which they have gotten—'*Christian religion, devil religion; Christian*

* India House Records. The letter is dated November 22, 1617.
† Mr. Terry, who accompanied Sir Thomas Roe to India. His account of what he saw there is affixed to the English translation of Pietro Delavalle's "Travels."

*much drunk; Christian much do wrong; much beat much abuse others.'"*

The passage has been often quoted. It declares, in unmistakeable language, the immorality of the first Englishmen who went out to trade with the people of India, or were sent thither by their friends, " that so they might make their own graves in the sea, or else have graves made for them on the Indian shore."* Doubtless there were some honest, decent

---

* The writer referred to in the preceding note says, that " many that have been well born, when their friends knew not what to do with them, have been sent to East India." " A very cleanly conveyance," the writer adds, " for parents to be rid of their unruly children ; but I never knew any who was supposed to be sent thither, but he outlived that voyage." In Sir Thomas Roe's letters there are some significant allusions to the young-gentlemen adventurers, who brought him out letters of introduction from noblemen at home, and with whom, not being able to make them Members of Council or Inspectors-General of Cavalry, he did not know what to do. " You have many young gentlemen," wrote the Ambassador in 1616, " come that will not know how to bestow themselves here. The country is mistaken. There are no inns, no chambers to hire ; every man must build a house ; and the Company's, by express order, can be no refuge for them. As many as you can continue at sea, so many burdens you take off mine and the Company's shoulders. To enter into these wars is a poor hope. Their pay is not like ours—so much trouble, so much servility as no free heart can endure. Besides, these people are so proud, that they despise any art or form of war but their own. One or two men cannot break ancient customs of a nation wedded to their own discipline. I am sorry for them, and can only help them by my counsel. . . . My credit here is sufficient to do my nation right, provided it be not blasted with our own disorders, which I entreat you earnestly to look into, and, on my part, I will not fail." In another letter (Nov. 11, 1616) the ambassador says: " There is a young gentleman in your fleet, Mr. Herbert, for whom some of his friends, *that have such interest in me as I dare not disobey,* have written. I shall be extreme glad to do him any courtesy, but the preferment is so mean here that I dare not encourage, nor advise him to land. But if that be his desire, and that he will come up to me, he shall be very welcome, and he shall find I will do him all courtesy in my power. My house and diet shall be free for him until I can either settle him in the Prince's service, or that his curiosity to see this place be gratified ; and then he shall return with me at his pleasure. If he affect any other course, if it be in my power to stand him in stead, upon advice from him I will not fail him. I pray let him know this much, that besides the respect I bear his noble brother, the name of Herbert, and being of the blood of that honourable earl (Pembroke) whom I ever loved, and from whom I ever received undeserved favours, is such a tie to me to requite upon him, that I will not lose any occasion to do it." We are not unlikely, after a lapse of two centuries and a half, to see something of the kind enacted over again.

men from the middle classes amongst them—as old
Joseph Salbank, of whom mention has been made,
and Thomas Kerridge, who came to be chief of the
factory at Surat. But many, it appears from contemporary writers, were society's hard bargains—
youngsters, perhaps, of good family, to which they
were a disgrace, and from the bosom of which, therefore, they were to be cast out, in the hope that there
would be no prodigal's return from the "great
Indies." It was not to be expected that men who
had disgraced themselves at home would lead more
respectable lives abroad; but if their career would not
be better, it might be briefer; and so they were sent
out to show not only how a Christian might live, but
how a Christian might die—blaspheming. It is
truly a matter to be looked back upon with shame
and sorrow. There had been two Christian nations
in India before us. We found the name of Christian
little better than a synonym for Devil; and for some
time we did nothing to disturb the popular belief in
the Satanic origin of our saving faith. Compared
with the lives of many of our own people, those of
the natives of the country really appeared to glow
with the "excellent moralities" with which early
travellers were wont to invest the meek and patient
Gentoos. And so not only was nothing done for
Christianity, during the first century of our connection
with India, but very much was done against it.
We made for ourselves impediments to the diffusion
of Gospel light.

We may deplore this now, after a lapse of two

centuries, for there is much in it to account for our
tardy progress in the great work of evangelization;
but there is nothing that can reasonably surprise us.
In the first place, England herself was not, at that
time overburdened with morality.  In the middle of
the seventeenth century our countrymen at home
were but little distinguished for the purity of their
lives; and there was small chance of British virtue,
dwarfed and dwindled at home, expanding on foreign
soil.  The courtly licentiousness of the Restoration
had polluted the whole land.  The stamp of White-
hall was upon the currency of our daily lives; and it
went out upon our adventurers in the Company's
ships, and was not, we may be sure, to be easily
effaced in a heathen land.  Society in our distant
dependencies commonly reflects, with an added coarseness, the prevailing tone of the morality of the mother
country.  England herself is chargeable with a large
share of the vices which her children import into
foreign lands.  But there is something still which must
be attributed to the deteriorating influences of the
social position of the exile. . The more isolated he is,
the more probable becomes the decay of all high principle in his breast.  Self-respect is a choice plant; but
few are at the trouble to cultivate it.  A man, cut
off from the society of his countrymen, is not only
removed beyond all the obstructions of immorality,
but is doubly exposed to all its temptations.  There
is, in fact, everything to allure—and nothing to stay
him.  He seeks, in the pursuit of sensual enjoyment,
occupation and excitement; and, as there are none

whose opinion he regards, to watch his descent, he
cares not how low he descends. In his solitude he
takes " a harem for his grot," or he flies to the companionship of the bottle. Regarding the natives only
as so many graven images, or so many ingenious me-
chanical contrivances, he sinks lower and lower in the
slough of immorality, until he is utterly debased.
Even in these times, the demoralising effects of
segregation are not unfrequently apparent. In
remote out-stations men do what they would shrink
from doing in the crowded Presidency. Now this
dangerous segregation in a large degree distinguished
the lives and influenced the conduct of our earliest
European settlers. It is true that they met together
at the few stations, which were accessible to them,
but even then they were mere scattered fragments
broken off from the mass of European humanity.
There was among them little dissimilarity of taste,
feeling, and habit. There was no society, whose
frowns the sensualist could dread. His doings, on
those far-off shores, were unknown to his countrymen in England; perchance there may have been
a parent, or a brother, or a friend, in whose eyes
the adventurer might desire to wear a fair aspect;
but in India he was as far beyond the observation of
that parent, brother, or friend, as though he dwelt
in another planet. There were, in truth, no outward
motives to preserve morality of conduct, or even decency of demeanour; so, from the moment of their
landing upon the shores of India, the first settlers
cast off all those bonds which had restrained them in

their native villages; they regarded themselves as privileged beings—privileged to violate all the obligations of religion and morality, and to outrage all the decencies of life. They who went thither were often desperate adventurers, whom England, in the emphatic language of the Scripture, had spued out; men who sought those golden sands of the East to repair their broken fortunes; to bury in oblivion a sullied name; or to wring, with lawless hand, from the weak and unsuspecting, wealth which they had not the character or the capacity to obtain by honest industry at home. They cheated; they gambled; they drank; they revelled in all kinds of debauchery. Associates in vice, linked together by a common bond of rapacity, they still often pursued one another with desperate malice, and, few though they were in numbers, among them there was no fellowship, except a fellowship of crime.

All this was against the new comer; and so, whilst the depraved met with no inducement to reform, the pure but rarely escaped corruption. Whether they were there initiated, or perpetuated in destructive error, equally may they be regarded as the victims of circumstance. They left a country of checks—checks imposed not only by civil polity but by the more stringent code of opinion—to seek a country where no checks existed: what wonder then that they fell?

As the English in India increased in numbers, and something like a society began to form itself, affairs began a little to improve. There are saving influences in a multitude. The variety of character, of motive,

and of habit, which it presents, can scarcely fail to
exercise a restraining power over the individual.
When a man knows that he is surrounded by others
whose opinions, tastes, and habits are widely different
—who will turn away with disgust from open profligacy, and religiously keep aloof from the profligate
—he restrains those natural impulses, and subjects
himself to a course of moral training, which he soon
acknowledges to possess its worldly advantages, even
in a vicious state of society. The value of a fair
character is appreciated even by those who have no
abstract veneration for what is beautiful and excellent
in religion and morality; and good example, where it
does not generate virtue, often obstructs vice.

It is only from incidental allusions in the few works
of travel and fewer political memoirs, which our
ancestors have bequeathed to us, that we can gain
any insight into the moral condition of the English
in India, previous to the conquest of Bengal. Many
writers, who have described the rise and progress of
the rival East India Companies, have given us somewhat startling accounts of the official rapacity of our
predecessors—of the fierce contentions of the opponent
companies, of their unscrupulous conduct towards
the natives, and towards each other—of their commercial dishonesty, their judicial turpitude, and their
political injustice—all these things are broadly stated;
but to the immorality of their private life we have
little but indistinct allusions. But the quaint old
despatches of the earliest servants of the Company,
still preserved in the records of the India House,

supply, in their marvellous truthfulness and unreserve, much that is wanting in the printed materials of history. One fact, however, may be gathered from the latter—our countrymen managed to work through the first eighty years of the seventeenth century without building a church. Old John Mandelslo, who wrote in 1640, tells us that at the chief factory prayers were said at the President's house. "The respect," he writes, "and deference which the other merchants have for the President was very remarkable, as also the order which was there observed in all things, especially at Divine Service, which was said twice a day, in the morning at six, and at eight at night, and on Sundays thrice. No person in the house but had his particular function, and their certain hours assigned them as well for work as recreation. Our divertisement was thus ordered. On Fridayes after prayers, there was a particular assembly, at which met with us three other merchants, who were of kin to the President, and had left, as well as he, their wives in England, which day being that of their departure from England, they had appointed it for to make a commemoration thereof, and drink their wives' healths. Some made their advantage of this meeting to get more than they could well carry away, though every man was at liberty to drink what he pleased and to mix the sack as he thought fit, or to drink *palepuntz*, which is a kind of drink consisting of *aqua vitæ*, rose-water, juice of citrons and sugar."

It would have been well if these carouses had been

permitted to come off only "after prayers." But sometimes they interrupted Divine service even on the Sabbath. The Deputy-Governor of Bombay was tried in 1669, and found guilty of the offence of obstructing public worship by holding drinking-parties at church-time on Sundays, and keeping them up on week-days "to two or three of the clock in the morning, to the neglecting of the service of God in the morning prayers."* I am afraid, however, that not many of his countrymen in England at that time were very fit for matutinal devotions.

They were not all, however, of this kind. Some good, God-fearing men were, at intervals, to be found among these local Presidents and Governors. There was, for example, Sir George Oxenden, of whom Hamilton wrote, that when he died "piety grew sick, and the building of churches unfashionable."† These

---

* The wording of the charges is so curious, that I am tempted to give a portion of them in a note:—

"3rd. That he (Deputy-Governor Young) hath on the Sabbath day hindered the performance of public duty to God Almighty at the accustomary hour, continuing in drinking of healths, detaining others with him against their wills; and whilst he drank, in false devotions upon his knees, a health devoted to the Union, in the time appointed for the service belonging to the Lord's-day, the unhappy sequel showed it to be but the projection of a further disunion.

"4th. That to the great scandal of the inhabitants of the island, of all the neighbours round about, both papists and others that are idolators, in dishonour of the sobriety of the Protestant religion, he hath made frequent and heavy drinking meetings, continuing sometimes till two or three of the clock in the morning, to the neglecting of the service of God in the morning prayers, and the service of the Company in the mean time had stood still while he slept, thus perverting and converting to an ill private use, those refreshments intended for the factory in general."— *Consultations held at Surat*, January 22, 1669.

† I may as well give entire the passage in Alexander Hamilton's travels, from which these words are taken. It will be gathered from them that Sir George Oxenden had actually commenced the erection of the church:—

" Notwithstanding the Company was at so much charge in building of forts, they had no thoughts of building a church for many years after Sir George Oxenden began to build one, and charitable collections were gathered for that use; but when Sir George died, piety grew sick, and the building of churches was grown unfashionable. Indeed,

E

words have a double meaning. The writer might have intended either to glorify Sir George, or to sneer at the propensity of the smaller people of the Factory to follow the example of the great man. In either sense the passage is honourable to Oxenden, who strove hard to compass the erection of a church at Bombay. There is on record his appeal to the Directors in England in behalf of his proposal to erect an edifice of a "form proportionable to the small churches in England," the "main design" of which, although the spiritual good of the factors themselves was not forgotten, was that the natives should be induced to enter the building " and observe the purity and gravity of our devotions." The settlers themselves had collected a good round sum for the purpose, and they asked the Court to make up the balance, and to despatch an experienced English builder to superintend the work.* This was just at the close of the third quarter of the seventeenth century; but Bombay had yet to wait many years more for the erection of a Protestant church. No wonder that our progress was slow. The Portuguese had churches everywhere "thwacked full," we are told, " of young blacks singing vespers;" and there were convents, and colleges, and religious libraries,

it was a long while before the island had people enough to fill a chapel that was in the fort, for as fast as recruits came from Britain they died in Bombay, which got the island a bad name. There were reckoned above 5,000*l.* had been gathered towards building the church, but Sir John Child, when he came to reign in Bombay, converted the money to his own use and never more was heard of it. The walls were built by his predecessors to five yards high." It should be stated that the stories which Hamilton tells of Sir John Child are to be accepted with some qualification.

* See Anderson's " English in Western India."

nd other indications of a living and ostentatious faith.

The church-building scheme, however, was not neglected by Sir George Oxenden's successor, another President, worthy of exceptional notice. This was Gerald Aungier, who urgently pressed upon his honourable masters at home the expediency of building a church at Bombay, hoping, as he wrote, that "when the merciful pleasure of God shall think good to touch them (the natives) with a sense of the eternal welfare of their souls, they may be convinced of their error, sensible of their present dangerous, uncertain wanderings, and desirous to render themselves happy in a more sure way of salvation, which we pray God grant in his good time."[*] It was not however for Surat—it was not for Bombay—to see the erection of the first Protestant church. That honour, a few years afterwards, was conferred on the Factory at Madras.

Under Presidents Oxenden and Aungier served one Streynsham Master—a devout man, of generally good repute, who was afterwards appointed chief of

---

[*] Letter from the President and Council at Surat, January 17, 1675-6, quoted in Anderson's "English in Western India." The same accurate and entertaining writer gives another passage from the Surat papers of the time, which illustrates the earnest character of this good man's piety and morality. When he was about to leave Surat for Bombay, he handed over charge of the Surat factory to Mr. Streynsham Master (another pious man, of whom mention will presently be made), saying, that "a blessing may attend you in all your proceedings, we recommend to you the pious order observed in our family, to wit, morning and evening prayer, the strict observance of the Lord's-day, the preventing of all disorder, profaneness, and debauchery, the preservation of the peace, and good government among our fellow-servants; in all which we shall not doubt your careful observance, being well acquainted with your own inclination thereunto; and therefore need not mind you thereof, but as it is one of the most essential parts of your charge."

the Factory at Madras. In the year 1681 he laid
the foundation stone of the first edifice ever erected
for Protestant worship in India. He commenced and
carried on the great work at his own charge, and
never rested until he had brought it to an end. I
doubt not that there are some, who think, that when
it was done, it was after all no better than a barn
or a riding school; for, assuredly, it was not episco-
pally consecrated; and Streynsham Master had probably no very accurate notion of the necessities of a
due observance of the points of the compass. But it
is no small thing to have built the first Protestant
church in India—single-handed, as it is said; or even
with such help as he could obtain from his brother-
settlers. It was not an achievement the less meritorious on his part, because we wonder that it should
have taken the English residents in India eighty
years to build a church at all. They do not, however,
appear to have been altogether destitute of respect for
the Church. Among the earliest of the Company's
records I find an entrance of the fact that a small
party of adventurers had subscribed "200*l.* for the
church at Wapping;" and I learn from Mr. Anderson's book, that Sir George Oxenden sent home 500*l.*
for the repairs of the church and chancel of Wing-
ham. Our missionary enterprise in those days seems
to have set from east to west; and as I have learnt
since I commenced this chapter, from a circular left
at my door, that my own parish of St. Pancras has
a population of 190,000 souls, with church accommodation for not one third of them; that " New Zealand

is higher in the scale of Christianity" than this great metropolitan parish; and that the "central organization for the diffusion of infidelity throughout Great Britain is within its bounds,"* I am almost tempted to think that some of this missionary enterprise might advantageously set in the same direction still.

But although up to this time (1680) there were no Protestant churches, there were some Protestant ministers in India. The Company sent out chaplains, but in no great number. Up to the beginning of the eighteenth century the entire list of ecclesiastics did not contain more than nineteen names. The sufficiency of the supply, however, is not to be judged by the actual number, but by the proportion it bore to the general list of Englishmen at that time in the Company's service; and one chaplain to each Factory, by this reckoning, would have been ample for the spiritual wants of the settlers, if death, the great interloper, had not so often cut off the supply. Of the character of these men, with one or two exceptions, we have no very clear idea. The Courts of the second Charles and the second James were not peculiarly favourable to the growth either of sound morality or sound Protestantism: but the advent of William of Holland inaugurated a new era; and the settlers in Western India took advantage of the occasion to assert their Protestantism, and to beg that the Governors of the Company would send them out "two good orthodox ministers, we having not one on this side of India;' " a little good English beer, called stout; and a little

* Circular of the City Mission.—April 1858.

wine from your honours," for their stomachs' sake and their often infirmities.[*]

The orthodox ministers were sent, and soon afterwards, not only was the appointment of a sufficiency of chaplains to the Indian stations, but the conversion of the Gentoos by these chaplains, decreed in letters patent from the Crown. The Dutch, although they do not appear at this time to have done anything for the advancement of Christianity on the continent of India, had been active and successful in Ceylon and in the Malayan archipelago ;[†]

[*] The passage here quoted, which I have extracted from the old records of the Company, is worth giving entire : — " We observe what your honours are pleased to write us concerning the Prince of Orange being arrived at St. James's, &c. God of his mercy send all things for the best, and keep our native country from civil wars, and grant that the true Protestant religion may flourish there as long as the sun and moon endureth. . . . . We humbly beg your honours will supply us with two gunners, able men that understand their business. You will truly lose nothing by it, and if you will keep fortifications, 'tis very fit you have at least one, if not two, able gunners in each fort. We likewise petition your honours for two good orthodox ministers; we having not one on this side of India, as formerly advised to your honours. We likewise beg you will yearly supply us with good paper and quills. . . . . If you do please to send us a little good English beer, as they call stout, it will be very welcome ; and a little wine from your honours as you were pleased to favour us with formerly, would not be amiss."

[†] Mr. Crawford, in his admirable " Dictionary of the Indian Islands," shows that their Dutch converts were principally at Amboyna, where, he says, some 30,000 Christians are to be found. " These belong," he adds, " to the reformed Lutheran church, and are with justice considered as the most moral, best educated, and best conducted people in the whole Archipelago."—See article CHRISTIANITY. In this paper Mr. Crawford gives a passage translated from Pigafetta's First Voyage, which contains so curious an account of the manner in which Magellan converted the Philippines, that I am tempted to give it entire, as an illustration of Portuguese propagandism :—

" A great cross was then erected in the plain. The Captain-general had previously advised all who desired to become Christians, that it was necessary to destroy all their idols and substitute for them the cross, which they were to adore on their knees daily, morning and noon. He taught them also, how to make the sign of the cross on their foreheads, and admonished them to confirm these forms by good works. The Captain-general, who was entirely clothed in white, said that he was habited in this colour in order to show his love and sincerity to them. Of this they appeared sensible, but without knowing what to answer. He then took the King by the hand, and conducted him to a stage, where he, and those that were with him, were baptised. The King (of Cebu), who was before called Rai (Raja) Humabon, was named Don Carlo,

and there seemed no reason why the English should
not achieve similar successes. So the new charter
granted to the second East India Company, in 1698,
contained a clause, enacting that the Company should
constantly maintain one minister " in every garrison
and superior factory," that they should "in such
garrisons or factories provide or set apart a decent
and convenient place for divine service only," and,
moreover, that " all such ministers as shall be sent to reside in India, shall be obliged to learn, within one year
after their arrival, the Portuguese language, and shall
apply themselves to learn the native language of the
country where they shall reside, the better to enable
them to instruct the Gentoos, that shall be the
servants or slaves of the said Company, or of their
agents, in the Protestant religion." Perhaps, it may
be inferred from this that the chaplains were expected

after the Emperor,—the prince, Don
Ferdinando, after the Emperor's
brother,—the King of Massana, Gio-
vanni, and one of the principal chiefs
got the name of our captain, that is,
Ferdinando. The Moorish merchant
(master of a junk from Siam) was
named Christoforo, and others had
other names given to them. Five
hundred islanders were baptised before saying mass. The captain invited the King and some of his chiefs
to dine with him: they excused themselves, but accompanied us to the
beach, where they took leave. In
the meanwhile there was a general
discharge of artillery from the ships.
After dinner, the priest and many of
us went ashore, in order to baptise
the Queen and other ladies. We
mounted the same stage where the
Queen was seated on a cushion, and
the other ladies around her on mats.
When the priest made his appearance, I called the attention of the
Queen to a portrait of Our Lady, and
to a wooden statuette representing
the Infant Jesus, and a cross, at the
sight of which things she felt a
movement of contrition, and weeping, entreated to be baptised. Other
ladies of her train were baptised
along with her. She was named
Joanna, the name of the Emperor's
mother. Her daughter, wife of the
prince, was named Catherine, and
the Queen of Massana, Elizabeth. A
particular name was given to all the
rest. We baptised that day, between
men, women, and children, about
eight hundred persons. The Queen
asked me to have the Bambino (the
same alleged to have been found
forty-four years after by a soldier of
Legaspi), in order to keep it in room
of her own idols, and I gave it to her.
At a later hour the King and Queen
came down to the sea-side, where we
were assembled, and took pleasure in
listening to the harmless discharge of
cannon, which had before produced
so much fear."—Primo Viaggio in-
torno al Mondo, p. 87.

to make converts among the Romanists as well as among the heathens. I do not learn from any authentic records, that they were very successful in either direction.[*] And assuredly there was enough to do among their own countrymen, not only to keep them Protestants, but to keep them Christians at all.

For that prodigal eighteenth century, which flung the vast empire of the Mogul at the feet of the British conqueror, dawned so cloudily upon the struggling fortunes of the English in India, that it seemed as though their career were about to close in a sudden and disastrous failure precipitated by their own crimes. There is no such gloomy period as this in the life of English adventure in the East. The two rival Companies were pursuing each other with terrible malignity; but there was no fellowship engendered in the ranks of either by the community of danger and of hatred engendered by this fierce strife. At no time, indeed, was there in our factories so much internecine strife, at no time were such scandalous

---

[*] It is certain that towards the close of the century, the Protestant religion made scant progress in India. There were occasional conversions; but, unhappily, they were entirely in the wrong direction. The Portuguese clergy made what proselytes they could; and much public scandal was created at Bombay by the perversion of a son of Sir Heneage Finch, who had been attorney-general and lord keeper in the reign of James the Second. The grief occasioned, however, by the fall of this misguided young gentleman was nothing in comparison with that resulting from the occasional apostacy of some of our people, who were attracted by the conveniences and enticements of the imposture of Mahomed. One example of this may be especially noted. In 1691, a man, rejoicing in a name which afterwards grew into better odour, vexed the spirits of the factors at Surat by openly embracing Mahomedanism. "In addition to our troubles," they wrote, "there is one of our wicked Englishmen, by name John Newton, that came out in the *Royal James and Mary*, and came from Umboor yesterday, and went immediately to the Cossys and declared his intention to turn Moor; and before we possibly could have an opportunity to send to the Governor, the business was done, and he circumcised, which was past our remedy of retrieving his wicked soul."

outrages committed, or was there altogether a more general defiance both of the laws of God and the decencies of man. They fought grievously among themselves; blows following words; and the highest persons in the settlement setting an example of pugnacity which their inferiors, under the potent influence of arrack punch, were only too well-disposed to follow.

As I write, the statesmanship of England is expending itself in a great effort to establish just relations between the President and the Council, to which the Government of our Indian empire is to be entrusted—to devise such constitutional checks as, whilst imparting some vital influence to the latter, will not impair the salutary freedom of action which it is sought to impart to the former. Our Indian Presidents, at the period which I am now describing, adjusted their relations with their councils after a fashion of their own, and their councils imposed checks, which, if not theoretically constitutional, were practically sufficiently effective. If a President exceeded his authority, or otherwise offended his colleagues, some adventurous councillor coerced him with a cudgel or endeavoured to vacate the chair by means of the dagger or the bowl;* whilst the President, on his part, if a man of muscle, sometimes kept a councillor in order by cuffing him to that extent

* Take for example the following pleasant incident, which I have extracted from the Company's records: —" We send your honours our consultation books from the 21st of August, 1695, to the 31st December, 1696, in which does appear a conspiracy against the President's life, and a design to murder the guards, because he would have opposed it. How far Messrs. Vauxe and Upphill were concerned, we leave to your

that scarce a sound place was left about his person.\* The dignified official who inflicted this severe punishment on the councillor was Sir Nicholas Waite, of whom afterwards the civilians said—and, no wonder, considering the perils of office under such circumstances—that they would " rather be private centinels at Fort St. George than serve as second in council under Sir Nicholas Waite."   The violence of such a man could not be tolerated for ever ; so in course of time the Court of Managers at home recalled him and appointed a new council to manage their affairs.

Whilst such was the propriety of those in high place, their subordinates in the several factories were equally dissolute in their lives and outrageous in their conduct.   There was a general complaint of the " sottishness " of the factors.   But for all this, there was an outward recognition of the duties of religion, and the Company's servants, however reluctantly, attended divine service, according to regulation, far more frequently than in a later and more decorous age.   They went to chapel, as boys at Eton, or men at Oxford, and were booked by the chaplain if they

honours to judge by this and depositions before mentioned.   There is strong presumption that it was intended first that the president should be stabbed, and 'twas prevented much through the vigilance of Ephraim Bendall; when hopes of that failed by the guards being doubled, it seems poison was agreed on, as by the deposition of Edmund Clerk, and all bound to secrecy upon an horrid imprecation of damnation to the discoverer, whom the rest were to fall upon and cut off."—*Surat, Feb.* 6, 1696-7.

\* See the complaint of Mr. Charles Peachey: " I have received from you (*i.e.,* the President) two cuts on my head, the one very long and deep, the other a slight thing in comparison to that.   Then a great blowe on my left arme, which has enflamed the shoulder, and deprived me (at present), of the use of that limbe; on my right side a blow on my ribs just beneath the pap, which is a stoppage to my breath, and makes me incapable of helping myself ; on my left hip another, nothing inferior to the first; but above all a cut on the brow of my eye."

were not present.   There were prayers, morning and evening, and every member of the factory was ordered to attend eight times in a week, exclusive of Sunday attendances.   If he failed in this he was fined, and the amount of fine cut from his pay.   Had our people led more decorous lives, these outward observances might have had some beneficial effect upon the minds of the natives in the neighbourhood of our factories —but, as it was, they had still too much reason to complain, " Christian religion, Devil religion," and to rejoice that they were not themselves as this publican.

The continued outrages and indecencies of their servants grievously afflicted the worshipful governors at home, and they did all that they could to control the licentiousness of the settlers, writing out to them that " The Governor, the Deputy Governor, and Committees of the East India Company having been informed of the disorderly and unchristian conversation of some of their factors and servants in the ports of India, tending to the dishonour of God, the discredit of our Lord Jesus Christ, and the shame and scandal of the English nation," had made certain regulations with a view to render " the religion we profess amiable in the sight of those heathens among whom they reside."   Then followed directions for religious observances.   The agents and chiefs of the several factories were, also, strictly enjoined " to prevent all profane swearing and taking the name of God in vain by cursed oaths; all drunkenness and intemperance, all fornication and uncleanness."   If any persisted in committing these sins, they were to bo punished, and if found incorrigible, to be sent to England.

In 1708, the Union of the two companies was accomplished; and from that time, the factories, subsiding into a state of comparative quietude, began to assume a more decorous aspect. It was not, however, until the United Company was ten years old that Bombay witnessed the erection of a Christian church. Meanwhile, Streynsham Master's great work had gone on prosperously at Madras;· and the new century had witnessed the unwonted sight of a party of English gentlemen, headed by the President, walking every Sabbath morning, in stately procession, through a street of sepoys, to a goodly temple dedicated to the Christian's God. Prayers were read twice every week-day. There were two ministers in the enjoyment of salaries of 100*l.* a year ; which I am afraid was not enough to enable them to reject the practice of other settlers, and to yield to the temptations of trade.*

Hitherto I have spoken only of the progress of Christianity on the southern and western coasts of the great Indian peninsula. It was not at first believed that there was very hopeful business of any kind in Northern India. The rich country on the banks of the Hooghly was laconically described as " Bengalla, a hot country—the most of the people very poor gentiles." The Portuguese had been before us in that, as in other parts, and had contrived, as

* See Appendix—" The First Protestant Church."

elsewhere, to impart a somewhat unsavoury odour to the reputation of Christianity. They had built churches and convents, and baptized people by hundreds; but it was only a new form of idolatry that they taught. As for our own people, they were in continual strife with the "papists," and spoke of themselves as the only "good Christians," but with small title to such a distinction. Bad as the English were on the Coast, it would seem that they were still worse on the banks of the Hooghly.

The earliest account that I have been able to find; and I believe the earliest account extant of the moral and social condition of the English in Bengal, is in an unfinished letter written by Sir John Gouldsborough from Chuttanutty (the old name of Calcutta) in 1692. Sir John went round from Madras to visit this outlying factory and to correct the disorders of which a lamentable account had reached him. Job Charnock had recently died; and the character which he had left behind was that of a man averse from business and prone to strife. History, somehow or other, has cast a halo of romance around the life of this man; but I am sorry to say that cotemporary records exhibit him only as a very indifferent public servant and a dissolute cruel-minded man, who having married a native wife, apostatised outright to Paganism.*
His death was conceived to be no loss to the settle-

---

* Hamilton says, "Instead of converting her to Christianity, she made him a proselyte to Paganism; and the only part of Christianity that was remarkable in him was burying her decently, and he built a tomb over her, where all his life after her death he kept the anniversary day of her death by sacrificing a cock on her tomb after the heathen fashion."

ment, and yet it was not easy to find a better man to take his place. Affairs at the time of his death were at all events in so bad a state, that it required all the efforts of the General to restore them to decent order. Let him tell his own story. It affords some curious glimpses into the social life of infant Calcutta :—

"On the 4th of August we set sail from Bengal, and arrived at Chuttanuttee the 12th ditto, where I found your honours' servants in great disorder, and that everyone did that which seemed good in their own eyes. . . . Such wretched men many of these are; but I have great hopes by removing the worst of them from hence to Madras I shall be able to work a thorough reformation among the rest. I have begun with Captain Hill, who was the Secretary and the Captain of the soldiers, who was allowed to keep a punch-house and a billiard table gratis, when others paid for it, and to make two false musters besides his pay for it, and his house gave entertainments to all strangers whatsoever, and he himself an open-tempered man, and debauched in his life, who hath let his wife turn papist without control, and this man neither Mr. Charnock nor Ellis dare contradict because they looked upon him as a fit man to dictate their consultations and letters, whilst the slothfulness of Mr. Charnock and the ignorance of Mr. Ellis would not let them do it themselves. He (Charnock) had a strange disposition, he loved everybody should be at difference, and supported a sergeant that set them to duelling, till Captain Dovrill told him the evil thereof; and always was a friend of Charles Pale, one of the factors, whose master-piece was to invent differences between man and man and deeply swear to the most extravagant lies he could invent; but God hath removed Pale a little while before I came, by death."[*]

The activity of the papists at that time was one of the evils, with which the reforming General had to contend. He found the merchants and factors marrying black wives, who either were or who turned papists and became the willing instruments of the priests. Sir John Gouldsborough, however, asserted his Protestantism in a vigorous manner. He turned the Romanist priests out of Chuttanutty and pulled down their " mass-house.". His own account of the matter is as follows :—

" One Messenger, an Englishman, who had a black wife here (who) died at Hooghly, and being a papist, the Padre Prior made her will, and gave to the Church (that is to himself) her estate. Mr. Hartop was sent to demand these effects from him, as being a silly Englishman's who knew not his own right by our law, was by the Prior wheedled into a consent to the will of his wife, yet complained of it here; upon which Hartop wrote a letter to Captain Hill, as then being a great man in the Government; by which letter your honour will see what a straite the papist priests were come to, even to threaten to command all the good Christians in this place, and our wives too, if they pleased; upon which I turned their priests from hence, and their masshouse was to be pulled

* M.S. Records of the East India Company.

down in course to make way for the factorie, when it shall be thought convenient to build it; and I disbanded all the black Christian soldiers and lowered their wages from five to four rupees a month, and made them intreat to be received again so; and all this came to pass by the poor regard which this and the former agent's wife had for our religion, and by the encouragement Hill's wife had put into the papists, by whose example several Englishmen's black wives turned papist and were not so before, which made the Padre Prior at Hooghly, who is Captain of Bandel, give such a pragmatic answer to Mr. Hartop."[*]

The last ten years of the seventeenth century saw the licentiousness of the. English in India at its height. The fierce contentions of the two rival Companies roused into more vehement action the bad passions of humanity; and there was neither inward scruple nor outward restraint. After the union of the two Companies, these animosities subsided, and in Northern India, as at the Southern and Western Factories, fewer outrages were committed, and there was more decency of life; but I am afraid that true Christianity still waxed slowly in Bengal.

* M.S. Records of the East India Company.

# CHAPTER III.

The First Protestant Mission—Ziegenbalg and Plutscho—Missionary Efforts at Tranquebar—Encouragement of the Company's Chaplains—Schwartz and Kiernander.

IN the meanwhile some hopeful symptoms of energetic religious action in the Reformed Church were slowly evincing themselves in the Western world. The Protestantism of Europe was beginning to bestir itself. The Hollander and the Dane preceded the Englishman in fields of missionary enterprise; but at the commencement of the eighteenth century, England herself was right royally connected both with the Hollander and the Dane; and now that Protestant ascendancy was securely established at home, it began to move, somewhat sluggishly it must be admitted, in new directions, and to feel its way towards propagandism in foreign parts. Cromwell had thought of this some time before; and at the end of the seventeenth century, Prideaux, Dean of Norwich, had put forth a scheme for the dissemination of Christianity in the East, of which the establishment of bishoprics was a more prominent feature than the Nonconformist Protector would have approved. But out of these good intentions nothing had really come; and it was

F

not until the year 1709 that England made a pecuniary contribution towards the support of missions in the East; and that contribution was made by the Society for the Propagation of the Gospel in Foreign Parts, which had been established in 1701; the amount of the contribution being 20*l.*, with a case of books and some encouraging letters.*

The mission to which this contribution was made, through the intervention of one of the chaplains of Prince George of Denmark, the husband of our Anne, was a Danish Mission. Early in the seventeenth century the Danes had established themselves at Tranquebar, on the Eastern coast of the Southern Peninsula of India. But it was not until the commencement of the eighteenth century that they turned their thoughts towards the evangelization of the heathen. In the year 1705, Frederick IV. of Denmark appears to have meditated much and deeply on the great subject of Gospel-diffusion; and before the year had worn to a close, two Protestant missionaries were on their way, in a Danish ship, to Tranquebar, full of high and solemn thoughts of the greatness of their enterprise.

The names of these two men were Bartholomew Ziegenbalg and Henry Plutscho. They had been educated at the University of Halle—that great centre of Evangelical Christianity—under the learned and pious Professor Franke, whose delight it was to train young men to the work of God; and by him they had been selected, at the instigation of the King,

* Hough's " Christianity in India."

to go forth into strange countries, and to disseminate among benighted nations the message of eternal truth. In a true Christian temper they took up the burden, as a privilege, and girded themselves to leave all and follow Him. It was their mission not to baptize, but to convert the heathen. They had sound Protestant ideas of Christian teaching; and they laboured for God, not for the Church. They reverenced and they used the Bible. In the great warfare they were about to wage with falsehood and idolatry, they looked upon that holy book as at once their sword and their buckler. They went forth with the truth in their hand; and they sought the aid of no shams and disguises. It was their desire to place the Word of God before the eyes of the dark-minded people; to declare the glad tidings of salvation, and to bring them face to face with their Maker, high above the dense mists of idolatrous superstition, on the clear mountain-peaks of revelation. In the full flush and energy of youthful enthusiasm, yet weighing well the difficulties they were about to encounter, and the sufferings it would be theirs to endure, they quitted the University of Halle, and embarked for the coast of Coromandel. The voyage was a lengthy and a perilous one; but Ziegenbalg and his associate found leisure and quietude to map out the scheme of their enterprise, and to gird themselves up for the great work that lay before them. The first sight of the natives on the beach at Tranquebar filled them with profound emotion. Their eyes glistened with tears; their hearts swelled with sympathy; and their souls were lifted up in prayer. Their reception was not encouraging. Their countrymen shook their heads; started difficulties; almost regarded them as madmen. But they comforted one another; sought strength from God; and remembered the example of the Apostles.

They did not expect to work miracles of genuine conversion; and they were content with no conversion that was not genuine. They saw at once that it was no easy task that they had set themselves. The language which they spoke was high Dutch; that of the natives was low Tamul. To open out a medium of communication was necessarily their first object. As they could not expect the natives to learn their language, they began at once to learn the language of the natives. In these days this is no difficult matter. Dictionaries, grammars, and vocabularies to aid the student of almost any Oriental dialect, are to be bought for a few rupees, and competent instructors are to be had by any one who will send for them. In Ziegenbalg's time, the vernacular literature of the Coromandel coast was only to be studied upon palmyra leaves. These Danish missionaries did not learn the language with a sleek Moonshee by their side, a freely-going punkah overhead, and an odorous hookah between their lips. They put themselves to school again. They joined a children's class under a common native schoolmaster, and sitting on the ground traced the Tamul character on the sand, or repeated the words after the master, whilst their little schoolfellows stood a-gape with astonishment at the new comrades with whom they found themselves so strangely associated.

In a short time they had made such progress, and, in spite of the difficulty of obtaining access to the Vedas, had gained such an insight into Hindoo literature and theology as greatly to alarm the Brahmans. It was hard to say whether the intolerance of the native priesthood or the immorality of the European laity at Tranquebar were the greater obstacle, at the outset, to the success of the mission. But the pure lives of Ziegenbalg and his associate triumphed at last over the latter difficulty; and it may be questioned whether the remarkable contrast which their temperance, soberness, and chastity, their gentleness and humility, presented to the arrogance and immorality of their brethren, did not ultimately work mightily to their advantage. They lived down a great national reproach; and won the confidence of all by the blamelessness of their Christian deportment.

The enmity of the Romanist priests was another obstacle to their progress—as was also the opposition of the Protestant divines, who were "on the Establishment," and had a church and congregation of their own. But when it was discovered that the humble missionaries were under the especial protection of the King of Denmark, the Governor himself went to call upon them; and the chaplains, becoming suddenly overtaken with courtesy, lent them their church, for the performance of a special service for the Germans of the settlement, whose language the chaplains did not understand. Soon, however, the missionaries began to think of erecting a church of their own. A wealthy native offered to build it at his own charge, but the rage of heathenism was so furious against him, that he was fain to desist from his pious purpose, and to hide himself from the malice of his enemies by running away from Tranquebar.

On the 12th of May, 1707, their first converts were baptized. The victory in this case was one of no great difficulty, for the proselytes were poor slaves, in the possession of Danish masters, purchased perhaps in infancy, and willing, at any time, to belong to " master's caste." But after this, the fame of their teaching spread mightily ; and, their own humble residence being too limited to meet the requirements of their increased congregation, they determined, in spite of the scantiness of their funds, to erect for themselves the church of which their native patron had been compelled to abandon the design. " We began in great poverty," they said, " but with faith and confidence in God." And assuredly the pious work did not halt for want of money or of anything else. The first stone was laid on the 14th of June, 1707, and on the 14th of August, of the same year, it was complete. At this the natives wondered greatly, looking upon it as something truly miraculous that the Christians' temple should thus spring suddenly out of the ground—or, as Ziegenbalg himself phrased it, " visibly discovering the finger of God attending us all along in carrying on the work." The church being built there was never any want of a congregation. The two young missionaries preached, in Tamul and in Portuguese, to crowds of Papists and Protestants, Mahomedans and Hindoos.

Doubtless many went from mere idle curiosity; some, perhaps, simply to scoff. Ziegenbalg and Plutscho were prepared for this. They did not expect to make genuine converts by miraculous thousands; and they were content only with genuine conversion. They numbered their proselytes slowly, by units and tens. And they met with the usual disappointments in the way of selfishness and hypocrisy —and, still worse, of backslidings. One tremendous difficulty met them at the outset — a difficulty, perhaps, but little appreciated in the learned atmosphere of Halle. Christianity they soon found to be, in the understandings of the natives of the country, only a synonym for *ruin*. It was a deplorable truth; but they looked it boldly in the face. "If any one resolves on entering into our religion," they wrote to their friends, "he must forthwith quit all his estates and relations, and suffer himself to be insulted as the vilest and most despicable fellow in the world." Their converts were commonly, therefore, made from among men who had nothing to lose but the privilege to labour; and, if no one else would employ them, the missionaries provided them with food and raiment. This brought some about them eager to belong to master's caste, as a short and easy road to a provision, and naturally threw suspicion upon some of their true conversions. Never destitute of resources, and quick to meet every new difficulty as it arose, Ziegenbalg and Plutscho then bethought themselves of establishing

manufactories, " chiefly," as they said, " on account of
employing the new-converted heathen about some
useful business at home." With all their spiritual
enthusiasm, these young Danish missionaries were
eminently practical men; and I am not sure that we
should not have done much better in India, if we had
imitated them in this good practice of providing work
for our heathen converts.[*]

But all this great work could not be carried on
with the insufficient means at the disposal of the two
missionaries. How could churches be built, and
schools maintained, and converts supported, upon the
slender resources of the Mission? Communication
with Europe was irregular in those days, and often
there were long intervals between the arrivals of
expected vessels. So it happened, that trouble fell
upon the missionaries, and that Ziegenbalg was cast
into prison. The governor and the chief people of
the settlement had begun to doubt whether the King
of Denmark was really interested in the fate of the
pauper missionaries. It seemed, indeed, as if they
had no influential friends at home; and so of what
use was it to encourage them?[†] Ziegenbalg spent
four months in prison; and then succours arrived

[*] Commenting upon this incident in the lives of Ziegenbalg and
Plutscho, Dr. Duff says (in the " Calcutta Review"): " The subject of
providing lawful means of support
for converts from heathenism, without encouraging hypocrisy, exciting
cupidity, or impairing that spirit of
independence and honest industry
which all ought to desire to cherish,
... of the most perplexing con-
... with successful missionary
... one, moreover, which,
... has awakened far less sympathy and attention than its importance merits, or its dormant necessities must eventually demand."

[†] Afterwards, when times had
changed—when the royal patronage
was plain and unmistakable — and
Ziegenbalg was going home for the
benefit of his health, the Governor
became alarmed lest the missionary
should report unfavourably of him
to his Majesty of Denmark. He
asked Ziegenbalg, therefore, to sign
an amnesty before his departure.

from Europe. His faith had never been, for a moment, obscured. He knew that the light would shine again upon him. Money came; books came; fellow-labourers came; and the Mission grew in prosperity.

There was no fear, after this, of any further tribulation; for orders came from the King of Denmark, enjoining the Governor of Tranquebar at all times to assist and to protect the Christian missionaries. This must have lifted a burden of anxiety from off Ziegenbalg's mind, and enabled him to carry on the great literary work, on which he was engaged, with greater freedom of thought and intensity of labour. He was translating the New Testament into Tamul. Commenced in October, 1708, it was completed in March, 1711. The Old Testament, as far as the book of Ruth, was translated by him at a later period. These were the first efforts ever made to render the natives of India familiar with the literature of the Bible through the vernacular languages of the country. If it were only for this, he would be entitled to a place in the foremost rank of Indian missionaries.

It would be a pleasure to trace, step by step, the progress of such men; but I am compelled to pass rapidly on through this history of the Danish Missions. It is the glory of Ziegenbalg and Plutscho that they were the first to attempt the conversion of the natives of India by those means which are now recognised as the only agency by which the great end is likely to be accomplished—by the translation of the Scriptures and the education of youth. The Romanists had relied on an unintelligible preaching, and an equally unintelligible ceremony of baptism. The first Protestant missionaries sought, above all things, to render the great truths of the Gospel intelligible to the dark minds of the heathen ; so they transfused the wisdom of revelation into the vulgar tongue of the natives, and in due course the words punctured on the primitive palmyra leaf were perpetuated and multiplied, in enduring characters, by the magic agency of the printing-press. There are few more interesting or suggestive chapters of missionary history than that which contains the narrative of the first establishment of the printing-office of the Danish missionaries at Tranquebar. After much trouble, funds were raised ; the press and the types were shipped ; but the printer who accompanied it died on the voyage. A young man attached to the Mission qualified himself to undertake the superintendence of the press. But paper was not to be procured. Nothing daunted by this, the missionaries looked the difficulty boldly in the face, and made paper for themselves.

Ziegenbalg died at his post while yet a young man, worn out by the intensity of his application and the severity of his labours. In the month of February, 1719, that pure spirit entered into its rest. Some years before, Plutscho had returned with broken health to Europe ; and now that the two men whose names will ever be remembered as those of the first Protestant missionaries in India had been removed from the scene, the charge of the Mission devolved on M. Grundler, whose apostolic zeal, not unworthy of those whom he succeeded, burned strongly and brightly in a frail shattered body, which soon succumbed to the weight that had been cast upon him. In March, 1720, he put on immortality. Other able and energetic men succeeded him, and year after year the influence of the mission extended itself more and more over the southern Peninsula, winning the confidence and obtaining the assistance of the English authorities on the coast.

At different periods of his apostolic career, Ziegenbalg himself had made occasional visits to Madras, and had been received there with the courtesy and kindness to which he was so eminently entitled, but which he was not, therefore, more likely to meet. Neither the English authorities nor the English chaplains looked askance at him or his successors. Of two English clergymen at Madras especial mention is made in all the records of Ziegenbalg's life. The Rev. George Lewis received the Danish apostle on his visits to the English settlement; and recommended the Mission to the good offices of his countrymen both in India and in England. A letter which he wrote to the secretary of the Christian Knowledge Society is on record.* The Tranquebar Mission, he wrote, " ought and must be encouraged. It is the first attempt the Protestants ever made in that kind. We must not put out the smoking flax. It would give our adversaries, the Papists, who boast so much of their congregations *de propagandâ fide*, too much

* I am indebted for it to that indefatigable historian, Mr. Hough, in whose third volume it is to be found.

cause to triumph over us. I do design by the January ships to let the society and yourself understand that I am a hearty well-wisher to your honourable, pious, and Christian undertaking." This was written in 1712. Two years afterwards, Ziegenbalg was compelled to visit Europe for the restoration of his shattered health.[*] On his return to India, he touched at Madras, where he was "welcomed by the governor and the chaplain." But his old friend Mr. Lewis had by this time been succeeded by Mr. Stevenson, who, imbued with the same good missionary spirit, had, during Ziegenbalg's absence, been aiding and encouraging the remaining members of the Tranquebar family; and was now rejoiced to extend the hand of fellowship to the young apostle himself. A true friend had Stevenson been to the mission ; for having learnt in the course of Ziegenbalg's furlough, that the establishment at Tranquebar was likely soon to be in want of funds, he authorised M. Grundler to draw upon him for any money that he might require before the arrival of his expected remittances.[†] Truly, was the first Anglican Church in India served by some godly ministers.

[*] Both in Denmark and in England the first Protestant missionary was received with becoming honour. He was introduced to George I., who assured him of his Majesty's sympathy, and of his great desire to promote the cause of missions. The Archbishop of Canterbury and the Bishop of London were among his kindest friends and warmest supporters.

[†] Mr. Stevenson visited Tranquebar in August, 1716, and wrote an interesting account of it to the Christian Knowledge Society, of which he was an industrious correspondent.

Among other things, he stated that "the people" (*i.e.*, the native converts) "seemed far more serious, attentive, and composed in their behaviour than our European congregations generally are. The children, whom I have heard catechised in Portuguese, have juster notions of religion, and are greater proficients in true Christian knowledge than those of a more advanced age among us. I have no time," he added, "to enlarge on the order and good discipline that are kept up in the three schools, nor on the successful labours of the missionaries."—*Hough.*

It was owing greatly to the encouragement of these worthy chaplains that the Danish Mission, which up to this time had found a home only in Tranquebar, was extended in 1726, under the auspices of the Christian Knowledge Society, to the English Presidency of Madras, and also to their factory at Cuddalore. In these undertakings they appear to have received good support from the English, the King himself acting as their fugleman and giving the time from the throne. The heaviest blows which they received were from the hand of Death—one master workman after another having been removed from the scene. When Grundler followed Ziegenbalg to his rest, Mr. Schulze took charge of the mission, and the number of labourers steadily increased, and with them the number of converts. They were, as I have said, too conscientious to make any great show of their successes. They numbered their converts at first only by tens; but when in the year 1756, they celebrated their jubilee, it was shown that during the ten years which had preceded that event nearly three thousand souls had been brought over to the Christian faith.*

It was a few years before the celebration of the jubilee that there was added to the Mission one whose name is associated with all that is best and noblest in the history of Christianity in India. Christian Frederick Schwartz had been trained for missionary work. At the University of Halle he had studied the Tamul language, and with such success as to

* By this time the number of the missionary stations had greatly increased. There were branch establishments at Madras, Cuddalore, Negapatam, Tanjore, Seringham, Trichinopoly, &c.

enable him to preach to the natives within four months from the time of his arrival at Tranquebar. From this date until the year 1798, a period wanting but two years of half a century, did this holy man labour earnestly and diligently in Southern India, presenting an example of Christian rectitude that inspired native princes and European functionaries with an equal measure of admiration and respect. It is with the history of the Tanjore Mission that his name is most intimately associated. It was in 1759 that his first visit was paid to that place, "with the Rajah's permission, and at the request of some German soldiers in his army." A few years afterwards (1762), the Rajah, whose interest was awakened by what he had heard of the character and conduct of the missionary during this and subsequent visits to Tanjore, invited Schwartz to his palace, and, seated behind a purdah, listened with rapt attention to the conversation relating to the great truths of the Gospel which passed between his officers and the Christian teacher. Those were times of trouble for Tanjore; little space was left for doctrinal discussions; and it was not until ten years afterwards that the Hindoo ruler openly sought an interview with the Christian priest. A remarkable meeting indeed was this—remarkable in itself, remarkable in its results. It would be a fine subject for a painter. Seated in the midst of a crowd of officers and Brahmans, the Rajah received the missionary with every manifestation of kindness and respect. The inquiring, interested expression of the prince's countenance—the puzzled look of the attendant courtiers —the eager, penetrating glances of the Brahmans, resentment struggling with alarm in their shrewd, crafty faces—the quiet, self-possessed attitude of the Christian priest, sitting on a chair opposite the Rajah, his face beaming with mild intelligence and spiritual hope—would afford fine scope for the genius of an artist great in the expression of human character. The first question of the Rajah was a pregnant commentary on the system of the Roman missionaries : " How came it," he asked, " that some missionaries worshipped with images, and some without them ?" There could be but one answer—that Christianity utterly rejected all idolatry. In due course, Schwartz unfolded, in plain intelligible terms, using the Tamul language, the whole scheme of Christian redemption. The pleasurable interest, with which the Rajah obviously listened to his discourse, alarmed the Brahmans. All their influence was put forth to counteract his growing desire for further enlightenment from the same source. Their surest plan was to keep the Christian teacher far from the presence of so candid an inquirer. And they succeeded for a time. New dangers threatened, and new convulsions agitated the Tanjore state; but throughout all the vicissitudes of his chequered career, the Rajah never forgot his Christian friend.

Better days began to dawn upon the Rajah and upon the Mission. In the year 1777, Schwartz took up his residence at Tanjore; and for a time it seemed that his work was advancing under happier auspices.

But those were not times when any long continuance
of tranquillity could be looked for in Southern India.
Hyder Ali ravaged the Carnatic, and the European
power in India was shaken to its very centre. But
in the midst of all this desolating warfare the Christian missionary pursued his work, and only quitted
it for a time when called upon to play the unaccustomed part of mediator between the two contending
powers. The fierce Mahomedan zeal of the tyrant
of Mysore had not been proof against the holy
rectitude and mild enthusiasm of the apostolic
Schwartz. He had heard of the good man, to whom
money was no temptation, and whose lips never
uttered guile; he had heard of one meek, lowly, yet
full of courage, who had suffered much and done
much for God and man, but had sought nothing for
himself; and when he was now told that the English
wished to treat with him, he said, "Let them send
the *Christian* to me; I need fear no deceit from
him." So Schwartz was summoned from Tanjore,
where the erection of his church was then mainly
occupying his thoughts, to play the part of an ambassador of State; and the one man who was deemed
incapable of falsehood and fraud—the one Christian
who, it was believed by the Mussulman ruler, would
not violate an engagement with a native prince,
proceeded to Seringapatam. His mission was not
successful. The war was not to be stayed. Schwartz
returned to Tanjore. His presence was needed there.
The inhabitants had no confidence in the Rajah—
no confidence in the British authorities. In the

extremity which then threatened the place, Schwartz alone was trusted — Schwartz alone was believed. The word of "the Christian" was as magic everywhere. Supplies came in at his bidding. Even in the midst of the fiercest paroxysm of this sanguinary war, Hyder issued a decree to his officers commanding them to treat the holy man with kindness and respect. And over the country, ravaged and desolated by Hyder's troops, even through the midst of the encampments of a sanguinary and remorseless enemy, went the Christian missionary about his godly work uninjured and unmolested.

In the settlement of Tanjore, which followed the peace of 1784, Schwartz took a conspicuous part— everywhere exerting himself to obtain justice and protection for the poorer inhabitants, but never losing sight of his missionary obligations. The secular work which he had done was held in just subordination to his more extended spiritual aims. His heart was in the business of conversion; he yearned to bring all by whom he was surrounded, the highest and the lowest, to the saving faith; he never relaxed in his exertions, and never lost an opportunity. Of the Rajah himself, he had ever been the cherished friend and teacher. But the days of that docile prince were numbered; and a question of succession arose. The Rajah being without an heir, nominated a successor, and declared his intention to place the boy under the guardianship of Schwartz. There were political objections to this course, for an aspirant to the throne presented himself in the person of the half-brother of the deceased Rajah; and it was considered expedient to appoint this man regent and guardian during the minority of the prince. But the regent grossly neglected his charge; and from a life of wretched imprisonment and restraint, which was crippling the limbs, destroying the health, and benumbing the faculties of the boy, Sivajee was rescued by the intervention of the Christian missionary, and placed under his charge. Beautiful was the relationship that thenceforth subsisted between the venerable Schwartz and the youthful Hindoo prince — great the lessons that were taught, and abiding the influence of the teaching. The pupil regarded his master with unbounded reverence and affection; and if he did not openly adopt the faith of his Christian parent, he at least learned to respect both the doctrines and the professors of Christianity, and to shape his conduct, in some sort, according to the precepts of his revered instructor. And when, at last, full of years, and full of honour, Schwartz bowed his grey hairs upon the bed of death, and prepared to resign his soul into the hands of his Maker, no tears of more genuine emotion were shed than those which fell from the dark eyes of the young Rajah. All classes of men, from the Directors of the great Company, beneath whose power all the states of India were fast succumbing, to the little dark-faced children who had flocked around him with up-looking filial affection, and abundant faith in his kindness and gentleness, deplored the good man's death, and revered his memory. Our two greatest sculptors, Bacon and Flaxman, carved the image of the holy man in marble, the one for the East India Company, to be erected in the principal church of Madras, the other, for the Tanjore Rajah, to be placed in the Mission Church, where daily the young Rajah visited the monument, and delighted to point to it, exclaiming, " There is the image of my father." There are old men still living in Southern India who remember the silvery hairs and seraphic countenance of the venerable apostle, whilst thousands, who have never seen him in the flesh, still venerate his name.

There were people in those days who spoke sneeringly of the " saints " and " puritans " of Leadenhall Street, whilst others were fain to describe the Directors as an ungodly, anti-Christian set of men. But whatever may have been their errors at other times, and under other circumstances, their recognition of the virtues and the services of Schwartz was honourable to the body.   When they sent out Bacon's statue to be erected in St. Mary's church, they inserted in " a general letter " some paragraphs announcing its despatch, and declaring that "on no subject had the Court of Directors been more unanimous than in their anxious desire to perpetuate the memory of this peminent erson, and to excite in others an emulation of his great example."   At the same time, they directed the Madras Government to adopt, in conjunction with Dr. Kerr, any measures which might tend to give effect to the Court's intentions, and " to render them impressive on the minds of the public." A sermon was to be preached on the character and career of Schwartz on the first Sunday after the erection of the monument; and it was especially stated that the native inhabitants were to be permitted and encouraged to view the monument, and that translations were to be made of the inscription "into the country languages and published at Madras, and copies sent to Tanjore and the other districts, in which Mr. Schwartz occasionally resided and established seminaries for religious instruction." This inscription set forth that Frederick Christian Schwartz had been employed by " the Society in England for the promotion of Christian Knowledge," that during fifty years, he had gone about doing good; that he had built a Christian church and established Christian seminaries, and that " the East India Company, anxious to perpetuate the memory of such transcendent worth, and gratefully sensible of the public benefits which resulted from its influence," had caused the monument to be erected to his memory.*

If this letter, and the " four packing cases, numbered 1 to 4," sent " by our extra ship the *Union*," had reached Madras before, instead of after, the Vellore massacre, it is not to be doubted that the disaster would have been attributed in no small measure to this public exaltation, in the face of the nations, of a Christian missionary. But Bacon's

* It may be mentioned here that the Company were wont to forward the packages of the Christian Knowledge Society, containing " valuable stores and presents " for the Tranquebar missionaries, " freight and duty free."

statue did not arrive before the excitement attending
that catastrophe had considerably subsided; and
Dr. Kerr's sermon was not preached till more than
a year after the event. But there had never been
a more open demonstration than this in favour of
Christianity—never before, and never since, I believe,
so direct an appeal to the people by the Government
of the East India Company. It was not likely that
the great corporation, which in 1806 thus declared
their common delight to do honour to the venerable
Schwartz, would, at any time, take pleasure in the
humiliation of his brethren. They had, indeed, no
prejudice against the good men who had been labouring so diligently for the diffusion of the Gospel, or
any other than a sincere desire to see Christianity
spread itself over all the dark places of the earth.

As was the "traditionary policy of the East India
Company" half a century ago, so is the imperial policy
at the present moment. It was not merely the desire
of the Directors as Christian men, but it was their
interest also, as rulers of a great empire, that the
blessed religion of Jesus should make its way among
the people—and the more rapidly, the better. But
they believed that any direct and open identification
of the Government with the efforts of individuals
for the evangelization of the heathen, would have
the effect, not of promoting, but of retarding the
growth of Christianity, whilst, at the same time,
such intervention might be regarded, constructively,
as a violation of the pledges given to the people.
They believed also that any indiscreet manifestations

of zeal on the part of individuals, having a tendency
to alarm and to irritate the national mind, would be
a stumbling-block in their way—that wherever there
was the greatest prudence, there also would be the
greatest success;—and, therefore, they counselled
caution. Rashness is not valour. The cross, which
Queen Victoria has decreed as the prize of personal
bravery in the face of the enemy, is forfeited by
the foolhardy; because foolhardiness advantages the
enemy. And so he who would bear the Cross of
Christ, and fight the good fight bravely and successfully, must take heed lest he advantage the enemy
by his indiscretions, and give the battle at last to
the heathen.

A few more words about the Southern Missions:—
Whilst Schwartz was labouring with holy zeal at
Tanjore, his associates were carrying on the good
work in other parts of Southern India. Among the
most distinguished of his brethren were Gerické,
Kohloff, and Kiernander. In Tinnivelly and in
Southern Arcot the Gospel had made great progress.
In the former place, which was the scene of Schwartz's
early labours, it had taken root, perhaps more deeply
than in any part of the Peninsula; and still, when
proof is sought of the efficacy of Christian missions,
the advocate of these pious labours, answering the
doubts and objections of those who speak scorn of
such efforts to evangelize the heathen, points with
pride and exultation to the 40,000 Christians who
are said to worship the true God on the arid plains
of Tinnevelly.

## CHAPTER IV.

Progress of Christianity in Bengal—Kiernander—His labours in Calcutta—State of society there—Hastings and Francis—Drinking, gaming, and duelling—Female society—Nautches—The Press.

WHILST during the last quarter of the eighteenth century Schwartz and Gerické and Kohloff were labouring diligently and successfully in Southern India, the other member of the Tranquebar mission, of whom mention has been made, was performing, though with less important results, the functions of his high calling in Calcutta. The name of this man was John Kiernander. He is remarkable in the history of Christianity in India as the first Protestant missionary to Bengal. Like Ziegenbalg, Plutscho, and others of the same heroic band, he had been educated at the University of Halle. Receiving from the son of Professor Franke those credentials which the venerable father, then gone to his rest, had presented to the first Protestant missionaries, he sailed, in the year 1740, to the coast of Southern Arcot, and took charge of the Cuddalore mission. The surrender of the place to the French crushed the hopes, in that direction, of Kiernander and his brethren; but there were other fields of missionary enterprise before him; and, in the full vigour of active manhood as he was, he turned his thoughts towards untrodden paths on the banks of the great rivers of Northern India. Clive invited him to plant the Cross in Bengal, and in 1758 he left the pleasant sea breezes of Cuddalore for the dust-charged atmosphere of Calcutta. The Company's chaplains* received him kindly and encouragingly; and Clive placed a house at his disposal, in which he resided rent-free.

Between the period of the union of the two Companies and the time of the conquest of Bengal, but few noticeable events had occurred to mark the progress of Christianity in Northern India. In 1715, the settlers built God a church, but laughed his word to scorn for many years afterwards. The Christian Knowledge Society, among other good works, aided the erection of the first Protestant house of worship in Bengal; and the Society for the Propagation of the Gospel sent out a silver chalice, in commemoration of the event; but the chief amount of the money was subscribed by private liberality. There had been chaplains in Bengal before this time,—the first name on record being that of Samuel Brereton; but death often left the settlement without a minister; and then one of the merchants undertook to perform the duties on a Sunday, not purely as a labour of love, for there was a salary attached to the office of lay-chaplain, and we may be sure that it was punctually

* The Rev. Henry Butler and the Rev. John Cape, who arrived in the earlier part of the same year to replace Messrs. Belamy and Maple-loft, the former of whom had been suffocated in the Black Hole, and the latter died soon afterwards.

drawn. When the Church was built, the Rev. S. Briercliffe, seemingly a devout man, was chaplain to the Factory at Calcutta; and we may be sure it rejoiced his heart to see the President and all the chief servants of the Company walking, every Sabbath, in solemn procession to the house of God. Captain Hamilton says that at that time, all religions were freely tolerated except the Presbyterian; "and that they browbeat."\* There must have been a much smaller proportion of Scotchmen at the Presidency than there is at the present time.

In 1737, the steeple of the first English Church in Bengal was demolished by the great hurricane of that year; and in 1756 the building was altogether destroyed by the fury of Surajáh Dowlah. When, therefore, Kiernander arrived at Calcutta, the presidency was without a church. Society was, doubtless, at that time, less scandalously depraved than it had been in the time of Job Charnock, but it was a long way off from a becoming state of morality, and the religion of the settlement was mainly the worship of gold. After the terror created by the great convulsion of 1756 had subsided, men gave themselves up as absorbedly as before to the pursuit of wealth, and traded for their masters and for themselves with an earnestness which commanded success. Perhaps this kept them from something worse. "We looked

* "In Calcutta, all religions are freely tolerated but the Presbyterian, and that they browbeat. The Pagans carry their idols in procession through the town. The Roman Catholics have their church to lodge their idols in; and the Mahometan is not discountenanced; but there are no polemicks, except what are between our high churchmen and our low, or between the governor's friends and other private merchants on points of trade."

no further," wrote Mr. Verelst, "than the provision of the Company's investment. We sought advantages to our trade, with the ingenuity, I may add the selfishness, of merchants. . . . All our servants and dependants were trained and educated in the same notions; the credit of a good bargain was the utmost scope of their ambition." That this was intended to be high praise, is not the least suggestive part of the matter.

Slow, indeed, was the growth of religion and morality among the English in India. Hospitality, kindliness, generosity, nay, even a sort of conventionality, which might have been mistaken for something better, sprang up among our people; but it was long before Christian piety and its fair fruits began to bless our adopted land. The natives of India marvelled whether the British acknowledged any God.* And

* "These people," writes Mr. Forbes, in his *Oriental Memoirs*, " in their own artless, expressive style, often asked me this important question, ' *Master, when an Englishman dies, does he think he shall go to his God?*' My answer in the affirmative generally produced a reply to this effect—' Your countrymen, master, seem to take very little trouble about that business; they choose a smooth path and scatter roses on every side. Other nations are guided by strict rules and solemn injunctions, in those serious engagements, where the English seem thoughtless and unconcerned. The Hindoos constantly perform the ceremonies and sacrifices at the Dewal; the Mahomedans go through their stated prayers and ablutions at the mosques; the Parsees suffer not the sacred fires to be extinguished, nor neglect to worship in their temple. You call yourselves Christian; so do the Roman Catholics, who abound in India. They daily frequent their churches, fast and pray, and do many penances; the English alone appear unconcerned about an event of the greatest importance.' " And again, the same amiable writer, a little further on, proceeds to show that there was something worse than mere indifference. " What may be the prevailing practice, I cannot say; certainly, the spirit of Christianity was not (in my time) the actuating principle of European society in India. A thoughtlessness of futurity, a carelessness about religious concerns, were more prominent. Highly as I esteemed the philanthropy, benevolence, and moral character of my countrymen, I am compelled to add that a spirit of scepticism and infidelity predominated in the younger part of the community, especially in the circle of those who had received what is called a good education."

in truth a large number of our countrymen, whatever may have been their creed or their no-creed, practically ignored the fact.* Numbers became more or less orientalized. Acquiring Oriental tastes and Oriental habits, they soon began to look with bland toleration upon the religions of the country, and ceased to see anything either very absurd or very revolting in the faith of the Hindoo or the creed of the Mussulman. Of this school were the men who, at a latter period, endeavoured to persuade the world of the pure religions and the excellent moralities of the natives of India, and declaimed against the wickedness and the danger of attempting to wean them from such blessed conditions of knowledge and belief.

It was not to be expected, whilst such was the state of society, that any great amount of encouragement would be extended to the efforts of a foreign missionary by the English inhabitants of Calcutta. Fortunately, Kiernander was not in need of assistance of one kind. He was independent of the pecuniary contributions of his fellow Christians; for he was a rare, perhaps a solitary instance, of an affluent missionary. He married a wealthy widow; and though not altogether free from the weaknesses of

* In the preceding note, Mr. Forbes, whose experience was acquired in Western India, states that the irreligion or infidelity of his countrymen was far greater than their immorality. Mr. Shore (afterwards Lord Teignmouth), writing from Calcutta, in 1772—probably about the period to which Mr. Forbes refers—speaks of the "too great prevalence of immorality in the settlement," and of "the disregard with which religion is treated;" but adds, "You will, perhaps, conclude that the number of freethinkers must be great—they are, in fact, but few." This relates to a time antecedent to the French Revolution, which soon lighted up a fire of infidelity in every settlement in the country.

humanity, he turned his worldly possessions to profitable Christian account.

His labours were chiefly confined to Calcutta, where he established a mission-school, and preached to men of all sorts and conditions. His converts were mainly from among the degraded mass of Portuguese Romanism settled in the outskirts of that increasing city. These conversions brought a hornet's nest of Papal priests about the Protestant missionary. Kiernander retaliated by converting three of them to the religion of the Reformation and enlisting them as auxiliaries in the work of the Mission. As to the people of the country, if we compare Kiernander's successes with those of Ziegenbalg and Schwartz, they dwindle down into slender proportions. But it is no small thing that, mainly at his own expense, he erected a Protestant church, where no church was, and thus restored to the English inhabitants of the chief city of British India the long-forfeited privilege of worshipping God in a public place consecrated to His service.*

It has been seen that the first church which the British residents erected was doomed to a brief and calamitous existence. From the time when, in 1756, the entire building was destroyed by the fury of Surajáh Dowlah, up to the year 1770, Calcutta was without a Protestant church; and without a Protestant church it would probably have remained many

* From December 1, 1758, to the end of 1766, Kiernander reported to the Christian Knowledge Society, that he had made 189 converts; of whom half were Romanists, one-third children of Romanist parents, and thirty were heathens.

years longer, if Kiernander had not bethought himself of erecting one for missionary purposes at his own expense. He did bethink himself of this good work, and he soon carried the design into execution. He had calculated that it would cost him 2,000*l.* But with the usual uncertainty attending affairs of brick-and-mortar, it cost nearly 7,000*l.*, of which 5,000*l.* were contributed by himself. It was three years in course of erection;* the architect having died before the work was complete; and when, at last, it loomed out in all its full proportions, it was at best an unsightly edifice. Somewhat uncouth in form, and glaring in colour, it goes even now by the name of the "red church," though it no longer justifies the description.

In 1775, the Christian Knowledge Society sent out a colleague to Mr. Kiernander in the person of Mr. Diemer, who also had been educated at the University of Halle. The president of the society stated that they "highly glorified" in Mr. Kiernander, "accounting him worthy of every commendation, praising God for having been pleased to send them such a servant of His, so great a friend to religion, and of such a generous disposition; worn out by his continual labours, yet still of a cheerful and courageous mind, strengthened by long experience:"—a tribute that was well deserved. The assistance of Mr. Diemer was most welcome to Kiernander, and most serviceable to the cause. Every year saw a considerable addition to the number of converts—converts to Protestantism

* It is worthy of mention that Kiernander would never allow the heathen workmen to prosecute their work upon the Christian Sabbath—a "refinement" very little understood in India at that time.

and converts to Christianity. The number of scholars at the mission-schools increased—schools which were erected and supported mainly, I believe entirely, at Kiernander's own expense. The buildings, indeed, were paid for from the proceeds of Mrs. Kiernander's jewellery, which she had directed in her will to be sold for that good purpose.

Little sympathy and less encouragement did Kiernander's labour meet with in Calcutta; for, in truth, the professing or the unprofessing Christians of that growing settlement were but a godless community. Their morals were no better than their religion. Of the state of Anglo-Indian society during the protracted administration of Warren Hastings, nothing indeed can be said in praise. The Regulating Act was not designed to regulate the private lives of our administrators, and nothing could have been much more irregular than they were. I am afraid that they who ought to have set a good example to the Presidency, did grievous wrong to Christianity by the lawlessness of their lives. We must not, however, judge them too harshly. The age of Hastings and Francis was not a moral age. Duelling in those days was a creditable occupation; and acts of what was then called "gallantry" raised a man in the estimation of his fellows. It is something, indeed, to be noted in favour of Anglo-Indian society, that the morality which was imported fresh from England was not a shade better than that which had grown up in our Eastern settlements. Hastings was not better disposed to shoot Francis, than Francis to shoot

Hastings. And if there was any difference between the "gallantries" of the two men, it is rather in favour of Hastings than of Francis. Hastings took another man's wife with his consent; Francis did the same without it. Hastings resorted to a convenient deed of divorce, Francis employed only a rope-ladder. The external moralities of the Indian Nabob were not worse than those of the war-office clerk, and his heart was a good deal better.

It was scarcely to be expected that, with such examples before them, the less prominent members of society would be conspicuous for morality and decorum. In truth, it must be acknowledged that the Christianity of the English in India was, at this time, in a sadly depressed state. Men drank hard and gamed high. Concubinage with the women of the country was the rule rather than the exception. It was no uncommon thing for English gentlemen to keep populous zenanas. There was no dearth of exciting amusement in those days. Balls, masquerades, races, and theatrical entertainments, enlivened the settlements, especially in the cold weather; and the mild excitement of duelling varied the pleasures of the season. Men lived, for the most part, short lives, and were resolute that they should be merry ones. If they survived the fiery trials to which they were subjected, they commonly realised large fortunes, and returned to England to make no very favourable impression on the popular mind. In truth, Nemesis then became over-active in her ministrations. The Nabob may have done some bad things in his day, and probably many foolish ones; but he was neither the miscreant nor the idiot, in the garb of one or other of which dramatic characters he commonly appeared in the bad plays or the worse novels of the last century.

He was, indeed, more sinned against than sinning. His failings were commonly exaggerated, the better part of his nature ignored. In England, the victim of the bitterest prejudice, he found himself isolated, and he was unhappy. Disappointment grew into discontent. The climate—the people—the social customs —all were strange and distasteful to him. Harpies and parasites gathered round him, but he had no real friends. They who were not bent on plucking the Nabob, religiously kept aloof from him. A sort of superstitious awe attached to his person; he was looked upon as an unholy being doomed to drag out a miserable existence, haunted by the grim shadows of his victims, and tortured by relentless furies. If he shut himself up on his own premises, it was said of him that he shunned the light of day, and rustic ignorance drew strange pictures of unhallowed rites and unearthly ceremonies within the precincts of the Nabob's domain. If he wandered abroad, it was said of him that he was endeavouring to escape out of himself—to drown the fearful memory of the past. His very sufferings were arrayed in judgment against him. The ravages which pain, and sickness, and toil beneath a scorching sun, had committed upon his frame; the strangeness of manner which long absence from home and much intercourse with a foreign people had naturally engendered; the eagerness with which he sought by lavish expenditure and luxurious profusion to compensate for the absence of friendship and kindly sympathy;—all these things, the misfortunes of the returned exile, were imputed to him as grave offences, and sober moralists held up their hands, without the charity even feebly to acknowledge "that what to them seemed vice, might be but woe."

I think that the Nabob of the old times may fairly claim to be regarded with more toleration than has commonly been bestowed upon him. It was, doubtless, very foolish to call for more curricles, and to think that he had any right to cut roads through his neighbours' grounds. But my lord, with the home-staying wits of his home-staying order, was scarcely less foolish when he turned his back upon the Nabob, and called him a purse-proud upstart. The poor man was not purse-proud. It is not easy to divest one's-self suddenly of the habits and associations of a life, and to cut one's new coat in accordance with the cloth of a strange state of society. What would have been arrogance and affectation in his brother, was pure simplicity in him. He said and did foolish things without knowing it, and acted in perfect sincerity and good faith when he appeared to be violently pretending.

But it must be admitted that he brought home with him from India very hazy ideas of a living Christianity. Of the conversion of the people he had never thought for a moment. Insensibly, as has been said, he had glided, when in India, into their "excellent moralities" and "pure religions;" he had even taken part in their ceremonies without a misgiving;* and had become what has since been familiarly called "half a native." Not that in those days he knew much about the creeds of the people. It was reserved for a later generation to drag the deformities and impurities of Hindooism into the clear light of day. But he had come to think that it little mattered whether he were a Hindoo, a Mahomedan, or a Christian; and, in point of fact, he was not one of the three. If any one questioned him on the subject of the religion and morality of the people of India, his testimony was generally favourable to both. He had not learnt to look with horror and detestation upon the hideous idolatries of the pagans, but saw something, on the other hand, sublimely heroic in the most revolting of their superstitions He idealized into saints and martyrs the poor victims of a barbarous faith, and smiled contemptuously when enthusiasts talked about converting them to Christianity, declaring it "better to leave them as they are."

It is not to be doubted that there was, as I shall

* A curious illustration of this fact is to be found in the autobiography of Mr. Robert Lindsay, given in "Lives of the Lindsays." He was a civilian, in the time of Warren Hastings, and was sent as Resident to Sylhet. Of his initiation into his new office he gives the following *naïve* account :—"I was now told that it was customary for the new Resident to pay his respects to the shrine of the tutelar saint, Shaw Juloll. Pilgrims of the Islam faith flock to this shrine from every part of India, and I afterwards found that the fanatics attending the tomb were not a little dangerous. It was not my business to combat religious prejudices, and I therefore went in state, as others had done before me, left my shoes on the threshold, and deposited on the tomb five gold mohurs as an offering. Being thus purified, I returned to my dwelling and received the homage of my subjects." This kind of thing, in a modified form, has, I am sorry to say, existed ever since. Frequent mention will be made of it in the course of the ensuing chapters.

have occasion to show, in this notion, so prevalent among old Indians, of the impossibility, and the inexpediency, if possible, of converting the people, much that at a later period tended greatly, by the diffusion of prejudice and ignorance, to retard the progress of Christianity in India. And it was, in truth, not altogether unreasonable that, seeing what the Christianity was to which, if to any, at that time, the people were to be converted, some doubts should have been entertained of the value of such conversion. It was of little use to think of christianizing the people, until the English in India had begun in some measure to christianize themselves.

What the natives of the country thought of the earlier settlers has already been seen. Little reason had they, in the days of Warren Hastings, to think much better of the English than when they first said: " Christian religion, devil religion: Christian much drunk; much do wrong; much beat, much abuse others." The drunkenness, indeed, was general and obtrusive. It was one of the besetting infirmities—the fashionable vices—of the period; national rather than local in its character, and only more destructive of human life than at home. In the earlier times, wine and beer had been scarce and costly commodities, obtainable only by those in high place. Arrack punch was the ordinary potation throughout the seventeenth century, and, indeed, far into the eighteenth.* During the admi-

* See Lockyer's " Account of the Trade in India" and other works. Lockyer, who was at Madras at the commencement of the eighteenth century, says, " Every one has it in his power to eat well, though he can

nistration of Warren Hastings there appears to have been no scarcity of wine, but it was irregularly supplied; and a large importation was sometimes followed by a succession of carouses, which materially increased the bills of mortality.

Contemporary writers state that it was no uncommon thing for purchasers of a new investment of claret to invite a few friends to taste it, and for the whole case to be consumed at a sitting —a feat dependent upon the number of sitters and the quantity of wine, which I do not find particularly mentioned, but which, judged by the stated result, the death of one or more of the consumers, may be presumed to have been something terrific. At the larger Presidency towns—especially at Calcutta—public entertainments were not unfrequent. Ball suppers, in those days, were little less than orgies. Dancing was impossible after them, and fighting commonly took its place. If a public party went off without a duel or two, it was a circumstance as rare as it was happy. There was a famous club

afford no other liquor at meals than punch, which is the common drink among Europeans, and here made in the greatest perfection. Wine and beer may be had; but it must be good business that will afford a constant supply of it. The Governor keeps a generous table, nor is that where the factors and writers dine less regarded,—differing only in this, here you have a great deal of punch and little wine, there, what wine you please and as little punch."

Mr. Forbes tells us that, when he first arrived at Bombay, in 1765, "the cadets, who were soon promoted, and whether stationed at the presidency or the subordinate settlements, perhaps mounted guard once or twice a week, and did no other duty, had abundance of leisure time. On those idle days, the morning was generally occupied in calling upon each other at their different quarters, and at each visit taking a draught of punch, or arrack and water, which, however cool and pleasant at the moment, was succeeded by the most deleterious effects; indeed, from its fatal consequences, it might be called a slow poison; and from this cause alone it may be confidently asserted that a number proportionate to the Berampore estimate were annually committed to an untimely grave."

in those days, called Selby's Club, at which the gentlemen of Calcutta were wont to drink as high as they gamed, and which sometimes saw drunken bets of 1,000 gold mohurs laid about the merest trifles. Card parties often sat all through the night, and if the night chanced to be a Saturday, all through the next day.

These were what may be called the social vices. There was another vice very common in those days, which morality is bound to reprobate, but which, all circumstances of temptation fairly considered, all charitable allowances rightly made, is not without its claim to be regarded with mercy and toleration. Honourable marriage was the exceptional state, concubinage with the women of the country the rule. In tracing the Christian progress of the English in India fitting mention should be made of the influence of Christian womanhood. The earliest adventurers were, doubtless, solitary men ;* but the old records of the East India Company inform us that during the second half of the seventeenth century the exile of some of the principal merchants was shared by their wives. Whether the first wives of Englishmen known in Western India were Portuguese or Dutch women whom they found in India, or Englishwomen whom they brought from home or imported into the country, is not very apparent; but the presumption is, that

* Pietro della Valle, an Italian, who visited Surat about 1623, says that on landing there he was immediately invited to the house of the English President, but he declined the invitation, "for that it was requisite for Signora Marinecia to be amongst women, of which there were none in the English house."—By which was signified the house in which the principal merchants lived together.

there was an intermixture of both classes.* There is proof, indeed, that some at least were Englishwomen, and very troublesome specimens of their class. Their contentions, especially when, as often happened, they fell into a state of widowhood, and remained to wind up the concerns of their late husbands, were very harassing to the minds of the local councils, who did not know how to deal with them.† But it was held to be a greater grievance still that Protestant Englishmen, high and low, should marry Papistical Portuguese —a heresy into which our people, and especially our soldiers, were wont incontinently to fall.

* The earliest mention of the residence of fair strangers from the West, which I have been able to find in any work open to my researches, is contained in the Travels of Pietro della Valle, who visited the country in 1623, and whose work is referred to in the preceding note. According to this authority, the king of Portugal took upon himself to send a small annual investment of female orphans to India, for the especial use of the settlers on the western coast. "We were no sooner come to the Dogana," says the noble Roman, after describing his voyage to Surat," but, the news of our arrival was, I think, by Sig. Alberto's means, carried to the house of the Dutch, many of which have wives there which they married in India purposely to go with them and people a new colony of theirs in *Java Major*, which they call *Batavia Nova* ; where very great privileges are granted to such of their countrymen as shall go to live there with wives and families; for which end many of them, for want of European, have taken Indian, Armenian, and Syrian women, and of any other race that falls into their hands, so they be, or can be made, Christians. Last year the fleet of the Portugals, which went to India, was encountered at sea, and partly sunk, partly taken by the Hollanders; amongst other booty, three maidens were taken of those poor but well-descended orphans, which are wont to be sent from Portugal every year at the king's charge, with a dowry which the king gives them, to the end they may be married in India, in order to further the peopling of the Portugal colonies in those parts. These three virgins falling into the hands of the Hollanders, and being carried to Surat, which is the principal seat of all their traffick, the most eminent merchants amongst them strove who should marry them, being all passably handsome. Two of them were gone from Surat, whether to the above-said colony, or elsewhere, I know not. She that remained behind was called Donna Lucia, a young woman, fair enough, and wife to one of the wealthiest and eminentest Hollanders."

† There are some amusing passages in the old records of the Company respecting one "Madam Harris," widow of President Harris (described after his death as the greatest impostor that ever lived), who gave the council at Surat vast trouble by secreting her husband's property, and cheating the Company, who had an equitable claim upon it.

Strangely impressed with a sense of the evil of these marriages, Gerald Aungier, of whose piety and good conduct honourable mention has been made, brought the matter to the notice of the worshipful Directors, and suggested that the Court should obviate the difficulty by sending out a supply of Protestant womanhood. The Court at this time were engaged in the good work of reforming the morals of their settlements; and thinking that the means of forming respectable marriages would be an important auxiliary, they acceded to the President's recommendation, and sent out not only a supply of the raw material of soldiers' wives, but some better articles also, in the shape of what they called gentlewomen, for the use of such of their merchants and factors as might be matrimonially inclined. The venture, however, was not a successful one. The few who married made but indifferent wives; whilst they who did not marry,— and the demand was by no means brisk,—were, to say the least of it, in an equivocal position. For a time they were supported at the public expense;[*]

[*] See Anderson's "English in Western India." Mr. Anderson says, "Of course they supposed that the Company were their honourable guardians, and that if they could not find husbands, they would at least have the protection of Government. Not so the Company. To the first party, indeed, a guarantee was given that they should be supported for the first year, and if, at the expiration of that time, they were still unmarried, they should be allowed their diet for another year. This engagement was faithfully kept. But there came out a second party, fondly expecting that they would be treated like their predecessors; indeed, they affirmed that 'so much was declared to them at the India House by Mr. Lewis.' Nevertheless, their claims were not recognised. After considerable agitation on their part, and reluctance on the President's part, six or eight pagodas a month were allowed to such as were actually in distress. The President and Council, in writing to the Court, made a merit of this base and cruel economy:—'We have refused to put you to this charge,' they wrote, 'declaring we have no order from you, which hath caused some discontent among them; only we have thought fit to assist those who are more objects of charity, to keep them from perishing for want of sustenance.'"

but they received only sufficient to keep them from starving, and so it happened naturally enough—it would have been a marvel, indeed, if it had been otherwise—that the poor creatures betook themselves to vicious courses, and sold such charms as they had, if only to purchase strong drink, to which they became immoderately addicted, with the wages of their prostitution. The scandal soon became open and notorious; and the President and Council at Surat wrote to the Deputy-Governor and Council at Bombay, saying: "Whereas you give us notice that some of the women are grown scandalous to our native religion and government, we require you in the Honourable Company's name to give them all fair warning that they do apply themselves to a more sober and Christian conversation;—otherwise the sentence is that they shall be deprived totally of their liberty to go abroad, and fed with bread and water, till they are embarked on board ship for England."

This attempt to establish a marriage-market in Western India having thus discreditably failed, Government withdrew from all interference and left matters to take their course. For more than a century after this period the number of English-women who were induced to make trial for themselves of the delights of an Indian settlement was small in proportion to the wants of the growing European community. In time, a mixed race sprung up; and the settlers not seldom found wives among the half-caste girls whom an elder generation had bequeathed to them. But these poor children, though seldom wanting in personal comeliness, were uneducated, undisciplined, and little fitted for domestic life. It was, however, a step in advance—better than alliances with the Portuguese women, who made Papists of their husbands and brought up their children in the same faith. In the children of English fathers there was not likely to be much Romanist zeal of this kind; although, mixing as they did with the Portuguese, their Protestantism may have been of a dubious character.

That during the administration of Warren Hastings there were at the Presidency towns a considerable number of Englishwomen—and some, too, of great personal attractions, and at least as well educated as Englishwomen commonly were in those days,—may be gathered from contemporary publications. The first English newspaper published in India, of which I shall speak presently, announces an arrival of spinsters, "eleven in one vessel—too great a number for the peace and good order of a round-house," and describes a grand Christmas party at Government House, at which "the ladies were all elegant and lovely;" and, it is added, "it is universally allowed that Calcutta never was decorated by so many fine women as at present."* But when we read of one lady being attended to a ball by no less than sixteen admirers, all "wearing her colours," we may presume that the ladies of Calcutta bore but a small proportion to the gentlemen; and that

* Memoirs of M. Grand, husband of the well-known Madame Grand (afterwards Madame de Talleyrand), the object of Francis' amorous regards.

English wives were only to be obtained by the very rich or the very lucky.

If the opportunities of contracting honourable marriage even at the large Presidency towns were few, at the out-stations it may be fairly assumed that there were none. It must not be asserted that this admitted want justified a general resort to concubinage with the women of the country, but Charity may suggest that it extenuated the offence. In some cases it may have assumed so offensive a character, that nothing can be said of it except that it was gross and revolting profligacy; but in others, there was something that seemed almost to hallow the connexion, or at least to divest it of all the attributes of a degrading licentiousness. Charity cannot recognise the logic any more than the morality of the assertion that, because a man cannot find a wife to his liking, he is justified in peopling a zenana.* But many a man was wont to make the native

* Capt. Williamson, who, fifty years ago, published an Indian *Vade Mecum*, dedicated to the Court of Directors, and professedly "undertaken with the view to promote the welfare and to facilitate the progress of those young gentlemen who, from time to time, may be appointed to situations under the several Presidencies," thought it rather a joke than otherwise that European gentlemen should keep harems. "I have known," he wrote, "various instances of two ladies being conjointly domesticated, and one of an elderly military character who solaced himself with no less than *sixteen* of all sorts and sizes. Being interrogated by a friend as to what he did with such a number, 'Oh,' replied he, 'I give them a little rice, and let them run about.' This same gentleman, when paying his addresses to an elegant young woman lately arrived from Europe, but who was informed by the lady at whose house she was residing, of the state of affairs, the description closed with, 'Pray, my dear, how should you like to share a sixteenth of Major ———?'" It is something very significant of the author's morality that in this book, written "to promote the welfare" of the young gentlemen of the Company's service, Capt. Williamson enters upon an elaborate dissertation on native women, gives a detailed account of the expenses attendant upon the keeping of a coloured mistress, and devotes fifty pages to a catalogue of the ornaments worn and unguents used by these ladies.

concubine the companion of his life, and to worship her with his body, in all fidelity, as truly as though the Church had sanctioned the bond. With this fidelity often went unfailing kindness—even tender affection, surviving the youth and beauty of the mistress; and when circumstances, as they sometimes did, prevented the permanence of the union—when the English officer returned to England, or when he married an English wife, he was sure to make provision for the woman who had shared his bed. It was for a higher state of social civilization and Christian morality than that of which these much-reviled Anglo-Indians boasted, to sanction the practice of casting adrift upon a cruel world the unhappy victim of the sated lust of an English gentleman. Such victims added in India none to the list of public prostitutes.* The concubinage, which custom sanctioned, may have been reprehensible in itself; but there was not seduction at the one end of it and desertion at the other.

And here I may not disadvantageously digress to offer a few remarks on a subject, peculiarly illustrative of the progress which the English have recently made in social morality. No one who is familiar with descriptive works of the seventeenth and eighteenth centuries, can have failed to observe the very prominent place which the *nautch* occupies in every picture, not only of native, but of European

---

* I see that there is a proposal, emanating from a high quarter, to put down public prostitution in India. I can imagine, if the Legislature were to undertake so to maintain public decency in India, not only the feelings but the exclamations of an intelligent native of that country, on finding himself, some night, at the junction of Coventry-street and the Haymarket!

social life in India. A traveller, on first landing there, was pretty sure to be entertained with a *nautch;* and a nautch, too, differing widely from the dull and decent affairs of the present century. Even European gentlemen sometimes entertained troops of nautch-girls, and thought it no discredit to possess such appendages to their domestic establishments. Indeed, there were some who imagined that without such adjuncts the duties of hospitality could not be properly performed, and sent out troops of dancing-girls to welcome their expected guests.*

. What would the European of the present day think, if when about to enter the house of a friend, in quest of his hospitality, he were to be met in the compound by his host and a troop of these damsels? The English gentleman, who were now to entertain his guests with this well-nigh exploded abomination would surely infamize himself. He cannot, indeed, attend such exhibitions at the house of the native gentry, without lowering himself in

---

* I give, but with the omission of an over-warm description of the performances of the dancing-girls, one illustration of this unhappy truth from a work published in the last century. The writer is Capt. Donald Campbell, who was cast away on his voyage to India, and imprisoned by the officers of Hyder Ali; and, after a series of most distressing adventures, returned to England to write his Memoirs. The date referred to is 1783:—" Leaving Anjengo, I set out for Madras, designing to go all the way by land—a journey of near eight hundred miles. I accordingly struck through the kingdom of Travancore, whose Sovereign is in alliance with the English; and had not long entered the territories of the Nabob of Arcot, before Major Mac- neal, an old friend of mine, and commandant of a fort in that district, met me, proceded by a troop of dancing-girls, who encircled my palanquin, dancing around me until I entered the Major's house. . . . That such incitements to vice should make part of the system of any society is to be lamented: yet, at all ceremonies and great occasions, whether of religous worship or domestic enjoyment, they make a part of the entertainment; and the altar of their gods, and the purity of the marriage rites, are alike polluted by the introduction of the dancing-girls. The impurity of this custom, however, vanishes in India, when compared with the hideous practice of introducing dancing-*boys.*"

the estimation of his brethren.* The more respectable portion of the British community scrupulously abstain from attending the nautches, which even in my recollection were graced by the presence of many of the first gentlemen and ladies in India. Those nautches, I have said, were very different from the nautches of the last century; for nothing could be more staid and decorous—more dull and unexciting—than the native dances with which the present generation has been regaled. To the eye, at least, there was no violation of decency: compared with a ballet on the boards of an European theatre, the only nautches which I ever remember to have seen were outward propriety itself. But setting aside the very important consideration that these nautches are for the most part given on the occasion of some idolatrous ceremony, and are performed in actual adoration of a graven image, it is unquestionable that in the minds of the natives—indeed, of all who are acquainted with the character of the class—the nautch-girls, who are professional courtesans, are associated with all that is impure; and that the European lady, who gives the sanction of her presence to such exhibitions, however outwardly decorous, must infallibly lower her own character and the character of her countrywomen in the eyes of every native looker-on.

In this state of society the ministrations of a few zealous Christian ministers might have done much good, but, in truth, the Pulpit had no living influence,

* Of course, I except the nautches given on the occasion of visits of ceremony to native princes.

and the godly example of those whose special duty it was to guide and to instruct their brethren was not anything for the historian to dwell upon with pride and gratification. For many years Calcutta itself had but one Protestant church, and that was the property of an individual. In 1784 was laid the first stone of another church, the funds for the erection of which were raised by public subscription. In the absence of Warren Hastings, the stone was laid by Mr. Wheler, Acting President, " with the usual ceremonies." A public breakfast was given on the occasion, and all the chief people of the settlement went in state to see the *tomasha*. It is not improbable that the breakfast had more attraction for the majority than any other part of the proceeding, for it was considered by Mr. Kiernander a fact of remarkable omen that Lady Coote had actually attended and received the sacrament at the Mission Church. " This good example," said the missionary, " is attended with a very happy influence, and gives great encouragement to the congregation."

The very few English chaplains, whom the Company sent out, at this time, were so frequently absent from their posts that even in the large Presidency towns their clerical duties were commonly performed by laymen. Of the personal character of these men no very high estimate is to be formed from the perusal of contemporary records. Even at a much later period,* it was said that " neither the number nor the choice of the clergymen sent out by the Court

* See *post*, page 121.

of Directors was in proportion to the number of their
servants or the importance of the object in view."
That they were considerably engrossed with the
thought of heaping up worldly store, appears to be
no mere matter of conjecture. From an entry in
Kiernander's journal we learn that Mr. Blanshard,
who was a chaplain on the establishment during the
administration of Warren Hastings and Lord Cornwallis, carried to England, after a service of little
more than twenty years, a fortune of 50,000*l.*
Another chaplain, Mr. Johnson, after thirteen years'
service, took with him from Calcutta 35,000*l.*; and
Mr. Owen, after ten years' service, 25,000*l.* Unless
they performed a vast number more burial and
baptismal services, and married more Christian
couples than there is any good reason to believe,
and unless the fees received for such offices were
exorbitantly high, it is not clear how such fortunes
could have been accumulated from the ordinary
wages of clerical labour. A slight suspicion of
profitable trade must therefore disturb the reflections even of the most charitable.

That such was the character of all the Company's
chaplains at that period is not to be confidently
affirmed; there may have been bright exceptions
among them, as there was among the laity. Even
in those days there were in Bengal some shining
examples of godliness among the servants of the
Company and the other European residents, the
chief of whom were connected with the Supreme
Court. At the head of these were Mr. Charles

Grant, Mr. Udny, and Mr. William Chambers, of whom mention will be made more fully in another chapter.  One incident, however, illustrative of the genuine earnestness of the first of these, may be here mentioned.  Before the close of the administration of Warren Hastings sorrow fell on Mr. Kiernander and the Protestant mission.  He was an old man, and his sight had failed.  The wealth which he had once enjoyed had passed away from him. He was over-liberal, and a bad manager, and mainly, I believe, owing to the misconduct of others, a coil of debt gathered around him.  His creditors became importunate.  They looked to his property—no matter of what kind—for the discharge of their claims ; and the Mission Church—*Beth Tephellah*, as it had been named ; the one " house of prayer " in the settlement —fell a prey to the Sheriff of Calcutta.  The appraiser came in.  He valued the building—moderately enough, at ten thousand rupees, for it had cost seventy thousand—and Mr. Charles Grant stepped in and paid the money to redeem it.  It was afterwards, with its school and burying-ground, made over to the trustees ; the first being Mr. Grant himself, Mr. William Chambers, and Mr. David Brown.* Mr. Kiernander lived many years after this—but the days of his utility were past ; and the mission, which once had given some promise of success, faded away into a mere shadow.

* This incident occurred at the commencement of Lord Cornwallis's administration, and properly belongs to the next chapter.  I have narrated it, however, by anticipation, here, in connexion with the life of Mr. Kiernander.

I think that something should be said in this place about the birth of the Indian press and the character of its infancy. From the prevailing tone of the journalism of any particular period a just conception of the character of society may generally be derived. In the year 1780 was published the first number of the first Anglo-Indian newspaper. The publication was started by a man named Hicky; and was called *Hicky's Gazette*. Society must have been very bad to have tolerated such a paper. Full of infamous scandal, in some places so disguised as to be almost unintelligible to the reader of the present day, but in others set forth broadly and unmistakeably and with a relish not to be concealed, it appealed to all the worst passions of humanity. It is difficult to bring forward illustrative extracts. The most significant passages are too coarse for quotation. Moreover, a clear impression of the state of society, as represented by the journal, can only be derived from the perusal of a considerable file of *Hicky's Gazette*. Many of the worst libels appeared in the shape of fictitious race-meetings, law-cases, warlike engagements, and other pseudo-narratives of events; or were set forth in the shape of advertisements. Most of these paragraphs, doubtless, contained or insinuated atrocious falsehoods; but what is to be thought of the people who employed themselves in fabricating these infamous calumnies, and of the larger circle who were delighted to read them?

That the writers, at least, thought well of themselves is matter of reasonable conjecture. "I con-

I

gratulate this settlement," wrote one, " in having so amusing, so entertaining a channel for conveying the sentiments of some amongst us, who generously sacrifice a portion of their time for the benefit. of their fellow-subjects." These generous sacrifices of time were often made for the purpose of outraging the feelings of some young lady, who, not improbably, had rejected the suit of the generous libeller. One unlucky damsel, whom a contemporary manuscript note asserts to be Miss Wrangham, figured in a succession of offensive paragraphs, assuming every variety of scandal, under the designation of " Hookah Turban." This young lady, a Mr. Tailor, translated into " Durgee," and Kiernander, the missionary, were three of the most conspicuous victims who appeared in these " generous sacrifices." Hastings, and Colonel Pearse, who acted as his second in the memorable duel with Francis, the dignitaries of the Supreme Court, and the Admiral on the station, were handled with equal severity. Thus continually striving to murder reputations, no man in such a state of society could long have been safe; so it happened that the assassin of reputations was well nigh assassinated in the flesh.

One morning the journal came out with an announcement that " Mr. Hicky thinks it a duty incumbent on him to inform his friends in particular, and the public in general, that an attempt was made to assassinate him last Thursday morning, between the hours of one and two o'clock, by two armed Europeans, aided and assisted by a Moorman."

"Mr. H.," it is added, "is obliged to postpone the particulars at present for want of room, but they shall be inserted the first opportunity,"—that is to say, when the "generous sacrifices" of the slanderers should fall short of their wonted abundance.

Altogether, this chapter is a painful one. The administration of Warren Hastings, whatever may have been the greatness of his political career, was not distinguished by any striking progress in the moral and religious character of the English in India. The earlier adventurers may have committed more heinous crimes, and may have participated in scenes of more offensive debauchery; but in those more remote times the English settlers were so few that they are to be spoken of rather as individual offenders, than in the concrete as constituting a depraved state of society. At a later period affairs were so much in a transition-state, there was so much of the turmoil and excitement of war and revolution, that the English in India might be properly described as living in a great encampment. Their manners, therefore, were more the manners of the camp than of the drawing-room or the boudoir. But during the long reign of Warren Hastings, affairs were comparatively in a state of quiescence, and the ordinary manifestations of what is called society began to be evinced. People had time to think of amusing themselves, and they consorted for the purpose; but their experiments were, to say the least of them, unsuccessful. It could hardly be otherwise. Hastings erred grievously against morality. There may have been circum-

stances to divest his connexion with Madame Imhoff
of some of its ugliest features; and even the greatest
and best of men may fall into temptation. But his
determination not to regard the evil he had done
as a social offence, to be hidden as much as possible
from the eyes of his countrymen, had nothing to
justify or to excuse it. He was Governor-General
of India, and as such he could not openly offend
against morality without offending as a ruler no
less than as a man. Evil example in high place
is a deadly evil, for vice, always infectious, dif-
fuses itself with virulence a hundredfold when the
disease breaks out on an eminence. In no place,
perhaps, in the world, is bad example more pernicious
than in India; for in no place is personal character
more mighty an agent for evil or for good. By the
force of that personal character, every European who
embarks for India must do either harm or good, not
merely to himself and to his brother exiles, but to
the nation which he represents. The higher his
position the greater the amount of good or of harm;
but for the Englishman in India, whatsoever his position, there is no such thing as the harmlessness of
obscurity.

# CHAPTER V.

Progress of Morality and Religion—The Administration of Lord Cornwallis—Charles Grant and John Shore—The Malda Mission—The Clapham Sect—The War of Pamphlets.

LORD CORNWALLIS entered upon his administration in 1786; and a considerable improvement in the tone of society very soon began to be apparent. He was a high-minded English nobleman; the first who had ever carried out to our Eastern settlements the conventionalities and the moralities of aristocratic English life. I am inclined to think that he carried out something still better—the sterling integrity of a thoroughly honest man, and the pure example of a blameless way of life, not reflecting the common morality of his countrymen at home, but greatly outshining it. Such an example was much wanted in India. It is impossible to turn over the Indian journals of 1788, and the few following years, immediately after laying down those of 1780-81, without being struck with the very different kind of reading which the society had begun to relish. The journals of 1788 are highly decorous and respectable. They contain no private slander; no scurrilous invective;

no gross obscenity.  There appears, at that time, to
have been more than enough of worldliness; but it
was much better regulated than it had been a few
years before.  The papers abound in descriptions of
balls and plays; but in these there is nothing offensive.  They bespeak far greater decorum and sobriety
than those of the Hastings' administration.  There
are extant detailed accounts of two grand balls—one
given in 1781, the other in 1788.  In the former, we
are told that the ladies took their departure, " accompanied by the danglers, at about half-past 12;"
whilst the "jolly bucks remained behind to seek for
charms in the sparkling juice of the grape, who, like
the true sons of Bacchus and Comus, kept it up until
four; and in all probability their happiness had continued until Sol in his journey towards the West had
bid them good morning, had they not been disturbed
by two carping sons of Mars, who began to quarrel."
Then comes an account of an altercation, a pugilistic
encounter, and a dénouement, as offensively gross in
description as anything I have ever seen in print.
In the other, we are told that " the ball opened about
half-past nine in the evening, which was graced with
a numerous assemblage of ladies.  The dances continued till near twelve, when his lordship (Cornwallis) and the company adjourned to supper.  The
pleasures of the dance are always preferred by the
ladies, and the repast afforded but a short interruption
to their renewing them, which consequently attracted
their partners and left the solitary swains to the enjoyment of the bottle, though to the praise of their

moderation it must be observed that the dancing-room seemed to engage the most of their attention." This was no small improvement; for only a few years before, dancing was not thought to be possible *after supper*. There was room, doubtless, for a great deal more improvement, for even in these comparatively decorous accounts we see somewhat too much of " choice spirits" and " votaries of Bacchus ;" but the change which I have indicated must have been considerable, for I find a public journal—the *India Gazette* (1788) commenting editorially upon the palpable improvement in the state of society, and congratulating the settlement upon it :—" We are not surprised at the various changes of fashion, as they arise from fancy or caprice, but the alteration of manners must be derived from a superior source ; and when we find that the pleasures of the bottle, and the too prevailing enticements of play, are now almost universally sacrificed to the far superior attractions of female society, can we fail to ascribe the pleasing and rational distinction to that more general diffusion of taste and politeness which the company and conversation of ladies must ever inspire ? — this was the sentiment of the all-accomplished Chesterfield, and there are few who were better acquainted with the science of attaining the *graces*."

This may be accepted as a very fair indication of the period at which a palpable improvement in the social morality of the English in India first began to be discernible. It will be gathered, from the above extract, that before the close of 1788 gambling and drinking had gone out of fashion.*

But at this time, although the English in India were emerging from that absolute slough of profligacy and corruption in which they had so long been disgracefully sunk; though great social changes had supervened; though knavery and extortion were no longer dominant in their offices, and rioting and drunkenness in their homes; though men walked more decently before their fellows, making outward show at least of honesty and sobriety, and living as though it were no longer incumbent upon them, habitually and unreservedly, to break *all* the commandments of the decalogue, there was little real Christianity in India. Few were the altars erected to the true God; few the ministers of the true religion. Living in a heathen land, they were still contented to live as heathens. Of anything like a state religion there was but the faintest shadow. Here and there a solitary chaplain, if he chanced to be at his post, and off the bed of sickness, ministered to an

* I do not know the precise date at which the first regular race-meeting came off at Calcutta, or at the other presidencies. Mr. Stocqueler, in his " Handbook," says: " The first record of the existence of racing in Calcutta may be dated from the origin of the Bengal Jockey Club, in 1803 "—but in the volume of " Hickey's Gazette" for 1780 there are accounts both of races and of race-balls. A few years later they appear to have fallen into desuetude in Calcutta, though carried on with great *éclat* at Madras. " We have continued scenes of gaiety," writes a newspaper correspondent from that presidency, in 1788; " and may boast a competition even with your more populous settlement. The races take place soon, from which much entertainment is expected. This is an amusement which seems to be exploded in Calcutta, as we hear no mention made of them in any of your public papers." How soon the custom was revived I do not know; but Lord Valentia stated, early in the next century, that "on Lord Wellesley's first arrival in that country, he set his face decidedly against horse-racing and every other species of gambling; yet at the end of November, 1803, there were three days' races at a small distance from Calcutta."

unwilling congregation in some riding-school or court-house; married and buried the few who were within his reach, and left the rest to the good offices of laymen.*

It would hardly express the truth to say that in those days men systematically broke the Sabbath. They did not recognise—they were barely conscious of its existence. All the daily concerns of life went on as usual, with the exception, perhaps, that there was somewhat more than the ordinary abandonment to pleasure. At our military stations the flag was hoisted, and they who saw it knew that it was Sunday. But the work-table and the card-table were resorted to as on the week-days. Christianity cantered to the races in the morning and in the evening drove to a nautch. If there were any talk of divine worship, the subject was dismissed with a profane sneer or an idle excuse. One lady claimed great credit to

* Some years later, that is, in 1798,—Mr. Tennant, one of his Majesty's chaplains in India, wrote: "It is certain that neither the number nor choice of the clergymen the Court of Directors have appointed in Bengal, has been in proportion to the number of their servants, nor the importance of the object in view; whether you regard keeping up the appearance of religion among Europeans, or disseminating its principles among the natives. On this establishment their full complement of chaplains is only nine; their actual number seldom exceeds five or six. Two of these being always fixed at the presidency, all the other European stations, dispersed over a tract of country much more extensive than Great Britain, are committed to the charge of the other three or four individuals. In consequence of this, the presence of a clergyman is seldom seen, or even expected, to solemnize the usual ceremonies of marriages, baptisms, or funerals. Prayers are read sometimes at the stations where a chaplain happens to reside; but I have seldom heard of any sermon delivered, except by his Majesty's chaplains, and those at Calcutta. Hence, it must happen that many persons have left England at an early age, and resided in India perhaps for twenty or thirty years, without once having heard divine service, till their return." To this passage Mr. Tennant, in the second edition of his *Indian Recreations*, published in 1804, appends the following note:—"Since writing the above this negligence has been corrected, yet many, from indolence, or contempt of the institutions of their country, have wilfully neglected the opportunity when offered of attending on the offices of religion."

herself as a venerator of the Sabbath, because she
read over the Church service whilst her ayah was
combing her hair. Another, who had. lived twelve
years in Calcutta, where there was a church, said
that she had never gone all that time, because no
gentleman had offered to escort her and hand her to
a pew.

When Lord Cornwallis assumed charge of the
Government of India, there was only one church in
Calcutta—the old, or Mission Church, of which I
have spoken in the last chapter. But in 1787, the
erection of St. John's Church—then called the "new
church," now known as the "old cathedral"—was
completed. It has been stated that the first stone was
laid in April, 1784, when Warren Hastings was
Governor-General. In June, 1787, the edifice is said
to have been "consecrated" in the presence of Lord
Cornwallis, Messrs. Blanshard and Johnson being
the officiating chaplains. Truly was this an important epoch in the history of Christianity in India.
The mere brick and mortar of St. John's Church
were but a small matter. There were living and
enduring influences then at work in men's breasts,
which wrought mightily in God's good time for the
diffusion of the Christian faith. The new church saw
on every Sabbath a number of empty pews. In the
year after its completion, Lord Cornwallis told one of
the Calcutta chaplains that " he thought St. John's
a pretty church; but it had many critics." The
reverend gentleman thought that he might have fitly
replied, that it had not many critics—*on Sundays*.

The man who thought this, and in heaviness of spirit, was one of a little knot of good Christians who often took sweet counsel together—Mr. Charles Grant and Mr. William Chambers* being members of the conclave. He had so much to do with the nativity of Christianity in this part of India, that I may well be excused for giving some account of his antecedent history.

David Brown was the son of a Yorkshire farmer. His father seems to have designed that he should follow some trade; but the boy, happening to make the acquaintance of a clergyman at Scarborough, who discerned his early piety and promising abilities, was reserved to follow a higher calling. This new friend took young Brown by the hand, removed him to his own residence, imparted to him enough of preparatory education to fit him to prosecute with advantage his studies in a public academy, and then removed him to the grammar school at Hull, which was superintended by Joseph Milner. Such acts of beneficence are not so common that I can allude to them here without deploring my inability to record the name of the benefactor. The biographer of David Brown lends me no assistance. He is content that the benevolent patron of the farmer's son should remain in his pages an anonymous "stranger."

From the Hull school, where young Brown soon won upon the affections of his excellent preceptor, he was removed to Magdalen College, Cambridge. This

* Mr. William Chambers was a brother of Sir Robert Chambers. He held the appointment of Protho- notary in the Supreme Court of Calcutta. He died in 1793.

must have been about the year 1782—the year in
which Charles Simeon was ordained.  Brown appears
to have been a frequent attendant at Trinity Church,
to have formed an intimacy with the then persecuted
preacher, and subsequently to have entertained some
idea of accepting a curacy under him.  But it so
happened that he had not very long taken his degree,
before an accidental circumstance turned his thoughts
towards Indian labour.  That noble institution, the
Military Orphan Asylum, was then in course of
establishment.  Captain Kirkpatrick was in England,
as the delegate of the Bengal army, and among other
duties entrusted to him was that of obtaining the
services of a young clergyman as superintendent of
the institution.  A common friend introduced Mr.
Brown to a Major Mitchell, who recommended him to
Captain Kirkpatrick as a fit person to fill the appointment.  After some doubts and misgivings and
consultations with friends, he resolved to start for
London, and, at all events, to communicate personally
with Major Mitchell.  The result was a visit to
Captain Kirkpatrick, and the acceptance of the
proffered appointment.

The Military Orphan Society required the services
of a clergyman and a married man.  Brown, at this
time, was neither.  But it appeared sufficiently easy
to attain to the fulfilment of both conditions.  He
received a check, however, which greatly disheartened
him, and for a while dispersed all his visions of an
Indian ministry.  The Bishop of London refused to
ordain him.  He had known so many, he said, or-

dained ostensibly for colonial ministrations, who had loitered about London and never made their way to the promised field of labour. But what the Bishop of London refused, the Bishop of Llandaff at length consented to do. Early in 1785, David Brown was ordained. About the same time he married.

He continued for some months in London waiting for a passage to Calcutta. His circumstances were, at one time, so straitened, that he scarcely possessed the means of purchasing food for himself and his young wife. The repayment by a friend of a trifling loan, which Brown had made to him some time before, and since wholly forgotten, was viewed in the light of a very Godsend, and acknowledged as such in a devout spirit of gratitude and love. Wanting money, however, he did not want friends. He enjoyed the privilege of familiar intercourse with Cecil and Newton; and had he not seen before him his appointed work, he might, under the ministry of either of those two good men, have obtained pleasant and profitable employment.* "Moneyless, friendless, healthless, and helpless," he described himself at this time, but friendless he was not; and there was a very present help in trouble to which he turned, and in the very extremity of his failing fortunes found succour. He

---

* See Mr. Brown's Journal: "Went to town—called on Mr. Cecil; Mr. C. offered to make me his curate; or, if I would stay in England, procure me a very important and valuable one, namely, at Maidley, where the pious Fletcher has long been labouring." The Editor of the "Memorial Sketches" adds, in a note: "In a separate memorandum of occurrences at this period, Mr. Brown likewise mentions a similar offer having been made to him by the Rev. John Newton. With these honoured friends he maintained an affectionate correspondence during their lives."

prayed,. and his prayers were answered. Having applied to the Court of Directors for an advance of money,. he received from. that body three hundred guineas, paid his passage money, and very soon was fairly on his way to India. Simeon came from Cambridge to see Brown embark, an office of friendship which many years afterwards he performed for Martyn and Thomason.

At the close of the month of November, 1785, Brown commenced his voyage to. Calcutta. The vessel appears to have been constantly in danger, from fire, from storms, from rocks, from collisions, from all sorts of bad management. The passage was altogether very much what a consideration of the time at which it was undertaken would lead us to expect—in many respects a source of constant pain to a pious minister of the Gospel. The captain and the passengers quarrelled with him, because he would not sing a jolly song and drink his bottle of claret. Some argued in support of infidel opinions, some in defence of their favourite sins ; and, though service was sometimes performed on Sundays; it was always shirked when there was a decent pretext, and often when there was none. On the 8th of June, 1786, Mr. Brown "landed with his dear family at the Orphan House," and at once took charge of his appointment.

This appointment he continued to hold until August 1789, when the Management thought fit to dismiss him. He had been appointed, some time before, a chaplain on the establishment, and the troops in Fort William had been placed under his care. When the Mission Church in 1787 fell into the hands of the Sheriff of Calcutta, and was rescued by Mr. Charles Grant, it was transferred to the hands of three trustees—Mr. Grant himself, Mr. Chambers, and David Brown; the latter consenting to take charge of the European congregation for a time. He continued to discharge the duties of all the three offices; but it appeared, and not unreasonably, to the managers of the orphan institution, that they were entitled to a larger share of his time; and he was called upon to take his choice—to abandon either the Mission Church or the superintendence of the Orphan Asylum. After much thought, much prayer, and much counsel with his friends, he resolved to cleave to his Calcutta congregation. He could not persuade himself to forsake the Mission Church; so the Orphan Institution was abandoned.

But eager as was this good man for the spiritual edification of his own countrymen, neither his sympathies nor his efforts were bounded by his desire to bring Christian men to a sense of their Christian duties. He had not been long in India before he bethought himself of doing something to enlighten the dusky millions who had been brought so mysteriously under our sway. In counsel with Mr. Grant, Mr. Chambers, and Mr. Udny, he devised a scheme for a Church of England Mission to India. It was expedient, in the first instance, to seek the assistance of some zealous coadjutor in England. Little difficulty had David Brown in naming one sure to enter into such a project with all due evangelical earnestness, and to carry it out with an equal measure of perseverance. His thoughts wandered back to Cambridge, and fixed themselves upon an old and a beloved friend, whose words of holy encouragement had never ceased to vibrate in the heart of the young Indian chaplain. Any sketch of Christianity in India would be incomplete without some account of this Cambridge friend, and the work that he did to promote the diffusion of the Gospel.

It was at the end of the month of January, 1779, that an Eton boy, named Charles Simeon, awoke one morning to find himself a Cambridge man. The son of a Berkshire squire, he had been sent, at a tender age, to endure the hardships of foundation life at a public school, and had emerged thence at the age of nineteen, none the worse for the conflict, a sturdy scholar of King's. He had eaten the college mutton; knelt on the flogging-block; breasted the Thames; worn the grass off the playing fields at football, and the surface off the chapel walls at fives;—fagged and fagging, from the lower school to the sixth form, he had roughed it to some purpose, had gained strength of body and of mind, and among his brother *" tugs "* had obtained some repute as a hard-headed, straightforward fellow, and an athlete of the first class. There was muscle in young Simeon—but beyond that, there was something strange about the boy, which his class-fellows did not find it quite so easy to fathom. He was not moody; he was not unsociable; but there was at times a solemnity in his manner which puzzled the young collegers. They laughed at him too, as schoolboys will laugh, at what they cannot quite understand. And no blame to them for not understanding: young Simeon himself knew not what it was that he felt stirring within him.

In January, 1779, the school boy grew into the university man. Three days after the attainment of this new dignity, he was told that, in accordance with university custom, it was expected of him that he should receive the sacrament of the Lord's supper. The announcement seemed to startle him. There was something awful in the obligation. Satan, he said to himself, might as well think of attending this solemn service. But there were three weeks before him—three weeks allowed for preparation; and what might not be done within that time to school and discipline his erring nature? With all his soul, he applied himself to the work. He made himself, in his own words, "quite ill with reading, fasting, and prayer." He humbled himself and groaned in spirit —but God at length smiled upon him. Hope sprung up in his breast and a light dawned upon his soul— a light which was never obscured.

Three or four years afterwards, the same young man might have been seen slowly wending his way from the church of St. Edward's, Cambridge. He had taken the first great step: his ministry had commenced. The weight of new responsibilities was upon him; but he felt equal to the burden. He had strength, and he was now suffered to put it to the proof—to try the temper of his Christian courage. As he threaded St. Edward's passage, the jarring

K

notes of strife issued from a mean house and smote
harshly on his ear. The young minister paused and
listened. A man and his wife, in loud railing tones,
were disputing and accusing one another. It was a
time to use the passport of his Master. He entered
the house; reproached the disputants, first, for
absenting themselves from Church; then for disturbing those who had been more mindful of their duties;
and, this done, he knelt down and earnestly prayed
for them. The door was open; and a crowd collected.
But the young minister was not abashed; he prayed
on:—they stared and they scoffed at him, but his
courage did not depart. He was about his Father's
business; and he neither fainted nor failed. It was
an earnest of his future career. His strength never
forsook him. From that day he persevered with the
dauntless valour — the inflexible resolution of one
whom no selfish fears, no doubts and misgivings, no
love of the world, no dread of its opinions, could
drive or tempt from the straight path. And he
proceeded bravely to the end. Men might marvel
and stare at him; might scoff at and calumniate him.
And they did so—but his constancy was not shaken;
he " bore up and steered right on."

A place was prepared for him. Very early did the
young enthusiast see before him his appointed work.
Within a few months from the date of this little
incident, Charles Simeon was called to take up the
crook which he held to the latest day of his life.
For more than half a century was he the shepherd
of that same flock. Entering, in very youth, upon

the ministry of Trinity parish, Cambridge, he only relinquished the cure, when at the age of seventy-seven, he closed his eyes upon the world for ever. No temptation—no promise, no certainty of worldly advantage;—not declining years, nor failing strength; not wealth in possession, nor ease in prospect, could induce him to forsake the temple in which he had worshipped at the outset of his career—in which, with God's blessing, he had redeemed so many erring souls, and out of which had gone forth a spirit to evangelise the University and to work a mighty influence upon the whole Christian world.

Stormy, indeed, was the dawn of that long day: but how tranquil its close! Cambridge began by scouting him as a mountebank and a madman, and ended by honouring him as a monarch. They broke the windows of his church, when he first ascended the pulpit; they closed their own, when that pulpit was vacant. They had made the Sabbath, on his account, a day of tumult and uproar; but when he passed away from them, an unaccustomed quiet reigned over Cambridge even on a market-day. When Simeon entered upon the ministry of Trinity Church, there was fierce antagonism to encounter—antagonism which would have appalled a heart less true to itself and less strong in devotion to its Saviour. Appointed in opposition to the wishes of his parishioners, he was received with enmity and with insult. The people locked up their pews, and the church-wardens tore down the seats which the minister erected in vacant places. For months and months,

until months had swelled into years, he bore up
against this persecution—preaching to a scanty congregation, with an energy and impressiveness which
enchained the attention and often touched the hearts of
the listeners collected in the aisles.   The parishioners
complained to the Bishop that he frightened them,
and that strange people crowded the church.   They
could not, poor souls, drowze comfortably in their
cushioned pews; and so, compelled to abandon them,
they petitioned for a more considerate, a more oily
preacher.   But Simeon stood his ground manfully.
For years and years, he was calumniated, ridiculed,
insulted.   With the parochial authorities he was at
open war.   They closed the church against him, and
he called in the locksmith to his aid.   The University, too, was against him.   Young gownsmen went
to his church, as they would go to a fair; there was
excitement to be gathered from the "hot-gospellings"
of the preacher, who in vehement tones, and not
without some grotesqueness of manner, consigned
them all to the bottomless pit.   And there was always
too — rare attraction for Cambridge men — a good
chance of a *row*.   Outrages of the most indecent
description were committed by men who came to scoff
and to riot.   There was tumult and uproar within
the church; stones were thrown in at the windows.
From the University authorities Simeon had nothing
to hope; they looked upon him as a methodist—a
schismatic.   His zeal was a rebuke to their supineness.   They denounced him as a perilous disturber
of the dreamy quiet of scholastic life.   University

preaching had always been in a different style; University Scripture had always been differently interpreted. They could not countenance such a dangerous innovation upon established rules of procedure.

But better than all support from heads of colleges, Simeon had his own Christian courage to lean upon. And it sufficed to sustain him. He lived down the enmity which assailed his opening career—he preached down the ridicule which greeted his early ministrations. One by one, the men who had scoffed at and insulted him, became listeners and then proselytes. New hearers flocked to the church, and stood in breathless silence, to catch the eager, impassioned words of a preacher who had once been received in that place with noisy derision. It became the fashion for young gownsmen to crowd the aisles of Trinity Church, and, in time, the magnates of the University condescended to do honour to the once despised fellow of King's, who had raised himself so far above them.*

* "It was Mr. Simeon's peculiar happiness," observed the late excellent bishop of Calcutta, Daniel Wilson, in his eloquent tribute to the memory of Mr. Simeon, "to live long enough to see the prejudices which assailed him in his earlier ministry, changed throughout almost the whole university to respect and veneration. Contrast the commencement and the close of his course. He stood for many years alone—he was long opposed, ridiculed, shunned —his doctrines were misrepresented —his little peculiarities of voice and manner were satirised—disturbances were frequently raised in his church, he was a person not taken into account, nor considered in the light of a regular clergyman of the church. Such was the beginning of things. But mark the close. For the last portion of his ministry, all was rapidly changing. He was invited repeatedly to take courses of sermons before the University. The same great principles that he preached were avowed from almost every pulpit in Cambridge. His church was crowded with young students. When the new Chancellor of the University placed a chaplainship at the disposal of the Vice Chancellor in 1833, Mr. Simeon was the person applied to to make the nomination. In 1835, the University went up to present an address to the King. The Vice Chancellor wished him to attend; and when the members of the senate were assembled, made a public inquiry as to whether Mr. Simeon was present, that he might be presented to his Majesty as one of the deputation." "The writer of

It took half a century to consummate this change; but it was a half-century pregnant with blessings to the world—a half-century, in which the cause of Christianity made progress as it had only once made progress before.

It was from that centre of Trinity Church, Cambridge, and of Mr. Simeon's own college rooms, that radiated so much of that apostolic spirit, to which India is now so eminently indebted. It was his privilege to awaken the hearts and to engage the affections of men destined to achieve great spiritual triumphs. Bound as he was to the narrow limits of the University—seldom going forth beyond them, it was his to impress himself, through the agency of others, upon the minds of a people with whom he had never held communion, and to shed a broad light over a country which he had never visited in the flesh. In India comparatively little is known of Charles Simeon. His name is scarcely associated in men's minds with the history of the evangelical progress of the English in the East. The student who would trace the changes which have passed over Anglo-Indian society — the moral and religious advancement of professing Christians, and the silent but sure decadence of the worst forms of Hinduism — seldom travels back to that Cambridge church in which

these lines," adds Bishop Wilson, "can never forget the impression made upon his mind, when Mr. Simeon delivered one of his sermons on the Holy Spirit before that learned University about six years since. The vast edifice was literally crowded in every part. The Heads of Houses, the doctors, the masters of arts, the bachelors, the under graduates, the congregation from the town, seemed to vie with each other in eagerness to hear the aged and venerable man. . . . And at his death, when did either of our Universities pay such marked honour to a private individual?"

Charles Simeon preached the gospel, or those college rooms in which he took sweet counsel with his friends. But he was the spiritual father of many of those who during the last half-century have shaped the religious destinies of India—the sender-forth of many of the great sent-forth who have laboured in that vineyard. "In every part of the kingdom," wrote Bishop Wilson of Calcutta, many years afterwards, "he had children, as it were, in the gospel, who had derived benefit from his unwearied labours during a long life. Multitudes had first been led to serious religion under his energetic ministry or had been awakened to greater earnestness. These recommended others, when going into residence, to seek his acquaintance. In various ways did he labour for the highest welfare of those who were thus brought within his influence. His public ministry was directed very much to their edification — an evening party each week was known to be open to any who wished for his counsel; and he delivered twice in a year a course of lectures upon preaching to such as had passed the earlier division of their college course. Thus he drew around him a constant succession of pious youth, whose minds he imbued with his own sound and laborious views of ministerial diligence. The last day alone will reveal the aggregate of good he thus accomplished. If we take only four or five cases now before the world — David Brown, Henry Martyn, John Sargent, Thomas Thomason, and Bishop Corrie—we may judge by them, as by a specimen, of the hundreds of somewhat similar ones which occurred during the fifty-our years of his labours."

At the head of this list, it is thus seen, was David Brown, who was but little younger than his friend. Simeon, indeed, was still in the earlier years of his ministration when, in 1788, he received from the little conclave in Calcutta, of which I have spoken, a spirit-stirring letter on the subject of a mission to the heathen. They sent him the outline of a scheme, saying, "We understand such matters lie very near to your heart, and that you have a warm zeal to promote their interest. Upon this ground, we take the liberty to invite you to become agent on behalf of the intended mission at home. We humbly hope you will accept our proposal, and immediately commence a correspondence with us, stating to us, from time to time, the progress of our application." * The invitation was cheerfully accepted; and from that time, to provide for India became, in his own words, as written more than forty years afterwards, a principal and incessant object of his care and labour.

But the project moved slowly towards accomplishment. Earnest as Simeon himself was in the good cause, his letters did not give very hopeful assurance of the support it would meet with at home. And in Bengal there was but slight encouragement. The high position of Mr. Grant enabled him to feel the pulse of Lord Cornwallis.† It beat but languidly.

---

* Carus's "Life of Simeon."
† The Presidency chaplains (Mr. Johnston and Mr. Blanchard), it should be remarked, were, to their honour, willing to lead the way, and addressed Government on the subject of the proposed mission.

The Governor-General had a very bad opinion of the natives of the country, and he seems to have thought that they were not a convertible people. "It does not seem that his lordship," wrote Brown to Simeon, in February, 1789, "is disposed to forward our wishes; however, we have the consolation to know that he will not oppose them. He has no faith in such schemes, and thinks that they must prove ineffectual; but he has no objection that others should attempt them, and promises not to be inimical." This neutrality was all that ought to have been expected. Rightly considered, indeed, it was all that ought to have been desired. It does not seem to have damped the ardour of Charles Grant and David Brown. "It is proposed," continued the latter, "that forthwith two young clergymen be sent missionaries to India. They will come immediately to Bengal, and remain with us a few months at Calcutta. It will then be advisable that they remove to that famous seat of Hindoo learning, Benares. There they will spend about three years in study, and furnish themselves with languages. After which they may begin their glorious work of giving light to the heathen with every probability of success."* It was proposed that each missionary should receive 300 rupees a month; from a public fund, if such a fund could eventually be raised; but in the meanwhile from Mr. Grant's private purse. This was, at all events, a plain, practical suggestion, with some hope of realisation. But, although others

* Carus's "Life of Simeon."

besides Simeon had been appealed to—and amongst
those others William Wilberforce*—the response from
England was very feeble, and the great design, as far
as it is to be judged by immediate results, then fell to
the ground. There was, however, strong vitality in
it, and though prostrate it was not defunct. Out of
this correspondence between the little handful of
Christians in Calcutta and their friends in London
and Cambridge, ere many years had passed, grew that
great fact—the Church Missionary Society.

Whilst this correspondence was passing between
England and India, the one solitary missionary in
Bengal (for Mr. Kiernander was then old and indi-
gent, and had ceased to labour) was doing his best
among the factories at Malda—and with much strong
will and sincerity of purpose—to convert the heathens
to Christianity. But Mr. Thomas had not learnt to
temper his zeal with discretion; and he made neither
converts among the people of the soil, nor friends
among his own countrymen. Mr. Grant was disappointed. He had contributed large sums of money to
the support of this mission, and he was compelled at
last to confess that it was a failure. Some parts of
the New Testament were translated by Mr. Thomas
into scarcely intelligible Bengalee; but it may be
doubted whether he ever made a single real convert.
Hoping long against hope, Charles Grant continued
his grants in aid; but the missionary betook himself
to commercial speculations, failed utterly, and in-

* "Our hopes are particularly fixed on Mr. Wilberforce," wrote ~own to Simeon, in 1789. "It is to his influence alone we hope the minister will regard such a project, and ask for it the countenance of Majesty."

volved himself in debt. It was obvious, therefore, that he was one, in no sense, to be trusted; so when Charles Grant prepared to betake himself to England, he wisely determined to wind up the affairs of the Malda mission.

During the remaining period of the administration of Lord Cornwallis, it does not appear that anything more was done to promote the cause of Christian missions in Upper India. It was at the close of 1793 that this estimable nobleman retired from the Government of India. Far different from that in which he found it was the state of the country which he left. The improvement in civil affairs was great, but the social improvement was no less striking. Party animosities seem to have died out altogether during his benevolent administration. He was hospitable, courteous, humane; a nobleman by birth, yet more a nobleman by nature; and his contemporaries appear to have admired his public, and venerated his private character. The journals of 1793 abound with records of Cornwallis's hospitalities, and of the entertainments given in return by a grateful society to the ruler they loved. In these accounts is observable an increased and increasing decorum.* From year to year the progress of propriety is distinctly marked. Fashionable

* Mr. Tennant, an English clergyman, writing in 1798, bears willing witness to the ameliorative influence of Lord Cornwallis' personal character. "A reformation highly commendable has been effected, partly from necessity; but more by the example of a late Governor-General, whose elevated rank and noble birth gave him in a great measure the guidance of fashion. Regular hours and sobriety of conduct became as decidedly the test of a man of fashion as they were formerly of irregularity. [Mr. Tennant means to say, "as irregularity formerly had been."] Thousands owe their lives, and many more their health, to this change, which had neither been reckoned on nor even foreseen by those who introduced it." Another and later writer, though apparently no admirer

dissipation was there in abundance, and no small amount, doubtless, of secret vice; but there was outward decorum, and there were social checks, which wrought a certain moral improvement. The Roman actor, who wore the mask so long that his features caught its likeness, is no bad type of the society, which constantly wears the semblance of morality. In process of time, it becomes what it appears; and morality takes the place of decorum. People do not suddenly change their natures; but to change, or even to conceal their habits, is a great thing gained; and it is unquestionable that this much at least was gained, under the government of Lord Cornwallis.

What was thus auspiciously commenced during the administration of one good man progressed steadily under the administration of another. Sir John Shore's character and example were no less worthy of admiration than those of his predecessor; and society, under the wholesome influence of his virtuous dominion, was placed beyond the perilous chance of backsliding. His administration extended over the next four years; and although the religious movement, commenced during the reign of his predecessor, made

of Cornwallis's administration, gives equally strong evidence on the same point as the above. "Gambling was formerly," says Captain Williamson, in his *Vade Mecum* (1810) "one of the most prominent vices to be seen in Calcutta, but of late years has considerably diminished. Those who recollect the institution of Selby's club, and who now contemplate the very small portion of time dissipated, even by the younger classes, at cards, &c., by way of profit and loss, cannot but approve the salutary reform introduced by the Marquis Cornwallis, who certainly was entitled to the approbation of the Company, as well as to the gratitude of their servants, for having checked so effectually a certain licentious spirit, which had till his arrival been totally uncontrolled, indeed unnoticed, in any shape by his predecessors."

no great demonstrations, it was quietly and successfully encouraged. Christianity owes much, indeed,
to John Shore. He was eminently a Christian man.
Like his contemporaries, he had been exposed in early
life to every kind of temptation, but he had bravely
resisted them all. At a time when to be corrupt
was only to be like one's neighbours, he had preserved,
in poverty and privation, the most inflexible integrity.
Thoroughly conscientious, simple-minded and unam-
bitious, he had made his way, without any brilliant
talents or masculine energies to advance his progress,
to the summit of the ladder of official promotion.
How it was that he at last found himself on such an
eminence, he must, at times, have been somewhat
perplexed to determine. But now that he was there,
by whatever mysterious process, occupying the seat of
Clive, of Hastings, of Cornwallis, he regarded his
elevation to high place and power in a humble and
a trustful spirit, not at all dazzled, not at all inflated,
but prayerfully and painfully endeavouring to do his
duty in that state of life to which it had pleased God
to call him. He entered upon his high office in
October, 1793. At the end of the year, he wrote in
his private journal, " As Governor-General, I have
refused to transact any business on Sundays, and have
devoted portions of them to religious duties and
reading." So far, his duty as a Christian ruler was
clear to him. It was clear to him also that it was his
duty to provide his countrymen with the means of
hearing God's word in decent edifices set apart for
holy uses. One of his first acts, therefore, was to

sanction the building of a church in the Fort. "I
have at last," he wrote to Charles Grant in May,
1794, "gratified your friend Mr. Brown's impatience
and my own feelings in the appropriation of a place
for divine worship in the new fort." He was anxious,
too, as he wrote in the same letter, that the Company
should erect chapels "at Patna, Dacca, and Moor-
shedabad, and at the military stations of Berhampoor
and Barrackpoor, for the use and edification of Christians." But he did not see his way clearly much
beyond this. Lord Cornwallis had either esteemed
the natives of India to be an unconvertible people, or
had thought that they were not worth converting.
But Sir John Shore—who knew the country and the
people far better—looked at the matter in a more
inquiring spirit, and drew back alarmed at the first
sight of the difficulties and dangers which met his
eye. Charles Grant and William Wilberforce were
by this time eagerly discussing the great question at
home; and, believing that they would find in John
Shore an earnest and an active auxiliary, they wrote
stimulating letters to him, which were answered, as
some may think, coldly and cautiously; but, at all
events, with a due sense of the responsibility of his
position. "The difficulties," he wrote, "to be encountered and surmounted are many. Our countrymen in general are by no means disposed to assist the
plan; some from indifference, others from political
considerations, and some from motives of infidelity.
Some would view the attempts without concern;
others would ridicule or oppose it. . . . If the attempt

were made with the declared support and authority of Government, by the aid of misrepresentations it would excite alarm."*

To Mr. Wilberforce he wrote much in the same strain. He considered it to be the first duty of the English in India to christianize themselves. "The Company," he wrote, "expect principle and honesty in their servants without endeavouring to establish the foundation of them. Why do they not direct churches to be established?" And to those who were intent upon the great thought of diffusing the blessed light of Christianity over the dark places of the earth, such language as this, doubtless, appeared cold and discouraging. But, at that time, to set an example of Christianity, and openly to avow Christian principles was no small thing. For Christianity was threatened in its own home. The civilization of the Western world, in that momentous conjuncture, seemed to be madly in love with the foulest infidelity. The hideous blasphemies of the French revolutionary school—the new philosophy of the Age of Reason—were tainting men's minds even in the remote dependencies of the East; and it was with the growing scepticism of his own countrymen that Sir John Shore now conceived that it was his first duty to contend. Both by precept and by example the Governor-General strove to keep alive the smouldering religion of his countrymen†; and I believe that it was no small gain to the cause of Christianity that

---

* Sir John Shore to Mr. Charles Grant. May 5, 1794. "Life of Lord Teignmouth, by his son."

† "I have no hesitation," he wrote to Wilberforce, "on any occasion, and on some find it a duty, to declare

such a man was then at the head of the Government of our Indian possessions.

In the spring of 1797, Sir John Shore, glad to divest himself of the cares and the pomps of high office, turned his back for ever on the shores of India. It was with no lukewarm feelings of pleasure that he found himself again in the society of his friend Charles Grant, who had ere this become an honoured member of the Court of Directors of the East India Company, and who was exerting himself, in Leadenhall Street, right manfully in the good cause. Grant had taken up his abode at Clapham, among the magnates of which pleasant suburb were Wilberforce and the Thorntons, and from the pulpit of which that eminent Christian, John Venn, preached the Gospel to a loving congregation. From Calcutta, Sir John Shore had written to Mr. Grant :—" I think it more than possible that we may be, under Providence, your neighbours at Clapham. Lady Shore's affection for Mr. Grant, her obligations to you both, and my own predilection for a society than which I know no better, are inducements which will hardly submit to others ;" and now, as Lord Teignmouth, he gratified this long-cherished desire, and taking a large, unsightly brick house, now converted to Romanist uses, on the outskirts of the Common, he became one of the " Clapham Sect."

myself a disciple of Christ, in whose Gospel, and in the Bible, I look for my religion; and in that for tranquillity, confidence, and happiness." But his health was precarious at that time; and he confessed that during the hot weather he was scarcely able to attend church. He gave a bad account of the chaplains. " Our clergy," he wrote, " with some exceptions, " are not very respectable characters. Their situation, indeed, is arduous, considering the general relaxation of morals; and from which a black coat is no security."

He found his new associates earnestly and vigorously at work—Grant, Wilberforce, the Thorntons, Zachary Macaulay, John Venn, and other able and pious men, were all full of great thoughts of the conversion of the heathen. The religious Associations, too — the veteran Christian Knowledge, and the Gospel Propagation Societies, and the younger Church Missionary Society — were making grand exertions, in the face of every kind of difficulty, to diffuse the light of truth through the dark places of the earth. It was a period of the deepest interest to all who then had the cause of Missions at heart, or who now trace the progress that has been made during the present eventful century. And it is hard to say how much Christianity in India owes to the social meetings and friendly discussions which were continually taking place in the pleasant suburban villas skirting the green area of Clapham Common.

Charles Grant, as I have said, had by this time become a Director of the East India Company. His active habits, his persevering industry, his steadfast resolution, and it would be just neither to him nor to his colleagues not to add, his high integrity, soon rendered him one of the most influential members of the Court. His views of religious questions were not generally popular in Leadenhall Street; but he was a man not easily to be put down; and his strong convictions, his earnestness of purpose, and his indomitable perseverance, soon made head-way against the feebler wills and the idler habits of his associates. And so it happened, that after he became a member

L

of the Home Government of India, a marked improvement in the tone of the Court's despatches became apparent. There was a more distinct recognition, than before, of the duty of every Christian officer in a heathen land to illustrate his national religion by his own purity of conduct, and by his outward observance of the ceremonial decencies of his faith. Ready assent was given to the extension of the means of church-worship, as recommended by both Sir John Shore and Lord Wellesley. One celebrated despatch, written before Grant had been more than a year in the Direction, bears the unmistakeable impress of his mind, if not of his hand. It was a dignified protest against the systematic profanation of the Sabbath; against Sunday racing and Sunday card-playing, and other desecrations of the Lord's day.*

This was something; but there was much more than this in the accession of such a man to the ranks of the great corporation which then traded with, and administered the affairs of, our Indian empire. In Charles Grant the great cause of Christian Missions had an earnest advocate and a resolute supporter. Out of his own private resources he had maintained the first English missionary that had laboured in Bengal. He had no fear of the results of Christian teaching, if conducted with due discretion. In India, if he had been less cautious than his friend John Shore, it was mainly, perhaps, because he was in a less responsible position. As a member, and after-

* A portion of this despatch is given in the Appendix.

wards as Chairman of the Court of Directors, his zeal had not abated; but he had probed with a steadier hand, and a more searching eye, the depth of the difficulties which beset the propagation of the Gospel in regions peopled with vast millions wedded to hostile creeds; and he had pursued the great object of his life under an increased sense of responsibility, which did not give less force, but more steadiness and system to his exertions. People called such men as Grant and Teignmouth "saints" and "fanatics" in those days; but how calmly and sensibly they thought of the great subject of Gospel-diffusion, may be gathered from their correspondence.* Such prudence and moderation would in these days incur no small risk of being stigmatised as the lukewarmness, if not as the frigid indifference, of mere empty professors.

Yet no small privilege would it have been, in the

---

* Take for example the following passages from Lord Teignmouth's letters, given in his Life, published by his son. "I cannot bring myself to believe," he wrote to Mr. Wilberforce, "that the public would ever deliberately put a veto on the introduction of Christianity in India. . . . But," he added, "I regret that the conversion of the natives of India has been brought forward so conspicuously by the publications of Dr. Buchanan and his premiums for prize disputations. That Christianity may be introduced into India, and that the attempt may be safely made, I doubt not; but to tell the natives we wish to convert them, is not the way to proceed." Again,— "Whether the natives of India will be disposed to receive or to reject the Scriptures when offered to them is at their option and concern; but I should certainly consider a disposition on their part to accept them as an omen of a most favourable nature to the permanency of the British dominion in India. On the other hand, if this country should so far disavow the obligations of its religious profession as to prohibit the promulgation of the Scriptures among the natives of India, I should deem it a fatal prognostic. . . . But although I consider the country called upon both by duty and policy, to attempt the diffusion of Christian knowledge, as far as circumstances will admit, amongst the natives of India, I am equally sensible that the attempt should be regulated by the greatest caution and prudence, and that it can only succeed by a due attention to these maxims."

earlier years of the present century, to form a part of
the Clapham Council, which discoursed on these high
topics when the worldly business of the day was done;
when Thornton had left his Bank, and Grant had
sat out the day in Leadenhall-street, and Venn had
written his sermon, and Macaulay had corrected the
proofs of the *Christian Observer*.* It was anything
but the idle abstract talk of amiable dreamers which
then flowed so freely among them, as they sate round
the winter's fire, or strolled on warm summer evenings
round the green lawn of Thornton's villa, parochially
in Battersea, but socially and historically in Clapham
all the same.   They were emphatically doers and not
dreamers.   They were always doing something to
give an impetus to Christianity in the East.   Perhaps,
Grant had a chaplaincy to give away, and good Charles
Simeon had been invited to recommend one of his
young Cambridge friends; and Henry Thornton
rejoiced in the thought that, if he could do nothing
else, he had money in the Bank to start the young
pilgrim on his godly journey.   Then there were the
affairs of those two young, but now most potential
institutions—the Bible Society and the Church
Missionary Society, to suggest unceasing topics of
discourse.   Lord Teignmouth, to the great scandal of
many, who were not improperly called the "advocates
of Heathenism," had become President of the first;
and the second had grown out of the correspondence,

* If anyone has not made himself
familiar, either in the *Edinburgh
Review* or in the "Essays on Ecclesiastical Biography," with Sir
James Stephen's graphic picture
of this Clapham Council, I would
recommend him to do so forthwith.

which a few years before had passed between Grant and his Christian friends in Bengal, and Wilberforce and Simeon in England. And then, there was sometimes news from India to be discussed; good news of missionary successes; bad news, perhaps, of official obstructions. And the Clapham Council then had to consider what could best be done in Leadenhall-street, and in Westminster, by despatch-writing and by speech-making, for Grant had enlisted under Wilberforce's banners in the House of Commons, to stem the tide of ignorance, and prejudice, and irreligion, which was threatening to bring the missionary efforts of these good men to a disastrous close.

Much, too, was there to engage their thoughts in the controversial aspects of the question. The early years of the nineteenth century were distinguished by a great strife of pamphlets—a war prosecuted with some earnestness, perhaps with some acrimony, by both the contending parties. In 1805, Claudius Buchanan, of whose history I shall speak presently more in detail, published his Memoir on an Indian Church establishment. From that time the subject stood prominently before the public: and, in spite of the necessary obtrusion of more exciting topics throughout those stirring times of European war, there were circles in which the progress of that great battle between truth and error was regarded with livelier interest than the contest between the Corsican Adventurer and the Allied Sovereigns of Europe.

Having exhumed a considerable number of these long-buried pamphlets, and very carefully and conscientiously examined their contents, I am bound to declare my conviction that they are very heavy affairs. One wonders, in these days, how so interesting a subject could have been treated in so uninteresting a manner. So feeble was the light that illumined these weighty discourses, that if it had not been for the Reviewers, the controversy would have been the dullest, perhaps, on record. Foremost among these anonymous writers were Sydney Smith and John Foster. A dread of the biting sarcasms of the *Edinburgh Review* extended even to the Northern Provinces of India; but I would rather have fallen under the hands of the former, than have been consigned to the tender mercies of the latter. The canon of St. Paul's cut sharply with a polished razor; the dissenting divine clove down with a hatchet. Foster was not a witty man; but there was a certain dry humour about him, which he turned to profitable account. His sneer was a mighty one. It came down upon its victim, very quietly but very crushingly, like the paw of an elephant. I have never risen from the perusal of one of his reviews of Scott Waring, without being haunted by a vision of that unhappy gentleman, flattened and forlorn, like a hat that has been sat upon, gasping in a state of semi-animation, and feebly articulating "quarter!"

Yet this Scott Waring held the chief place in the little army of pamphleteers that fought with such good will, in defence of genuine Hindooism. On the other side, there was Mr. Owen, Secretary of the Bible Society; and there was its President, Lord Teignmouth.

The latter wrote with most knowledge of the subject; but he was not a brilliant writer; he was in earnest after his kind, but he was not an earnest man. He was not an enthusiast; he was not a hero;* but he was something better than a hero; he was an eminently good and honest man; and, at a time when lies were being tossed about so prodigally, the truisms which dropped from his pen were not without use and significance, though the sentences which contained them had sometimes an official dreariness about them.

I have no intention to detain the reader with a long recital of the narcotic details of this war of pamphlets. A few specimens will suffice. Among other pamphleteers was Mr. Thomas Twining, "late Senior Merchant of the Company's Bengal Establishment," whose patronymic has since become familiar to the consumers of tea throughout the whole British world. His "Letter to the Chairman of the East India Company" exploded like a shell in the enemy's camp. It consisted mainly of extracts from the Reports of the Bible Society and the publications of Claudius Buchanan. The original comments were brief, but pungent; and, it was remarked by a controversialist on the other side, not without some show

---

* "India House traditions," writes, Sir James Stephen in his "Ecclesiastical Essays," "tell, that when a young aspirant for distinction there requested one of the chairs to inform him, what was the proper style of writing political despatches, the chair made answer 'the style we prefer is the *hum-drum.*' This preference for the hum-drum, enjoined perhaps by the same high authority, clung to Lord Teignmouth, even after his return to Europe. He wrote as if to baffle the critics, and lived as though to perplex the biographers. —He was in fact rather a fatiguing man—of a narcotic influence in general society, with a pen that not rarely dropped truisms; sedate and satisfied under all the vicissitudes of life; the very antithesis and contradiction of a hero."

of truth, that "no such letter was ever before written in a Christian country, under a Christian king, by a gentleman professing the Christian religion."

It may be worth while to exhume, and to examine, a few passages of Mr. Twining's pamphlet. There is a fine antiquarian flavour about them. As relics of a by-gone age, as fossil remains indicating a pre-existent condition of the religious mind of England, they will be pored over with wondering curiosity. The establishment of the Bible Society called forth the following explosion of horror and alarm :—

" I must observe, that my fears of attempts to disturb the religious systems of India have been especially excited by my hearing that a Society exists in this country, the ' *chief*' object of which is the ' *universal*' dissemination of the Christian faith ; particularly among those nations of the East to whom we possess a safe facility of access, and whose minds and doctrines are known to be most obscured by the darkness of infidelity. Upon this topic, so delicate and solemn, I shall for the present make but one observation. I shall only observe, that, if a Society having such objects in view does exist, and if the leading members of that Society are also leading members of the East India Company—and not only of the East India Company, but of the Court of Directors—nay, sir, not only of the Court of Directors, but of the Board of Control !—if, I say, these alarming hypotheses are true, then, sir, are our possessions in the East already in a situation of most imminent and unprecedented peril ; and no less a danger than the threatened extermination of our Eastern sovereignty commands us to step forth, and arrest the progress of such rash and unwarrantable proceedings."

After twenty-two pages of extracts from the Bible Society's Reports and Mr. Buchanan's Memoir (the entire pamphlet consists only of thirty), Mr. Twining thus comments upon the latter :—

" Here, sir, ends the second chapter, which Mr. Buchanan has devoted to this subject, and here, sir, my extracts from the work must terminate, for *I really cannot cut open the leaves, which contain the sequel of this sanguinary doctrine.* Again and again, sir, I must insist upon the extreme danger to our very existence in India, from the disclosure of such opinions and views to the native inhabitants of that country. Let Mr. Brown, and Mr. Buchanan, and their patrons at Clapham and Leadenhall-street, seriously reflect upon the catastrophes at Buenos Ayres, Rosetta, and Vellore; and let them beware how they excite that rage and infatuation, which competent judges describe as without an example among any other people."

And then we have the following ominous notice relative to the Buchanan Prize Essay, which Mr. Twining describes as a " most improper and most alarming fact :"

" What must the natives of India think, when they shall know, as most assuredly they will, that Mr. Buchanan has been permitted to engage the national universities of this country, in discussing and determining the best means of diffusing the

Christian religion throughout India? It is a fact, and I think, a most improper and a most alarming fact, that the Vice-Provost of the Company's College at Fort William has actually bestowed a prize of 500*l.* at each of the Universities, for the best disputation on the following question, viz. ‘ *What are the best means of civilising the subjects of British India, and of diffusing the light of the Christian Religion through the Eastern world?* ’”

The Letter to the Chairman concluded with the following peroration, in which there would have been something not wholly impertinent, if it had ever been intended to force Christianity upon the heathen :—

“As long as we continue to govern India in the mild and tolerant spirit of Christianity, we may govern it with ease; but, if ever the fatal day should arrive, when religious innovation shall set her foot in that country, indignation will spread from one end of Hindustan to the other, and the arms of fifty millions of people will drive us from that portion of the globe, with as much ease as the sand of the desert is scattered by the wind. But I still hope, sir, that a perseverance in the indiscreet measures, I have described, will not be allowed to expose our countrymen in India to the horrors of that dreadful day : but that our native subjects in every part of the East will be permitted quietly to follow their own religious opinions, their own religious prejudices and absurdities, until it shall please the Omnipotent Power of Heaven to lead them into the paths of light and truth.”

This pamphlet called into the field a small regiment of rejoinders. I have now before me, "Cursory Remarks on Mr. Twining's Letter"—"A Letter in answer to Mr. Richard Twining, Tea-dealer"—"An Address to the Chairman of the East India Company, occasioned by Mr. Twining's Letter," and other similar publications. The last named was the production of Mr. Owen, one of the Secretaries of the Bible Society, and is principally directed to the defence of that institution. In so far, it is a triumphant reply to Mr. Twining's tirade. Mr. Twining had especially commented on the fact, that Lord Teignmouth, Mr. Grant, and Mr. Thornton were on the Committee of the Society— the first being at its head; Mr. Owen, with reference to this, replied that neither Mr. Grant nor Mr. Thornton had once attended a meeting of the Committee, during the period of three years and a half for which the society had existed; and he successfully exploded a surmise, to which some weight was attached, that a certain letter from Mr. Brown was addressed to Mr. Grant, by declaring that it was written to himself. Bishop Porteus followed Mr. Owen; and, Scott Waring having taken the field on the other side, Lord Teignmouth sate down to write his "Considerations" on the duty and expediency of communicating a knowledge of Christianity to the natives of India. It was said, at the time, and with undeniable truth, that if this pamphlet had appeared at the beginning of the controversy, no other need have been written. It was sensible, argumentative, conclusive; and it demolished the Waringites.

I think that it may be serviceable to exhume one or two of these "considerations"—considerations not the less worthy of regard in these days, although, as I write, they are just half a century old.   In answer to the assertion that the natives of India would identify peaceful missionary efforts with a desire, on the part of Government, to convert the people to Christianity by force, Lord Teignmouth very pertinently remarked :—

"The natives of India, whether Hindoos or Mahomedans, have the clearest possible demonstration that no such idea as their *forcible conversion* can be entertained by the British Government.   They enjoy the most complete religious toleration: and the performance of the rites and ceremonies of their respective religions is unmolested and without restriction, even in Calcutta, under the very eye of the ruling power.   They see this principle avowed in the laws by which the country is governed; their experience tells them that it is practically observed by all the officers of Government, whether civil or military—by judges, collectors, and commercial agents, and by the officers of the army; and they are sensible, that if any violation of it were attempted, redress for the injury might be obtained."

He was of opinion that the toleration of the Government imparted both security and efficiency to the Christian efforts of private individuals and religious societies: that it was because authority never sought to interfere, that the missionaries would be enabled to prosecute their efforts in perfect safety and with good success. That our position in India must always be surrounded with more or less of danger, he thus admitted :—

" The situation of a Government exercising a dominion over a population of fifty millions of natives (I am contented to take the calculation of Major Scott Waring) through the means of a few Europeans, and natives trained by European discipline, is obviously at all times a situation of peril; and the peril of the situation is greatly enhanced by the consideration of the moral and physical distinctions between the European rulers and their native subjects.

" Our dominion is built on the subversion of the Mahomedan power; and all the toleration which can be granted to the followers of Mahomed, all the benefits of a mild and equitable government, will never make them forget that they once possessed the empire of Hindostan, and have now lost it. Europeans, in their estimation, are câfers, or infidels; and if they receive a respect from them in India, which is denied in all other parts of the globe where Islamism is the religion of the sovereign, it is merely the homage to power, and proceeds from no principle of gratitude or attachment.——With respect to the Hindoos, who constitute much the largest portion of the population, the case is somewhat different. They had for centuries been the slaves of Mahomedan despotism, and saw with little emotion a revolution, which emancipated them from the rigour of its coercion. But the substantial benefits which they have derived from it, will not obliterate the impression of those distinctions in manners, customs, country, colour, and religion, which so widely discriminate the people and their rulers."[*]

One more " consideration "—it is the final one; the closing passage of a sensible essay by a good man :—

"Anxious as I am that the natives of India should become Christians, from a regard for their temporal happiness and eternal welfare, I know that this is not to be effected by violence, nor by undue influence: and although I consider this country bound by the strongest obligations. of duty and interest, which will ever be found inseparable, to afford them the means of moral and religious instruction, I have no wish to limit that toleration which has hitherto been observed with respect to their religion, laws, and customs. On the contrary, I hold a perseverance in the system of toleration not only as just in itself, but as essentially necessary to facilitate the means used for their conversion; and those means should be conciliatory, under the guidance of prudence and discretion. But I should consider a prohibition of the translation and circulation of our Holy Scriptures, and the recall of the missionaries, most fatal prognostics with respect to the permanency of the British dominion in India."

Wise and good men will do well to take this as their confession of faith with respect to evangelising

---

[*] " A minute detail of these distinctions might throw an air of ridicule on the argument. I shall, however, venture to observe that a European meal is not less disgusting to a Brahmin, than a festival of anthropophagi would be to us."

efforts in India. To go beyond this, on the one side or the other, will be assuredly to go wrong.

This war of pamphlets lasted for some years. It was rightly described as "a contest between the friends of Christianity and the advocates of Heathenism."* The outcry against the missionaries was most preposterous; for, in fact, there was but a handful of missionaries in the country. Major Scott Waring had contended that the Danish missionaries had done no great harm, because the temporal power of their Government was so slight; but that the appearance of English missionaries on the scene must fill the breasts of the people with alarm. Had it not already done so? Had not the dangers of such interference, the awful signs of the resentment of the people, been written in characters of blood? Was not the massacre of Vellore a damning proof of the terrible calamities which might be brought down upon the nation by the follies of those zealots and fanatics who were continually casting fire-brands among the most inflammable people in the world? Of this great

* Foster's Contributions to the "Eclectic Review:"—Speaking of those advocates of Heathenism the Essayist says: "It should be distinctly recorded, as it may probably be a fact worth knowing long after their pamphlets and names have perished, that they have not only represented that the effort to supplant paganism by peaceful Christian instruction may be politically mischievous; and insisted that to political considerations all others are without hesitation to be sacrificed, but shown an explicit partiality to paganism itself. In speaking of its fables, institutions, and ministers, they have carefully employed a language not only of forbearance of 'abuse,' as they call it, but of marked veneration; and they have been violently angry that the friends of Christianity should assume the truth of that religion in terms implying that all other religions are therefore necessarily false. . . This direct homage to paganism itself, abstractedly from all consideration of policy in our management of Pagans, appears to us the distinguishing circumstance on account of which the recent paroxysm of enmity to religion merits a more marked record than those ordinary manifestations of it, in which it is perfectly common to misrepresent religion and true policy as incompatible, and insist that the former must be sacrificed."

bugbear of Vellore I shall speak in another place.
The answer given by Lord Teignmouth and other
writers to Scott Waring and his associates was that
there were really no English missionaries in the
neighbourhood of Vellore, or anywhere, indeed, in
that part of India. If the progress which had been
making in the practice and in the diffusion of Christianity in India had been sufficient to excite the
apprehensions of the people, the alarum would have
been sounded in Bengal, rather than in Southern
India.

It is time now to trace this progress. Returning
to the chief Presidency of India, I shall speak first of
the labours of our Anglican divines, and then of the
efforts of the Nonconformist ministers, who established the first English Mission, worthy to be
so-called, in the neighbourhood of the Anglo-Indian
capital.

# CHAPTER VI.

Dawn of the Nineteenth Century—The Protestant Church in Bengal—
Brown—Buchanan—Henry Martyn—Corrie—Thomason.

AT the dawn of the nineteenth century, though in
the provinces of India there were few signs of the
presence of Christianity, in Calcutta a great and important change was every year becoming more per-
ceptible. The ministrations of some pious clergymen, and the practical encouragement of Lord Wellesley, may have done much to foster the growth of
the true religion at the Presidency; but the French
Revolution had done still more to arrest the progress
of infidelity and impiety. Scepticism had once been
the fashion in India; but the brutal excesses of that
great struggle, which had convulsed all Europe, filled
the minds of Anglo-Indians with disgust and detestation; and the doctrines professed by the revolutionary
leaders, though at one time received amongst them with
consideration and encouragement, now began to sicken
and alarm. The reaction was sudden—but salutary.
" The awful history of the French Revolution," wrote
Mr. Brown, in 1805, " prepared the minds of our
countrymen to support the principles of religion and

M

loyalty which our late Governor-General considered it his most sacred duty to uphold with the weight of his authority; he resolved, to use his own words, to make it be seen that the Chrisian religion was the religion of the State; and, therefore, at different times, he appeared in his place as chief representative of the British nation, attended to church by all the officers of Government, to give the Christian religion the most public marked respect of the Governor of the country." And referring to a somewhat earlier period, Claudius Buchanan wrote to a friend in England, "It became fashionable to say that religion was a very proper thing, that no civilized state could subsist without it; and it was *reckoned much the same thing to praise the French as to praise infidelity.*"[*] The Governor-General went regularly to Church; the principal people of the settlement soon followed him there, and the place, which had once been said to be fit only for the reception of stable-boys and low Portuguese, began to open its doors wide to the quality, and to require enlargement for the accommodation of the people of condition who flocked to the temple they had once avoided and the priest they had once despised.

Those opening years of the present century were,

[*] And, in a thanksgiving sermon, preached about the same time (1800) —copies of which were distributed throughout the country by order of Government, to the great astonishment of the Company's servants, the same truth was set forth with still greater emphasis. "The contest in which our country has been so long engaged hath, in one particular, been of essential service to her. It has excited greater respect for Christian institutions and Christian principles. . . . Scepticism and infidelity are not now so well received in society as they once were. It was formerly thought a mark of superior understanding to profess infidelity," &c. &c.

indeed, important ones in the history of Christianity in the East. "The state of society among our countrymen here," wrote Mr. Corrie, in 1806, "is much altered for the better within these few years. The Marquis Wellesley openly patronised religion; whether from motives of State policy or not, it is not ours to judge. He, on every possible occasion, made moral character a *sine quâ non* to his patronage, and sought for men of character from every quarter to fill offices of trust. He avowedly encouraged, and contributed to, the translation of the Scriptures into the native languages, and wherever he went paid a strict regard to divine worship on the Sunday." And Mr. Brown has recorded a conversation which took place, a short time before, between himself and Sir J. D. (D'Oyly) which is still more significant. "Sir J. D., by whom I was seated, said, 'it was very true that the worst opinion had been formed of us at home, and though he had written the truth to his friends, he did not think he should be believed, prejudices ran so high.' He then told me his own feelings and grateful wonder on finding the society here so highly improved from what he had left it so many years before; and further observed that there was no society in England, which he had seen, more correct in all respects. He added, you have full churches, and the most serious attentive audiences I ever saw; and in company I never hear an offensive expression. I believe there is nothing like it in any part of the world." And yet a few years before, Mr. Obeck, when asked by Buchanan if he could produce "ten

M 2

righteous to save the city," replied that he was not sure he could produce ten, but he thought he could produce five.[*]

That the ministrations of David Brown and Claudius Buchanan conduced in no small measure to this consolatory change, it would be manifest injustice to those eminent servants of God to deny. Mr. Brown, during a quarter of a century, laboured, with scarcely a week's intermission, in the same once-deserted field. Other ministers belonged to India— he was wholly of Calcutta. There was all his work done; there he died; there he was buried. By unwearied industry and unfailing zeal; by a steady and consistent course of conduct; by a life of ministerial activity and personal holiness, he achieved more than many, who have had the advantage of more lustrous talents and more exalted station, have proved themselves able to accomplish. He arrived in India when things were at their worst; he lived out a quarter of a century pregnant with the most consoling changes; and the sorrow which was felt for his death, and the reverence entertained for his memory, declare the good part which he had taken in bringing those happy changes about.

Sketching the progress of Christianity in Calcutta, during the concluding years of the last century, I have sufficiently shown the difficulties with which Mr. Brown had to contend and the triumph which he achieved over them. The history, indeed, of the

[*] Mr. Obeck had been steward in the family of Mr. Charles Grant. He was, at the time to which we are referring, one of the oldest inhabitants of Calcutta, and one of the most pious men in the city. He died in 1803, in his 75th year.

religious improvement of the European community of Calcutta, during the quarter of a century which followed the transfer of the Mission Church to the new body of trustees, is the history of Mr. Brown's life. In the results of his teaching we read the career of the man. In all other respects his life was most uneventful. For five and twenty years he was never more than once absent from his post; and then but for a brief passage up the river. Between Calcutta and Aldeen his life was spent; between the Mission and St. John's church his labours were divided. Having been appointed a presidency chaplain, his Sabbath duties were most onerous. Twice he officiated every Sunday at the Mission Church; once at the cathedral; once in the fort. At one period, he had a school in his own house. He was a constant attendant at the hospital and the gaol; an active agent of the Bible and Church Missionary Societies in the East; and ever zealous in his efforts to promote the translation of the Scriptures. In the religious progress of the European community he found his reward. He lived to see the streets opposite to our churches blocked up with carriages and palanquins, and to welcome hundreds of communicants to the supper of the Lord. He lived to see the manners and conversation of those by whom he was surrounded purified and elevated; the doctrines of his master openly acknowledged in word and deed, where once they had been scouted by the one and violated by the other. And when he died it was in the full security that his mantle had descended to more than one who was worthy to wear it—that the field which he had so long and diligently cultivated would never be suffered to be over-run with weeds, for want of labourers to follow his example.

During, perhaps, the most important period of his ministry—for it was at the very turning point of the religious fortunes of the English in India—Mr. Brown enjoyed the solid advantage and the unspeakable comfort of the support and assistance of Claudius Buchanan. The son of a Scottish schoolmaster—born and educated in Scotland, and at the early age of fourteen appointed private tutor to the sons of a gentleman of fortune—this able and excellent man had been originally designed for the Presbyterian ministry. Having spent some time at the Glasgow university, he would there have taken his degree, but happening to fall in love with a young lady, of superior worldly station, he conceived the romantic idea of leaving his native country, carving out his fortune in foreign lands, and returning with wealth and honour to claim the idol of his youth. It appears that his chief stock in trade was a lie and a violin! With the former he deceived his parents; with the latter he intended to fiddle his way through the world; but had scarcely reached the borders of England before he repented of his preposterous design. His success, as a wandering minstrel, was considerable; but at the best he felt it but a sorry way of life; and if he had not been so overwhelmingly ashamed of himself he would even then have returned to his home. But the die, as he said, was cast. He went on—though not as a fiddler by the wayside, or as an enthusiast swelling with thoughts of foreign travel. Those visions had passed away. He obtained a passage, on board a collier, from North Shields to London, and was nearly drowned before he reached his destination. Arriving safely at last, he found himself in the great metropolis; and there, after the common fashion of adventurers, he was brought to the extremity of wretchedness and want. After selling his clothes and his books, he appeared to be on the very brink of starvation, when he obtained employment in an attorney's office; and subsequently he secured a situation under another solicitor, with a salary of forty pounds a year. He designed, at this time, to make the law his permanent profession; and so little was his future career foreshadowed in his then way of life, that it is recorded of him that although he sometimes wanted a dinner, he had money to spend on theatres, spouting clubs, and other public amusements.

A year after the date of his exile from Scotland, while leading this unprofitable life, Buchanan received intelligence of the death of his father. The lie, with which he had set out on his journey, was not yet to be suffered to die. He wrote to his mother soon afterwards from London, and dated his letter from *Florence*. In the summer of this year (1788) he was prostrated by a severe fever; and whilst on the bed of sickness made many wise resolutions to be broken upon his recovery. He read Homer and Virgil; but neglected his Bible. Occasionally he found an hour, snatched from the severe studies of the law, to devote to literary pursuits; but none to pious meditations. His heart was as hard as ever.

In 1790, some higher thoughts and better feelings found entrance to that God-deserted shrine. He saw the sinfulness of his way of life as in a glass; he withdrew from evil society; he reflected much, read much, prayed much. Beneath the sanctifying influence of Mr. Newton's ministry his deepening convictions took firm root in his mind. He wrote to that good man; and from the pulpit of St. Mary Woolnooth the preacher replied to his nameless correspondent. The invitation to come unto him was gratefully accepted by the heavy-laden lawyer's clerk. There he found what he had long sought—some one to guide him, some one to instruct. The old man took him by the hand, became his friend and his counsellor; and, in a happy hour, recommended him to the good offices of one who with the will united the power to turn the best gifts of nature and of fortune to account in doing the will of his master. This was the late Henry Thornton, already mentioned with honour, whose life was mainly spent between his office in the city and his villa on Clapham Common, but whose good deeds went forth in a perennial stream to the uttermost parts of the earth. A man of enlarged sympathies, of unbounded charity, with the most reverential love of truth, and a sense of justice, not severe towards others but unstinting in self-sacrifice, he was for years the centre of that noble group of philanthropists, from which the venerable faces of William Wilberforce, Thomas Clarkson, Granville

Sharpe, and Zachary Macaulay, beam forth with benignant expression.* In this group were men who possessed more brilliant talents, more fluent eloquence, more energy and enthusiasm of character— altogether more of that heroic spirit which originates great deeds and courts dangers and privations, which sets before it some great object to be achieved and girds itself up to encounter every obstacle, strenuous in the purpose to beat them down with the strength of an unconquerable will—but in Henry Thornton there was that which rendered him the ally, the counsellor, the friend of all. With the strongest sense to advise, the most unfailing generosity to aid, and the kindliest sympathy to encourage, he promoted every good work; he rallied around him the friends of humanity; and from his villa on Clapham Common went forth many a great scheme for the relief of his suffering, and the evangelization of his benighted fellow-men in all parts of the world; and whilst he was ever ready to promote these great and comprehensive schemes, his individual charities, often noiselessly, secretly administered, brightened up many a dreary hearth and infused new vigour into many a drooping soul. He gave not by hundreds, but by thousands; and how well and wisely his wealth was distributed, the memoirs of Buchanan, Martyn, and others, abundantly declare.

To Claudius Buchanan he was indeed a friend. He sent the young Scotchman to Cambridge. Out

* Grant and Shore had not returned to England at the time of Buchanan's first introduction to Henry Thornton. When they arrived, they pitched their tents at the extreme corners of Clapham Common.

of his abundance he supplied funds to one who was
worthy of such patronage. Buchanan paid back the
money which was thus generously advanced. Out of
his first savings, he remitted to Henry Thornton the
four hundred pounds which had been spent upon his
college education. Nor did he stop there. In grateful
remembrance of the aid which he had derived from
one wealthier than himself, he placed a sum of money
at the disposal conjointly of Mr. Newton, Dr. Milner,
and Henry Thornton, to educate for the ministry any
young man, whom they might think fit to select.

At Michaelmas, 1791, Claudius Buchanan entered
Queen's College, Cambridge. He was regular in his
habits and indefatigable in his studies. He kept but
little company, and the few whose society he sought
were men of approved godliness. Among these was
Charles Simeon,* who invited him to those Sabbath
evening parties, at which so many of the young men
of the day were encouraged to take up the cross, and
strengthened in all their good resolutions by the
affectionate exhortations, and by the godly example of
their friends.

Great as were his abilities, and assiduous as was his

---

* "In addition," says Mr. Pearson, in his biography of Claudius Buchanan, "to the society which has been just mentioned, Mr. Buchanan was invited to spend an hour on Sunday evenings at the rooms of one excellent person, who has been distinguished during many years for his active and zealous support of religion in Cambridge, and to whom a numerous body of clerical and other students have been successively indebted for the most important in-struction and encouragement during their academical progress. Of the kindness of this gentleman, and of the benefit which he derived from his conversation and example, Mr. Buchanan wrote to more than one of his friends in terms of the highest respect and gratitude." Why the name of this "excellent person" should be so studiously suppressed, we cannot even conjecture. Why should not Mr. Simeon's name take its proper place in the biography of Claudius Buchanan?

attention to his studies, he took no University honours. There were those who thought that he might, had he so willed it, have taken the highest. This, however, he always denied. "Those who think," he said, "that I might have been Senior Wrangler are not well informed. There are few instances, I believe, of any persons arriving at this eminence who had not studied mathematics before they went to Cambridge."* Honours, though not the highest, *were* within his reach; but he seems to have had no academical ambition. Perhaps, the warnings and admonitions of his venerable friend, Mr. Newton, may have deterred him from a conflict which is not without its snares. He did not despise human learning, but he entered with chastened ardour upon the pursuit. Other objects had been set before him. It was not to obtain a name but to prepare himself for the ministry that he had entered the gates of the University. And by much prayer, much self-discipline, much searching of the Scriptures, much converse with holy men, he had prepared himself for the great race which Providence had so significantly ordained him to run.

The first idea of Indian labour seems to have been suggested to him, whilst yet an undergraduate, by Mr. Newton. "I decline giving any opinion," was his answer: but he added in all humility—"It is with great pleasure I submit this matter to the determination of yourself, Mr. Thornton, and Mr. Grant. All I wish to ascertain is the will of God." And again,

---

* A few years later, Henry Martyn added another to the "few instances" then on record.

in another letter, "I am equally ready to preach the Gospel in the next village or at the ends of the earth." His friends decided the matter for him. Mr. Grant was by this time in the East India direction. He had the power and the will to serve Buchanan; and early in 1796 a chaplaincy was presented by him to the young minister. "On the 3rd of July, he preached for Mr. Newton at St. Mary Woolnoth." Strange, indeed, must have been the sensations with which he ascended that pulpit, to which years before he had turned his streaming eyes, and from which had come forth the announcement—the invitation, which was the settling point of his religious career. Little could the lawyer's clerk have dreamt that one day he would himself be uttering Gospel-truths from that very spot which seemed to him radiant with glory and instinct with inspiration—not to be profaned by unhallowed footsteps, and scarcely to be gazed at by unveiled eyes.

On the 30th of that month of July, 1796, Buchanan embarked for India. Of his voyage no particulars remain. On the 10th of March, 1797, he landed at Calcutta. Mr. Brown, to whom he was the bearer of a letter of introduction, received him with a hospitality which would have been equally extended to him had he carried no such recommendation. His residence in Calcutta was but brief; for shortly after his arrival he was appointed military chaplain at Barrackpore.

There a great disappointment awaited him. The appointment he held was in one respect, at least, a sinecure: there was no church and there was no

congregation. Divine service was never performed.
" Barrackpore," he wrote soon after his arrival, " has
been called the Montpelier of India. Here I enjoy
everything that can minister to comfort or elegance,
except society; we have society too, but it is only
polite society: there are not many here, I fear, whose
hearts are awakened to the love of virtue and truth.
Nevertheless, I possess two companions of inestimable
value. I mean those two books which are written
by the finger of God, the book of God's *word* and the
book of God's *works*. These are treasures which are
inexhaustible, and which afford me in my retirement
pleasure, company, and comfort."

The spirit of Claudius Buchanan was severely tried.
He had believed that a wide field of utility had been
opened to him—that his zeal and devotion were about
to be put to the test, his energies called forth, his
abilities proved, by circumstances at once novel and
inspiriting. Instead of this, he found himself thrown
into the midst of uncongenial society, drawing a good
salary from Government, doing little or nothing for
it, pining in dreary inactivity, his energies running to
waste—his mission shown to be no more than a mission to drowse away life on a salary of twelve hundred
a year. Another trial was soon to be added to the
pile. His friends in England began to mistrust him
—to feel and indeed to express some disappointment.
They expected that he would do so much; they could
not hear that he was doing anything. There were
those who understood his position too well to blame
him for that which was only his calamity; but others

had a vague sort of idea that he had gone out to
preach the Gospel to the heathen, and that tidings
ought to have reached England of conversions on a
grand scale. They thought, perhaps, that he had, in
the language of a recent missionary writer, "apostatised to a chaplaincy." But he had never been
anything but a Company's chaplain. It was simply
Buchanan's duty to obey orders; to bury the Company's officers when they died, to marry them when
they turned their thoughts towards marriage (which
was not very often in those days), and to baptize their
Christian children. The only work that he could add
to this was the study of the Scriptures and of the
native languages, hoping one day to turn his acquirements to good account. It was, I repeat, a sore
trial; but what could Buchanan do? "I suffered,"
he wrote to Mr. Grant in 1798, "a long struggle
before I could resign myself passively to my unex-
pected destination. But the struggle is now over;
and I view myself as one who has run his race; to
whom little more is left to do. I have known some,
who in such a case would have extricated themselves
with violence, and sought a new fortune in the Gospel.
But it will require a very evident interposition of God
indeed to bring me out of this Egypt, now that he
has placed me in it: I shall esteem myself highly
favoured if I be enabled to pass my days in it with a
pure conscience, endeavouring to do a little where
much cannot be done."—The language this of deep
despondency—probably the result of failing health.
He had suffered from severe attacks of fever, and was

afflicted by a disorder of the chest. "I have now," he wrote to Mr. Newton, "been a year and a half in India, and have not yet engaged in the ministry; and I know not when I shall. At present indeed, I should scarcely be able, were I called to it." But better times were in store for him.

In 1799, Buchanan was united in marriage to Miss Whish, the daughter of a Suffolk clergyman—a young lady of amiable temper, gentle manners, and the soundest Christian principles imbibed in early youth and since cherished upon conviction. Here at least was an addition to his stock of happiness! For some time he continued to reside at Barrackpore, doing occasional duty in Calcutta. "My public ministrations," he wrote to Henry Thornton in 1800, "have been rare; but perhaps not so rare as from my situation might be expected. Of the three years I have been in India, including the number of times I have officiated at the hospital in Calcutta, and in my own house at Barrackpore, I have preached on an average once a fortnight." But soon other duties were assigned to him. Lord Wellesley had conceived the design of that noble institution, the College of Fort William. Mr. Buchanan was desired to draw out a sketch of the constitution of the college, and to prepare a justificatory minute. In the month of August, 1800, the college was formally established, Mr. Brown was soon afterwards appointed Provost, Mr. Buchanan Vice-Provost and Classical Professor.

From Buchanan's letters to his friends in England, despatched about this time, we gather a few interesting particulars of the state of the Church in Calcutta, at the commencement of the present century. "Both the churches," he wrote to Mr. Grant in 1801, "are generally full, particularly in the cold weather. The College chapel has punkas, which will probably draw a great number of the townspeople during the hot season. Lord Wellesley has fitted up a pew for himself in chapel." And again, "Lord W. has had serious thoughts of building a larger church. But the College institution has deranged his plans a little. If you cannot give us a new church at present, we shall thank you for a clock and bell; and also for a singing man and organist. The charity boys sing in the two churches and in the College chapel every Sunday. And there are organs in each, but only one organist. . . . Sir Alured Clarke has just left us. He is entitled to the thanks of your Court for his attention to Divine service; and for the general good example he has set to your settlement here."* And later in the same year he wrote to the same excellent member of the Court of Directors: "Our church continues in much the same state in which I described it to be in my last. We have had an addition of some communicants, principally from college. The church thins a little always in the hot months of May and June. Lord W. has proposed to use punkas and tatties; and it is probable that we shall have recourse to them next season." In the following year, writing an apology for infrequency of correspondence, he says

---

* And in another letter it is set down—"General Lake has just arrived. He and his family were at church yesterday."

—" I have less time now than ever. The chief labour of the churches is devolving fast upon me. My religious correspondence in India is greater than at any former time. The whole direction of the College is with me; every paper is drawn up by me; and everything that is printed is revised by me. In addition to this, I give Greek and Latin lectures four times a week." And again early in the same year, " Our churches during this cold season are more crowded than I ever saw them before. Even on Wednesday evening there are a great number, and good is done. Some of the students attend on that evening. Their presence warms the heart of old Mr. Obeck. ' How would Mr. Grant rejoice,' he sometimes says, ' to see these things.' The pillars are removed, and a number of additional seats made, to accommodate the many who come."

And from that time, every year saw a more numerous attendance in our churches, and a more devout spirit pervading the congregations. In 1805, Buchanan wrote, " We have had Divine service at the Mission Church lately for the settlement. The punkas make it very pleasant; but it was found to be too small for the auditory; many families going away every Sunday morning; seats being in general occupied an hour before service;" and to this he added, as another evidence of the progress of vital religion among the European inhabitants of Calcutta: " The demand for religious books, particularly of evangelical principles, has been very great these two last years. Messrs. Dring told me they had sold an investment

N

of fifty 8vo Bibles in the course of three months."
And in other letters, written about the same time, he
thus described his congregations:—" On account of
the increase of our congregations we are about to
have two morning services on Sunday; the first at
seven o'clock in the Old Church, and the second at
the usual hour of ten at the new.   This is very agreeable to a great majority.   Only Mr. Brown and
myself will officiate at the Old Church.   We shall
of course (at least I shall) continue to officiate as
usual at the new. . . .   We have some of all sects
in our congregations; Presbyterians, Independents,
Baptists, Armenians, Greeks, and Nestorians.   And
some of these are of my audience at the English
Church.   But a *name* or a *sect* is never mentioned
from the pulpit; and thus the word preached becomes
profitable to all. . . .   Even among the writers in the
College there are Presbyterians, Independents, and
Methodists.   Their chief difficulty at first is from the
ceremonies of the English Church, which few of them
ever witnessed till they came here.   I must lie down
awhile and dictate to an amanuensis, for it is very
hot.   The thermometer is to-day near 110."

In the hot weather of this year (1805) the failing
health of Mr. Buchanan rendered it necessary that
he should determine on a brief cessation of labour—
a brief absence from the enervating, exhausting
climate which had so reduced his strength and
diminished his activity.   A visit to the Malabar coast
was accordingly planned ; but before it could be put
into execution, an alarming accession of illness brought

the invalid down to the very brink of the grave.
The hour of death seemed to be at hand.   Buchanan
himself, assured that his earthly race was run, sent
for his friend and colleague, David Brown, resigned
into his hands all his worldly affairs, commended wife
and children to his care, ran over the history of his
past life, spoke of the interpositions of an especial
providence discernible in it, said that he was ready,
nay eager to depart, and gave directions about his
burial, his monument, and his funeral sermon.   In
this trying hour did he exhibit the utmost tranquillity
of mind and an assured belief of his acceptance
through the merits of Jesus Christ.   In "a humble,
submissive, patient and fervent" spirit he gave himself up to prayer ; but not his alone were the suppli-
cations which then ascended to Heaven.   Other
prayers were offered up in faith—other prayers were
blessed to the supplicants—and Claudius Buchanan,
almost by a miracle, rose up from the bed of
death.

The fever left him.   In the steamy month of September, he was removed from Calcutta to Barrackpore and thence to Sooksaugor.   Here a new trial
awaited him.   He received intelligence of the death
of his wife, on board the vessel which was to have
conveyed her to England.   "I am now a desolate old
man," he wrote, "though young in years.   But my
path will, I doubt not, be made 'clear as the noon-
day.'"   Resigned to his hard lot, he turned his
thoughts into new channels, and never was his mind
more busy with great projects than during this season

of affliction. " My chief solace," he wrote, " is in a
mind constantly occupied; and this is the greatest
temporal blessing I can expect even to the end."*
To Mr. Grant he wrote to recommend the enforce-
ment of certain regulations for the better government
of writers and cadets on board-ship; and to the Archbishop of Canterbury he despatched a lengthy and
elaborate epistle on the religious prospects of Hindustan and the necessity of an episcopal establishment
for India—the darling project of Buchanan's life. He
did not labour for himself; but there were those who
hoped and expected to see in him the first Bishop
consecrated to the Indian Church. " I must inform
you," he wrote to Mr. Grant early in 1806, " that
since my late illness I am become infirm in body and
in mind: and I am scarcely fit for those public duties
in this place which require the heart of a lion and a
countenance of brass. I trust my excursion to the
Deccan, which I meditate next month, will be beneficial to me. . . . As to returning (to England) in
order to receive episcopal dignity, my soul sinks at the
thought of it. I trust my lines will rather be cast in
a curacy. Place the mitre on any head. Never fear;
it will do good among the Hindus. A spiritual bishop

---

* The manifestations of genuine
sorrow are so variously shaped by
individual character, that it would
argue little charity, and indeed but a
limited knowledge of humanity, if I
were to say more than that the following words, which I find in the
same letter, grate somewhat harshly
on my own feelings: " Whilst I was
thus engaged (in the study of the
Syriac language), the news of Mrs.
Buchanan's death arrived. I found
some consolation in writing a few
lines to her memory in the Hebrew,
Syriac, Greek, and Latin languages,
which I inscribed on a leaf of her
own Bible—the best monument that
I could erect; for the body was buried
in the deep." This is the pedantic
side of sorrow; but all I wish to say
about it is that, although I do not
question its sincerity, I have no sympathy with such polyglot woe.

will appear in due time!" The prophecy has been amply accomplished.

Repeated attacks of fever and ague, and some difficulty in handing over his several appointments, detained him for some time in Bengal, and it was not until the beginning of May that he was enabled to commence his voyage to the southward. "The principal objects of this tour," he subsequently wrote in his *Christian Researches*, "were to investigate the state of superstition at the most celebrated temples of the Hindus; to examine the churches and libraries of the Romish, Syrian, and Protestant Christians; to ascertain the present state and recent history of the Eastern Jews, and to discover what persons might be fit instruments for the promotion of learning in their respective countries, and for maintaining a future correspondence on the subject of disseminating the Scriptures in India." With this great design occupying his thoughts, Buchanan set out on his voyage along the coast. At the Sandheads, the vessel, in which he sailed, passed within sight of another then steering towards the mouth of the river. It was one of an outward-bound fleet; and it bore the name of the *Union* on its stern. Among the passengers in that vessel was a young man of whose great talents and signal piety Buchanan had heard much from Mr. Charles Grant, and whom he now yearned to embrace as a friend, a brother, and an associate.

The son of a self-taught Cornish miner, who had raised himself to a seat in a merchant's office, Henry Martyn had passed through the Grammar-school of

Truro with the character rather of a docile than of a studious boy. Quiet and inoffensive, of a delicate frame and of retiring habits, he had paid the common penalty of the gentleness which does not resent, and the weakness which cannot resist, injustice. To his master he had recommended himself by the quickness of his parts and the sobriety of his disposition; but thus early he had given no sign of the brilliant talents which distanced all competitors at Cambridge, and the energy of character which supported him throughout so great trials in the Eastern world. Unsuccessful, at the boyish age of fifteen, in an effort to obtain a scholarship at Oxford, he had returned to the Truro Grammar-school, and directed his thoughts towards the sister university. Two years after the Oxford failure, he was entered at St. John's, Cambridge; but so little was he aware of his own capacity for the exact sciences, that he commenced his academical career by committing to memory the problems of Euclid, as lessons which he could not understand. Such was the inauspicious dawn of his Cambridge life; but before he had completed his twentieth year he had attained the highest University honours. No man ever wore them more meekly. Senior wrangler of his year, he felt the emptiness of the distinction. In his own words, he had but " grasped a shadow."

His talents were of a remarkable order. He seems to have combined, in an extraordinary degree, the imaginativeness of the poet with the exactness of the man of science. Intellectual eminence he had attained.

Social eminence was within his reach. But he had no such aspirations. The promptings of worldly ambition never disturbed the serenity of his mind. Human learning and earthly fame appeared before him as mere baubles. New desires had sprung up in his heart—new thoughts were busy in his brain. Another path was opening out before him—another hand was beckoning to him ; other voices were making music in his ears.

He was one of those students who, attracted in the first instance by mere curiosity to Trinity Church, listened with deep attention to the Gospel truths there uttered by Charles Simeon. He was one of those who in due time became constant attendants at Mr. Simeon's rooms, on those ever-remembered social occasions, when he mustered his young friends around him, inquired into their wants, and gave them the counsel they needed. In the young student of St. John's, Simeon soon discerned the brilliant talents and the apostolic character which we now contemplate with so much interest and veneration. Loving Martyn as a son, he was soon enabled to testify the genuineness of his affection by appointing him curate of Trinity Church.* In October, 1803, Martyn was ordained. And how truly may it be said that no man ever entered upon his ministerial career with a more solemn sense of the responsibilities he had

* In succession to Mr. Sowerby, another senior wrangler, who had shortly before died of consumption. Mr. Thomason was, at this time, an associate of Mr. Simeon in his ministerial duties. "What," says the biographer of the latter, "must have been Mr. Simeon's consolations in the ministry at this period, enjoying as he now did, the rare privilege of the devoted affection and invaluable co-operation of two such friends as Thomason and Martyn."

undertaken with his ordination vows—a more holy desire to render himself worthy of the honour and the trust that had devolved upon him.

It would seem that he had already determined to devote himself to missionary work. The great outline of an undetailed scheme of action had been grasped with the tenacity of an unalterable resolution. He was called to preach the gospel to the heathen. It was whilst listening to a sermon by Mr. Simeon, in which were set forth in impressive language the immense blessings which had flowed from the endeavours of a single labourer* in the vineyard, that his thoughts had leaped up to embrace the grand idea of a missionary sacrifice.† In his study it had gathered strength and significance. Pondered over, prayed over, wept over, it had swelled into the one desire of his soul. He read with ecstacy the outpourings of David Brainerd's saint-like spirit, and felt his " heart knit to the dear man," rejoicing in the thought of meeting him in heaven. His imagination traversed the burning sands and confronted the fiery skies of

* That single labourer was Dr. Carey—*clarum et venerabile nomen*—of whom I shall speak presently.

† Henry Martyn, like Brown and Buchanan, like Thomason and Corrie, was a *Chaplain* on the establishment —and in no accepted sense of the word a missionary. It was not his mission to preach the Gospel to the heathen, but to perform Church service in the presence of the Company's servants, to marry them, to bury them, and to baptize their children. The error, which assigns to Martyn the character of an ordinary missionary, has recently been in some measure endorsed and perpetuated by the biographer of Mr. Simeon, who writes: " The deeply-cherished desires of his (Martyn's) soul were at length gratified by an *appointment to missionary labour* in India." Martyn's own biographer, indeed, says: " God, who has appointed different orders and degrees in his Church, and who assigns to all the members of it their respective stations, was at this time pleased by the Almighty and gracious influence of his Spirit to call the subject of this memoir to a work demanding the most painful sacrifices and the most arduous exertions—*that of a Christian missionary.*"

the Eastern world. He saw before him mighty victories to be achieved over ignorance and superstition —but he saw with equal distinctness the cost at which they must be purchased; not the perils and privations—these he disregarded—but the severance of ties which, enlacing a heart of no common tenderness, bound him to his own native England. He had a beloved sister—and there was one still dearer to him than a sister. The sacrifice was great; but he was prepared to make it—prepared to leave his family, his friends, his betrothed; and, perhaps, for ever.

With feelings most chequered, but honourable in their varying shades alike to the man and the Christian, Henry Martyn turned his back upon Cambridge. A chaplaincy had been procured for him in the service of the East India Company—from the same source as that which had supplied Buchanan with his credentials, the discriminating benevolence of Mr. Charles Grant. In the summer of 1805, he prepared to embark. Mr. Simeon met him at Portsmouth, and accompanied him to the vessel, remaining some days on board, sustaining his young friend with kind words and wise counsels, preaching to the passengers and sailors, fixing the attention of all and touching the hearts of some. On the 17th of July, the two friends parted for ever. It was a bitter moment when Henry Martyn awoke, next morning, to find himself alone on the great waters. "My feelings," he wrote, "were those of a man who should suddenly be told that every friend he had in the world was dead. It was only by prayer for them that I could be comforted."

The vessel was detained, for some weeks, off Falmouth. New excitements, new trials, new joys, new sorrows, were now unexpectedly opened out before him. The temptation was not to be resisted; he went on shore. He knew what it would cost him. He knew how great the agony of that fresh divulsion of the closing wounds of his lacerated heart. Who would not have done as he did—snatched a few brief hours of enjoyment even at the cost of such after pangs. He sat beside his betrothed again.* For-

---

* Henry Martyn's biographer has shadowed forth the individuality of this young person with an indistinctness which we cannot suppose to be accidental. She was a Miss Grenfell. In the following extract from one of Simeon's letters, in his published biography, we catch a glimpse of the truth:—

"With her mother's leave Miss G. accompanied us to Col. Sandys'; when I had much conversation with her on Mr. Martyn's affair. She stated to me all the obstacles to his proposals; first, her health; second, the indelicacy of her going out to India alone, on such an errand; third, her former engagement with another person, which had indeed been broken off, and he had actually gone up to London, two years ago, to be married to another woman; but as he was unmarried, it seemed an obstacle in her mind; fourth, the certainty that her mother would never consent to it. On these points I observed, that I thought that the last was the only one that was insurmountable; for that first, India often agreed best with persons of a delicate constitution; e. g., Mr. Martyn himself, and Mr. Brown. Second, it is common for ladies to go out thither without any previous connection; how much more therefore might one go out with a connec-

tion already formed. Were this the only difficulty, I engaged, with the help of Mr. Grant and Mr. Parry, that she should go under such protection as should obviate all difficulties upon this head. Third, the step taken by the other person, had set her at perfect liberty. Fourth, the consent of her mother was indispensable; and as that appeared impossible, the matter might be committed to God in this way: If her mother, of her own accord, should express regret that the connection had been prevented, from an idea of her being irreconcilably averse to it, and that she would not stand in the way of her daughter's wishes; this should be considered as a direction from God in answer to her prayers; and I should instantly be apprised of it by her, in order to communicate it to Mr. M. *In this she perfectly agreed.* I told her, however, that I would mention nothing of this to Mr. M., because it would only tend to keep him in painful suspense. Thus the matter is entirely set aside, unless God, by a special interposition of his Providence (*i.e.*, by taking away her mother or overruling her mind, contrary to all reasonable expectation, to approve of it), mark his own will respecting it."—This was written shortly after Martyn's departure. The picture is not an getful of the past, regardless of the future, he gave himself up to the happiness of the present hour. But the dream was soon dissolved. A sudden summons to rejoin his ship called him back to the dreary reality of actual life. With all speed he hurried to Falmouth, and again, in solitude of heart, sinking beneath the burden of his sorrows, he looked out over the wild waters, and called on God to comfort his soul.

The agony he endured was excessive. He seemed as one sinking in deep mire, where there was no standing; as one who had come into deep waters, where the floods was overflowing him. He wept and groaned till he was weary of his crying; till his throat was dried, and his eyes failed him. We must know the nature of the man to appreciate his sufferings. A strange, sensitive being—*all nerve*—was this young Cornish priest. Irritable and impulsive, of varying moods, sometimes sanguine and hilarious, at others despairing and dejected, he was wrenched and torn by gusts of passion which seemed almost to threaten his existence. His health was delicate, and he had over-worked himself. He seemed to be always in an extreme state of tension vibrating to the slightest touch. His soul never rested. Ever alive with emotion, trembling with deep joy or deeper

agreeable one. To many it is simply that of a prudent, calculating mother,
" Old and formal, fitted to her petty part,
With a little hoard of maxims preaching down a daughter's heart."
But the truth, I fear, is not to be disguised: that daughter's heart required little preaching down. She did not love Henry Martyn. Love never deals in reasons after this fashion. In all probability her heart had never wholly given up her old idol. Perhaps, when she first listened to Martyn's addresses, she thought herself stronger than she really was, and subsequently discovered her mistake. Let no man ever trust to such appearances.

sorrow, with wild hope or profound despair, he should
have had the frame of a giant to sustain the shocks
of so tempestuous a spirit.    But his physical organization was of the most delicate kind; his body was
feeble and diseased.    Much, indeed, that was strange
and unaccountable in his character may be attributed
to this constitutional weakness; his irritability, at one
time so extreme, that the life of a friend was endangered by an attack which young Martyn made upon
him with a knife—his dreadful fits of despondency,
which at times almost seemed to threaten his reason—
were but so many indications of the constant presence
of disease.    But for the saving influence of Christianity, it is probable that the curse of madness would
have descended upon him.    That influence made
him a hero—a martyr.    The Christian character has
never, in these later days, worn a more heroic aspect.
He had the courage to do and to endure all things;
he was the true soldier of the Cross.    From the day
on which, from the deck of the *Union*, he gazed, for
the last time, with swimming eyes, on the dim outline
of St. Michael's Mount and St. Hilary's Spire, to
that hour when he sat in the Armenian orchard,
and thought with sweet comfort of God, in solitude
his company, his friend and his comforter,—his life
was one long season of self-sacrifice—of self-sacrifice
mighty in the struggle between the strength of his
earthly affections and the intensity of his yearnings
after the pure spiritual state.    The subjugation of
the human heart was finally accomplished—but what
it cost him who can tell?

The voyage to India was a long and a tedious one: to Martyn it was inexpressibly painful. For weeks and weeks he had not even the consolation of that sense of progress, which has always an exhilarating influence on the mind. At last the fleet began to make some way. Rising from the depths of despondency in which he had been sunk, Martyn began to bestir himself. He saw that there was work to be done and he flung himself upon it with a whole-hearted energy to be admired whilst it is deplored. The truth must be told; Martyn lacked judgment and discretion; he lacked kindliness, not of heart, but of manner. He wept for the sinners by whom he was surrounded, but he did not weep with them. The earnestness—almost the ferocity, with which he preached against the companions of his voyage, exasperated rather than alarmed his hearers.* Some assailed him with bitterness—some with ridicule. It was a failure to be utterly deplored.

On the western bank of the Hoogly, not far from the settlement of Serampore, where in those days

---

* Simeon, at the outset of his career, had erred in the same manner as his disciple. But his more matured judgment had pointed out the danger of this intemperance. "I am arrived at the time of life," he wrote, in 1817, "when my views of early habits particularly in relation to the ministry, are greatly changed. I see many things in a different light from what I once did; such as the beauty of order, of regularity, and the wisdom of seeking to win souls by kindness rather than to convert them by harshness, and what I once called fidelity. I admire more the idea which I once had of our blessed Lord's spirit and ministry." And again, writing to a clergyman of whom it was reported that his style was "unnecessarily harsh and offensive," he observed:—"It is not by coarseness of expression, or severity of manner, that we are to win souls, but by speaking the truth in love." And again, a short time afterwards, he thus remonstrated with another, who had the same taste for strong preaching: "What is your object? Is it to win souls? If it be, how are you to set about it? by exciting all manner of prejudices, and driving people from the church? How did our Lord act? He spake the words in parables, '*as men were able to hear it.*' How did St. Paul act? He fed the babes with milk, and not with strong meat."

toiled with unintermitting energy, regardless alike of
the frowns of Government and the apathy of the
people, those eminent servants of God, Carey, Marshman, and Ward, stood a garden-house, in which there
dwelt the venerable minister, David Brown.  At no
great distance from this house, a deserted idol-temple,
on the banks of the river, stands out shadowy and
grand against the setting sun.  It had once been the
temple of Radha-Bullub—an eminent ·shrine in its
day, not wholly unconnected with pseudo-miraculous
associations; but the encroachments of the Hoogly
had driven the idol to seek a residence further inland,
and the once sacred abode had been given up to the
profaning hands of the stranger.  David Brown
bought it, as a mass of brick and plaster; and turned
it into a bungalow.  Being a hospitable man, in the
true spirit of Christian hospitality, the number of
his guests often outgrew the dimensions of the
Aldeen house;  and  the  idol-temple  soon  grew
into  a  supplementary  place  of  reception.  Here
Henry  Martyn  was  presently  located  as  the
honoured guest of David Brown; and here, before
many weeks had passed, he was joined by Daniel
Corrie.

Martyn's first public discourse, delivered at the New
Church of Calcutta, produced no little sensation.  It
was one of those bold, uncompromising sermons, which
had so exasperated his auditors on board the *Union*.
Here he not only gave offence to his congregation, but
drew down upon himself the enmity of some of his
brother-chaplains.  His doctrines did not consort

with their notions, so they preached at and against him. They pronounced his discourse a rhapsody—a mystery; said that he would drive men to despair, destroy their hopes of salvation, and speedily empty the church. All this was gall and wormwood to poor Martyn; but there was boundless comfort in the conviction that God was on his side. Right or wrong, Martyn was always sure of this. What he did was done at immense sacrifice of self. He may have had subsequent misgivings; but he ever acted, in all sincerity, according to the light that was in him at the time.

These unseemly pulpit contentions were not new to the settlement.* Brown and Buchanan had been preached at in the same manner. It appears that they had offended by offering "strong meat" to their congregations. The former, we may be assured, did it very sparingly; and not before he had long fed his people with "milk." And it was not very difficult to persuade Henry Martyn that there might be wisdom in moderating his fiery zeal. Corrie,

* Lord Valentia, alluding to a time prior to the arrival of Martyn, observed:—" It will hardly be believed that in this splendid city, the head of a mighty Christian empire, there is only one church of the establishment of the mother-country, and that by no means conspicuous, either for size or ornament. It is also remarkable, that all British India does not afford one episcopal see, while that advantage has been granted to the province of Canada; yet it is certain that from the remoteness of the country, and the peculiar temptations to which the freedom of manners exposes the clergy, immediate episcopal superintendence can nowhere be more requisite. From the want of this it is painful to observe, that the characters of too many of that order are by no means creditable to the doctrines they profess, which, together with the unedifying contests that prevail among them, even from the pulpit, tend to lower the religion, and its followers, in the eyes of the natives of every description. If there be any plan for conciliating the minds of the natives to Christianity, it is so manifestly essential that it should appear to them in a respectable form at the seat of Government, that I presume all parties will allow, that the first step should be to place it there upon a proper footing."

on his arrival, found that a " great opposition was raised against Martyn, and the principles he preached,"* but adds soon afterwards, " Martyn preached from Rom. iii. 21—23, the most impressive and best composition I ever heard. The disposition of love and good-will which appeared in him must have had great effect: and the calmness and firmness with which he spoke raised in me great wonder. May God grant a blessing to the word. Oh, may it silence opposition, and promote religion, for Jesus Christ's sake, amen !"

And now that we find them together—those two friends, Martyn and Corrie—located beneath the same roof, comforting and sustaining each other, each at the outset of his apostolic career, sprung from the same seat of learning, the sons of the same " father in the Gospel," the same bright rays of glorious promise descending on either head ; so similar and yet so dissimilar, so firmly knit together in common bonds, and yet in human character so inharmonious : let us pause to think of the latter of the twain, of the fainter, but of the steadier light. Daniel Corrie was not a man of great genius or gigantic enthusiasm. His mind was in nowise cast in the heroic mould ; but for ordinary purposes of life it was sufficiently strong and serviceable. He was the model of an useful colonial chaplain, rising at last to the highest ecclesiastical rank, and whether in a humble or an elevated condition of life, blameless in all relations and admirable in some. He was the

* " Lord, grant me wisdom," exclaimed Corrie, " that I may act with discretion, and in nothing give unnecessary offence."

son of a Scotchman who had become a Lincolnshire clergyman. Cast early upon his own resources, and subsequently redeemed from a profitless London life, and sent to Cambridge, he had done his best to repair the defects of a neglected education, and had passed out of college with credit to himself, but with no distinguished success. Attracted by the preaching of Mr. Simeon, he had become a constant attendant at Trinity Church, and was one of the little band of disciples which gathered around the teacher in his rooms. With Martyn he had formed an intimacy, which had ripened into affection on either side, and with another predestined fellow-labourer, not the least loveable of the group, the excellent Thomas Thomason, he had united himself in brotherly bonds, which were only broken by death. Some two or three years spent in a country curacy had strengthened his convictions and endeared to him his office; and when Simeon pressed upon him the acceptance of an appointment to ministerial labour in India, it was with the assurance that he was in every way fitted to bear the burden and to perform the work.

Daniel Corrie was the man of all others to glide easily through a voyage to India. He gave offence to no one, and endeared himself to many by the kindliness of his heart and the gentleness of his manners. There was nothing more remarkable, nothing more loveable in his character, than his affectionate concern for the welfare of young people. He took a deep interest in all that related to the cadets on board the *Asia;* and his friendly condescension was not without

o

its results. All respected him; many loved him; some were converted by him. And as at the commencement so to the very close of his career, he was emphatically the friend of the young. Many and many an eye, as it is fixed on this page, will glisten in grateful recognition of the truth which I have just uttered.

A few weeks spent together in the enjoyment of the Christian hospitality of Mr. Brown; and Martyn and Corrie parted. The former had been appointed to the Dinapore station, and in the middle of October he set out on his voyage up the river, accompanied some little way by Corrie, by Brown, and another chaplain, Mr. Parson. " Mr. Marshman seeing them pass the mission-house (at Serampore) could not resist joining the party, and after going a little way left them with prayer." Martyn was soon fairly launched on his solitary journey. How easy is it for all who have read the memoir written by Mr. Sargeant,—and who has not read it?*—to accompany him as he goes. We see him, we sympathise with him, now immersed in deep study, translating the Scriptures in his boat; now sauntering along the shore with gun in hand, the student bent on active exercise; now listening to the wild discordant music which marked the approach of some heathen procession; now deploring the idolatries which he was forced to witness; now mixing with the deluded people, con-

---

* My pen was arrested before I had finished writing this question by the recollection of the ludicrous fact that, some fifteen years ago, an English journal, commenting on a list of certain books which had been ordered by Government to be supplied to soldiers' libraries in India, asked, indignantly, what the authorities could be thinking of, when they proposed to supply the soldiery with the life of Henry Martyn *the regicide?*

versing with them as best he could, distributing his
tracts among them, often with exquisite griffinism
unwittingly offending their prejudices, but always
regarding them with the deepest feelings of commiseration and love. Yes; and easy is it to penetrate
into the deeper recesses of that warm human heart—
to take discursive flights with the imaginings of that
ever active human brain. What memories, what
hopes, what aspirations! Now his thoughts travel
back to his college rooms; he is face to face with the
revered Simeon, or the beloved Thomason—he is
taking sweet counsel with one in whom he sees, as in
a glass, himself reflected—one as delicate, as sensitive, as earnest as himself, with his genius and his
holiness blended together—the early-called Kirke
White. Now he is at home again in his father's
house, sitting beside his dear sisters—hoping all
things, yet trembling much, for sad events already
are casting their mournful shadows before;—now,
still as his eye ranges over the wild scenery of his
native Cornwall another female figure passes before
him, and his heart leaps up to embrace it; he is in
an ecstacy of wild hope, and then in the very slough
of abject despair.* He spreads his books out on the
little table of his narrow cabin; the lamp is set before
him; the unfamiliar characters of strange languages
are before his eyes; strange sounds are in his ears,
the howlings of the jackalls, the scarcely more melo-
dious music of the boatmen, the clanging gongs on

* "Thought at night more than   exaggerated these ideal joys, the
usual of dear L——; but the more I   more I treasure up subjects of woe."

the river side—but the sights and sounds loved long ago still distract him. He cannot quiet that throbbing heart.

At Berhampore his Christian courage and his Christian patience were severely tried. The rebuffs of the natives on whom he obtruded himself pained him little, but his sensitive nature shrank from the insulting ridicule of his European fellow-countrymen. He knew what it was to force his way among hard-hearted English soldiers; but what he had done on board the *Union*, he was prepared to do at Berhampore. He went to the European hospital; but the inmates would not listen to him. "Rose very early," he records in his journal, "and was at the hospital at daylight. Waited there a long time, wandering up and down the wards, in hopes of inducing the men to get up and assemble; but it was in vain. I left three books with them, and went away amidst the sneers and titters of the common soldiers. Certainly it is one of the greatest crosses I am called to bear to take pains to make people hear me. It is such a struggle between a sense of propriety and modesty on the one hand, and a sense of duty on the other, that I find nothing equal to it. I could force my way anywhere in order to introduce a brother minister; but for myself I act with hesitation and pain." The failure here described is as characteristic as the tone in which it is recorded. The passage may advantageously be compared with one in another journal. Two months afterwards, Corrie, on his way to the Upper Provinces, visited that same hospital. "In

the afternoon," he writes, " we visited the hospital.
I drew near the bed of a man apparently in the last
stage of disease, who received the word with tears and
requested me to pray with him. Having made this
known, P. (Parson) invited the others to draw near;
*a large party collected from all parts of the hospital.*
I expounded the third chapter of St. John's Gospel,
and prayed. *Much attention in the poor men.*"
Corrie could find hearers, where Martyn could find
none. With a lower order of intellect, and less heroic zeal, he abounded in what Martyn most wanted,
the tact to conciliate and the cordiality to attract.
He was, in the more honourable Christian acceptation
of the phrase, "all things to all men"—from the
Governor-General to the youngest cadet. Henry
Martyn, in his ministrations, was always the same
Henry Martyn. The inward zeal rode rough-shod
over the outer manner. He failed so often, because
to his spiritual earnestness he did not impart an
exterior grace.

Arrived at Dinapore, and surrounded by an uncongenial society, Martyn found his chief solace in
the letters of his Calcutta friends and the translation
work in which he was engaged. The duties of the
chaplaincy were not very onerous. There was no
church; but he " read prayers to the soldiers at the
barracks from the drum-head, and as there were no
seats provided, was desired to omit the sermon." A
building better adapted to the purpose being subsequently found, he managed to collect on the sabbath
a number of Christian families, but they did not like

his extempore preaching, and intimated to him that
it would please them better if he would read them a
written sermon.  This excited the natural irritability of the man; but his anger soon passed away,
and he saw clearly the wisdom of conciliation.  "He
would give them," he said, "a folio sermon-book,
if they would receive the Word of God upon that
account."

The year 1807 opened and closed upon Martyn at
Dinapore.  He saw little society; there was, indeed,
but one Christian family with which he was on terms
of intimate friendship; but in his solitary bungalow
how busy he was, how active, and, in thought, how
social.  He could people his room at will with beloved forms, and fence himself around with loving
faces.  "I am happier here in this remote land," he
wrote, "where I hear so seldom of what happens in
the world, than in England, where there are so many
calls to look at 'the things that are seen.'  How
sweet the retirement in which I here live!"  Shadows
there were, doubtless; but perhaps at no period of
Martyn's career was there more of sunshine to irra-
diate his path.  Now discussing points of faith with
his Moonshee and Pundit; now dreaming of his beloved; now in deep humiliation contrasting himself
with David Brainerd; now cheering himself with the
thought that as a translator, at least, his labours were
not profitless; now endeavouring to obtain redress
for the injured; now submitting to injury himself;
now rejoicing in the affection of his friends; now
weeping over cruel disappointments—he passed from

one state of feeling to another; but ever in weal or
woe there was a sustaining power, a cheering influence
in the thought of *work* done or doing—of something
already accomplished, of something more *to be* accomplished, by human brain and human hand active in
the cause of their Maker.

And it was at this period that he succeeded in
obtaining the greatest mastery over himself. Never
had he been so resigned—never so hopeful—never so
assured that God is love—never so eager to see Him
face to face. Tried in the furnace of human affliction, he had come forth purer and brighter, longing
for that great and glorious hour when God will wipe
away all tears from the eyes of his beloved children.
The victory was not complete. We dare not say it
was. How could it be, with that warm human heart
still beating against his side ?

From Dinapore, early in 1809, Martyn was removed
to Cawnpore. Here was much to vex his spirit and
to assail his health. The arid, dust-charged atmosphere of that sultry place pressed upon him with a
weight which sunk him to the earth. He had seen
a Christian church rise up before him at Dinapore.
He was now at a station where was no Christian
church. He performed service, in the open air, to
the European troops, and sometimes saw them
dropping around him under the influence of the
intense heat. Among the natives he was at this
time unusually active. His heart was always with
them. In spirit, at least, he was their minister; not
a mere military chaplain. We see him preaching to

crowds of mendicants whom he assembled around his house. They came to receive alms, and he distributed to them. Then they listened to what he said—those naked, squalid heathens—the halt, the maimed, and the blind—they flocked around him and listened. Or they pretended to listen—for what could they do less? And Martyn spoke to them, as one who could not help speaking; as one who felt it would be a sin to be silent. From the full heart gushed forth a torrent of words — not always perhaps with the strictest philological propriety—and, in sooth, only by rare snatches intelligible to his congregation. But the numbers increased, and so did the plaudits : and far be it from me to say that no seed fell upon good ground.

In the meanwhile Corrie, who had been appointed chaplain at Chunar, was steadily pursuing his course, contented with small successes. There was much to discourage and dishearten; but for this he was prepared. The invalids were, at best, but a careless, godless, set of men; and they were slow to welcome the *Padre*. The officers of the station had not much more piety than the men; and Benares, to which Corrie occasionally went, had about as much Christianity as Chunar. At the latter station there was public worship in the Fort, but the greater number of the invalids remained away; and the officers made all manner of excuses. To preach openly to the heathen he hesitated. He had the fear of the supreme Government, of the Court of Directors, and above all of the *Edinburgh Reviewers* before his eyes. "I suppose," he wrote, " we should be taken to task were we to preach in the streets and highways ; but other methods, not less effectual, are to be used and less likely to produce popular clamour.    Natives themselves may and can be employed with the greatest advantage in evangelizing their brethren, whilst the minister superintends and directs and encourages."    And again, hearing that a letter to his friend Mr. Buckworth had been published in England, he writes, " I heard some time since, by a friend, that a letter from one of the Bengal chaplains who came out in 1806 had been published, and in the then state of the Court of Directors towards the evangelization of this country might be of great detriment ; Mary (his sister) brought me word who the offending chaplain is, and who the friend is that has published his letters.    I confess that for a time I found myself wounded in the house of friendship.    In the eyes of the world, pride told me that my character would suffer ; and I still expect to see myself caricatured by the *Edinburgh Reviewers*, or by some such enemies to all serious acknowledgment of God."    Sydney Smith's well-known article had recently been published.    It seems to have alarmed Corrie more than it pained him.*

Corrie was then on a visit to Calcutta ; his sister having arrived from England.    His sojourn at the presidency was but brief : and we soon find him again among his people at Chunar.    His residence was on

---

* I must distinctly be understood not to reproach any chaplain on the establishment for abstaining from preaching, at such a time, to the natives of the country.    It was not the business of the Company's chaplains to give themselves up to such work.

the banks of the river; and his hospitality was constantly extended to passing travellers, proceeding by water to the Upper Provinces—especially to young officers, recently arrived from England, whom he was always eager to advise and to assist. " Our dwelling," he wrote " is on the banks of the Ganges. The common mode of travelling is by water, in commodious boats, dragged when the wind is adverse, like barges. At this distance from home, hospitality to strangers seems to me a peculiar though painful duty, as it breaks in too much upon my leisure. There is no such thing as an inn, and very many of the passers-by are young officers, whose situation is in general far from being comfortable. To these I would be especially kind, as being also less noticed by many who judge of the attentions due to them by the wealth and rank they possess. Those youths who are now here join readily in our family worship, and delight me when I hear them repeating the Lord's Prayer after me with seriousness. Dear lads, my heart yearns over them, exposed as they are, to every kind of temptation, without a rudder or a pilot." A passage in every way most characteristic of this amiable and excellent man.

Though the fruits of his ministerial labours were not very palpable at first, in due time they began to develope themselves, both at Chunar and Benares.*

* Of Corrie's first attempt to establish himself at Benares, we find this account in his journal: " I came down on Friday evening, with the view to perform divine service on Sunday. On Saturday morning I waited on the General, who received me with most chilling coolness. He told me that he had nothing to do with divine service or the Artillery men; and that he should not interfere; he had heard nothing of divine service except from my application Mr. ——, who had been forward for

Still there was much to discourage his efforts—much
painful opposition to encounter. " We have for some
time," he wrote, "been engaged about a Church at
Benares; a subscription of about 3,000 rupees has
been made, and a spot of ground is fixed on. I trust
now all opposition is silenced, though not entirely
done away. The hearts of some haters of all good
have been brought to give money even. One family
is highly respectable and regular in religious duties.
One young officer has become a new creature. Of
the rest, few, alas! seem willing to go any further."
Still counting by units!—But other good work was
done. He had opened several schools; and was
diligently engaged in studying the native languages
with the view of translating the Scriptures. And he had
a congregation of native women, principally soldiers'
wives, to whom he read and discoursed. But he was
soon removed to another field of labour. Government
appointed him, in 1810, to the ministerial charge of
the Agra station.

On his way to join his new appointment he halted
at Cawnpore. There he took up his abode beneath
the roof of his beloved Martyn. Twice had he seen
him at Dinapore, and then had cause to tremble for

my coming down, on hearing of my
arrival, flew quite off, and said they
could do quite as well now, as before,
without divine service; he, however,
came yesterday in the morning. A
congregation of at least sixty assembled; and after service Mr. A.
thanked me, and said he hoped they
should give me encouragement to
come oftener amongst them. Afterwards the Brigade-Major came with
a message from the General (who

did not come to church) saying, I
was 'at liberty to come and go as
I pleased, but the Artillery-men
and officers could not be permitted to
attend so far from the lines, for fear
of the natives seizing the guns whilst
they were at a distance. If the
Court House were used to assemble
in, or a place of worship erected near
the lines, he should have no objection;
but all this was to be *kept a secret.*"

the safety of his friend. But even with this preparation, the altered aspect of poor Martyn greatly startled and alarmed him. "When I arrived here," he wrote to Mr. Brown, "Martyn was looking very ill, and a very little exertion laid him up. Since then, you will know that I have been ordered to remain here for a time to assist him ; and he is already greatly recovered." Three weeks later he wrote, "On my first arrival, Martyn recruited greatly for a fortnight, but is now, to say the best, at a stand . . . The state of his health seems to be this : he is easily fatigued and then gets but broken rest, with confused and distressing dreams. A very little exertion in speaking produces pain in the chest, with almost total loss of voice, and all these symptoms are produced by the evening of every day."[*]

* In another letter (to his English friend, Mr. Buckworth) Corrie gives the following refreshing account of their way of life at Cawnpore. It need scarcely be said that the initial S. represents the name of *Sherwood :* "The account of one day will give you a general idea of our whole manner of life. We usually rise at daybreak and ride out. Martyn and I breakfast between six and seven o'clock : then read the Scriptures with a Polyglot before us, and pray. Martyn then goes to his study. I go to see Mary (Miss Corrie); and she and Mrs. S. are learning Hindustani, in order to be able to speak on religion to their female servants; and, if circumstances favour, to get a school of female native children. I am their teacher. Mrs. S. has a school of European children belonging to the regiment. I return to reading, usually Hindustani or Persian. At eleven, my Christian children come to me to say the lesson they have been learning with the native schoolmaster. In the middle of the day we have a repast, and then resume reading till four, when the Christian children come again to read in the Hindustani Gospels. In the evening we meet, usually at Captain S.'s or Martyn's, when we sing some hymns, with reading and prayer before we separate. This is the peaceful tenor of our way. At the intervals, two days in the week, I visit and pray with the sick in the hospitals. On the sabbath, public worship; in the morning at the drum-head of one of the three European corps lying here, in rotation. In the evening of Sunday and Wednesday we have social worship with a goodly number of pious soldiers in a public building fitting up, but not yet ready to open as a church: besides the (services) once a fortnight, there is public worship in the General's house. Except the soldiers, all our other English rank as gentlemen. We have here only these two classes, except a very few persons in trade."

Most unwilling was Martyn to leave his post, and difficult, indeed, was it to persuade him even temporarily to lay aside his work. He thought that a brief river-trip would suffice to restore him, and when he felt, under the influence of excitement, a little temporary accession of strength, he said that even that was unnecessary. But the truth was not much longer to be disguised. He was absolutely dying at his work. The affectionate solicitude of his friends prevailed over his own reluctance; and he at last consented to obtain leave to proceed to Calcutta and to try the restorative effects of a sea-voyage. On the 1st of October, he commenced his journey down the river. It was some consolation to him to leave his flock under the care of one whom he so dearly loved, and in whom he reposed so much confidence. He had smoothed the way for his friend. A church had sprung up during his ministry. He had remained long enough to see it opened; and when he turned his back upon Cawnpore he felt that he had not sojourned there in vain.

For Martyn's affectionate heart there was other comfort in store. He was about again to partake of the hospitality of his venerable friend, Mr. David Brown. He was about to meet for the first time in this land of exile a cherished friend and associate of former days—one whom he had loved and honoured at Cambridge, a fellow-disciple in the great Simeonite school: a fellow-labourer in the ministry at the outset of his career. Let me break off for a while to speak of this last accession to the saintly band. There are few of my readers who have not already syllabled in thought the name of Thomas Thomason.

Left in infancy, by the death of his father, to the care of his surviving parent, a woman of sound understanding and matured piety, he had imbibed whilst yet a boy those lessons of wisdom, which, however slowly they may seem to fructify, or however destructively they may be choked up for a time by the weeds of worldly engrossment, are never instilled wholly in vain. In the case of Thomas Thomason the good fruit was seen early upon the boughs. When only twelve years old he had in his conversation and in his manner of life evinced signs of a settled piety almost unprecedented at so immature an age. Like Buchanan he had been engaged in teaching others, whilst himself yet a boy; but the offer of a situation as French interpreter to a Wesleyan establishment then proceeding to the West Indian islands, had carried him for a time from his native country; and it is probable that he might long have remained in a Western settlement and subsequently attached himself for ever to the Wesleyan ministry, but for the advice of a lady, bearing the honoured name of Thornton, who had directed his thoughts towards the Episcopal Church, and pointed out the especial advantages of the Elland institution to one who, like young Thomason, had not the means of obtaining, out of his independent resources, the benefits of an University education. To this institution, therefore, he had endeavoured to gain, and had succeeded in gaining, admission; and, after some time spent under its tutelage in the house of the venerable Mr. Clark, of Chesham, he had been sent up by the society to Magdalene College, Cambridge, and had distinguished himself by the successful exercise of talents of a high order.* Whilst yet an undergraduate, a chaplaincy had been offered to him by Mr. Charles Grant, but reasons of a domestic nature had induced him to decline the tempting invitation, and the appointment had been given to Claudius Buchanan in his stead.†

After taking his degree, Mr. Thomason had accepted a tutorship in a private family; and from this, having received ordination, had been raised to the more honourable office of assistant to Mr. Simeon. The curacies of Trinity Church and of Stapleford had both been intrusted to him; for, of all Simeon's disciples, I must pause to observe, Thomas Thomason was the one whom the master most loved. He had such a loveable spirit, he was so gentle, so humble, so little selfish, so little envious, it would have been difficult not to love him. Simeon, indeed, always "clove" to him. It was to Thomason, that in after days he delighted to write—to record all that he felt, to narrate all that he did. Thomason was his own familiar friend—his brother, not simply by Gospel bonds, but by the ties also of human affection. He felt the tenderest concern for all that related to him. He became a son to Thomason's mother—a father to Thomason's child. Of others it may be said,

---

* He was *fifth* wrangler of his year—and had he commenced earlier the race for university honours, he would have gained a more forward place.

† Thomason's biographer says, that the offer made to him was that of an appointment "to fill the *Mission* Church of Calcutta"—but the context shows this to be a mistake.

that Simeon loved the Christian—of Thomason, it is emphatically to be remarked, that he loved the man.

In the companionship of a loving wife and of his dear friend and master; and in the continued performance of his ministerial duties, the stream of Thomason's life flowed placidly on until the spring of 1805, when the great idea of Gospel-labour among the Heathen rose up and took possession of his mind —" This year he resolved under God, with the Bible in his hand, and his Saviour in his heart, to go where the darkness was dense and the sphere extensive for the diffusion of light." But there had then been no vacancy. Mr. Grant's patronage for the time was exhausted; and it was not until the spring of 1808, that an Indian chaplaincy had been placed by that Christian gentleman at Mr. Thomason's disposal.

He sailed soon afterwards for Calcutta, and was shipwrecked before reaching it; but most miraculously delivered, and suffered to come face to face with his beloved friend and associate, Henry Martyn. There was deep joy in the meeting; but with it how much of human sorrow mingled! He saw in poor Martyn but the wreck of his former self—he saw one whom sickness, and sorrow, and much toil in an exhausting climate—the strong spirit ever battling against the weakly frame—the carnal wretchedness of the man at strife with the heavenly ecstacy of the immortal—had brought down to the very borders of the grave. " This bright and lovely jewel," wrote Thomason to Simeon, " first gratified our eyes on

Saturday last. He is on his way to Arabia, in pursuit of health and knowledge. You know his genius, and what gigantic strides he takes in everything. He has some great plan in his mind, of which I am no competent judge. But as far as I do understand, the object is far too grand for our short life, and much beyond his feeble and exhausted frame. Feeble indeed it is! how fallen and changed! his complaint lies in the lungs, and appears to be incipient consumption. But let us hope the sea air will revive him, and that change of place and pursuit may do him essential service, and continue his life many years. In all other respects he is exactly the same as he was; he shines in all the dignity of love, and seems to carry about him such a heavenly majesty as impresses the mind beyond all description. But if he talks much, though in a low voice, he sinks, and you are reminded of his being dust and ashes. It would have filled your eyes with tears to have seen dear ——— (Mrs. Thomason) when she saw him; you know her smile and hearty countenance, and eyes darting good-nature, but you never saw them so called forth. We were all filled with joy unspeakable, and blessed God for the rich opportunity of loving intercourse. I immediately put into his hand your long and affectionate letter, in order that *you* might be of the party. Martyn read it in the corner of the sofa, ——— sat by him, and I sat looking on: so the letter was read and the tears flowed."

And Martyn left them, never to return. On the 7th of January he embarked on board a vessel bound for

P

Bombay. I do not think that his biographer records, but it is still worthy of notice, that the companion of his voyage to Bombay was Mountstuart Elphinstone. Arrived at the Presidency, he was introduced by his fellow-traveller to Sir John Malcolm and Sir James Mackintosh*. From Malcolm he must have learnt much concerning the new lands in which he was about to travel. In his philological pursuits, he was encouraged by his new friends; but his missionary enterprises were not countenanced by them. Malcolm especially cautioned him against endeavouring to convert the people, and entering into controversies with the Moollahs; and he thought that he had succeeded. "Mr. Martyn," wrote Malcolm to Sir Gore Ousely, to whom he had recommended the wandering chaplain, "assured me, and begged I would mention it to you, that he has no thought of preaching to the Persians, or of entering into any theological controversies, but means to confine himself to two objects; a research after old Gospels, and the endeavour to qualify himself for giving a correct version of the Scriptures into Arabic and Persian, on the plan proposed by the Bible Society. I have not hesitated to tell him that I thought you would require that he should act with

---

* Mackintosh called him "the saint from Calcutta," and said of him: "His meekness is excessive, and gives a disagreeable impression of efforts to conceal the passions of humanity." (See "Life of Mackintosh," by his son.) Perhaps the author would have written more correctly, if he had said to "suppress," not to "conceal" the passions of humanity. It is worthy of remark, too, that nothing about Henry Martyn made a stronger impression on Malcolm's mind than his cheerfulness. "I am satisfied," he said, "that if you ever see him, you will be pleased with him. He will give you grace before and after dinner, and admonish such as take the Lord's name in vain; but his good sense and great learning will delight you, whilst his constant cheerfulness will add to the hilarity of the party."— *Life of Sir John Malcolm.*

great caution, and not allow his zeal to run away with
him. He declares he will not, and he is a man of
that character that I must believe." But although in
all sincerity, Henry Martyn may have promised this
at Bombay, it was another thing to abstain from controversy at Shiraz and Ispahan. He could not be
silent; he could not be inactive; he could not refrain
from doing his Master's work. So Malcolm's exhortations were forgotten; and, surrounded by the disciples
of the great false Prophet of Medina, the Company's
chaplain soon again expanded into the missionary of
Christ.

My subject is Christianity in India, and I cannot,
therefore, now narrate the history of his travels and
his trials—what he did and what he suffered in other
lands. There is nothing grander in the annals of
Christianity, than the picture of Henry Martyn, with
the Bible in hand, alone and unsupported, in a
strange country, challenging the whole strength of
Mahomedanism to a conflict of disputation. He
seems at this time to have possessed something more
than his own human power; so cool, so courageous;
so bold to declare, so subtle to investigate; astonishing
the Mahomedan doctors with his wisdom,—gaining
the confidence of all by the gentleness of his manners
and the blamelessness of his life. There is a cheerfulness of spirit predominant in the Shiraz journal—
almost, indeed, are there touches of humour in it—
which would lead us to think that at this period of
his life he was more happy and self-possessed than he
had been for many years. His victory over the

Moollahs was complete; and it pleased him to think of it. In the translation of the Bible into the Persian tongue he had achieved a great work, which was a solace to him to the very hour of his death. He quitted Shiraz and new trials awaited him. Inclement weather—extremes of heat and cold alternating— weary travelling along rugged roads on ill-trained horses—little rest and bad food—every possible kind of exposure and privation, soon fevered the blood and exhausted the strength of one so sensitive as Martyn. From Shiraz to Ispahan—from Ispahan to Teheran —from Teheran to Tocat, he struggled onwards, hoping to reach his home; and he did reach his home—but it was in Heaven.

He died on the 16th of October 1812; but he is truly one to be held in perpetual remembrance. Of all the men who had gone before him on the same great Christian enterprise, Xavier alone can be compared with him in intensity of zeal and heroism of character. In both was there the same burning love of their fellow-men, the same eager spirit of adventure, the same vast power of self-annihilation, the same ecstatic communing with the unseen world. Had Henry Martyn lived three centuries before the time of his ministrations, he might have seen visions, such as appeared to Francis Xavier, and believed, with the same strong impulse of faith, that he had been commissioned to work miracles among men. It may be a scandal in the eyes of some Christian readers to name the two enthusiasts in the same sentence; for Henry Martyn is the very pink and

essence of the chivalry of Evangelical Protestantism;
and it may seem a shame to liken him to a Jesuit.
But Xavier was born in days when Protestantism was
not; and of Jesuits he was the least jesuitical. He
was, indeed, the very antithesis of a sham: and it is in
the reality of the two men that their likeness is most
apparent. Henry Martyn disputing with the Mahomedan doctors at Shiraz, and Francis Xavier contending with the Bonzes of Japan, each alone and
unsupported in a strange country, present images of
genuine zeal and devotion, the grandeur of which
may be admired, without a compromise, by Protestant
and Romanist alike. Both died with the harness on
their backs, far from home and all friendly succour,
broken down by much fatigue and much suffering, by
painful alternations of heat and cold, by the hardships
and dangers of journeyings in strange lands, and among
inhospitable people. And whether we look upon
the picture of the gaunt Jesuit, stretched beneath
a wretched shed on the barren coast of Sancian,
breathing out his soul with the uplifted crucifix before
his eyes in accents of hope and adoration, as one
longing to be blest; or watch over Martyn's dying
bed, as plague-struck he lay at Tocat, with his Bible
by his side, and saw close at hand the answer to that
great question which a few days before he had put to
himself with a thrill of eager exultation, " When shall
appear that new heaven and new earth wherein
dwelleth righteousness, wherein in nowise shall enter
anything that defileth ? "—we still see the grandest
of human spectacles, the triumph of the spirit over

the flesh—one who had crucified self throughout life, throwing himself with ecstacy into the arms of his Maker.

I have, perhaps, dwelt more minutely on the lives of these Bengal chaplains than is altogether consistent with the scope of such a work as this. They were not, as I have said, missionaries; and it may be doubted whether they were the direct means of converting any large number of heathens to Christianity. But still, it is difficult to say how greatly they contributed to the progress of Christianity in India. It was impossible for us to christianise our neighbours until we had in some measure christianised ourselves. The ungodly lives of our people and the practical non-recognition, if not the abnegation, of our national faith, had been, for two centuries, vast obstructions to the successful career of the Gospel. If, then, such Christian heroes as Brown, Buchanan, Martyn, Corrie, and Thomason had, by their bright example and by their appointed ministrations in regular official course, merely contributed to the amendment of their own countrymen's lives and to the better observance of the outward decencies of religion, they would have done a great thing. But they did much more than this. They awakened in the breasts of many that missionary spirit which now for half-a-century, unquenched and unquenchable, has wrought so mightily for the deliverance of the Gentiles; they taught their countrymen to believe that the propagation of Gospel truth in a heathen land was not a work becoming only dissenters and "methodists," but

one in which churchmen and official functionaries of
all kinds might engage without loss of caste, and that
there was not an ensign in the service, who might not
do something, if only by an exemplary way of life,
to plant the cross in heathen soil; and it is hard to
say how much that has since been done in the way
of direct missionary labour has resulted from the
Christian efforts of these missionary chaplains.

But what they did themselves towards the diffusion
of Gospel light was not contemptible.  If it were only
for what was done by them to transfuse the great
truths of Christianity into the languages of the East,
they would deserve honourable mention in the evangelical annals of the country.  They were earnest in
translation-work from the very commencement of their
career; and the achievements of one, at least, of their
band were crowned with remarkable success.  The
best linguists in the country acknowledged the ripe
oriental scholarship of Henry Martyn; and I cannot
help thinking it a source of regret that the chaplains
of the present day are so little eager to devote themselves to the acquisition of the "country languages."
It is not expedient that they should collect crowds in
front of their bungalows and preach to wandering
natives in broken Hindostanee.  There are mis-
sonaries now to do that work, as there were not in
Henry Martyn's time; and the chaplains of the
establishment are called to the performance of other
duties.  But there are more ways in which the knowledge of the languages may enable the Christian
minister to serve his Master; and, therefore, the

example in this, as in other respects, of such men as those of whom I have here spoken, may profitably be held in remembrance.

But there were others in those early years of the nineteenth century, not with the mark of the establishment upon them, who were labouring still more diligently in the great cause, and are still more worthy of distinguished mention in such a volume as this. They were not chaplains—they were not ordained ministers of any kind—they were simply, in the language of ecclesiastical wits, " inspired cobblers." But they wrought mightily for all that; and the lawn sleeves of the bishop could not have made them more potential agents of Christianity in India. Others who have since trodden the same paths, both chaplains and cobblers, might deserve equal notice for the thing done and the result obtained; but taking account of obstacles encountered and difficulties overcome, history delights to exalt the pioneer above all who follow after him :——

> " 'Tis on the advance of individual minds
> That the slow crowd must ground their expectation
> Eventually to follow—as the sea
> Waits ages in its bed, till some one wave
> Of all the multitudinous mass extends
> The empire of the whole, some feet, perhaps,
> Over the strip of sand which could confine
> Its fellows so long time: thenceforth the rest,
> E'en to the meanest, hurry in at once,
> And so much is clear gained."

# CHAPTER VII.

The Serampore Mission—First missionary efforts of the Baptists—William Carey—The Mission to Bengal—Marshman and Ward—Establishment at Serampore—Hostility of the Government—Eventual Success.

It was in the year 1793, when John Shore was preparing to enter upon the Governor-Generalship of India; and Charles Grant was striving to obtain a seat in the direction of the East India Company; and David Brown was ministering peacefully in Calcutta on a salary of 1,000*l.* a year—when Claudius Buchanan was still attending Charles Simeon's Sunday parties, and Martyn and Corrie were yet at school—that a member of the Baptist persuasion, sick at heart and weary of limb, might have been seen wandering about the streets of London, and entering, often vainly and disappointedly, house after house, in quest of contributions towards the support of a great, but a doubtful, enterprise. What he sought was pecuniary aid to enable him to launch a Baptist mission to the heathens on the banks of the Ganges. What he wanted was but a small sum—an amount that in these days would be the merest trifle in the accounts of any one of our great religious societies; but, foot-sore and heart-sore, this holy man passed from house to house, seeking help from brethren of his own persuasion or from religious friends of other sects, and, in spite of his abundant faith in the goodness of God and of his own unyielding perseverance, often obstinately questioning his eventual success and weeping over his repeated failures.

This good man was Andrew Fuller. A little while before, in conjunction with a few other members of the same church, a society had been inaugurated, under no very brilliant auspices, the object of which declaredly was "to evangelize the poor, dark, idolatrous heathen by sending missionaries into different parts of the world, where the light of the glorious Gospel was not then published;" and there were two labourers ready to go forth and shed that blessed light upon the dark places of Northern India. One of these was Mr. Thomas, who had already spent some time in Bengal; who had gone out as a ship-surgeon, had advertised for a Christian, had been planted, as I have already shown, by Mr. Grant in Malda, had failed both as a missionary and a merchant, and had irremediably forfeited the good opinion of his patron. The other was a younger and a better man. His name was William Carey.

He was the son of a village schoolmaster in Northamptonshire, and had early in life been apprenticed to a shoemaker. Of a studious disposition and an inquiring nature, he had acquired a stock of information rarely obtained in such humble circumstances at so immature a period of life, and it does not appear that the necessities of his new calling quenched the ardour of his thirst for knowledge, or wholly forbade its gratification. It is not on record that he achieved, or was ever likely to achieve, any great distinction as a craftsman. He said, indeed, years afterwards, when he was the guest of the Governor-General of India, that he had never been anything better than "a cobbler." But he rose to the dignity of journeyman (in which rank he accidentally attracted the attention of the well-known biblical commentator, Thomas Scott, who predicted that he would become a shining character), and afterwards married his master's sister —a wretched speculation—and did some business on his own account. His vocation, however, was towards preaching rather than towards cobbling; and his heart having been touched by an accidental circumstance, and afterwards softened by the pulpit oratory of Thomas Scott, he soon conceived the idea of teaching others; and, at the early age of eighteen, commenced, in an irregular sort of way, his ministrations in a dissenting chapel. His grandfather had been parish-clerk, and his father parish schoolmaster; so that he was bound by strong family ties to the Church of England. But the Church of England has no place for such men as William Carey, except as diggers of graves, or openers of pews, or utterers of "Amen!" and so his eager desire for the ministry drove him into the ranks of dissent. In October, 1783, he was baptized by Dr. Ryland, in the river Nene, near Northampton, and soon afterwards was placed in ministerial charge of a congregation in the village of Earl's Barton. He did not,

however, forsake his worldly calling until he found
his business falling away, and, in great pecuniary
distress, was compelled to sell his stock-in-trade.   The
Boston congregation was equally unprofitable; so,
after enduring considerable privation, he removed to
Moulton, where he took charge both of a congregation and a school; but neither being productive, he
fell back upon the old craft of shoe-making, and
carried to Northampton twice a month a bag full of
his professional performances.

But he was now at the turning-point of his career.
Whilst at Moulton he had conceived the grand idea
of illumining the dark places of the earth; and
intently did his mind brood over the sublime project
in his little workshop, whilst his hands were busily
plying the implements of his humble craft.   In this
state of mind he made the acquaintance of Andrew
Fuller—then minister at Kettering—an acquaintance
which soon ripened into a friendship only severed by
death.   He had previously become acquainted with
Dr. Ryland—another eminent Baptist divine; and to
both of these did young Carey now impart the great
scheme of evangelization which occupied all his
thoughts.

They were pious and able men with whom he
communicated; but they did not at first grasp that
mighty design.   Carey, however, had fast hold of it;
and would not let it go.   From Moulton he removed
to Leicester; but his thoughts travelled vast conti-
nents; and the changes neither of time nor place
could weaken the tenacity with which he clung to the

great idea of a heathen mission.   He wrote in aid of
it ; he preached in aid of it ; he talked earnestly and
continuously in aid of it to his older and more influential brother ministers ; and, at last, what had
been frowned or sneered down, began to be accepted
as a thing possible, perhaps a thing desirable ; and at
last it was agreed that, at the next meeting of the
Baptist ministers at Kettering, a project for the establishment of a society for propagating the Gospel
among the heathen should be formally discussed.

The meeting was held ; the subject was discussed.
Doubts and misgivings assailed the minds of many of
the ministers present ; but the earnestness of brother
Carey prevailed, and the Society was established.
This done, he at once offered to proceed to any part
of the world to which the Society might be pleased to
send him.   But before they could commence operations branch societies were to be formed ; money was
to be collected ; much was to be done.   London ever
delights to lead, and has small notion of being dictated
to by the Provinces.   So the metropolitan ministers
and magnates of the Baptist church looked coldly at
the Kettering mission—almost, indeed, thought it an
impertinence.   Fuller, who had been appointed secretary, and on whom, therefore, devolved the general
organization of the Society, was then little known to
his brethren, and Carey was not known at all.   So,
although some of the provincial churches responded
to the invitation, and money was collected, scant progress was made in London ; and it was plain that the
Society must content itself with a small beginning.

Where was the beginning to be made? Fortunately in some respects, unfortunately in others, Mr. Thomas, whilst this question was yet undecided, returned to England, and, hearing of the formation of the society at Kettering, recommended that they should commence operations in Bengal, and offered to be their first workman. The offer was accepted. It was determined that Thomas and Carey should go together to India; and it was to collect the amount necessary to defray the expenses attending their start in life, that Andrew Fuller went from door to door begging the contributions of unwilling givers.

There were other difficulties, however, in the way of the inauguration of the great enterprise. How were they to make their way to Bengal? The question is a surprising one in these days, when no one has anything to do, in such a case, but to take his passage in sailing vessel or in steamer, and go whithersoever he listeth. But at the close of the last century there was a wholly different order of things. India was a close preserve in the hands of the East India Company, and to go there without a license from the Company was to become a poacher, and to incur the risk of being ignominiously sent home again. Now, in 1793, although Charles Grant, not yet a Director, was infusing some better leaven into the Court, the Company were decidedly not the friends and favourers of missions. They were jealous of strangers of all kinds, especially of preachers of the Gospel. A man without a covenant was, in their estimation, a dangerous person; doubly dan-

gerous the man without a covenant and with a Bible.
The ships, too, which sailed for India were the Company's ships; and any captain of a vessel, carrying
out such unlicensed persons, might forfeit his appointment, and be ruined for life. How, then, were
Thomas and Carey to leap the great gulf which
separated the banks of the Thames from the banks of
the Ganges? Their only hope was in Charles Grant.
But Charles Grant knew nothing of Carey; and of
Thomas a little too much. In this strait the ready
help in trouble of John Newton was sought and
readily granted. Mr. Grant, however, still hesitated. Eager as he was to serve so good a man as
Mr. Newton, and earnest as he was in the cause of
missions, he would have nothing to say to an enterprise in which Mr. Thomas was concerned. So the
missionaries were driven back upon the necessity of
going to India without a license.

Their first attempt failed. Having embarked on
board one of the Company's vessels, commanded by a
friend of Mr. Thomas, they were compelled to unship
themselves in the Channel. An information against
the captain was threatened; so, to save him from
ruin, the missionaries were disembarked. It is hard
to say whether Thomas or Carey were the more disheartened by this failure, or grieved, in greater
anguish of spirit, when he saw the fleet sailing out of
the Channel; for Thomas was escaping from his
creditors; and Carey, with all the true apostolic
afflatus within him, was eager to begin his appointed
work. The disappointment, however, was but tem-

porary. They remembered Ziegenbalg and his associates; obtained a passage in a Danish vessel, and sailed for Bengal.[*]

After an uneventful voyage, they landed at Calcutta on the 11th of November, 1793. If, during the voyage they had entertained any apprehensions regarding the manner of their reception, their alarm soon disappeared. No kind of notice was taken of them. They took a house; and, whilst Mr. Thomas was trading, Mr. Carey was studying the languages of the country. Such ill-assorted companionship could not last long. The strenuous realities of missionary life lay before the inspired cobbler; and he was eager to embrace them. But, in spite of all his faith and all his courage, the trial was a hard one. The sufferings which, in the cause of his Master, he was now called upon to endure were something very different from the delicate distresses of the Bengal chaplains. That "awkward circumstance" in their lives—the salary of 1,000*l*. a year—did not stand in the way of the struggling Baptist. He found himself, with a wife, a sister-in-law, and a family of young children, under the burning copper skies of Bengal, without money, without friends, and, seemingly, without hope. A rich native lent him a miserable dwelling-house in one of the suburbs of Calcutta; and there for some time he bore, as best he could, the reproaches of his wife and her sister, and struggled to

* Their party was now increased by the addition of Mrs. Carey, her sister, and four or five children. Mrs. Carey, who had a soul above missions, had at first refused to accompany her husband, but had afterwards relented, yielding to her fears, rather than to her inclinations.

raise a few pounds to enable him to remove himself to a part of the country in which he might hide himself from his brother Christians, and find food for his family in the jungle. But even that excellent minister, Mr. David Brown, closed his heart against the applicant; not because he was a Baptist, but because he was, or had been, an associate of Mr. Thomas.*

But Carey was a man of a robust nature; not one to turn back. With a small sum of money obtained from Mr. Thomas, who bore the purse of the Mission, and was bound to render more assistance than he did, the good man went forth literally into the howling wilderness. He betook himself to the Soonderbuns —a place of forests, and jungles, and intersecting streams, where the alligator basks in the sun, and the tiger watches for his prey. Having obtained possession of a convenient clearing, he built himself a hut; and, as game of all kinds was abundant, and there were heathens in the neighbourhood to whom he could preach, when not marketing with his gun in the jungle, he would probably have remained there until carried off by a fever, if that worthy Christian, Mr. Udney, having heard of his forlorn condition, had not invited him to Malda, and given him charge

---

* I gather this, as almost everything else that is interesting in this chapter, from Mr. Marshman's "History of the Serampore Mission." Mr. Marshman says: "He (Carey) waited on him (Mr. Brown) on the 24th of January, but without any satisfactory result. 'He is an evangelical minister of the Church of England,' writes Mr. Carey, 'and received me with cold politeness. I found him a very sensible man; but a marked disgust prevails between him and Mr. Thomas, and I left him without his having asked me to take any refreshment, though he knew I had walked five miles in the heat of the sun.' Such conduct on the part of the generous and hospitable David Brown could be attributed only to the calamity of Mr. Carey's being associated with Mr. Thomas, whom he regarded with feelings of incurable mistrust."

Q

of an indigo factory, a few miles distant, with full permission to convert as many people as he could. There he spent five quiet years, attending to the business of the factory, honestly and usefully, and yet not neglecting the weightier concerns of the Mission. There he improved his knowledge of the languages; preached to the natives, probably with no great success; opened a school for heathen children, and devoted such time as he could spare to the important work of translating the Gospel into Bengalee.

But the factory which Mr. Carey superintended was not successful as a commercial speculation; and he was, therefore, compelled to seek other employment. So he purchased from Mr. Udney a small factory, to work upon his own bottom; and, having heard, to his extreme delight, that four fellow-workmen were on their way to join him, he proceeded to erect mat-houses for the whole party, with the idea of forming something like a Moravian settlement. This had, for some time, been a cherished idea, and he now proceeded to carry it out, under the encouragement of the society at home, who could not perceive at the time any other means of supporting what, in the slender state of their finances, appeared to them so extensive a Mission.* As for brother Carey, he was full of joy at the thought of the associates who were about to join him, and of the great work which such a body of labourers would accomplish. To overcome

* Mr. Marshman, in his "History of the Serampore Mission," gives the following suggestive extract from the Society's letter, adopting the idea of the Moravian settlement: "Now we apprehend you will find it necessary to form what you have proposed, a kind of Moravian settlement, as

all official difficulties he proposed that they should
come out to India ostensibly as his assistants—for he
had obtained a license as a free-merchant, and that
his little factory in the obscure village of Kidderpore
in Malda, should be the nucleus of the Mission station.
There he believed that he might set up his printing
press—there strike off innumerable copies of his
Bengalee version of the New Testament—and thence
" diffuse the blessed light of the Gospel through all
the dark places of heathen India."

Whilst full of these great thoughts, early in the
cold weather of 1797, William Carey received a
stirring letter, intimating that his new colleagues had
arrived in an American vessel; but that the authorities had come down upon them at the very threshold,
and that they were in sore tribulation. They had
refused to give any other than a thoroughly honest
account of themselves. Not only were they resolute
to tell the truth, but to declare the whole truth. To
have registered themselves as assistants to Mr. Carey,
indigo factor, at Kidderpore, in Malda, would, under

otherwise we do not see how the
missionaries can be supported. Our
hearts rejoice at the character of
these young people; and in anticipating the joy it will afford you
if God should prosper their way,
and carry them in safety to Mudna-
butty. We shall be able, through
the good hand of God upon us, to
support you, if you form a settlement according to brother Carey's
proposal,—that is, you may draw on
Messrs, Weston and Co., bankers,
London, for 360*l.* a year for your
whole number, in which we do not
include Mr. Thomas, who will probably not be with you. We shall
also, we trust, be able to get through
the printing of 2,000 copies of the
New Testament, for which we have
already sent the paper; and if a
larger edition be wanted, we shall
find the money. We have now
nearly 3,000*l.* in hand, above 1,000*l.*
of which will go in sending out the
missionaries. But the Lord is our
provider. We shall not want." This
letter was addressed to Mr. Carey,
and to a Mr. Fountain, who had
gone out to join the Mission, but had
taken to politics, abused the authorities, and well-nigh brought the missionary enterprise to disgrace and
disaster.— See Marshman's " History,"

the prevailing notion of a self-supporting Mission upon the Moravian plan, have been no actual untruth. But there would plainly have been a *suppressio veri*; and so, after much counsel and much prayer, they entered themselves as missionaries, and as missionaries were reported in Calcutta. But they had taken good advice from Mr. Grant and others, before they left London; and had determined not to land at the English capital and fling themselves naked into the lion's den.

Some sixteen miles above Calcutta, on the opposite bank of the river, lies what was once the little Danish town of Serampore. It has now lost its ancient privileges as a foreign settlement; but not many years ago it was a sort of Alsatian receptacle for outcasts of all kinds. Fugitive debtors from Calcutta found there an asylum where English law could not reach them; and it was believed that even that most perilous and pestilential of all suspected persons at that time in India, the missionary of the Gospel, might lie there without molestation So the little party of Baptists, when they descended the ship's side in the Hooghly, put themselves and their worldly goods on board a river boat, and made their way to Serampore. There they were received by the Danish governor with all courtesy and kindness; but they had not found a sanctuary which English authority would willingly respect. The privilege of the fraudulent banker and the low swindler was not to be extended to them. So they had scarcely had time to congratulate  themselves on the kindness of their new friends when alarming tidings reached them from Calcutta. The intelligence of their arrival had dismayed and incensed the Government; and now the missionaries wrote to brother Carey in Malda, that they were all to be sent home again by the first ship, and begged him to come down to the presidency to aid them in the crisis of their fate. The storm, however, passed over. Good Governor Bie had resolved to refuse, if demanded, the extradition of the missionaries; and great Governor Wellesley had, on calmer consideration, decided that it might be better to leave them alone.

So they waited for an answer from brother Carey; but before it arrived, trouble fell upon the Mission, for one of the little party died. Three or four days afterwards, the expected communication was received. Mr. Carey was still sanguine as to the success of the missionary settlement in Malda; but grave and reasonable doubts had assailed his colleagues whether they would be permitted to preach, and to itinerate, and to set up printing-presses in that part of the country; and as Governor Bie pressed upon them the hospitality of Denmark, offered them the rights of Danish citizens, and declared that they should always have the protection of his flag, it became matter for serious consideration whether they should not establish themselves permanently at Serampore. But they acknowledged the chiefship of brother Carey, and were unwilling to oppose themselves to what obviously lay so near his heart. Agitated by these conflicting opinions and desires, they did the best thing they could—they sent one of their party on a deputation to Malda to talk over the matter with their chief.

The deputy was William Ward. The son of a carpenter and builder at Derby, he had received a decent education, and had been apprenticed, in early youth, to a printer in that town. From this humble position he had risen to the responsible office of editor of the "Derby Mercury," which, under his superintendence, soon developed into an influential political organ. He was a high-pressure liberal, dallying on the brink of revolutionary doctrines, and on more than one occasion, well nigh involving himself, by the utterance of his extreme opinions, in personal trouble. From Derby he had afterwards betaken himself to Hull, where he conducted, with good success, a second newspaper, and, living in a pleasant lodging on the banks of the Humber, enjoyed much literary leisure, and the cheerful companionship of friends. But, in the year 1796, when he was twenty-seven years of age, he began to take more serious views of Christian life, and, utterly ceasing from the strife of politics, turned his thoughts towards the ministry of Christ. In the August of that year, he was baptized, and soon afterwards began to instruct the poor and to preach to rustic congregations open-mouthed in the open air. In this condition, he attracted the attention of an influential gentleman, who, at his own charge, placed Mr. Ward at Dr. Fawcett's well-known training establishment of Ewood Hall. There he was visited by a member of the Baptist Missionary Society, who spoke to him of the labours of Carey in Bengal, and filled him with an earnest desire to go to the dark places of the earth and to do likewise. He believed that he might turn to good account, in his Master's service, the knowledge of the trade in which he had been brought up; so he offered himself to Mr. Fuller, as one willing to join Carey in Bengal and to aid him in the printing of the Scriptures. He had met the "inspired cobbler" some years before, and had conversed with him on the subject of his contemplated mission—little thinking that he would one day be his associate. But so it was willed; and now they met again, face to face, in Carey's bungalow, and talked over the present fears and future prospects of the Mission; they reverted to the time of their first meeting, when they walked together "from Rippon's chapel one Lord's day," and inspired each other with a feeling of mutual liking and trust.

The great question now between them was, whether it were better to cling to the Malda factory, where they were at the mercy of the British Government, which might at any moment revoke their licenses and send them all to England; or to gather themselves together under the protection of the Danish flag, and to plant the Mission at Serampore. Reluctantly and regretfully, Mr. Carey abandoned his cherished scheme of the Moravian settlement in Malda, and consented to remove himself and his family—his press and his types—to the Danish settlement. Early in the new year (1800) he arrived at his new home, and there embraced his other associates

in the great missionary enterprise.  One of the four
who had left England had fallen a victim to the
climate.  Another (Mr. Brunsdon) was soon afterwards cut off at the outset of his career.  The
fourth, of whom no mention has yet been made,
was Mr. Joshua Marshman.

Descended from a good family, but born in very
humble life—his father being a weaver in Wiltshire
—this remarkable man had acquired all the knowledge ever derived from the tuition of others at a
village school, whose academical capacity did not
extend even to the power of teaching its scholars
to write or to cast up a sum in simple addition.
He was one, however, little dependent upon others
for intellectual nourishment.  He taught himself
thoroughly to read; and, under difficulties scarcely
to be appreciated in these days of much and cheap
printing, he borrowed books from whomsoever he
could, and at an early age had indulged extensively
in desultory reading.  Great, indeed, was his delight
when, at the age of fifteen, a London bookseller, who
happened to be a native of Joshua Marshman's own
borough-town of Westbury, offered to take him into
his shop and bring him up to the business of a
bibliopole.  The boy had begun to follow his father's
occupation—and the change from the loom to the
book-shelf appeared to him to be little less than a
transfer to Paradise.  But the experiment was, after
all, only a disappointing failure.  In his new situation he saw more of the outside than of the inside of
books.  He acquired, in a short time, a wonderful

knowledge of titles; but he had scanty literary leisure, and he did not find that his knowledge increased as rapidly as in the little Wiltshire borough. So, after brief trial of metropolitan life, he returned to the loom, and for many years lived the life of a weaver, increasing largely in intellectual wealth and growing strong in his religious convictions. His parents were pious, god-fearing people of the Baptist persuasion; and Joshua had become a great reader of the old Puritan divines. But the magnates of the Westbury church had high views of church fellowship. They looked suspiciously at the book-learning of the young weaver; and were fain to keep him in a state of probation, though he was eager to be baptized.

But another field of labour was now ready for him. He was offered the mastership of a school at Broadmead, Bristol—under the shadow, as it were, of the great Baptist University over which Dr. Ryland presided. He had taken to himself a wife by this time —the daughter of a Baptist minister, the Reverend John Clerk of Crockerton—and he was pleased to enter upon a sphere of extended usefulness which at the same time increased his means of subsistence. Permitted to take private pupils, he had no difficulty in finding them; and as the privilege of attending the classes of the Bristol Academy had been granted to him, he contrived, whilst earning a comfortable income by tuition, to increase his stores of knowledge, and especially his acquaintance with the classical and the Hebrew languages, and so to fit himself for higher pursuits. At Broadmead he was baptized; and there, conversing with Dr. Ryland on the great subject of missionary enterprise, he conceived the idea of becoming a labourer in that vineyard. Having once formed the resolution, he was not slow to carry it into effect. He made an offer of his services to the Society; his offer was accepted; and three weeks afterwards, accompanied by Mr. Ward, Mr. Grant, and Mr. Brunsdon, he was on his way to Calcutta.

Such, briefly narrated, were the antecedents of those distinguished Indian missionaries — Carey, Marshman, and Ward. I have brought them now together at Serampore, which their labours have since made illustrious.* They dwelt together in utter unselfishness, as one great Christian family. Never have men addressed themselves to the Holy work of evangelisation in a purer spirit, or with more earnestness of purpose; and yet at the same time with more sound good practical sense and more steady perseverance in the adaptation of all legitimate means to the great end which they had set before them. In this, as in other respects, they greatly resembled Ziegenbalg and his associates. They expected no miracles to be wrought in their behalf. They hoped to make their way only from small beginnings. They knew that much toil was necessary to the attainment even of scanty success. But they never spared themselves. They gave up

* Mr. Fountain and Mr. Brunsdon were also, at this time, members of the Mission. Mr. Grant had previously died.

everything to the one great object of their lives. Most thrifty in their own expenditure, casting everything into a common stock, they were glad, by any fitting labour, to realise this world's wealth, that they might devote it to the somewhat costly requirements of the printing of the Scriptures in the native languages. Carey had translated nearly the whole of both testaments. The presses and the types were ready, and Ward had all the knowledge of a first-rate printer. So, whilst Carey went out into the highways to preach, Ward, studying hard, with Marshman as his fellow-student, at the vernacular languages of the country, undertook to set up the New Testament in good Bengalee; and on the 18th of May, to the inexpressible joy of the whole party, the first sheet was struck off in clear legible type. In less than a year from that date, the whole of the New Testament had been printed in Bengalee.

This was a great thing accomplished; for they believed that only by sowing the Scriptures broad-cast over the land, could the conversion of the heathen, on any great scale, be accomplished without a miracle. They did not fail utterly; but the results of their teaching were at first so limited that it would have taken, at such a rate of progression, a century to fill a church with their converts. It was something even to " save some." Nay, at the outset of their career, one convert was a matter of great rejoicing. The first-fruits of the labours of the Serampore Mission was the open avowal of Christianity by a Bengalee carpenter, named Krishna Pall. The occasion was a great one; and Mr. Thomas, who had recently come down from the Mofussil on a visit to the Serampore missionaries, was so greatly excited, that he literally went mad with joy. When the baptism of the convert took place in the Hooghly, the ceremony, so touching in itself that the Governor of Serampore shed tears as he witnessed it, was rendered terible by the blasphemous shoutings of the madman, who had been brought down on a litter to witness the spectacle, and by the screams of Mrs. Carey, who had gone mad with grief sometime before, and who now responded to the bellowings of Mr. Thomas from an adjoining house. The gentleman expiated his enthusiasm in a lunatic asylum; but was released, after a time, to pursue his varied occupations with renewed vigour. Mrs. Carey died not long afterwards; and her husband, in due time, linked himself with a more fitting helpmate.

Other successes, but still numbered slowly by units, were accomplished; and, in the meanwhile, the missionaries, waiting hopefully the results of the distribution of their Scriptures and tracts, increased greatly in worldly prosperity. Mr. and Mrs. Marshman had established boarding-schools at Serampore, and such was the confidence reposed in those excellent persons, that in course of time their establishments yielded to the Mission a revenue of 1,000l. a year. Mr. Carey, too, was adding by his exertions largely to the common stock. Lord Wellesley's magnificent design of a college in Fort William for the education of the younger members of the Company's service, had been inaugurated, and a staff of learned professors and teachers appointed to give practical effect to the scheme. At the head of this staff, as I have already shown, were the chiefs of the English Church in Calcutta, David Brown and Claudius Buchanan. There was no sectarianism in those days among the English in India, and neither did the Governor-General look askance at learning and merit in a dissenting guise, nor did the English Churchmen on the Establishment refuse to be associated, in this or in other enterprises, with pious men of different denominations. It was enough for them that Mr. Carey was a learned man, of a blameless way of life. So, on the recommendation of Mr. Brown, he was appointed teacher of Bengalee at the College of Fort William on a salary of 600*l.* a year; but with the distinct understanding that the acceptance of such an office was in no wise to be regarded as a constructive pledge of his intention to cease from his missionary labours. The proceeds of office, like the scholastic earnings of the Marshmans, were thrown into the common stock—20*l.* a year, however, being set apart to enable the Government servant to appear "in decent apparel" at the College, and at the levees and parties of the Governor-General which he was sometimes expected to attend.

The Mission was now thriving to the full extent of the expectations of its most sanguine members. They were not unreasonable. They did not look for great and sudden gains to the cause of Christianity. They were well content, at the end of 1802, to

know that they had thirteen native communicants
and nine "inquirers." Early in the following year
they baptized their first convert of the great sacerdotal caste of Brahmans. Important as was the
event in itself, it was still more important as the
inauguration of a great principle, to which the
Serampore missionaries, unlike some of their predecessors, had determined rigidly to adhere. The
Christianity which they taught utterly rejected the
distinctions of caste. Converts of all classes were
to meet together in fellowship and to communicate,
at the Lord's table, as members of the same family.
The Danish missionaries on the coast had suffered
their proselytes to maintain the social distinctions of
their abandoned faith in the presence of the sacred
elements; but Carey and his associates regarded
this as an unworthy compromise, and laid it down
as a fundamental maxim that Christianity is of
but one caste; and so successful was the teaching,
that soon after the first Brahman convert joined the
congregation, he married the daughter of a carpenter,
who had been for some time a member of the
Christian Church.

I cannot afford to trace in minute detail the
progress of the Baptist Mission in Bengal, nor is
it necessary that I should do so, for the son of Joshua
Marshman has done the work with such authority
and with such ability, that this great chapter of
evangelical history can never need further illustration.
It is sufficient to record here, that as time advanced,
the Serampore missionaries beheld, more and more

clearly, the way that stretched before them and the
manner in which it behoved them to tread it.
Becoming with increased experience increasingly
sensible of the little impression to be made upon
the dense mass of Indian life by a few European
strangers, they exerted themselves to train up native
missionaries, and believed that they themselves would
do more good by transfusing Gospel truth, either in
the way of pure Scripture, or of simple elementary
tracts, into the common languages of the country,
than by expending themselves in the exhausting
labour of itinerating under a burning sun.   At a
later period, encouraged by the Bible Society, which
had grown up in full vigour and activity at home,
they suffered themselves to be carried away by this
leading idea, to an extent which, at this distance of
time, it is hard to decide whether most to admire
or to regret.   Carey and Marshman were eager to
translate the Bible into no less than seven of the
chief languages of India; and, as if this were not
enough, the list was subsequently increased, at the
suggestion of Mr. Buchanan, by the addition of the
Chinese ; and Mr. Marshman gallantly undertook
to bring out a Bible in the language of Confucius.
Against this extended scheme of translation work
Mr. Ward earnestly protested.   He took brother
Carey and brother Marshman severely to task:
telling them that whilst they were expending their
lives in this scheme of translations for China, Bootan,
and other remote places, "the good in their own
hands and at their own doors would be left undone."

It must be admitted that they were attempting too much; and that, in the main, brother Ward was right. But there was something grand and heroic in the enterprise, though the polyglot enthusiasm of the brethren might have led them away from the more legitimate objects of the Mission.

But, right or wrong, there was one great advantage in this display of Orientalism: it endeared the missionaries to Lord Wellesley. It seemed to be the natural growth of his darling scheme of a mighty collegiate establishment in the metropolis of British India, from which was to go forth a perennial stream of learning to fertilise the soil, and to generate the best fruits of civilization. It matters little whether the Governor-General over-rated or not the benefits to be conferred on India by the College of Fort William. The enthusiasm with which he promoted the cherished design made him look kindly on whatsoever could be rendered auxiliary to its accomplishment, and inclined his heart, therefore, towards the missionaries who were deep in the study of the Oriental languages, and turning their acquirements to the best practical uses by widely disseminating the truth through the medium of the common vehicles of barbarism and error. A little startled at first by the idea of a small party of Englishmen, within twenty miles of the Government house and public offices of Calcutta, setting up an unlicensed printing-press, and, with no fear of the censor before their eyes, issuing freely their papers and tracts for general circulation among the people, he soon began to tolerate what he had no legal power to prevent, and ere long his toleration expanded into something very like encouragement. The stamp of the College appears to have covered in his lordship's estimation a multitude of political sins. He even suffered under the roof of Government House, one of those disputations, which were among the leading features of the periodical public displays of the college, to take the shape of an attack upon the religions of the country; so that then, for the first time in the history of the British empire in the East, it was reported that the Government intended forcibly to convert the natives to Christianity. Nothing that had been done at any other time, or in any other place, had occasioned any public alarm, though it may, in some instances, have provoked private resentment. English missionaries had preached in the bazaars, had circulated the Christian Scriptures, had distributed Christian tracts, had publicly baptized heathen converts in the sacred river of the Hindoos; but the people had not been alarmed. No sooner, however, was there an appearance of Government connection even with so trifling a matter as an anti-Mahomedan thesis, intended only to display the logical acumen and philological attainments of the stripling disputants, than there arose a cry that Mahomedanism was in danger, and the pundits caught up the cry which the moulavees had commenced. The alarm was soon dissipated; but the incident was instructive. It was demonstrated that the natives of India have no fear of the persuasive efforts of Christian ministers, that

R

the arguments and exhortations of individual men
or of private societies create no apprehensions in
their minds; but that they are keenly sensitive of
anything that even faintly resembles coercion by the
State, and that the least appearance of authoritative
Government interference, therefore, excites, first in
the teachers, and then in the followers both of Hindooism and Mahomedanism, the most unreasonable
emotions of alarm.

So, all through the period of history occupied by
the administration of Lord Wellesley, the Serampore
Mission, if it did not actually bask in the sunshine of
viceregal favour, encountered no storms and was
chilled by no frosts.* The missionaries increased in
number and relaxed not in diligence. The Serampore Mission had, indeed, become a great fact. It
made no vast pretence of multitudinous conversions.
But it supplied the means of converting nearly the
whole Oriental world.

Nor should it be forgotten that the Baptist missionaries at Serampore were forward to do battle
against all those cruel abominations, which were
among the outward and visible signs of the tremendous superstition, which they were endeavouring
to destroy. What were then called the "Saugor
sacrifices," the present generation knows only by
name. At the mouth of the Ganges, Hindoo mothers,
at the commencement of the present century, threw

* It was a great thing for the Mission that Mr. Udney, a man of the highest Christian character, was then a member of the Supreme Council. Charles Grant's mantle had descended upon him, and he wore it with becoming dignity.

their babes into the river on a festival day, as a propitiation to the deity. In accordance with the general system of toleration then observed by the British Government, this iniquity, like the kindred horror of widow-burning, was suffered to continue without molestation. A report upon the subject of this abominable rite, drawn up for Lord Wellesley by Mr. Carey, fixed the Governor-General's determination to suppress it; and on the occurrence of the next festival a detachment of soldiers was sent down to the point of massacre, to enforce the law passed for the prohibition and punishment of the crime. It was no fault of the missionaries that Suttee was not extinguished at the same time. From the very commencement of their career they had exerted themselves, actively and laboriously, to drag into the clear light of day all the realities of this fearful rite. With that love of truth, which rendered them so accurate and precise in all their doings, they made explorations in the neighbourhood, or sent out native agents to report to them the exact number of immolations within a certain circle around the capital; and they were then enabled clearly to ascertain that, year after year, from three to four hundred widows were annually sacrificed within thirty miles of the Government House of Calcutta. These and other facts illustrative of the same important subject were duly supplied to Government, in the hope that something might be done to root out the iniquity. The duty of a Christian government in such a case was strongly urged upon Lord Wellesley by Mr. Udney; but the

Governor-General was then on the eve of departure, and it was reserved for another statesman, who was then on the coast of Madras, to give, a quarter of a century afterwards, the death-blow to the abomination.

That statesman was Lord William Bentinck. I do not know that at any more fitting point of my narrative than that which it has now reached, the attention of the reader could be diverted for a while from the chief presidency of Bengal to the southern peninsula, where that worthy nobleman and his pious wife were by the rectitude and propriety of their own lives and the encouragement given to Christianity, in all its aspects, upholding the character of our national faith. There were some complaints, in those days, of the social quietude and decorum of the little court at Madras. The Governor and his wife were sneered at, by the licentious, for the drab-coloured domesticity which was the prevailing attire of their own lives and which they sought to render fashionable throughout the society over which they presided. But there were others, who spoke with delighted approbation of the good example thus prominently set to the people of the settlement, and diligently endeavoured to follow it.

By the exercise of the power and the authority of the Governor, no less than by the example of the man, did Lord William Bentinck endeavour to promote the progress of Christianity in India. The senior chaplain, on the establishment at that time, was Dr. Kerr, a man of distinguished piety, zealous, laborious, and not wanting in the true missionary spirit. In him the Governor found a willing and an indefatigable agent. Under the instruction of Lord William Bentinck, Dr. Kerr made a circuit of the Syrian churches on the Malabar coast, and sent in a long and interesting report to Government on the subject. He, also, under the orders of the same benevolent statesman, drew up, at a later period, a memoir on the state of the ecclesiastical establishment in the Madras presidency, and commented forcibly on the lamentable spiritual destitution of the greater number of stations at which European officers were posted. It was obvious that the Christian welfare of his fellow-men lay very near to his heart; and that although in some measure necessarily held in control by his official position, the missionary spirit was strong within him. Few men better deserve honourable mention in such a volume as this.

About the same time, Claudius Buchanan was prosecuting his researches into the state of Christianity in Southern India. He found the Tranquebar mission in a very decayed condition. The missionaries blushed when he reverted to its former glories in the days of Ziegenbalg and Grundler. But he heard the praises of the Christian's God sung in Tamul by two hundred voices, and saw native listeners taking down on the palmyra leaf the heads of the Tamul sermon. At Tanjore, which he described as the " grand scene of all "—" the garden of the Gospel," he found Mr. Kohloff still labouring, with a goodly congregation of Christians around him. The Rajah received Buchanan with the kindness and courtesy which he

extended to all the co-religionists of Schwartz, and
conversed with the English chaplain on the good
deeds and saintly life of his old friend. From Tanjore, he proceeded to Travancore; and thence made
a circuit of the Syrian churches of Malabar. He
found them, in some places, much Romanised; their
priests performing the services in languages unknown
to the people. In others, they appeared to be trem-
blingly apprehensive of Romanist interference, and
not without suspicion that Buchanan himself was an
agent of the Pope in disguise. He found the Syrian
Christians for the most part a simple-minded, guileless
people, timid and suspicious from the results of long
oppression; poorly instructed in the truths of the
Gospel, but willing to be taught and willing to
believe. What they most needed was the circulation
of the Scriptures in the vulgar tongue; and this
Buchanan diligently promoted. He persuaded the
bishops of the Syrian Church to undertake this most
necessary duty, and he was able to report before he
left that part of the country, that learned Syrian and
Malayalim scholars were engaged in the translation
of the Bible into the language of Malabar, and that
there were 200,000 persons ready to receive it.

It was during the time of Buchanan's visit to
Madras, that there came to pass that great and
terrible event known as the Vellore massacre—an
event, which during fifty years held undisputed
prominence as the saddest domestic tragedy which
the English in India had witnessed since the night of
the Black Hole; but which has now been dwarfed

by the tremendous calamity which has overtaken the present generation of Anglo-Indian Christians. The tidings of the mutiny met Buchanan as he advanced. He had well nigh been among its victims. He had intended to have visited Vellore two days before the eventful night of the massacre; but Providence, as he wrote soon afterwards, retarded his steps. He was seized by one of the fevers of the country and kept a prisoner at a dawk-bungalow, until the crisis had passed. How much his own researches had to do with the causes of the tragedy may be gathered from the fact, that it occurred on the 10th of July, and that he only crossed the frontier of the Madras presidency on the 29th of June.

I believe that I should best convey my opinion of the connection of the Vellore massacre with the subject of this work by taking no further notice of it. But although it was in no degree the result of Christianity in India, it was the cause of many grievous charges, and much dire hostility against Christianity in India. " A rumour," wrote Buchanan to Henry Thornton, in September, 1806, " has for some months pervaded India, that all castes are to be made Christians. I know the alleged causes of the rumour, but I consider them as inadequate to produce the effect without a concurring Providence. This strange rumour of conversion is perhaps auspicious to the event itself; as the shaking of an old building announces its approaching fall. It was attempted to be shown that the massacre at Vellore, which happened when I was in the neighbourhood, was in some measure caused by

this rumour.   But it has been proved by the evidence
of the conspirators that the design of resuming the
Mahomedan dynasty in Mysore was planned by the
princes immediately on their hearing the joyful news
that the tiger Wellesley, as they called him, had
returned from India."

The massacre of Vellore was the growth of a
number of concurrent circumstances.   That an insane
hope engendered in the breasts of the princes of the
house of Tippoo—a hope of recovering their lost
dominion in Mysore—was the origin of the movement
is not to be doubted.   Surrounded by adherents of
the family, who chafed under the galling loss of all
their powers and privileges, and who hated with the
bitterest Mahomedan hatred the infidels who had
trodden them down, these unfortunate princes were
induced to listen to evil counsel, and to suffer themselves to become the focus of a sanguinary intrigue
which resulted, after much loss of life, only in a
strangling failure.   It was thought that the time,
which had arrived, was propitious for such a movement.   Not because Christian missionaries were
itinerating in Southern India; not because Lord
and Lady William Bentinck were known to be good
Christians; not because Dr. Buchanan and Dr. Kerr
were making their inquiries into the state of the
Christian churches: of all these things, as far as
they existed (and in part, at least, they did not exist,
for the missionaries were by no means active, at this
period, in Southern India), the conspirators themselves
were, in all probability, profoundly ignorant.   But,

because, just at that period some changes had been introduced into the external equipment and discipline of the native army; and designing people, on the alert to discover any demonstrations on the part of the paramount power, which might be tortured into aggressive movements against the religious faith or the social observances of the soldiery, insidiously circulated a report that the object of these changes was to violate the caste of the Hindoo and to defile the purity of the Mussulman. The principal cause of excitement and alarm was a change in the head-dress of the native troops. A leather *chacot* had been substituted for the old turban; and a report was industriously circulated, firstly, that the shape of the head-piece, resembling as it did, the round hat, which was considered by the people as the distinguishing mark of the feringhee (whom they called a topi-wallah or hat-wearer) was intended to fix upon them the outward mark of Christianity; and, secondly, that the materials of this head-piece being leather—that is the skin of the cow, or the skin of the pig—was intended to outrage the Hindoo and to pollute the Mahomedan soldier, by placing a portion of the sacred or of the unclean animal on the top of his head. Other innovations, unfortunately, were attempted, mostly in ignorance, about the same time. Whilst the round hat of the Christian was being placed on the sepoy's head, his own distinguishing marks of caste were rubbed off his forehead; he was despoiled of his necklaces; and ordered to divest himself of his beard. In some stations the beating of taum-taums, an almost invariable attendant of native religious ceremonies, was prohibited; and English martinets forbade Hindoo soldiers, when on duty, to strip to their meals. Under such circumstances as these, it was not strange that the native soldiers of the coast army should have been readily pursuaded by the emissaries of the deposed family of Mysore to believe that their European conquerors purposed by these and similar means to endeavour to convert the sepoys to Christianity, after compelling them to violate their ancestral faith. Meanwhile, other agencies were set at work to excite the public mind and to prepare the people to rise against their white-faced masters. Wandering faqueers uttered wild prophecies in the bazaars. Wandering minstrels sung stirring ballads in the soldiers' lines. And puppet-shows were carried from place to place, representing in a series of dramatic scenes, the restoration of the imperial house of the Mogul, and exhibiting the European stranger as an object of detestation and contempt.

Now all this had nothing to do with chaplains or with missionaries. Perhaps, the sum of the whole would not have excited a single regiment to revolt, if the emissaries of the house of Mysore had not gained over a number of Mussulman officers in the Company's service, and through them excited the religious fears of the soldiery. The Mysore princes, or the courtiers surrounding them, thought that the time was propitious; for the army was in course of rapid reduction, the finances of the British Government were in a state of alarming depression; and "Tiger Wellesley" had gone to England. They who delight to pursue historical parallels will have no difficulty in tracing many remarkable points of resemblance between the antecedents of the mutiny of 1806, and the far more disastrous revolt of 1857. I have only to do with the fact, that in both cases, an apprehension of what is called "the forcible conversion of the native army to Christianity," was excited, by the machinations of designing persons, under circumstances favourable in the extreme to the successful dissemination of the dangerous lie. Current, however, as is the phrase, it by no means represents the real nature of the alarm of which I speak. We cannot forcibly make converts to Christianity. What is dreaded is the destruction of Caste. The appearance of a Christian missionary in every village in the country would excite little apprehension in comparison with even a rumour that the Government are greasing the cartridges in the magazines with animal fat, or mixing animal bones with the flour sold in the bazaars. The natives know that they may meet the missionary with argument, or that they may turn a deaf ear to his charmings, charm he never so wisely; but covert attempts to destroy caste they can neither grapple with nor evade; and when they believe that the immense machinery of a powerful foreign Government is set at work to compass their pollution, no wonder that a panic is engendered, and that panic rapidly ferments into revolt.

The same process appears to have gone on in the

minds of the chief people of the Bengal Government,
and of Anglo-Indians generally, alike in the east and
in the west.   A mighty panic was engendered ; and
panic rapidly grew into revolt—revolt against Christianity.   In all such cases, when anything goes
wrong, whether in the affairs of nations or in the
affairs of individuals, it is always Christianity that is
to blame.   If a man catches cold, he is sure to say
that he caught it at Church ; such accidents never
happen at the Theatre.   It was certain that there had
been a great disaster at Vellore ; and it was said to
have arisen, and perhaps it did arise, in some measure,
from a vague fear of certain offensive proceedings
hostile to the integrity of Caste, but which were as
little influenced by the spirit of Christianity as by
Brahmanism itself.   The Supreme Government, however, discovered that the massacre of Vellore was
the growth of the diffusion of Christianity in India ;
and as there were living, only sixteen miles from the
doors of the council-chamber, a little party of devout
men, whose lives were given up to that diffusion, it
was easy to find some culprits—accessories, at all
events, before the fact—ready to the hand of the
executioner.   The Serampore missionaries were to be
visited, therefore, with condign punishment—the
heaviest punishment that could be inflicted upon
them.   They were to be shut up in Serampore, and
peremptorily forbidden, under pain of expulsion from
the country, to prosecute their blessed work anywhere
in the Company's dominions.

It happened unfortunately, just in this adverse

conjuncture, that two more Baptist missionaries arrived, to join the society at Serampore. They were speedily ordered to leave the country. The mandate, however, was not obeyed without a resolute attempt, within the limits of Christian resistance to authority, to obtain a revocation of the order. They had gone out on board the *Criterion*, which had done the same pious service before, and good Captain Wickes was refused his clearance order, unless he carried back his dangerous passengers to the place from which he had brought them. This order, however, was subsequently rescinded. The ship went; the passengers stayed—but only under a constructive arrangement for their voluntary withdrawal. And this was the origin of the Burmese Mission. They had come out to evangelise the heathen, and all heathendom was not under the orders of the Company. Heathen Governments might tolerate what a Christian Government had ejected; so Mr. Chater betook himself to the Burmese country and there planted the mission.

Those years succeeding the mutiny at Vellore are not years to be dwelt upon with pleasure by the annalist of Christianity in India. There was, in truth, what appears in these days, a silly panic in high places; and England, as I have already shown, caught up the alarm. But, in what light did the collective wisdom of the East India Company look upon the contest between the great Government of India, and the humble missionaries shut up in Serampore. Differences of opinion there doubtless

were among the Directors, and, probably, some sharp
discussion. But the practical result was a despatch
to India, in which the question was considered, in a
calm judicial spirit, and instructions issued, in my
opinion, admirably suited to the requirements of the
case.

The despatch, which, after much careful preparation,
was signed on the 7th of September, 1808, expressed
the wish of the Court that it should be distinctly
understood that they were very from being averse to
the introduction of Christianity into India, or indifferent to the benefits which would result from a
general diffusion of its doctrines. "But," said the
Court, "we have a fixed and settled opinion, that
nothing could be more unwise and impolitic—nothing
even more unlikely to frustrate the hopes and endeavours of those who aim at the very object, the
introduction of Christianity among the native inhabitants—than any imprudent or injudicious attempt to
introduce it by means which should irritate and
alarm their religious prejudices." And having enlarged on these propositions, they went on to counsel
a course of non-interference on the part of the
local Government. "We rely on your discretion,"
they said, "that you will abstain from all unnecessary or ostentatious interference with their (the
missionaries') proceedings. On the other hand, it
will be your bounden duty, vigilantly to guard the
public tranquillity from interruption, and to impress
upon the minds of all the inhabitants of India
that the British faith on which they rely for the

free exercise of their religion will be invariably maintained."[*]

I am bound to say that I do not think that the Serampore missionaries were open to the charge of indiscretion. They conducted their weighty affairs with earnestness and with zeal, but with an amount of prudence—it may be almost said of forbearance—and with a regard for constituted authority and what is commonly called "public convenience," not only very creditable, but very surprising, considering the circumstances in which they were placed. Their whole bearing towards the Government was admirable. And it should never be forgotten, that Andrew Fuller, the mainspring of the Baptist Missionary Society in England, who was less, or rather not at all, within the reach of the powerful influences of a despotism like that of the British Government in India, never failed to counsel submission to the magistrate, as one of the first duties of a Christian. But a good time was now coming. It was decreed by Providence that a change in the law very favourable to the Christian enterprise, should be inaugurated by the British legislature; and in expectation of this event the missionaries laboured patiently and hopefully in the face of strong opposition. The instructions

[*] The despatch will be found entire in the Appendix. There is one passage in it which I think ought to be excepted from the general praise which I, at least, am disposed to bestow upon it. The Indian Government, in one of the despatches under reply, had expressed a hope that the Court of Directors would not "encourage any accession to the number of missionaries actually employed under the protection of the British Government;" and to this the Court now replied, "You are of course aware that many of the meritorious individuals who have devoted themselves to these labours were not British subjects, or living under our authority, and that none of the missionaries have proceeded to Bengal with our license." This appears to me to be an unworthy evasion.

from the Court of Directors, not to put forth the authority of the Government against the missionaries, if such a demonstration could possibly be avoided, were only operative for a time. After a few years, they were either forgotten or wilfully disobeyed. In the last two years of the old charter of 1793, the Supreme Government were more active and unrelenting in their hostility than at any former period. How this happened, I do not pretend to understand. The orders of the Court had not been revoked or superseded, and India was in a state of unwonted tranquillity. But in 1812, there was a raid against the missionaries in Bengal; and no less than five, partly Americans, partly English, were driven out of the country by the imperative orders of an unyielding government, who could find no other offence in them than that they had just arrived without a license.* I cannot understand this any more than I can explain it. But it was the last act of persecution permitted by the law. Events were then taking shape in England which deprived the Government of India for ever of this despotic power—events which I now proceed to describe.

* These were Messrs. Judson, Newell, and Rice, of the American Mission; and Robinson and Johns, of the Baptist Mission. For a detailed and very interesting account of their eviction, I would refer the reader to Mr. Marshman's forthcoming work. See also "The Lives of Dr. and of Mrs. Judson;" and the "Correspondence between the Supreme Government of Bengal and the Missionaries at Serampore," published in 1814.

# CHAPTER VIII.

The Emancipation Act of 1813—The Episcopal and Missionary Clauses—
The Committees and the Debates—The First Indian Bishop—His
Character and Career—The First Visitation Tour—State of the
Churches—Death of Bishop Middleton.

IN the spring of 1813 a great movement, which had
long been gathering strength and consistency in
England, seemed to have acquired an irresistible
impetus, which would command for it speedy success.
The harvest now appeared ready for the sickle.   The
labours of those busy workmen, Grant, Teignmouth,
Thornton, Wilberforce, Buchanan, and their companions, were at length about to be rewarded.   They
had toiled and striven manfully for years; they had
encountered public opposition and private ridicule;
they had been shouted at by the timid and sneered at
by the profane; they had been described as dangerous
intermeddlers, and as imbecile fanatics.   They had
contended only against the open official suppression
of Christianity in India; they had asked only for
toleration; they had demanded that, in the midst
of opposing creeds, the faith of the Christian might
be suffered to walk unveiled and unfettered.   They
had been seeking this liberty for many years; and

8

now at last the day of emancipation was beginning to dawn upon them.

The "Clapham Sect" were victorious. There was in truth everything to make them so. All the wit of Sydney Smith, and all the ponderous Orientalism of Scott Waring, could not long prevail against the steady efforts of that little band of strong-headed and strong-hearted Christians. They were not inexperienced novices, or mere idle dreamers. They had reason and experience on their side, and Christian England was with them. They had written much, and spoken much on the subject so near their hearts; and now they were bracing themselves up for a final effort—secure of victory in the end.

The old Charter of the East India Company was expiring. The provisions of a new Act were about to be considered and determined by the Parliament of Great Britain. Great changes of a commercial character were about to be introduced — but my business is with other changes. Twenty years before, Wilberforce had striven earnestly and resolutely to wring from Parliament a reluctant consent to the introduction into the India Bill of 1793 of a clause recognizing the duty of the country " to promote by all just and prudent means the interests and happiness of the inhabitants of the British dominions in the East," and to " adopt such measures as might gradually tend to their advancement in useful knowledge, and to their religious and moral improvement." But although he had contrived to bring about the passing of a resolution, declaratory of this as the opinion of the House, he was defeated at a subsequent stage of legislation. The East India Company were against the resolution. Proprietors of India Stock assembled in Leadenhall Street to denounce what was considered as nothing less than the first step towards the despatch of an army of missionaries to the shores of India; and when a clause, in accordance with Wilberforce's resolution was introduced, with some fatal specifications, into the Bill itself, it was opposed by the House and abandoned by the Minister. But the twenty years, which had passed away since that disheartening failure, had witnessed great changes in public opinion—changes brought about, it is hard to say how much, by the influence of such men as Wilberforce, Simeon, and the Thorntons. And now, having decisively routed the enemy in all their literary skirmishes in the open country, they girded themselves for a great effort to carry Parliament by storm. What they contended for was nothing very alarming—nothing very unreasonable. They sought the extension and the elevation of the Anglican Church Establishment in India, including the establishment of an episcopal see; and a removal of the restrictions which had so long impeded the progress of missionary labour in the Company's dominions. For these concessions to Christianity the battle was now to be fought. Churchmen and Nonconformists were on the same side. Thousands, who cared little for the extension of the Church establishment, except as a public declaration of Christianity which might, in some measure, favourably influence the minds of the heathen, were eager in the cause of Christian missions; whilst others, who had little missionary spirit, clamoured for the extension of the Church. The two questions were distinct from each other; but in the hands of Wilberforce and his friends they yielded mutual support, and many felt that the success of the one was identified with that of the kindred measure. And so, with this great union of Christian interests, there was little doubt of the issue of the conflict. It had virtually been decided before. Public opinion had pronounced, and was still pronouncing, the doom of the abnegation system. So emphatically were the people of England declaring themselves in favour of a more open recognition of Christianity by a Christian Government, and the concession of greater liberty to Christian missions in the East, that it was no longer possible to withstand the tide of popular feeling.

Petitions were pouring in from all parts of the country; from all classes of society; from all denominations of Protestant Christians. "On the subject of facilitating the diffusion of Christianity in India," wrote Mr. Simeon to his "dear friend and brother" Thomason, "there are going to be petitions from all quarters. Vast opposition is made to it: Lord Castlereagh is adverse to it; examinations are making in relation to it at the bar of the House of Commons; Mr. Hastings, Lord Teignmouth, and others have given their evidence; Hastings is very adverse. Lord Castlereagh's plan is to send out a bishop and three archdeacons; but whether it will be approved by Parliament I cannot tell." The war was now being waged in earnest.

A few days after Simeon's letter was written, the Protestant Dissenters of the country memorialised Parliament, setting forth that "to represent a system of idolatry and superstition as tending to produce moral virtue and human happiness, is no less contrary to the dictates of sound reason and philosophy, than irreconcileable with the first principles on which our faith is built; and that, entertaining a directly opposite sentiment, the petitioners are anxiously desirous that the light and blessings of Christianity should be gradually diffused over the immense Empire of Great Britain in the East, which, instead of being thereby endangered, would, as they believe on the ground of fact and experience, derive additional strength and stability from the spread of the Christian religion; and that the petitioners are fully aware of the mass of ignorance and prejudice to be encountered, and that the progress of knowledge must be proportionably slow; but whilst the means of persuasion only are employed (and all others they utterly deprecate), they are at a loss to discover from whence any such apprehensions of danger can arise, as to induce any wise and good government to discountenance the attempt." Local petitions poured in both from England and Scotland. Glasgow put forth an emphatic appeal, both in behalf of the general dissemination of Christianity throughout India, and, through its ministers and elders, of the claims of the Scottish Church to recognition in India. The Synod of Fife embodied both objects in one comprehensive petition. Mr. Whitbread presented a petition from "the Treasurer,

Secretaries, and Directors of *a certain voluntary Society, known by the name of the Missionary Society,* instituted in 1795;" but, half-ashamed of it, begged to be understood as giving no opinion on the subject. Warrington, Sunderland, Leeds, Weymouth, and other places in the north and south too numerous to specify, poured in their petitions both to the Upper and the Lower House. And whilst the two Houses were receiving these indications of popular opinion out-of-doors, they were busily engaged in taking the evidence of experienced members of the civil and military services, and of the commercial community, regarding the different points embraced in the charter of the great Company, which was now about to lose some of its dearest privileges, in spite of the most manful efforts to retain them.

Among the remarkable men examined by the Parliamentary Committees were Warren Hastings, Lord Teignmouth, Sir John Malcolm, and Sir Thomas Munro. When Hastings was asked by the Commons Committee whether he recollected any missionaries in India in his time, he said that he remembered Schwartz, "a very worthy gentleman" in the Carnatic; and another in Calcutta, Kiernander, who might not perhaps be properly described as a missionary. He stated also, that he remembered one conversion in Calcutta, effected by Kiernander, because it was announced "with great pomp and parade;" and that he remembered a catholic priest at Dacca, who boasted that he had a number of Christian converts, but did not seem to understand Christianity

himself.    When he was asked, what would be the
consequences, if persons were allowed to employ themselves, as missionaries, " unlicensed and subject to no
restraint;" he answered, that he could not suppose
such a situation; but, when told that the Committee
meant " unrestrained, as to the mode they may think
proper to adopt for effecting their object," he said,
that, if such people had demeaned themselves properly, he should have taken no notice of them; but
that, if they had given out that Government encouraged their designs, he should have exercised his
authority in controlling them, or, if necessary, have
sent them out of the country.    To the question,
" What is your opinion as to the political effect of the
measure proposed, respecting a Church establishment
for India?" he gave this answer :—

" The question is one of great intricacy, and of such
delicacy, that I should almost fear to speak to it, but
that my respect for this honourable House enjoins it;
because, though it specifically mentions only political
effects, yet it intimates no allusion to the nature of
the office itself.    Of the religious uses, or present
necessity, of such a creation I cannot be a judge, and
therefore can say nothing to it; and, unless I knew
both the circumstances and object of the creation, it
would be impossible for me to conjecture in what way
they could affect the peace of the country.    May I
say, without offence, that I wish any other time had
been chosen for it?    A surmise has gone forth of an
intention in this Government to force our religion
upon the consciences of the people in India, who are

subjected to the authority of the Company. It has pervaded every one of the three establishments of Bengal, Fort St. George, and Bombay, and has unhappily impressed itself with peculiar force upon the minds of our native infantry, the men on whom we must depend, in the last resort, for our protection against any disturbances, which might be the effect of such surmises. Much would depend upon the temper, conduct, and demeanour of the person devoted to that sacred office. I dare not say all that is in my mind on this subject; but it is one of great hazard."

And thus expressing his fears, the fine old man sat there, the embodiment of public opinion, as it was in India some twenty years before. Another Governor-General followed him; he spoke also, according to the light that was in him—but how different that light! Lord Teignmouth came forward, as the representative of a more enlightened era. The Committee seemed to know the kind of man they had to deal with, and assailed him at starting by putting an extreme case: " Would it be consistent with the security of the British empire in India, that missionaries should preach publicly, with a view to the conversion of the native Indians, that Mahomet is an impostor, or should speak in opprobrious terms of the Brahmins, or their religious rites?" To this, of course, Lord Teignmouth replied, that there might be danger in such indiscretion; but that no one contemplated the conversion of the natives of India by such means; and when, soon afterwards, the question was put, " Is your Lordship aware that an opinion prevails in India, that it is the intention of the British Government to take means to convert the natives of the country to the Christian religion?" he answered, without a moment's hesitation, "*I never heard it, or suspected it.*" One would have thought that there was little need after this to put the case hypothetically; but the witness was presently asked whether, allowing such an opinion to exist among the natives, the appearance of a Bishop on the stage would not increase the danger. "I should think," said Lord Teignmouth, "it would be viewed with perfect indifference." Determined to work the hypothesis a little more, the Committee asked him whether, "*were* the Hindoos possessed with an idea, that we had an intention of changing their religion and converting them into Christians, it would be attended with any bad consequences at all?" "I will expatiate a little in my answer to that question," said Lord Teignmouth; and he then delivered himself of the following explanation, the admirable good sense of which (as I have by anticipation observed, when citing almost similar words from his printed pamphlet,) is not to be surpassed by anything to be found in the entire mass of evidence elicited, throughout the inquiry, upon all points of the Company's Charter :—

"Both the Hindoos and Mahommedans, subject to the British Government in India, have had the experience of some years, that, in all the public acts of that Government, every attention has been paid to their prejudices, civil and religious, and that the freest toleration is allowed to them; that there are many regulations of Government which prove the disposition of Government to leave them perfectly free and unmolested in their religious ordinances; and that any attempt at an infringement upon their religion or superstitions would be punished by the Government of India. With that conviction, which arises from experience, I do not apprehend that they would be brought to believe that the Government ever meant to impose upon them the religion of this country."

But the Committee had not yet done with their hypothesis, and were determined not to let the witness, whatever might be his opinion of its absurdity, escape without giving a direct answer; so they assailed him again, by asking, "*Should the state of things be altered, and we not observe the conduct we have hitherto observed, but introduce new modes and enact new laws, for the carrying into effect the conversion of the natives to Christianity*, would not that be attended with disagreeable consequences?" To this, of course, but one answer could be given; and Lord Teignmouth gave that answer, leaving the Committee to make what use of it they could. "If a law were to be enacted," he said, "for converting the natives of India to Christianity, in such a manner, as to have the appearance of a compulsory law upon their consciences, I have no hesitation in saying that, in that case, it would be attended with very great danger." Who ever doubted it? Who ever contended for anything so preposterous—so insane? The Committee must have been *in extremis* indeed, to have fallen back upon such sciomachy as this. They supposed a case, which the warmest advocate of church extension and missionary liberty in India would never have contemplated in their most enthusiastic moments; and which the leaders of the Christian party, men of eminently sound practical good sense, would, if suggested to them, in those days, have repudiated with scorn. Such hypothetical questioning—such fighting with shadows, was quite unworthy of a Committee, whose object ought to have been to direct men's minds to the truth, and not to bewilder and lead them astray. No one ever dreamt of forcing Christianity upon the people of India: but the tendency, if not the object, of such questions, as have been cited, was obviously to induce an impression abroad that such intentions had absolutely existed. The Lords' Committee, when they examined Lord Teignmouth, did not touch upon the subject of religion, or Church establishments, at all.[*]

Meanwhile, the work of legislation was slowly proceeding. Lord Liverpool was at this time Prime Minister. Lord Castlereagh was Foreign Secretary, and leader of the House of Commons. The Earl of

[*] But, knowing the kind of answers that would be returned by their men, they had not shrunk from questioning Hastings on these points, though Teignmouth was discreetly left to himself. Warren Hastings was asked, "Would the introduction of a Church establishment into the British territories in the East Indies probably be attended with any consequences that would be injurious to the stability of the Government of India?" and he replied, "I have understood that a great fermentation has arisen in the minds of the natives of India, who are subject to the authority of the British Government, and that not partial, but extending to all our possessions, arising from a belief, however propagated, that there was an intention in this Government to encroach upon the religious rights of the people. From the information of persons who have recently come from the different establishments of India, your lordships will easily know whether such apprehensions still subsisted, when they left it, or

Buckinghamshire (known in India as Lord Hobart) was President of the Board of Control. It is believed that the Premier was more liberally disposed than his colleagues towards the promotion of Christianity in India. "Be so good," wrote Buchanan, in July, 1812, "as to tell —— and —— that I have received a letter from Colonel Macaulay this morning, informing me that a deputation of Messrs. Wilberforce, Grant, Babington, &c., had waited on Lord Liverpool, on the subject of evangelising India, and that his Lordship surprised them by offering almost more than they wished. He intimated his intention to carry the three following important measures:—1st. To establish a seminary at each presidency in India for instructing natives for the ministry; 2nd. To grant licenses to missionaries, not from the Court of Directors, but from the Board of Control; 3rd. To consecrate bishops for India." It is probable that Lord Castlereagh's pruning knife was applied to this scheme; and thence the modified form, which it subsequently assumed.

It had been determined to proceed by Resolutions, and on the 22nd March, they were announced by Lord Castlereagh. When he came to (what twenty years before had been, and still were irreverently

whether the report of them is groundless; but, if such apprehensions do exist, everything that the irritable minds of the people can connect with that, will make an impression upon them, which they will adopt as certain assurance of it. So far only, considering the question as a political one, I may venture to express my apprehension of the consequences of such an establishment *at this particular season*; in no other light am I permitted to view it. But I can conceive that, in a proper time and season, it would be advantageous to the interests of religion, and highly creditable to the Company and to the nation, if the Ecclesiastical Establishment in India were rendered complete in all its branches."

called,) the "pious clauses," he seemed somewhat
inclined to get over the ground, with as much rapidity
as possible. "Another Resolution," he said, "which
he should propose to the House, would be on the
subject of religion. He was aware that it was unwise to encroach on the subject of religion generally,
and that this, under the circumstances of our Government in India, was a most delicate question. But
there was one regulation on the subject necessary,
even for the sake of decency. The Company entrusted with the Supreme Government, in this as in
other matters, had permitted the free exercise of
religion at their settlements; but there was no sort
of religious control, and the members of the Church
of England could not receive the benefits of those
parts of their religion, to which the episcopalian
functions were necessary,—for example, the ceremony
of confirmation. He hoped that *the House did not
think he was coming out with a great ecclesiastical
establishment, for it would only amount to one bishop
and three archdeacons*, to superintend the chaplains
of the different settlements. The Company, he
hoped, would not think it an encroachment on their
rights, that while British subjects in India were
governed by British laws, they should be permitted
to exercise their national religion." Charles Grant
and Mr. Wilberforce both spoke (but briefly) on that
evening: the latter complaining—"that the Resolution of the 14th May, 1793, relative to the religious and
moral instruction of India, had not been attended to."
He was unwilling, he said, to leave the same power for

twenty years to come in the hands of the Directors, who had set their face against the introduction of preachers into that country, for twenty years past.

On the 9th of April, moving for certain papers, Lord Wellesley, in an able, and energetic speech, reviewed the whole question of Indian Government in the House of Lords. When he came to those especial points, which we are now considering, he gave his opinion, but not without some qualification, in favour of an extension of the Church establishment; and delivered himself of a well-deserved complimentary tribute to the missionaries. But he spoke as a man with a hobby of his own, which he was resolutely bestriding; and, thoughtless of any great comprehensive system calculated to advance the real glory of a Christian nation, he looked only to the carrying out of his favourite project of an extensive collegiate establishment, to be presided over by the dignitaries of the Church. The old bugbear of alarming the natives had possession even of his mind :—

"As to the last point," he said, "which regarded the ecclesiastical establishment in India, he always had thought that our ecclesiastical establishment there, did not rest on a footing sufficiently respectable. He was of opinion that a suitable ecclesiastical establishment would tend to elevate the European character in the eyes of the natives. Whether the proper establishment would be a bishop, or archdeacons, was a matter of detail which could be better discussed out of that House. But if it were intended to place the ecclesiastical establishment there on a more dignified footing, care should be taken to avoid all collision between the Government and the Church establishment, with respect to their authorities, by means similar to the connection between the Crown and the Church in this country and in Ireland. From recent events, which had taken place in India, it would, however, be certainly a matter of considerable delicacy: and, although no mischief might result from it, yet there was a possibility that the introduction of a very considerable novelty of this description in India *might occasion some alarm among the natives.*"

He lamented the absence from the scheme of the new Charter of any provision for the education of the civil and military servants of the Company. He expressed his conviction that there could be no better means of disseminating Christianity in India, than by placing the head of the Church establishment there at the head of the Collegiate establishment of Fort William; and he augured much from "the gradual diffusion of knowledge, which would result from this intercourse between learned natives and the dignitaries of our church in India." He then went on to speak of the missionaries :—

"With regard to the missionaries, he must say, that, while he was in India, he never knew of any danger arising from them; neither had he heard of any impression made by them, in the way of conversion. The greater number of them were in the Danish settlements; but he never heard of any convulsions, or any alarm being produced by them. Some of them, particularly Mr. Carey, were very

learned men, and had been employed in the College
of Bengal. He had always considered the missionaries, who were in India during his time, as a quiet,
orderly, discreet, and learned body; and he had
employed many of them in the education of youth,
and in translating the Scriptures, into the Eastern
languages. He however had issued no order, nor
given any authority for the dissemination of those
translations among the natives. He had thought it
his duty to have the Scriptures translated into the
languages of the East, and to give the learned natives,
employed in the translation, the advantages of access
to the sacred fountains of divine truth. He thought that
a Christian governor could not have done less, and he
believed that a British governor ought not to do more."[*]

[*] The influence of Mr. Wilberforce, an intimate personal friend of Lord Wellesley, had been exerted, in this direction, with good success. With admirable tact and *savoir faire*, he assailed the weak side of his lordship, appealing to his particular sympathies and predilections, and almost persuading him that the Anti-Christian party were attacking the ex-Governor-General's own system. "I know not," he wrote, "whether your lordship has heard of the unreasonable clamour, that has been raised by the Anglo-Indians in the House of Commons against all, even the most prudent, attempts to convert the natives of India; and more especially against missionaries. Now let me hope—a hope, which I share with, I am glad to say, a considerable number of men in the House of Commons, and with many more out of it—that your lordship, will to-morrow use your just authority in putting to flight these vain fears;— the rather, because the alarmists *are enemies of the system, which your lordship certainly established, and which, I trust, you will confirm and revive*, that, I mean, of diffusing useful knowledge of all sorts among the natives of India; and I confess, for my own part, that I have always held, and still retain the opinion, that education, the translation and diffusion of the Scriptures, and advancement in general knowledge, would be far the most powerful agents in the great work of Christianising the natives of India. Your weight thrown into the right scale will make it preponderate." To this he added a complaint, only too applicable to the Parliament of the present day, of the ignorance of both Houses—"I will only add, that your lordship can scarcely conceive (if I may judge of the House of Lords from the general condition of the members of the House of Commons) how ignorant their lordships in general are likely to be regarding India, and therefore how little they are qualified to ask questions in Committee." A wish was also expressed that the Marquis would attend that Committee, of which he was a member, but an ever-absent one. In replying to the speech,

The President of the Board of Control and the Prime Minister spoke upon that evening, and Lord Grenville made a very long and very able speech; but the religious points of the question were left untouched.

In the meanwhile the Commons had proceeded to the consideration of the Resolutions. On the 31st of March, they resolved themselves into a committee of the whole House (Mr. Lushington in the chair). A lengthy debate ensued, principally remarkable for a very dull speech by Mr. Bruce, and a very brilliant one by young Charles Grant.* Canning also spoke, characterising the free admission of Englishmen as traders in India, as a movement to "allow a few pedlars to travel in the country with a pack of scissors, or other hardware, at their backs;" and declared his conviction that "no system could be radically bad, which had produced such able and enlightened statesmen as had been examined on the part of the Company." But the "pious clauses" were not then touched upon. It was not, indeed, until the 16th of June, that the 12th Resolution— "That it is the opinion of this Committee, that it is expedient that the Church establishment in the British territories should be placed under the superin-

---

from which I have quoted in the text, the Earl of Buckinghamshire, then President of the Board of Control, taunted Lord Wellesley with his non-attendance. " A Select Committee had been formed, of which his noble friend was a member, but he never once had attended that Committee; with all the knowledge and all the information he possessed on that subject, he had not con-

descended to cast one ray of light on their proceedings, &c. &c." Warren Hastings, Mr. Cowper, and Lord Teignmouth, had all been examined at this time.

* The present Lord Glenelg. It must have been a fine thing to have seen the two Charles Grants—father and son—fighting side by side on the floor of the House of Commons.

T

tendence of a bishop and three archdeacons, and that adequate provision should be made, from the territorial revenues of India, for their maintenance," came under discussion. It passed without a division, but "after a long conversation," the particulars of which have not been reported by the Parliamentary historian.

The missionary clause came next. That was the field on which the great battle was to be fought between the Christian and the Philo-Hindoo parties. The resolution was thus worded:—" That it is the opinion of this Committee, that it is the duty of this country to promote the interest and happiness of the native inhabitants of the British dominions in India, and that such measures ought to be adopted, as may tend to the introduction among them of useful knowledge, and of religious and moral improvement. That in the furtherance of the above objects, sufficient facilities shall be afforded by law to persons desirous of going to and remaining in India, for the purpose of accomplishing those benevolent designs." It was thus cautiously worded, so as to contain no direct mention of missionaries and Christianity. Twenty years before, the effort to obtain a similar recognition of the duties of a Christian nation had broken down under the alarm created by the mention of schoolmasters and missionaries; and now profiting by experience, Wilberforce and his friends exerted themselves to obtain an official avoidance of the dangerous specifications which had ruined the good cause of old.

A special day (the 22nd of June) was set apart for the discussion of the clause. In a brief speech, expressive of his belief that no evil would arise from the admission of missionaries (under certain restrictions) into India, and of his hope that the question would be discussed with discreetness and moderation, Castlereagh introduced the resolution. He was followed by Sir Henry Montgomery, an old Indian, who declared that during twenty years' residence in the country, he had "never known an instance of any convert being made to Christianity, nor had he ever heard of any, except one, who was converted by that very respectable individual, Mr. Schwartz." "The attempt to introduce Christianity," it was said, "had never succeeded; but it had been productive of endless massacres and mischiefs." "The religion of the Hindoos," it was contended, "was pure and unexceptionable;" and Dr. Buchanan's account of its ceremonies was "an imposition upon England, and a libel upon India." And he concluded by declaring that "he was more anxious to save the lives of the 30,000 of his fellow-countrymen in India, than to save the souls of all the Hindoos by making them Christians at so dreadful a price."

After a brief maiden speech from the Honourable Frederick Douglas, who spoke in favour of the resolution, and contended that religion was not the cause of the massacre at Vellore, Mr. Wilberforce rose. He had girded himself for the conflict: and had gone down to the House with quite an encyclopædia of authorities in support of his favourite opinions. His whole heart was in the encounter. He spoke long and well, tossing about the testimonies of the learned with a prodigality that was quite overwhelming. He quoted the opinions of all the Governors-General, one after the other, to show that the people of India were the most abandoned people on the face of the earth. He quoted the historians ; he quoted the missionaries ; he quoted the civil servants of the Company ; he quoted Orme, Verelst, Scrafton, Bolts, Malcolm, Grant, Mackintosh, Colebrooke, Kerr, Marshman, Carey, Ward, and an infinite number of official reports. He piled up authority upon authority to demonstrate the claims of this unhappy and most benighted people upon the Christian sympathies of the British nation. It was a noble piece of special pleading, not exempt from exaggeration*—that exaggeration, which is perhaps seldom

* But it was characterized, at the same time, by a remarkable amount of acuteness and good sense. At the outset, he insisted upon the necessity of detaching ministers entirely from all connection with Government. Mr. Douglas had spoken of the expediency of employing the Company's chaplains as missionaries. After stating other objections to this course, Wilberforce said :—"It will not, I know, escape him, passing over other objections to the measure, that it necessarily implies that the missionaries who are to officiate in India, are to be expressly commissioned and employed by the State, or by the East India Company; whereas, I am persuaded we shall all concur in thinking that it ought to be left to the spontaneous benevolence and zeal of individual Christians, controlled, of course, by the discretion of Government, to engage in the work of preaching the gospel to the natives in our Indian territories; and that the missionaries should be clearly understood to be armed with no authority, furnished with no commission, from the governing power of the country." A little while afterwards he observed, with equal truth:—"After much reflection, I do not hesitate to declare that from enlightening and informing them (the natives), in other words, from education and instruction, from the diffusion of knowledge, from the progress of science, more especially from all these combined with the circulation of the Scriptures in the native languages, I ultimately expect even more than from the direct labours of missionaries properly so called." Most worthy, indeed, are these passages of consideration at the present time.

absent from the addresses of a man very full of his subject, very earnest and energetic, thoroughly convinced in his own mind, and intensely eager to bring conviction to the minds of others. The grandeur of the aims, the high character and pure sincerity of the speaker, imparted a dignity and solemnity to the address which it was impossible not to venerate. It made an impression upon the House; it made an impression throughout the country.*" Its course was successful, but not unopposed. The resolution was carried that night by a majority of 89 to 36; only 125 members having been induced to sit out the discussion.

The Bill was read a first and second time without a division. On the 28th, Castlereagh moved the order of the day for going into committee. After some brief speeches from Mr. Pascoe Grenfell and others, the elder Grant delivered a long and able address in defence of the Company; but he purposely avoided the discussion of "the religious question," thinking it wiser to leave it in the hands of Wilberforce and other independent speakers. Mr. Lushington followed with a reply to Wilberforce, and a defence of the Hindoos, to be answered by stout William Smith, who, with Mr. Stephen, had fought the battle of Christianity nobly, as Wilberforce's

---

* "The dogmas of some men," writes Sir James Stephen, who, in fulfilment of the mandate, *Thine own friend and thy Father's friend forsake not*, has borne touching and eloquent tribute to the worth of Wilberforce and his chosen associates, " the dogmas of some men are of incomparably more value (in the House of Commons) than the logic of others; and no member except the leaders of the great contending parties, addressed the House, with an authority equal to that of Mr. Wilberforce."

lieutenants. Mr. Tierney was the next speaker. Mr. Tierney often said very clever things in a very bad spirit. But the following is a very stupid thing in a very bad spirit. "He now came to the consideration of a clause for the appointment of an archbishop, who was never to apply himself to trade. Why, what was he to employ himself about? An arduous task — the jurisdiction from the Cape of Good Hope to remote Cape Horn. It would have been well, had any explanation been given, concerning what the archbishop was to busy himself about. He had no concern with morals and religion: these were confided in a separate clause to the missionaries. It appeared to him a gross job, the object of which was Church patronage in India." In such a spirit, and with such an amount of intelligence, was the episcopal question discussed by independent members of the House of Commons.

On the 1st of July, the House having gone into committee, the discussion was again resumed, and a very remarkable speech delivered on the wrong side of the question.

The speaker was Mr. Charles Marsh. This gentleman had formerly been a member of the legal profession at Madras. He had taken a conspicuous part in the discussions which had arisen, a few years before, out of the unhappy dissensions at that presidency, during the administration of Sir George Barlow, distinguishing himself by the bitterness with which he assailed that misjudged statesman. He was a writer and speaker of eminent ability; bold, earnest, and impetuous: but he wanted judgment, temper, and consistency. He used strong language, and he used it well. His declamation was forcible, vivid, picturesque. But the impression left upon the minds of his hearers was of a transitory character. They admired his eloquence, but were not convinced by his arguments. The address, which he delivered on the 1st of July, 1813 — an elaborate protest against Christian liberty in India—cannot be read, even now, without the strongest feelings of regret that such fine talents were turned to such bad account. With a more chastened fancy, a more calm and philosophic temperament, with a less dominant self-reliance, with less impatience, and with less intolerance, he might have taken a foremost place among the debaters of that epoch; but grievously lacking self-control and moderation, he failed by reason of his excesses, and after a brief meteoric display, disappeared altogether from the scene, and was speedily forgotten.

There was little or nothing in this address that had not been said before; but Mr. Marsh assuredly said it *better* than it had ever been said before. He said, indeed, everything that could be said upon the subject; and he said it extremely well. A dexterous allusion to the recent murder at Blackheath of Mr. and Mrs. Bonar by their footman, Nicholson, and to the still mysterious affair of the alleged attack upon the Duke of Cumberland by his valet, Sellis— two incidents which were then exciting the public mind—told with something of novel effect on the House. It was, of course, the object of his party to

exalt the Hindoo character. It must, in all candour,
be acknowledged that Wilberforce and his associates
had unduly depreciated it. There was consider
able exaggeration on both sides; but it may be
doubted whether the following eloquent picture
of Hindooism is not more painfully untrue than
anything that emanated from Mr. Marsh's antago-
nists :—

" Indeed, when I turn my eyes either to the present
condition, or ancient grandeur, of that country; when
I contemplate the magnificence of her structures, her
spacious reservoirs, constructed at an immense expense, pouring fertility and plenty over the land, the
monuments of a benevolence expanding its cares over
remote ages; when I survey the solid and embellished
architecture of her temples, the elaborate and exquisite skill of her manufactures and fabrics, her
literature, sacred and profane, her gaudy and ena-
melled poetry, on which a wild and prodigal fancy has
lavished all its opulence; when I turn to the philo-
sophers, lawyers, and moralists, who have left the
oracles of political and ethical wisdom to restrain the
passions and to awe the vices which disturb the
commonwealth; when I look at the peaceful and
harmonious alliances of families, guarded and secured
by the household virtues; when I see, amongst a
cheerful and well-ordered society, the benignant and
softening influences of religion and morality, a system
of manners founded on a mild and polished obeisance,
and preserving the surface of social life smooth and
unruffled—I cannot hear without surprise, mingled

with horror, of sending out Baptists and Anabaptists to civilize or convert such a people, at the hazard of disturbing or deforming institutions, which appear to have hitherto been the means ordained by Providence of making them virtuous and happy."

This speech called forth a rejoinder from Wilberforce, distinguished by no common ability. Southey had ransacked his marvellous common-place book to supply illustrations, drawn from Portuguese history, of the little danger that attends interference with the customs of the people of India. And now the speaker, thus fortified by the erudition of the newly-appointed laureate, cited Albuquerque with good effect; entered into an elaborate explanation of the causes of the massacre of Vellore (an event which Mr. Marsh had of course emphatically dwelt upon, for it was the stock-in-trade of his party); spoke of the suppression of female infanticide by Jonathan Duncan and Colonel Walker, and of the Saugor sacrifices by Lord Wellesley; rebuked Mr. Marsh for speaking of the missionaries as Anabaptists and fanatics; and compared the present contest with the great struggle, in which he and his friends had so long been engaged, for the suppression of the Slave Trade. He was followed by Mr. Forbes, Mr. William Smith, and other speakers, among whom was Whitbread, who spoke out manfully in favour of the religious clauses. " I am charmed with Whitbread," wrote Buchanan to a friend, a few days afterwards, " when he sounds the right note." The House divided; and there were fifty-four votes for the clause, and thirty-two against it. A hundred members could not be induced to sit out this important debate. Five hundred had divided a few weeks before on the Roman Catholic Relief Bill. The most important Indian questions were then, as at a later period, debated in attenuated and languid Houses. The clause, however, was not carried less surely for that in the Commons. In the House of Lords it passed without a division.

And so the victory was gained. A charter, embracing the establishment of an Indian bishopric and the concession of greater liberty to Christian Missions, passed into law ; and those good men, who had fought so valiantly in the libraries of their suburban villas, and on the floor of the Commons' House at Westminster, rejoiced with an exceeding great joy over their success. They all lived to see the end of the struggle ; but, the contest over, some soon descended to their graves. "John Venn," says the ecclesiastical biographer, "to whom the whole sect looked up as their pastor and spiritual guide, was at that time on his death-bed. He had been the projector, and one of the original founders, of the Society for sending Missionaries of the Anglican communion to Africa and the East—a body which, under the name of the ' Church Missionary Society,' now commands a wider field of action, and a more princely revenue, than any Protestant association of the same character."* Nor was he the only one of that band of Christian

---

* This society had exerted itself to the utmost throughout the glorious and successful contest. On the 21st of April, 1812, a special general meeting of the society had been held, at which 400 gentlemen were present, including several members of Parliament. Lord Gambier was in the

athletes whose days were well nigh numbered.   Henry Thornton did not long survive his honoured friend and pastor ; and Claudius Buchanan soon followed his early benefactor to the grave.   Neither lived to receive the tidings of the arrival of the first Indian bishop at the seat of his future labours.   In January, 1815, Henry Thornton entered into his rest.   Claudius Buchanan, whose strength had been for some time visibly declining, came up from the country to attend the funeral of his revered patron and friend. The effort was too much for him.   The inclement January weather told with deadly effect upon his decaying constitution, and he returned home only to die.

He was not an old man.   He had not, indeed, entered his fiftieth year.   But he had brought with him a debilitated constitution from India, and had encountered many severe trials since his return to his

chair. By this meeting, a committee, or deputation, was appointed to seek for interviews with his Majesty's Ministers, and to use all available means of obtaining a favourable reply to their petition. This deputation held various conferences with the Prime Minister, and other leading members of the Administration. Their success was mainly owing to the indefatigable labours of the secretary of the society, the Rev. Josiah Pratt. He made arrangements for large and influential meetings throughout the country, framed petitions, drew up resolutions, and himself appealed most effectively to the public, both from the platform and through the press; and with the most marked and happy effect, in January, 1813, he published the first number of "The Missionary Register." The admirable and judicious manner in which he brought the claims of the heathen before the public, his own high character, personal influence, and holy zeal in the cause, and the high and well-won reputation of the Serampore missionaries, did much to win the battle. Nor was Mr. Pratt, even in this life, without his reward. In one year after the publication of the "Register," the income of the society rose from 3,000l. to 14,000l.; and what its subsequent course has been, all Christians know. He lived to see a "spiritual" bishop: he lived to see his own pupil and friend at the head of the Indian ecclesiastical establishment; he lived to see his own son (the present Archdeacon of Calcutta), like-minded with himself, labouring in the same great field; and he died, lamented by good men of every persuasion, full of years and honour.

native land. The disappointments of worldly ambition were not, however, among them. He was not a disappointed man. If he had ever been ambitious, he had long outgrown his ambition. It was of course imputed to him that his zeal in behalf of the establishment of episcopal jurisdiction in India was fostered, if it was not actually generated, by a selfish desire to place the mitre upon his own brows. It would have been marvellous if this charge had not been brought against him; for in polemics forbearance is a rare quality. But I believe that there was no more truth in the accusation than in the ordinary shifts of defeated controversialists, who, when argument is lacking, betake themselves to abuse. Before leaving India he had written to Mr. Grant,—"As to returning in order to receive episcopal dignity, my soul sinks at the thought of it. I trust my lines will rather be cast in a curacy. Place the mitre on any head. Never fear; it will do good among the Hindoos. A spiritual Bishop will appear in good time."

What he thought of the selection that was actually then made from among the clergy of Great Britain to fill the episcopal chair, first planted on Indian soil, his biographer has not informed us. The state of Buchanan's health was a sufficient bar to his promotion, had no other impediments existed. But there is no reason to believe otherwise than that, had his constitution been unimpaired, his claims would equally have been passed over. He was not in good odour in high places. His zeal and ability were admitted; but, rightly or wrongly, he was supposed to be want-

ing in judgment and discretion.   He was not a safe
man.   A safe man was wanted; and one was found
in the parish of St. Pancras.   The first bishop of the
Anglican Church in India deserves detailed notice in
such a volume as this—I may be permitted, therefore, to pause and to speak of his antecedents.

Thomas Fanshawe Middleton, the only son of a
country clergyman, was born in January, 1769, at his
father's rectory, in the village of Kedleston, Derby-
shire.   At the age of ten he was sent to Christ's
Hospital (the "Blue Coat School"), whence he
emerged in due course to commence, at Pembroke College, Cambridge, his university career.   In January,
1792, he took his bachelor's degree—standing fourth
in the list of senior optimes.   In the following March,
he was ordained Deacon by Dr. Pretyman, Bishop of
Lincoln, and entered upon his duties, as a minister
of the Gospel, in the quiet curacy of Gainsborough.

Bishop Middleton was one of many eminent men,
who have owed their elevation in life mainly to their
connection with the press.   At Gainsborough, having
sufficient leisure for literary pursuits, he edited a
small periodical, entitled the "Country Spectator,"
which, short-lived as it was, endured sufficiently long
to recommend the writer of the principal papers to
the good offices of Dr. Pretyman, brother of the
bishop, who took the trouble to lift the anonymous
veil, and, having lifted it, was sufficiently well pleased
with the result to secure Mr. Middleton's services for
the domestic education of his sons.   The Pretyman
interest seems to have been the making of the young

clergyman. It introduced him not merely to ordinary church preferment, but to such scholarly society, as, under other circumstances, would not have been within his reach; and, from this attrition of erudite classical minds, emanated that work on the Greek article, which laid the broad foundation-stone of his reputation and his success. In those days, a treatise on the Greek article was not seldom the ladder by which men rose to the highest offices in the Anglican Church. How far it may have assisted in the elevation of Middleton, I do not undertake to determine; but his advancement, after that great feat of scholarship, was sufficiently rapid to warrant a conjecture that the Greek article helped him to ascend to the Episcopal climax. The Pretymans, as I have said, were his great patrons. Through them Middleton obtained the livings of Tansor and Bythams, a prebendal stall at Lincoln, the Archdeaconry of Huntingdon, the Rectory of Puttenham, in Hertfordshire, and the great parish of St. Pancras, London. In the last of these, Dr. Middleton exerted himself to compass the erection of a new parish church. It was deplorably wanted:—but, somehow or other, he failed. The good work, which he could not achieve, was left to his successor to accomplish;* and St. Pancras now rejoices in one of the most capacious religious edifices in the metropolis of England, and a large supplement of district churches, but still, I am told, greatly inadequate to the religious wants of the period.†

* Dr. Moore succeeded Dr. Middleton, and held the living for nearly five and thirty years. It is now held by Mr. Dale.
† See *ante*, pages 52-53.

His removal to London, which took place in 1811, enabled him to take an active part in the proceedings of the Christian Knowledge Society, to form many valuable clerical acquaintances, and to undertake the editorship of the *British Critic*—at that time a periodical of some repute in the literary and religious worlds.  He was in a fair way now to the highest honours of the church, and would, not improbably, have risen to the episcopal dignity in his own country, if the establishment of the Indian bishopric had not opened the road to more speedy preferment.  The nomination of the new bishop was in the power of the President of the Board of Control—then the Earl of Buckinghamshire; and the choice, upon the recommendation (it would seem) of Dr. Tomline, Bishop of Lincoln, fell upon Dr. Middleton, who held a prebendal stall in that diocese.  " Overpowered," says his biography, " by the vast magnitude and appalling novelty of such a charge, he was at first tempted to decline the offer.  His maturer thoughts, however, condemned this determination as unworthy of a Christian minister; and he found no peace of mind, until he had recalled his first decision, and had formed a resolution to brave the difficulties of the office, and the dangers of a tropical climate, in the service of his Saviour."

On the 8th of May, 1814, in the chapel attached to that venerable pile of buildings, which imparts something of interest to the dreary tracts of river-bank that lie between Westminster and Vauxhall —the archi-episcopal palace of Lambeth—the first

Indian bishop was formally consecrated. The consecration sermon was preached by Dr. Rennell, Dean of Winchester. The subject was a suggestive one; but what it suggested it is not permitted to me to write. There is no exhumation of the discourse practicable, search, as we may, in public libraries or old book-shops. It is customary to publish these things; but good Dr. Rennell's consecration sermon was *not* published. Christianity had triumphed; but still, in spite of its triumph, Christianity was compelled to walk with discretion. There were thorns and briars, and broken glass and sharp flint-stones, to be avoided with cautious tread. The bishopric had been wrung from Parliament; but it was dangerous to make a noise about it. The least said, the soonest mended. The enemy had been beaten, but not annihilated; and it was deemed prudent not to invite any new attacks. So the sermon was left to languish in the obscurity of manuscript, secure from the stolid assaults of the Warings, the Twinings, and other ingenious members of the same college of alarmists, who saw a massacre in every thread of the lawn-sleeves, which were now about, for the first time, to form an item of an Indian outfit.

Having been elected a fellow of the Royal Society —having been complimented by the Christian Knowledge Society, who placed 1,000*l.* at his disposal for the promotion of their views in India—and having received from his friends a parting memorial in the shape of a superb silver inkstand, Bishop Middleton embarked for Calcutta. Among the passengers in

the *Warren Hastings* were two of the new archdeacons. It might be thought, and not unreasonably,
that a selection for these subordinate offices would
have been made from among those ministers, who had
long been bearing, in India, " the burden and heat
of the day:" but, except in the case of the Madras
archdeaconry, which was bestowed upon Mr. Mousley,
a resident chaplain, the appointments fell to the lot
of new men—fellows of Oxford. The Simeonites
were not much in favour in those days. Among the
passengers, too, was Dr. Bryce, who had been appointed, under the new charter, Scotch chaplain, and
who was destined afterwards to fill no inconsiderable
part in the annals of Indian controversial literature.

The voyage out was a prosperous and a pleasant
one. Middleton fitted up a library in his cabin,
" furnished with more than a hundred volumes,
Hebrew, Greek, Persian, Latin, French, and English
—theological, classical, mathematical, historical, and
poetical;" he preached on Sundays to an orderly and
attentive congregation, and was well pleased with
his fellow-passengers and the captain. Stopping at
Madeira, he was induced to preach to the factory
there; but, as there was no regularly consecrated
church, the mind of the formalist misgave him. " I
rather hesitated at first about preaching in such a
place; but I recollected that the bishops in England
preach in proprietary chapels, which are not a whit
better, and have less excuse; for the Portuguese
Government will not allow anything having the
interior of a church to be built by Protestants."

Why, under such circumstances, he should have hesitated to preach "in a room, with seats for the ladies, and a sort of desk for the clergyman," more than in the cuddy or on the quarter deck of the *Warren Hastings*, with the dinner table or the capstan for a pulpit, it is not very easy to discern. And it is still less easy to understand how one, claiming to be a successor of the apostles, can have hesitated at all about doing what the apostles did of old, and a greater than the apostles did before them.

On the 28th of November, 1814, the first Indian Bishop ascended the steps of one of the ghauts of Calcutta.   His landing, in his own words, "was without any éclat, for fear of alarming the prejudices of the natives."   On Christmas day he preached his first sermon before a congregation of 1,300 persons, and administered the sacrament to 160 communicants, including the Judges and the members of Council. "The day," he wrote to his friends in England, "will long be remembered in Calcutta."

"And so commenced the episcopal period of Christianity in India.   There was no commotion—no excitement at its dawn.   Offended Hinduism did not start up in arms; nor indignant Mohammedanism raise a warcry of death to the infidel.   English gentlemen asked each other, on the course, or at the dinner table, if they had seen the Bishop; and officious native sircars pressed their services upon the 'Lord Padre Sahib.'   But the heart of Hindu society beat calmly as was its wont.   Brahmanism stood not aghast at the sight of the lawn sleeves of the Bishop;

he preached in the Christian temple on the Christian's *bara din;* and that night the Europeans in Calcutta slept securely in their beds: securely next morning they went forth to their accustomed work. There was not a massacre; there was not a rebellion. Chowringhee was not in a blaze; the waters of the *Lall Diggy* did not run crimson with Christian blood. The merchant took his place at his desk; the public servant entered his office: and the native underlings salámed meekly and reverentially as ever. In the fort the English captain faced his native company; and the sepoy, whatever his caste, responded to the well-known word of command, with the ready discipline he had learned under the old charter. Everything went on according to wonted custom, in spite of the Bishop, and his lawn sleeves, and his sermon on Christmas day. No one looked differently; no one felt differently; and it really seemed probable, after all, that British dominion in the East would survive the episcopal blow.

"The truth is, that those of the natives—the better educated and more intelligent few—who really thought anything about the matter, thought the better of us for evincing this outward respect for our religion, and have thought the better of us and our faith ever since. All the trash that was written and spoken about alarming the Hindus and weakening our hold of India; all the ominous allusions to the Vellore massacre, and anticipations of new catastrophes of the same class, now appeared in their true light, and were valued at their proper worth. Mr. Buchanan's 'sanguinary doctrines,' as Mr. Twining ludicrously called them in one of his pamphlets, had now been fully reduced to practice; and yet not a drop of blood had been shed—not a blow struck—not a menace uttered —not a symptom of disquiet had evinced itself. Our empire in India was then 'not worth a year's purchase;' and yet now for thirty-five years has it survived that first awful episcopal sermon on Christmas day."*

Of the condition of the church, on the arrival of Bishop Middleton, some idea may be gathered from what has been written in other chapters of this work. "The total number of clergy," says Mr. Le Bas, the biographer of Bishop Middleton, " both civil and military, did not, there is reason to believe, in 1814, exceed thirty-two; in the proportion of fifteen for Bengal, twelve for Madras, and five for Bombay. This number, small as it was, was subject to continual reduction, by illness, death, necessary absence, or return to England. Such, for instance, was the amount of these casualties at Bombay on the arrival of Archdeacon Barnes in 1814, that he found at that presidency only one efficient clergyman on the establishment; and was compelled himself for some time to undertake the ordinary duties of a chaplain." Mr. Whitehead says that this computation is too high; and makes the following statement on the authority of Mr. Abbott, the ecclesiastical registrar:

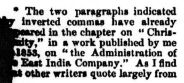

* The two paragraphs indicated by inverted commas have already appeared in the chapter on " Christianity," in a work published by me in 1853, on " the Administration of the East India Company." As I find that other writers quote largely from this book, sometimes with and sometimes without acknowledgment, I do not see why I should not quote from it myself, when it appears to me that I cannot say the same thing better in other words.

" On the arrival of Bishop Middleton in 1814, he found effective resident chaplains in Bengal, eight; in Madras, five or six; and in Bombay, one. Missionaries under episcopal jurisdiction, or licensed by the Bishop, there were none. India then possessed fifteen parochial clergy." We have now in the three presidencies more than two hundred clergymen of the Church of England.

" The grand evil," writes Mr Le Bas, " next to the want of the regular episcopal superintendence, was the insufficiency of the number of the clergy; it is painful to add that, few as they were, the churches, or places set apart for divine worship, were still fewer. At each presidency or seat of the local Governments there was one church, and one only; for the second church at Calcutta was private property, and the chaplain who officiated there was especially appointed to that service by the Court." [It was not less a church for all that]. " In the country there were one or two more churches at certain of the more important stations; but, in most of the places where the clergy were called upon to officiate, no such provision was made. A mess-room, a barrack, or, in some instances, the official court of the magistrate, was the only convenience that could be obtained for the assembling of a Christian congregation, and the public exercise of prayer and praise to the Almighty." Marriages were generally performed by commanding officers, or civil authorities, and the sacrament of baptism was often administerde by laymen. But there were worse things still in the opinion of the orthodox biographer ; for a minister of the Church of England—on one occasion certainly, perhaps on others—had " ventured on the performance of religious functions in a character, higher than that to which he had been ordained !"

The Bishop soon began to busy himself about forms, and to exhibit much orthodox zeal in the matter of church-building, " You will be glad," he wrote to Archdeacon Barnes, " to hear that, including a chapel at the gaol here, Surat chapel will be one of four now building in India. *Pray, direct that it be placed with the altar to the East;*" and again, " Pray request Mr. Carr to take care *that it be built in the proper direction, east and west; so that the altar be eastward.* The architects in India seem rather to affect variety than uniformity in this particular. *There has been sad irregularity !*" Sad, indeed !—But Brown and Buchanan, Martyn and Thomason, had not been much distressed by it ; or, at all events, had borne the affliction patiently and uncomplainingly. Perhaps, they had learnt no lessons in church architecture at Mr. Simeon's college rooms. The Simeon and Pretyman schools seem to have somewhat differed.

The Bishop was a martyr to the prickly heat. He complained piteously of it in his letters. " It has ignited," he said, " my whole frame ; and what with the sensations of pricking, and burning, and itching, and soreness, and lassitude, and irritability, I am little qualified for anything that requires attention." But there was something that irritated him even more than the prickly heat; and that was—Dr. Bryce. The same charter which tolerated a bishop tolerated also two Scotch clergymen; and the same ship which conveyed the Bishop to Calcutta, carried also the senior Scotch chaplain. The shipmates had not been long landed, before, as it is said, Dr. Bryce, lacking a presbyterian church for his own especial uses, applied to the bishop for the alternate use of the cathedral! The application, as might be expected, not proving successful, he obtained the use of the college hall, and there preached a sermon, in which little quarter was given to the predominance of episcopalianism; and he published it as a "Sermon preached at the opening of the Church of Calcutta." And to crown the whole, when the first stone of St. Andrew's Church was laid, with great national demonstrations and masonic ceremonials, Bishop Middleton was invited to attend.*

All this was gall and wormwood to the Bishop. It irritated him, as I have said, more than the prickly heat; and the irritation was kept alive by the astounding presumption of the Presbyterian community of Calcutta, who petitioned Parliament for the privilege of being married by their own ministers, and according to the rites of their own church. They

* Speaking of the appointment of the Scotch chaplains, and the erection of the Scotch churches in the three presidencies, Mr. Le Bas observes that "it was shown incontestably, that there was no occasion for such a movement, by the fact, that, when the new congregation was formed in Calcutta, it withdrew no more than 100 members from our communion, and that in the other presidences the defection was still more insignificant." This is very inconclusive. There may have been many others, not withdrawn from Episcopal communion, because never in it. Mr. Le Bas should have estimated the want by the number, who joined the Scotch congregation, when the church was erected.

gained their point too. The Scottish ministers at the presidencies were permitted to perform the ceremony of marriage for members of the Scottish church; and " it will easily be imagined," says the Bishop's biographer, " that occurrences of this description were not peculiarly animating or consolatory to Bishop Middleton."* Calcutta, indeed, was found to be a very hotbed of schism; and the Bishop thought it was very hard that the State should have conspired to disturb the even tenor of the Church's existence at so critical a time.

A new source of inquietude arose from the defective provisions of the letters patent. Bishop Middleton was a bishop without a clergy. There were clergymen in India—but there was no parochial clergy. There was no clergy over which he had supreme authority. The chaplains were Government chaplains, amenable to the orders of the secular authorities—sent hither and thither in general orders like a deputy collector, or a captain of engineers. The Bishop had really no power over them; and of this complaint was not unreasonably made. The Governor-General—Lord Moira—decided in favour of the authority of the Bishop; but the Court of

* In the celebrated "steeple" controversy also, the pugnacious Dr. Bryce was again victorious. The vexation of Mr. Le Bas, in relating this fresh instance of Presbyterian presumption, is not a little amusing. "St. Andrew's Church in Calcutta," he wrote in his Life of Middleton, "is a much more stately fabric than St. John's Cathedral, while the Scotch church at Madras is, perhaps, the noblest Christian edifice in Hindustan. It was built after the model of a church in Italy, with two fine domes, and to these, was added a spire, which, like that at Calcutta, towers very considerably above the steeple of every English place of worship!" The Bishop's biographer however consoled himself with the reflection, that the Court of Directors agreed to erect the Bombay spire as a matter of indifference not as a matter of right!—p. 347.

Directors repealed the decision: and the Bishop was no longer suffered to be commandant of the regiment of chaplains.*

In July, 1815, the office of confirmation was performed for the first time in Calcutta; and December of the same year witnessed the Bishop's first visitation. On the 18th of that month he left Calcutta for Madras. In the latter presidency, he found church affairs even in a less encouraging condition than in that which he had just left. In his own words, "within two years, a clergyman of good character was put under arrest by his commanding officer. In another instance, a military officer chose to have notice of the sacrament inserted in regimental orders; and, in a third, an officer ordered a chaplain to do the duty in a place so offensive, that no body could attend." The secular authorities were getting the upper hand sadly. But there was consolation and encouragement for him, at all events in one circumstance, that greeted his arrival at Madras. There was a splendid new church (St. George's) to be consecrated. "Yesterday," he wrote, "I consecrated a handsomer church than any which I recollect in London, supported on eighteen Ionic columns, which no English eye would distinguish from marble; with a lofty and elegant spire, and standing in a field (also to be consecrated) of five or six acres, surrounded with rows of palm trees. The whole conveys a magnificent idea of Christianity in the East. I was

* A later order of the Court, however, directed the Government to attend to the Bishop's recommendations.

assisted on this occasion by seven of my clergy, a great number to bring together in this country; and the solemnity seems to have been very gratifying to the inhabitants. This morning I confirmed nearly 300, of whom I rejoiced to find a large portion were adults. . . . A respect for the ordinances of our religion is gaining ground. To-morrow morning, I am to receive at ten o'clock a deputation from the Armenian nation who are numerous at Madras; and at eleven, no less a person than his highness the Nabob of the Carnatic who returns my visit; *and, on which occasion the guns will be fired from the fort.*" At these interviews the Nabob embraced him very affectionately, without, after the manner of Sivajee, sticking a knife into his bowels; and it does not appear that his highness, or any other potentate of heathendom, felt the least alarm for their hereditary faith from the appearance of the Lord Padre Sahib of the Feringhis at their gates.

But the secular authorities of Madras were not equally confident. They had not forgotten the Vellore affair. Visions of blood were still floating before their eyes. They thought a bishop a most dangerous, revolutionary personage—the representative of a pestilential heresy; and they anticipated that his visit to the southward would be the signal for another massacre. But the Bishop started with his family and his suite; visited the seven Pagodas, inspected the Capuchin Church and Jesuit's College at Pondicherry, where the Romanists with courteous toleration made him a present of books; halted at

Cuddalore, the seat of one of our earliest protestant missions; proceeded thence to the great Pagodas of Chillumbrum, where the Brahmans pressed forward to look at him, showed him the lions of their temple, and, instead of anticipating that he would demolish it, asked for a little money for its repair. It is not recorded in history that the episcopal tour produced either a rebellion or an earthquake.

At Tranquebar, where the first protestant missionaries had found a home, he was received with open arms. The population went out to meet him in the streets, or greeted him from the windows and the house-tops. "The place," he wrote, "is in great distress; and the people are living on incomes which, in this country, appear still smaller by comparison; but I never saw poverty more respectable. The mission there is everything, and the missionaries are the regular clergy of the place." Here he lived with the Governor; entertained him and the municipal officers in turn; contributed, at the expense of the Christian Knowledge Society, two hundred pounds to the mission; and then pursued his journey towards Tanjore, the seat of the illustrious labours of the apostolic Schwartz. The Rajah, who had been educated by the missionary, and who still called himself the good man's son, sent his Minister to the Christian Bishop, and invited him to the palace, where, descending from the musnud, he "received him at the steps of the durbar, embraced him with the warmest cordiality and courtesy, and, after the customary inquiries respecting his health, expressed the gratification with

which he saw the chief of our religious establishment
in his country and his Court." " He subsequently,"
says Mr. Le Bas, " assured an English officer, that no
occurrence, since he had occupied the throne, had
given him more lively gratification than this visit of
the English prelate ; and that since he must so soon
lose his society, he hoped to indemnify him by the
pleasure of his correspondence."

At Trichinopoly, the Bishop consecrated a church,
licensed the clergyman, confirmed about a hundred
persons, including several officers, and preached twice
on the Sunday.   At Palamcottah he was visited by a
deputation of Brahmans from the Tinnevelly Pagodas,
who came to pay their respects to the Lord Padre
Sahib, and  to represent that their church lands
yielded so little, after payment of Government demands, that the priests were in danger of starving :—
such being their lamentable position, they hailed with
delight the arrival of the English bishop, feeling sure
that he would interfere, as a brother, in their behalf.
Having dismissed this deputation with becoming
courtesy, he received another of native Christians,
who sung a hymn in Tamul; and the two parties
then quitted the camp together.

From Cochin, where the Bishop found " the Dutch
church shut up for want of a minister—the school in
the fort destroyed—the children left unbaptised—and
the sick unassisted ;" and where the Syrian church
was in an equally depressed state, he proceeded to
Cannanore, and thence to Bombay and Ceylon.  There
I need not follow him in detail.  In spite of the

ominous predictions of people who ought to have
known better, the first episcopal visitation produced
no sort of alarm or irritation throughout India, except in the puckah, well-verandahed houses of a few
professing Christians. Native princes received the
Christian bishop with reverence, and embraced him
with affection. Native priests came out from their
temples to welcome him, and implored his assistance
in their behalf. He came back to Calcutta again as
sound as he had quitted it. Not a hand had been
lifted up against him; not a stone had been cast at
him; not an affront had been put upon him. The
natives of India thought the better of us and our
religion — and the great question, which had been
discussed in scores of pamphlets and speeches, was
now set at rest for ever.

But the Bishop's troubles, which were of a different
class, were not yet quieted. There was much—in
Calcutta above all other places—to vex and to irritate
one of his peculiar frame of mind. Schism and in-
formality were the banes of his existence. It is
melancholy to read his complaints, and to think how
much cause of rejoicing there was, in at least some of
the circumstances which caused him so much annoy-
ance. I am afraid that in the affections of Bishop
Middleton, the Church was before the Gospel. Nay,
even the Church itself was a source of vexation to
him, where there was not proper episcopal control.

Unhappily for the peace of Bishop Middleton, the
missionary clause had been voted by Parliament soon
after the episcopal clause. The Church, it is true,

and were somewhat slow to respond to the invitation, or rather to avail itself of the permission of the Legislature. English clergymen were not eager to avail themselves of the privilege of imparting Christianity to the Gentiles. Two ministers, however, Greenward and Simmeon by name — the second probably a Swiss, were sent out by the Church Missionary Society in 1814. This was the beginning—others followed. But did the Bishop open his arms to receive the missionaries of the Church which he represented? No, they were thorns in his flesh. He talked of either licensing or silencing them, but he found it was beyond him to do either. He tolerated the missionaries in remote regions: he could even rejoice in their appearances upon the confines of civilization; but it was a different thing when they toiled at the very seat of the Supreme Government, and preached the Gospel without a license from any one but Christ, under the shadow of the episcopal residence itself. He did not recognise the value of the work done by Protestant ministers out of the pale of his own ecclesiastical jurisdiction. It was not Establishment work. It had not the stamp of the mitre upon it. It was not made legitimate by letters patent, or rendered lovely by lawn.

It was not likely that such men as Corrie and Thomason should regard these episcopal peculiarities without feelings of lively concern—perhaps, I might fully write, without lively contempt. That they d from him, on many points, is well known; situated as they were, it was only decorous that they should express themselves with moderation. " I was led," wrote the former, in a letter to his brother, " last Thursday into a long conversation with the Bishop respecting missionary proceedings, in which the Church Missionary Society and its views were brought forward and discussed. The Bishop's chief objection was, that the sending out of English clergymen as missionaries would prevent the East India Company from making such a provision of chaplains as they ought to make. As far as it goes, the argument is just; but I think he ought rather to adopt such missionaries, and, by pointing out to Government the benefits produced by them, to draw forth Government support which otherwise may not be afforded in any way."*

Mr. Corrie had returned to England, for the benefit of his health, a few weeks after the arrival of Bishop Middleton. Towards the close of the rainy season of 1817 he was again at his post. The Bishop had returned in the preceding cold weather. There being no vacancy at the presidency on Corrie's

* See also the Bishop's own letters *passim.* " But the missionaries in orders of the Church Missionary Society," he complains in one case, " are coming out continually. Three arrived very lately ; and they will become in a few years the parochial clergy. In one place the society have lately built a neat church, and appointed their minister ; and who can say anything against it ? . . Other cases of the same sort may be expected every day, and if the Church Missionary Society will supply ordained clergymen, wherever they are wanted, the Company may be relieved, indeed, of a heavy expense ; *but then what becomes of the Bishop's jurisdiction ?* " Again : " As to my recognising the missionaries, what can I do ? They will soon have in India a body of ordained clergymen, nearly half as numerous as the Company's chaplains ; *and I must either license them, or silence them—there is no alternative.* [The Italics are the Bishop's own]. But how can I silence men, who come to India under the authority of a clause in the charter ? " It does not seem to have occurred to Bishop Middleton, that they came to India, not merely under the authority of a clause in the Company's charter, but under the authority of a clause in the great Gospel charter of Christianity.

arrival, he was ordered to proceed to Benares.* At that time Brown and Martyn and Buchanan were dead. Thomason was at Calcutta. At Benares, as at Chunar, Corrie employed himself diligently; founding schools; correcting translations of the Scriptures; and doing incidentally as much missionary work as could be done without impairing his efficiency as a chaplain. Nothing could be more correct than Corrie's views of the relative claims to his services of the chaplaincy and of the mission. " If I were professedly a missionary," he wrote to Mr. Simeon, " and had the same prospect of entrance into this very citadel of idolatry, I should consider it a call to live and die in this place; but, as a chaplain of the Government, am I not to consider the disposal of Government as the voice of Providence to me? I can truly say that, in the prospect of leaving this place, I am oppressed; O Lord, undertake for me."

In the cold weather of 1818–19, Mr. Corrie was summoned to Calcutta to take his place there as a Presidency Chaplain. There the characteristic kind-

---

* On his way to Benares, he kept a journal. There is an entry, strikingly illustrative of the barbarity of those Ghat murders, which are so demonstrative of "the excellent moralities of the Gentoos," the "pure and unexceptionable religion," which had excited the enthusiasm of Sir Henry Montgomery. " During the 19th and 20th, we had an opportunity of witnessing two distressing instances of the unfeeling conduct of the Hindus towards the sick and dying. On one occasion, two women were employed at the river side, filling the mouth of a child with mud. Miss B. asked them, if the child were ill? One of them answered 'Yes;' Miss B :—'You are going to kill it outright.' On which they began to laugh, and talk with each other; and prosecuted their work of death. Farther on, a sick man was laid, with several people sitting round. A young and handsome Brahman was attempting to bind a weight round his neck, in order to sink him in the river, which the sick man was resisting, with marks of much remaining strength. Abdullah called out—'take him into some warm place, and he will recover;' to which the Brahman answered with a significant nod; 'Aye, aye; we will put him into a warm place;' on which the persons around laughed aloud."

liness and hospitality of his nature found such vent as was denied to them in the Mofussil. The social charities were largely cultivated by him. His doors were ever open to the stranger. He was continually surrounded by his friends. To the young he was especially accessible; and it was said of him, "as long as he lives, and wherever he lives, he will have as many people about him as fall in his way, until every corner is occupied, and he himself left without a corner."

It was about this time that the missionary zeal of Bishop Middleton began astonishingly to develope itself. The Archbishop of Canterbury had, in that year, 1818, as President of the Society for the Propagation of the Gospel, made a vigorous movement in favour of Indian Missions, by proposing to place 5,000*l.* at the disposal of the Bishop of Calcutta, to enable him to carry out the objects of the Institution —good hope being entertained of the result, now that the affairs of the Society were to be placed under " proper diocesan control." A Royal letter had been obtained on application to the Prince Regent, and large collections made on the strength of it. The biographer of Bishop Middleton says that "this intelligence was as the breath of life to him, as it showed that his urgent representations had at last succeeded in communicating a powerful impulse to the public feeling in England." It appears to me, that it would have been more correct if it had been stated that public feeling in England communicated a powerful impulse to Bishop Middleton.

x

These " splendid manifestations," it is said by the Bishop's historian, "confirmed him in the resolution to attempt the foundation of a Mission College at Calcutta." Here was a noble commencement of the Fund, which he had long wished to accumulate, for the establishment of a Collegiate Institution under Episcopal superintendence. The project was soon sketched out, and sent Home to the Propagation Society, the objects of the proposed college being thus represented :—

1. For instructing native and other Christian youths in the doctrines and discipline of the Church, in order to their becoming preachers, catechists, and schoolmasters.

2. For teaching the elements of useful knowledge, and the English language, to Mussulmans or Hindoos, having no object in such attainments beyond secular advantage.

3. For translating the Scriptures, the Liturgy, and moral and religious tracts.

4. For the reception of English Missionaries, to be sent out by the Society, on their first arrival in India.

The proposal was readily accepted by the Propagation Society, and the promised 5,000l. were placed at the Bishop's disposal. The Christian Knowledge Society also contributed 5,000l. towards the undertaking. Other large sums flowed in from other quarters. Government granted a plot of ground for the erection of the building—as noble a site as could have been found in the whole country—and the work of construction was speedily commenced. It has now been completed for more than a quarter of a century, during which time it has been, in its comely " Collegiate Gothic," an ornament to the river-bank upon which it stands. There is not perhaps a nobler monument of an unaccomplished purpose in any part of the world.

On the 15th October, 1820, the first stone of Bishop's College was laid, " with all due and impressive solemnity." It appears that the nature of the undertaking was not very clearly understood. One party " a sensible man, and a churchman too," much scandalised the Bishop, by asking him if his new college was a branch of the Baptist establishment at Serampore ! Mr. Jones, the contractor, died suddenly, whilst the edifice was in course of erection ; but, after a brief pause, it sprang up, none the less rapidly for this, under the superintendence of Captain Hutchinson of the Engineers. But they were getting on still faster at Serampore, and this made the Bishop a little anxious and impatient.

In 1821, Bishop Middleton went forth on a visitation-tour to Bombay and Ceylon. He arrived at the former place, towards the end of February, and remained there about five weeks—during which he held his visitation, consecrated two or three burial grounds, visited the caves of Elephanta, and received a vast number of visits of ceremony and invitations to dinner. Here he began to feel, more sensibly than before, that the climate was " telling" upon his constitution, and, in more than one letter, he complained of the lassitude which beset him, and of other dis-

tressing sensations, "symptomatic of decay." It was
whilst at Bombay, that he received intelligence of
the attempt, made at Queen Caroline's trial, to make
light of the imputation, that she had been present
during an indecorous exhibition of dancing by a
mountebank named Mahomet, on the plea that Bishop
Middleton and his family had attended a nautch at
the Governor-General's—the witness being a gentleman, who was a guest of the Bishop's at the time.
The Bishop wrote to a friend, requesting him to deny
the assertion in a London paper. "As his" (the
witness's) "topic," he wrote, "was no better, than that
Mahomet must have danced decently before the Queen,
because a Hindoo woman had danced decently at
Calcutta, his evidence might have been spared. *The
fact*, however, of my being there is utterly untrue.
He (the Governor-General) did me the favour of
taking charge of the ladies of my family, while I
remained with my books and business at home. I
am not quite sure that I was asked; but I could
safely swear that I was not there." The Governor-
General also thought it worth his while to deny the
imputation—in a very curious manner, too, according
to a statement in another letter from the Bishop:—
"Lord Hastings was very indignant at the dragging
in of the subject of Government House; and immediately wrote to the Lord Chancellor, explaining,
as was the truth, that there was no *dance* at his house
—the mere movement of the woman's feet, whilst she
was singing, not deserving the name." It may be a
question whether the singing, in such performances,

accompanies the dancing, or the dancing the singing ; but there are both singing and dancing ; and it is generally supposed that the latter, which gives the name to the exhibition, is, as grammarians say, " the more worthy " of the two. There are different styles of dancing ; a Hindustani nautch-girl does not dance like our Taglionis and Ceritos ; but if " movement of women's feet " to music, under such circumstances, does not constitute dancing, I do not know what does.*

Touching on his way at Cochin, to glance at the Syrian Churches there, the Bishop proceeded from Bombay to Ceylon, where he was hospitably entertained by Sir Eward Barnes, whose sublime intentions were, however, somewhat frustrated by the eccentricities of the weather. A magnificent fête had been prepared, some miles out of Colombo, and a gorgeous edifice, in the style of a large Gothic cathedral, had been erected, " after the Cingalese fashion of embellishment," in honour of the Bishop. Divers other preparations were made, on an equally grand scale, for the occasion ; but, on the evening before the fête, when the Bishop was dining at Government House, a tremendous storm arose, and entirely demolished the ecclesiastical structure. Foreshadowing the destiny of Bishop's College, the gorgeous Gothic edifice,

* At the same time I am bound to say that the dancing of nautch girls, on public occasions, at the Presidency, was, as far as my experience extends, never otherwise than decorous. I went to many nautches, when I first went out to India, and in my juvenile estimation they were dreary affairs. They were not even gracefully, much less licentiously attractive—differing greatly therein from the dancing of an earlier period, an account of which, partly quoted in a preceding chapter, I have been compelled to expurgate.

erected at so much expense, proved nothing but a magnificent failure. The Governor did the best he could under such circumstances; he substituted another kind of entertainment—but the disappointment was great and general. Better things, however, were done. "During my stay," wrote the Bishop, after his departure, "I had a visitation—two confirmations—three consecrations of churches, or buryinggrounds; I preached four times, and resuscitated the Promotion of Christian Knowledge District-Committee, and looked into the state of the schools; and, what is of most consequence, I got together a body of information respecting ecclesiastical affairs, which will furnish matter for a paper to be addressed to his Majesty's Government."[*] In June he sailed again for Calcutta.

On his arrival there, he found that Mr. Mill, Principal of the new College, and Mr. Alt, one of the professors, had already made their appearance on the scene of their future labours. The walls of the college had risen to an assuming height during his absence; and so far there was much to cheer him. But there were sources of inquietude too. Rammohun Roy was entering boldly the field of controversy: the Press—" that monstrous despotism, and tremendous

* Besides this, he ordained Mr. Armour, of whom an interesting account is to be found in Mr. Le Bas's book. "This extraordinary man," he says, "originally came out to Ceylon as a private soldier; but subsequently he took upon himself almost the work of an evangelist among the natives, who maintained a mere nominal profession of Christianity, always conducting his ministrations in strict conformity with the services and doctrines of the established Church. . . . . His heart's desire was that at some time he might be thought worthy to be received as an ordained missionary. . . . His whole soul was devoted to the service of God, and his truly Christian demeanour had won for him the cordial esteem of all ranks of men."

instrument of corruption, which some call the liberty
of the press "—was growing audacious; and he was
troubled about the question of precedence, the
authorities having given to the chief justices of the
three presidencies a place, on the social ladder, higher
up than that assigned to the Bishop of Calcutta.
Serampore, moreover, was flourishing in its rank soil
of heterodoxy; and a body of Christians had actually
built a chapel at Howrah, open to the ministration of
Protestant divines of all persuasions. His corre-
spondents, too, in England were very lax. Anxiously
expected communications, public and private, did not
arrive. All these evils—real and imaginary—preyed
upon his spirits, and affected his health. The hot
weather of 1822 found him in an irritable state, both
of body and of mind. On the 2nd of July, he
visited the college at an early hour of the afternoon; and, on the following day, went out with Mrs.
Middleton, before the sun was down, for an evening
drive. The slant rays shone distressingly upon him,
dazzled his eyes, and sickened him. He said that he
was struck; and he returned home. He passed that
night, and the following, in a state of extreme anxiety
and irritability: but it was not until the 4th, that, the
fever having increased to an alarming height, dear
Simon Nicolson was called in. It was then too late.
All the skill of that eminent practitioner—all the
unremitting attention of that kindest of men—could
not save the prostrated invalid. At one time certain
favourable symptoms developed themselves; but they
were only those delusive signs which so often are the

precursors of immediate death. And so it was. On the evening of the 8th of July, those favourable symptoms were followed by an alarming paroxysm of fever, attended with the most appalling agitation of mind. About nine o'clock, he was in a state of violent delirium; " his thoughts wandering, his articulation gone; his faculties, in short, a melancholy wreck, at the mercy of the tempest that had shattered them." To this succeeded a state of perfect serenity; and, a little before midnight, he died.

Such, briefly narrated, was the career of the first Indian Bishop. It will be gathered, perhaps, from the manner of my narration that I am not among the most ardent admirers of the prelate, whom Mr. Le Bas, with no great felicity of expression, described as " the father and the founder of the Protestant Episcopal Church of our Asiatic empire." He was the father of Protestant episcopacy in India, but he was not the father, and most assuredly he was not the founder, of the Episcopal Church. I do not know that he was the founder of anything but Bishop's College.

With every disposition to speak charitably of the prelatical character of Bishop Middleton, I am constrained to express my opinion that he was a cold and stately formalist. There may have been something in this very fact, especially to recommend him for employment, at a time, when it was apprehended, that Christian zeal would bring down upon us a sanguinary revolution, involving the forfeiture of our Indian empire. The alarmist party may have been somewhat

appeased by the appointment of so safe a man as
Bishop Middleton ; and his subsequent episcopal proceedings must have greatly confirmed the sense of
security, which his nomination engendered.   Nothing
was to be apprehended from the burning zeal of the
first bishop of Calcutta.   He was the man of all
others to uphold the dignity of our ecclesiastical
establishment, without exciting the fears, or offending
the prejudices of the natives of India.   He took
little interest in conversion-work ; and at one time
talked of silencing the whole missionary clergy.
Brahmanism was scarcely more offensive to him than
Protestant sectarianism ; and even a minister of the
Church of England, not on the Company's establishment, was a thorn in his episcopal flesh.   Puseyism
and Tractarianism were not known by those names,
when Bishop Middleton went out to India ; but he
was of the number of those, who esteem the Church
before the Gospel, who have an overflowing faith in
the efficacy of certain forms of brick-and-mortar, and
who believe that a peculiar odour of sanctity ascends
from prayers, offered up in an edifice, constructed
with due regard to the points of the compass.
No man could have had a higher sense of the
external importance of his office, or stickled more
rigidly for the due observance of the ceremonials
which he conceived to belong to it.   He had a decided
taste for military salutes, and struggled manfully for
social precedence.   In all this he was sincere.   He
wrought in accordance with his genuine convictions.   It
was not personal vanity that inflated him   Self was

not dominant over all. But he had an overweening
sense of the dignity and importance of his office.
He believed that it was his first duty to suffer nothing
to lower the standard of episcopal authority, or to
obscure its exterior glories. His zeal as a bishop
shot ever in advance of his fervour as a Christian.
This peculiarity was not without its uses. The
externals of religion had been too much neglected in
India. It was desirable that something more of
dignity should be imparted to the priestly character.
Lord Wellesley was described by Sir James Mackintosh as a *Sultanised* Anglo-Indian; Bishop Middleton would have *Sultanised* the episcopal office. He
was not without a motive—and a good one—in this.
But, doubtless, there are many good Christians, who
would fain have seen in his career a little less of the
bishop, and a little more of catholic Christianity.
He was an able and an active labourer in his way,
blameless in the relations of private life, and, as a
man, to be greatly respected. In a recent work on
the Anglo-Indian Church he stands labelled as "India's
first and greatest bishop." India's first bishop he
truly was, but who that has heard of Daniel Wilson,
can ever believe him to be her greatest?

## CHAPTER IX.

The Episcopate of Reginald Heber—The Bishopric in Commission—Heber's Early History—His Nomination to the See of Calcutta—State of Christianity on his arrival—His Tour in the Upper Provinces—Visitation in the South—State of the Southern Missions—Death of the Bishop—His Character.

It was in the steamy month of September, 1822, that Daniel Corrie, driven by ill-health from Calcutta, to seek a purer and more refreshing air upon the pleasant banks of the Hooghly river at Pultah Ghaut, took a pen one day into his hand, and wrote down the following words:—" This day sixteen years ago, I first landed in Calcutta.  How altered the state of society!  Then Mr. Brown was senior chaplain.  He had at that time, dear Martyn in his house, and received Parson and myself into his family.  Now he and his wife are numbered with the dead, and all their children returned. . . . How many other changes also, in the state of the religious society of Calcutta? so that Mr. U[dny] only remains of the friends of religion in his class of society of that day.  How varied has been the scene of my own Indian life!  In respect of public affairs, great changes, also, have taken place.  In ecclesiastical matters, great changes.  A bishop and archdeacon appointed in 1814, and Bishop's College has been the result.

The subject of missions has thus, by degrees, become one of acknowledged duty and advantage to society. The Bishop hurried off by sudden death, the Archdeacon taken off not two months after, more suddenly still; Parson and I appointed to exercise their functions *pro tempore*. I would, however, remark especially, the state of my own mind during this long period. I came to India chiefly with a view to the propagation of the Gospel; and that view, I trust I can say, has not been lost sight of. My time has been principally devoted to that object; my money, too, has chiefly gone in that cause. I trust a mission has been established at Chunar, Agra, and Benares, through my humble means, which will go on and increase with the increase of God."

Early in July, 1822, Bishop Middleton closed his eyes upon the world for ever. Early in October, 1823, his successor arrived at Calcutta. During fifteen months India was without a bishop. Throughout this interval the duties of the diocese were performed by Mr. Corrie and Mr. Parson. To the former it was a season of much suffering and much depression. Repeated attacks of fever prostrated his strength and turned his thoughts with eager expectancy towards the cool breezes of his native country. "God make you a greater blessing than ever to the Church," said one whose dying bed he was affectionately attending, "but don't waste your life in this country; go home and do good among the poor." To go home and do good among the poor were indeed a great thing to do; and if Corrie, at this time, in moments of sickness and depression, thought lovingly of the green villages of old England, where

> " The snow-white church upon her hill
> Sits like a thronèd lady sending out
> A gracious look all over her domain,"

and ever and anon embraced the idea of abandoning the scattered flocks on the wide arid plains of Hindostan, for one in some retired shady nook at home, where old men would have stood bare-headed before him, and children would have " plucked his gown to share the good man's smile," we must not think less admiringly of his fortitude and perseverance. He would have been a model of a parochial clergyman; and wherever his lot had been cast, he would have scattered blessings around him broad-cast, as the husbandman scatters the seed. But God willed it that he should labour upon Indian soil, that there he should live, and that there he should die. It was but for a little while that he thought of claiming his pension and ending his days as a parish priest. Bishop Heber came out to preside over the Indian Church, and one of his first public measures was the appointment of Mr. Corrie to the archdeaconry of Calcutta.

Reginald Heber, the second son of a Yorkshire gentleman of old family and good estate, was born at Malpas in the county of Chester, on the 21st of April, 1783. At a very early age he evinced signs of an amiable yet resolute disposition, a thoughtful inquiring mind, and such readiness of apprehension, and quickness of imagination, that he was a scholar and a poet before he was eight years old. He trans-

lated "Phædrus's Fables" into English verse in the
nursery; and being soon afterwards sent to the grammar-school at. Whitchurch, and after a little space,
to the care of a private tutor, resident at Neasdon,
in the western suburbs of London, he acquired the
character of a studious, thoughtful boy, eschewing
boisterous sports, delighting in long solitary rambles,
often with a volume of the "Fairy Queen" as his
companion; but still a favourite with his school-fellows,
for he was easily persuaded to tell them long stories,
drawn from memory or imagination, of deeds of
chivalry done long ago, in the old heroic times; or to
recite some romantic ballad of love and war, and marvellous self-devotion. He was very happy in the
choice of a friend; for the much-loved of his boyish
days was John Thornton, who carried back to school
after the holidays, reminiscences of the Clapham Sect,
and wrote to him about its members, after he had
turned his back upon academical Neasdon. "I think
that you are very lucky in your acquaintance with
Lord Teignmouth," wrote young Heber to his friend.
"They are such men as you have described him,
who are to keep us from sinking." He had surprising notions at that time of the might, majesty, and
dominion of the Church, and at the age of seventeen
wrote letters on ecclesiastical discipline and episcopal
supremacy, such as might have emanated from
Bishop Middleton himself.* It does not appear that

* Take, for example, the following
passage, which any reader now light-
ing upon for the first time might naturally suppose to belong to the preceding chapter, but for my positive
assurance that I have extracted it
from the "Life of Reginald Heber," by
his widow:—"The arbitrary suppression of ecclesiastical assemblies, the
disuse and contempt into which apos-

this disorder lasted very long. A healthier state of mind came with his wisdom teeth, and he was soon entirely cured.

In November, 1800, Reginald Heber was entered at Brazennose College, Oxford; and in the first year of his residence there, he obtained the University prize for Latin verse. In the spring of 1803, when he was just twenty years of age, he wrote, what is commonly regarded as the best prize poem in the English language. His "Palestine," at all events, is one of the few academical efforts of the kind that has survived the year—I might almost write, the day of its recitation. It gained for him great University distinction at the time, and is even now read with delight. He was not one, however, to be easily inflated by success; and he thanked God, in pure humility of spirit, only for the pleasure which his honours would impart to others. In November, 1804, he was elected a fellow of All Souls, in the hall of which college, his portrait is now suspended. In the following year, his "Essay on the Sense of Honour" gained the bachelor's prize for English prose. Soon afterwards, he accompanied his beloved friend, Mr. John Thornton, on a tour through the North of Europe, from which he returned in September, 1806. In the following year, he was ordained;

tolical censure and penances have fallen, and the number of chapels which, though many of them are served by episcopal clergymen, are yet independent of their spiritual head the bishop (and consequently equally schismatical with the ephod and teraphim of Micah), have, as you are no doubt well aware, stripped the Church so entirely of power, and rendered it in everything so dependent, that it has no ability to help itself on this or any other point. I sincerely pray that the Almighty would put it into the hearts of the nursing-mothers of the Church, to take some order for the comfort of her ministers."

and at once instituted to the family living of Hodnet, in the county of Salop. There for sixteen years he continued to perform, with unremitting devotion, the duties of a parish priest, greatly beloved by his flock, and loving them with parental tenderness. "Do not think that I fancy myself anything but what I am in truth," he wrote to John Thornton, "a prosperous man who has unremitted causes of gratitude, and whose principal apprehension ought to be that he has a greater share of earthly happiness than he knows how to manage." Sometimes in his humility, he was inclined to doubt whether he did not suffer his love of literature to beguile him from the quiet walk of the country pastor, and to devote too much, both of time and thought, to pleasant secular affairs unconnected with his ministry. There is something very attractive in quarterly-reviewing, and as it is attractive, so, for the time, is it absorbing, for quarter-day waits for no man; and, perhaps, the sermon was sometimes hurried over, or the round of visits curtailed, that the article might receive an additional polish, or be freighted with new matter. During this period of his life, he wrote many excellent papers in the *Quarterly*, some fugitive pieces in verse, and those hymns, which, in numerous places of public worship, are still, sabbath after sabbath, chaunted forth in praise and prayer to the Almighty, and of which it is small praise to say that while they are more poetical, they are not less devotional than any similar collection in the English language.

It was at Hodnet, in the December of 1822, that

Reginald Heber received from his old and cherished friend, Mr. Charles Wynn, who had recently been appointed to the Presidency of the India Board, a letter which raised a tumult of contending emotions in his breast. That letter related to the Indian Bishopric. Intelligence of the death of Bishop Middleton had arrived, and it had become necessary to appoint a successor. The epistle which Mr. Wynn addressed to the Rector of Hodnet did not contain an offer of the appointment, although it placed it within his reach. " I cannot expect," he wrote, " and certainly do not wish, that with your fair prospects of eminence at home, you should go to the Ganges for a mitre. Indeed, 5,000l. per annum for fifteen years, and a retiring pension of 1,500l. at the end of them, is not a temptation which could compensate you for quitting the situation and comforts which you now enjoy, if you were certain of never being promoted. You would, however, extremely oblige me by giving me, in the strictest confidence, your opinion as to those who have been, or are likely to be, suggested for that appointment ; and you would add to the obligation, if you could point out any one who, to an inferior degree of theological and literary quali fications, adds the same moderation, discretion, and active benevolence, which would make me feel that, if you were not destined, I trust, to be still more usefully employed at home, I should confer the greatest blessing upon India in recommending you."

Heber's answer to this flattering letter—more flattering, indeed, than a direct offer of the Bishopric,

Y

was one neither of acceptance nor of refusal. "I will confess," he wrote, "that (after reading missionary reports and some of Southey's articles in the *Quarterly*) I have sometimes been tempted to wish myself Bishop of Calcutta, and to fancy that I could be of service there. Had *you*, as was once reported, gone out to the East, I should have liked it beyond most other preferments. As it is, I am probably better at home, so far as my personal happiness is concerned, than in a situation, however distinguished and however splendidly paid, which involves so many sacrifices of health, home, and friendship." He added, that on such a question, it became him to consult those most nearly related to him—his wife, his mother, and his brother; and then went on to speak of the succession to the Bishopric, in a strain which we think every one will acknowledge to be highly honourable to the man. He urged the claims of those who had been long bearing the burden and heat of the day on the torrid plains of Hindostan. "There is one case," he wrote, "in which, however anxious I may be for the appointment, I should wish 'you to put me decidedly out of the question; I mean *if any eligible person should be found among the archdeacons and chaplains already in India*. The time may, perhaps, be not yet arrived for a division of the single unwieldy diocese into three, which otherwise might be done with ease and at no additional expense, by raising the three archdeacons to the episcopal dignity, and dividing the salary of the Bishop among them in addition to that which they already receive. If it were, such an arrangement might, I conceive, add greatly to the improvement and extension of Christian India; whilst, if the Bishop of Calcutta were made Primate, a unity of system and a power of appeal might be preserved as well as at present. But at all events it must be a great advantage to a Bishop to have been already for some time conversant with the wants, the habits, and the persons of his flock, his clergy and his heathen neighbours; and the advancement of a deserving man among their own number, might be a very beneficial stimulus to the activity and circumspection of the inferior clergy. Of the present archdeacons, however, I know nothing or next to nothing."

To this disinterested and sensible suggestion the answer was brief and conclusive. There was a practical difficulty in the way—if there were no other. It was urged that if one of the resident archdeacons were selected for the office, he would be compelled to return to England for consecration; and that in this way much time would be necessarily lost: whereas it was expedient to fill up the vacancy with the greatest possible despatch. This is not likely to have been the only consideration which had weight at the India Board; but there was no need to allege any other reason for not suffering promotion to go in the line of the profession. At all events, the elevation of one of the archdeacons was never seriously contemplated. Heber thought much and prayerfully on the momentous subject, and anxiously consulted his friends and his medical advisers. His wife readily consented to go, but there was a painful and embarrassing doubt about the health of his little daughter. The conflict, however, was not of long duration. He resolved not to accept the appointment. "Though I do not," he wrote to Mr. Wynn, "pretend to be indifferent to the power of raising a provision for my wife and child, and though this is the first point on which I should wish you to judge for me, I trust you will believe me when I say that there is a second, in my eyes, of far greater importance. I mean my probable comparative usefulness in India or in England. It has, indeed, been for several years a favourite day-dream of mine, to fancy myself conducting the affairs of an extensive mission, and by conciliation and caution, smoothing the difficulties, and appeasing the religious quarrels and jealousies which have hitherto chiefly opposed the progress of Christianity in the East." But considerations of a domestic character—considerations which have decided the fate of so many men against their own judgment, and against the interests of the public, pressed him strongly to remain in England. He was a husband and a father; and people told him that he must leave his little daughter behind, and that the mother must remain with the child. His friends, too, were all against the acceptance of the oriental appointment, and so a second time Reginald Heber declined the Bishopric.

But Mr. Wynn, still hopeful of his friend's eventual acceptance of the offer, abstained from filling up the appointment; and meanwhile, Heber was disquieted by the thought of the election he had made.

The evils of the state of exile, which had at first loomed in such gigantic proportions before him, began to dwindle down into comparative insignificance; he beheld more and more clearly the great work to be done in India; and his heart sunk within him, when he thought of the opportunities of extended usefulness which he had thus wilfully neglected. The missionary spirit burnt strongly within, and would not suffer him rest. "I hope I am not an enthusiast," he wrote at this time to John Thornton, "but I am, and have long been, most anxious for the cause of Christianity in India; and I have persuaded myself that I am not ill-adapted to contribute to its eventual success, by conciliating the different sects employed in the work, and by directing, and in some instances reining in and moderating their zeal." "Surely," he wrote to another beloved correspondent, "a priest should be like a soldier, who is bound to go on any service for which he thinks himself suited, and for which a fair opening occurs, however he may privately prefer staying at home, or may flatter himself with the hopes of a more advantageous situation afterwards; I may also say that, for many years, I hardly know how long, I have had a lurking fondness for all which belongs to India or Asia; that there are no travels which I have read with so much interest as those in that country, and that I have often felt that I should like to be in the very situation which has now been offered to me, as a director of missionaries, and ministering to the spiritual wants of a large colony."

With these feelings strong within him, doubtful exceedingly of the propriety of the course which he had adopted, and praying earnestly for guidance, he determined, if possible, to recal his refusal, and wrote, therefore, to Mr. Wynn, declaring that, if the appointment were still vacant, he was ready to respond to the call. The appointment was still vacant; and the President at once submitted his friend's name to the King. Heber said afterwards, that he should never have known peace of mind, if in this conjuncture he had turned a deaf ear to the call of duty.

On the 1st of June, 1823, Reginald Heber was consecrated Bishop of Calcutta. On the 8th, he preached his last sermon in England, in aid of the Society for Promoting Christian Knowledge, whose valedictory address he received a few days afterwards, declaring in his reply, that his great hope was, that he might be the chief missionary of the society in the East.* On the 16th, he embarked for Calcutta, on board the *Grenville*, and after an uneventful voyage, during which the Bishop prosecuted with some ardour his Persian and Hindostanee studies, he entered upon the duties of his diocese at the commencement of the cold weather.

And in what state did he find—not his diocese— but Christ's church in India, when he arrived and looked about him with the eyes of the chief mis-

* See Memorandum by Sir Robert Inglis, a dear friend of Reginald Heber, and one to whom the cause of Christianity in India is greatly indebted—"We shall long remember the sensation which he produced, when he declared that his last hope would be to be the chief missionary of the Society in the East; and the emotion with which we knelt down, sorrowing most of all that we should see his face no more."—"*Memoir of Reginald Heber*," *by his Widow.*

sionary? I fear that there was not much to rejoice
his spirit; for whatever apprehensions may, at one
time, have been entertained, that under the "religious
clauses" of the Charter of 1813, there would be a
vast flooding-in of Christian missionaries, they soon
disappeared before the barren, un-alarming fact. In
truth, the Christianity of England was slow to accept
the invitation. There had been, ever since the commencement of the century, a steady, gradual change
for the better, in the general Christian deportment of
the English in India; and, doubtless, some impression
had been made upon the dense mass of heathenism by
which they were surrounded.* But the toleration so
long sought, and so bravely contended for by the
great advocates of the Christian cause in England,
had not given that impetus to it which was so much
desired and expected. To such men as Daniel Corrie,
who had done so much single-handed, and who looked
eagerly to the time when fellow-labourers would crowd
in to aid him, this was mortifying in the extreme.
He was himself so emphatically a missionary chaplain, that he believed a large accession of churchmen

---

* "There is a growing respect for religion in this place," wrote Corrie, in 1817. Indeed, there are many instances of serious religion through-out the Presidency, both among the civil and military servants of the Company. The chaplains have en-tered into a regular communication with each other in common with the Committee of the Church Mis-sionary Society, and at some stations things seem wonderfully prepared for them. At one station where Mr. Spring is (Tellicherry) he found that through a native Christian, whom God had stirred up to read the Scriptures to his neighbours, thirteen of the heathen were anxious to be baptized. We hear, too, that near Delhi a company of about five hundred persons had collected to converse on the subject of the Christian Scriptures, which had been circulated among them, and that they had resolved to become Chris-tians, although they professed an unwillingness to associate with the English on account of their eating all kind of food. I hope they will learn the ways of God more per-fectly."

to the establishment would alone suffice to evangelise India. But the chaplains were not appointed; and ministers of the Church, not on the Establishment, were slow to avail themselves of the privilege that had been conceded to them, and to enter, as free lances, the service of their master in a heathen land. "The desirableness of some extension of our present establishment," wrote Corrie to his honoured father in the Gospel, Mr. Simeon, "is beyond all dispute. The most careless among us cry 'shame' on the want of attention of our rulers to this point. If we had a sufficient establishment of proper chaplains, we need be under no anxiety about evangelizing India; but who can supply the places of Brown, Buchanan, Jeffereys, and Martyn. It seems almost as if Mr. Carey's prophecy were coming true, that God would not employ us in the work of evangelization. Amidst the great attention we hear of excited to the distribution of the Scriptures, how comes it none of our brethren offer *themselves* to come and distribute the word of life? And what are we, who believe episcopacy to be the order of the primitive church, to do for duly ordained pastors from among the native converts."

But although missionaries came but slowly, the religious societies, which since the commencement of the century had been gathering strength in England, were actively at work. The Christian Knowledge Society, the Gospel Propagation Society, the Church Missionary Society, the Bible Society—had all ramified into different parts of India, and each in its own

way was diffusing the light of Truth.* Missionary
stations had sprung up in different parts of the
country, at greater intervals it is true than might
have been desired; and the great missionary college
on the banks of the Hooghly had at least " begun
operations." Then, too, a marked improvement was
visible in the outward manifestations of professing
Christianity. There was far more self-assertion in it
than there ever had been before. Several churches
had been built in the outlying parts of the country.
A place set apart for Christian worship was no
longer the distinguishing mark of a great presidential
town. Everywhere the natives of the country were
becoming more and more sensible of the fact that the
Feringhees had a religion of their own, and were not
ashamed to assert it.

To Heber, fresh from a country where from any
hill-top may be seen spire after spire, or tower after
tower, rising up from our quiet villages, the destitution of India in this respect may have been painful in
the extreme. But to Corrie, now his archdeacon,
who remembered a period of far greater destitution,
there was something encouraging in the change.
" When I arrived in Bengal," he wrote in 1824,

* See Correspondence of Daniel
Corrie, *passim — exempli gratiâ :—*
" First, there is the Diocesan Committee, which confines itself to supplying those only who understand
English, with bibles, prayer-books,
and tracts. Next, the Church Missionary Society, which supplies the
native Christians with bibles and
prayer-books in the native languages,
as well as its more direct objects.
Then the School Book Society,
which supplies elementary books in
all languages for all descriptions of
persons; and then the glorious
Bible Society, like ' the lion which
coucheth,' embracing all classes and
climes in the distribution of the
words of eternal life. If to these
be added the labours of missionaries
of different denominations, it will
appear that the Kingdom of God is
near to India. Of missionaries,
however, we have as yet but a scanty
supply." (July, 1818.)

"there was only one place of Protestant worship in Calcutta,* and not a building appropriated to worship, out of Calcutta, belonging to the English. There are now in Calcutta four places of worship in the established Church; besides the mission college and three dissenting chapels. There is a church at Dacca, Benares, Chunar, Futtyghur, and Meerut. Churches are in the course of erection at Agra and Cawnpore. Whilst at the old stations of Dinapore and Berhampore public worship is still performed in an empty barrack. There are at Monghyr and Benares dissenting chapels, and perhaps at some of the upper stations also. All this has not been accomplished without considerable individual exertion as well as public support; and though individual piety is still lamentably scarce, yet much more of public attention to religious observances prevails than formerly, and also much more of individual piety."

Such, stated by one who had watched with the deepest interest the progress here indicated, and had contributed perhaps more than any man living to the acceleration of that progress, was the state of the Anglican Church in Bengal, at the period of Bishop Heber's arrival. In the same letter, the good Archdeacon, whose true missionary spirit no ecclesiastical honors could quench, spoke also of the progress that had been made in the extension of the Christian Church in the dark places of heathendom. "With respect to the natives," he wrote, "when I arrived in

* This is surely a mistake. There were two Protestant churches in Calcutta at that time—the old or mission church and St. John's Cathedral.

the country, a few converts were found at Serampore; and a few, I believe, existed at Dinapore:
nor were there any attempts entered upon beyond
those places, except at Cutwah, where the late missionary Chamberlaine had settled.   Now we have a
few native converts in Calcutta, at Burdwan, and at
Cutwah and its branch in Beerbhoom; at Monghyr,
Buxar, Benares, Chunar, and Meerut.   In each of
these places a few converts are found; and what will
eventually work greatly for the good of the heathen,
some of the Roman Catholic converts and descendants
of Europeans, who had become quite native in their
habits and language, are attracted by the labours of
the missionaries at those places; and in some of
them, as at Chunar, where the native congregation is
the largest on this side of India, they constitute the
chief part.   Besides these I might mention Meerut
and Futtyghur,* where missionaries are labouring
and some converts have been gained.   Thus where
all was darkness, now here and there, a glimmering
of light begins to prevail."

Many, doubtless, will ask what the Baptist missionaries were doing at this time—they who had prayed
so earnestly, and waited so hopefully, and toiled so
bravely for that grand opening of the gates of
heathendom which was to give the Christian brethren
free scope for the exercise of their vocation in all

---

* I would call the attention of
those who have recently said and
written so much of special provi-
dences discernible in the incidents
of the recent military rebellion in
India, that not only were Meerut
and Futtehghur (now associated in
men's minds with some of the
saddest events of that calamitous
history) the first places in the North-
Western Provinces in which Christian churches were erected, but were
also among the earliest seats of our
Protestant missions.

parts of the great Indies. Truly, such a change as
this must have added vastly to their strength! They
were no longer at the mercy of a Government—no
longer on sufferance in a strange land. Whatever
might have been the self-imposed obstructions to the
free ingress into India of the "lordly Episcopalians,"
surely the "inspired cobblers" would be eager to
rush into their appointed work. Up the river and
down the river, on the opposite bank of the river,
and in remote places where no rivers were, they were
now free to itinerate; and it might be conceived,
therefore, that Serampore, having done such great
things in the face of almost every possible obstruction,
would, now that these obstructions were removed,
emerge into a state of far higher grandeur and glory.
But they who know the real character of the Serampore missionaries will hardly anticipate that result.
The missionary clause of the Charter of 1814 gave
them the security that they desired, but it imparted
to them no fresh vigour or new strength. It enabled
them to pursue, without alarm and anxiety, the
steady progressive course which they had marked
out from the first; and as they believed that their
success depended upon their gradual, well-considered
advances, they were not men to encourage any
impetuous notions of taking heathendom by storm.
It was a great thing for them that they now felt
secure of their position on the banks of the Hooghly,
for they had once seriously contemplated the necessity of seeking a new home on the Irrawaddy, under
the protection of an Eastern despot. Indeed, they

needed little else ; and they went on with their
translations, and they established mission stations in
Bengal and Orissa (principally under native converts);
and they multiplied their schools, and they distributed the word of God ; and, if they did not see
clearly before them the result of their teaching, they
still were sustained by the knowledge that they were
not labouring in vain.

There are some, I know, who will not be satisfied
with this general statement of their success, and will
ask for the statistics of the mission.  The success
of a missionary enterprise is not to be tested by
statistics.  It appears, however, that in the year
1815-16-17, the Serampore missionaries baptized into
their Church between four and five hundred persons ;
and that they had about 10,000 children in their
schools.  In the three years above mentioned, they
distributed not less than 300,000 copies of religious
tracts in twenty different languages, besides translations of the Scriptures, and there were at least
some gratifying proofs that all this good seed had not
been scattered in vain.

Up to this time, the Serampore mission and the
Baptist mission were identical.  All the Baptist
missionaries from England owned the supremacy of
Carey, Marshman, and Ward.  But the complete
Christian union, which had imparted so much strength
to the fraternity, was doomed to be dissolved ; and
before Bishop Heber arrived in Calcutta, there was
a Baptist Mission strenuously at work there, owning
no allegiance to Serampore.  The Serampore brother-

hood were at issue with the Committee of the Baptist Society at home, on some important questions connected with the government of the Mission. The younger missionaries sided with the Society, and left Serampore, to establish themselves in Calcutta. The first and foremost of these were Dr. Yates and Mr. Pearce, who lived to take a prominent place among the missionaries of Bengal. Into the history of this disruption, which was the work of years, and was not finally and formally accomplished before 1827, I do not purpose to enter. It is enough that henceforth we are to regard the Serampore missionaries and the Baptist missionaries as two separate bodies, having only a common faith and a common object.

And far off in the Burmese territory another little party of devoted Baptists were labouring bravely in the good cause. The Serampore missionaries had many years before turned their attention to that field of enterprise; Mr. Chater had laboured there for some years, and had translated the gospel of St. Matthew into the Burman language. But after a while he had removed himself to Ceylon; and others, also, after a brief residence at Rangoon, had betaken themselves to more alluring fields. Mr. Felix Carey, the eldest son of the patriarch of Serampore, had, at an early period, gone forth as a missionary to Burmah; but in the felicitous language of his father, he had "*shrivelled into an ambassador;*" and had scandalised the brethren on the banks of the Hooghly, by appearing at Calcutta, with the cortége of an Eastern prince "in the highest style of oriental splendour." The field, however, had not been deserted. Mr. and Mrs. Judson were labouring there, and Mr. Hough was aiding their efforts. They were Americans in communication with the Baptist connection,* and are worthy of all honour. The Judsons had been driven out of Bengal; and, after further wanderings in uncertainty and anxiety, had, at last, by God's providence, been cast upon the shore of the Burmese empire. When Bishop Heber arrived in India, they had been labouring among the Budhists for some ten years; and they had achieved no contemptible success. Their later history is well known. The captivity of Mrs. Judson is one of the most deeply interesting chapters in the whole history of missionary enterprise. Dr. Judson, who survived her for many years, and whose name was subsequently borne by two other ladies, with some claim also to mention in this book, has been called, and not without establishing his title to such a distinction, the "apostle of Burmah." The American Baptist churches have made that great field of labour their own, and will ever be honourably identified with the victories there achieved.

Such, as regarded by Reginald Heber, on his first arrival at Calcutta, were some of the most noticeable matters connected with the then existing state of Christianity in India. What he learnt upon the great subject was principally derived from the reports of others. But he soon determined to see what he could with his own eyes, and in the month of June,

* The Judsons had gone out to India as pædo-Baptists, but had been converted and baptised at Serampore.

he started upon a journey to the Upper Provinces. With the principal incidents of this journey, the English public have been rendered pleasantly familiar through the medium of one of the most attractive books ever devoted to an Indian subject. Every one has read Bishop Heber's Journal. I do not, therefore, purpose to indent upon it for illustrative matter. The impression made upon his mind by what he saw of the progress of Christianity, in the course of his journey, was of a favourable and encouraging kind. "There are," he wrote, in October 1824, "on the whole more native Christians than I calculated on finding when I last wrote to you. At Chunar there is really a large congregation, as many as seventy or eighty; still, principally women—soldiers' wives or widows, but who have most of them been actual converts, and retain many of their natural peculiarities. The women in receiving the sacrament would not lift up their veils, and even received the bread on one corner of them, lest their bare hand should be touched. All of a certain age appear to have been brought over by Corrie while he was in this neighbourhood; the present missionaries do little more, though decent and zealous men, than keep up his numbers. They are prudent, however, and conciliating, and everybody tells me, are respected and esteemed by the natives. The system of street-preaching, or obtruding themselves in a forward or offensive manner on the public notice, as is frequently done in Calcutta, is here quite unheard of; at least, among the missionaries of the Church of England. By this quiet way of proceed-

ing, it is probable that few opportunities of doing
good will be lost, and that many occasions of mischief
and danger will be prevented." He believed, indeed,
that caution was necessary to success; and that
nothing would so surely retard the progress of Christianity as the over-zealous and indiscreet efforts of its
professors.

But he was not one to suffer caution to degenerate
into timidity. Ever as he went, he remembered what
he had said before leaving England, about being the
chief missionary in the East. He took the liveliest
interest in the native converts, and never neglected
an opportunity of communing with them. To Corrie
all this was delightful. "His visit," wrote the good
Archdeacon, "cannot fail to increase the disposition
of the British to help on the work of missions. At
Buxar, he sat down in the hut of the native catechist
and heard the Christians read, and questioned them
in their catechisms; at Benares, he went in his robes
to the Hindostanee chapel, where Mr. Morris offi-
ciates, and pronounced the blessing; and the same at
Chunar. He has acquired sufficient Hindostanee to
give the blessing in that language. Also at Benares,
he administered confirmation to fourteen native
Christians, and afterwards the Lord's Supper: and
at Chunar to fifty-seven native Christians. He asked
the questions and pronounced the prayer in confirmation in Hindostanee, and also the words addressed
in giving the elements in the Lord's Supper. Some
of the old alarmists still remain, who, by these proceedings, are silenced, if not convinced; and scoffers

z

are put to shame. The Bishop also visits all the missionary native schools as he proceeds; and the missionaries are greatly encouraged by the interest he takes in their proceedings."

The progress of Bishop Heber through Central and Northern India, created no greater sensation than his predecessor's tour in the South. At Benares, the great stronghold of Hindooism, the Bishop was at first taken for the patriarch of Constantinople. As he proceeded upwards, holy men of all denominations made obeisance to him. Nothing, as he wrote to the Governor-General, occurred to excite the jealousy of the natives. " Of that jealousy, I must say," he wrote to Lord Amherst; "I have hitherto neither seen nor heard any indications. The very small degree of attention which I have excited has been apparently that of curiosity only. The King of Oude and his court expressed a wish to be present at Mr. Ricketts' (the Resident's) marriage, pretty much as they might have done, had it been a puppet-show; and as his Majesty is said to be curious in costumes, I suspect that the novelty of my lawn sleeves may have, in part, induced him to honour me, by asking for my picture. From the Brahmins and Fakirs," he continued, " of both religions, I have had pretty frequent visits. Some of the Mussulmans have affected to treat me as of nearly the same faith with themselves, and to call me their ecclesiastical superior, as well as of the Christians; but these compliments have generally concluded with a modest statement (like that of Sterne's Franciscan) of the poverty of their order. A rupee or two, with a request that they would remember me in their prayers, I have found, on such occasions, extremely well taken; and it has been, I hope, no compromise of my religious opinions." The Brahmins of Southern India had welcomed Bishop Middleton somewhat in the same way. Whatsoever their amount of religious zeal, they were not averse to Christian buxees.

But although Bishop Heber believed that the natives of Upper India had very little pure love for their several religions—although he saw that Hindoos and Mussulmans were being drawn closer and closer to each other in the bonds of a common bastard faith —he did not contend that, therefore, there was no danger in indiscreet interference. He seems, indeed, to have had an insight into the character and the temper of the people of Upper India, very remarkable considering his limited experience. "They are," he wrote to Lord Amherst, "a proud and irritable people; as yet, I apprehend, by no means thoroughly reconciled to the English or their Government; not unlikely to draw a sabre against any one who should offend their prejudices, and though caring little for religion itself, extremely likely to adopt the name of religion as a cockade, if induced by other and less ostensible motives to take up arms against their masters. Under such circumstances, Government certainly act most wisely in a careful abstinence from all show of interference; and it is still more fortunate that the inhabitants of these (the North-Western) Provinces have not at present the remotest suspicion that any such interference is contemplated." Viewed by the light of more recent history, there seems to be a suggestion of prophesy in this. The words are full of weighty significance and worthy at all times to be held in remembrance.*

The Christmas of 1824 was spent by Bishop Heber at Meerut. There, the elder Mr. Fisher, a chaplain on the establishment, a man of great piety and worth, had a considerable native congregation. The state of affairs at this large military station made a most favourable impression on the Bishop's mind. "I was

* There are some passages in this and other letters, written about the same time, which, although not bearing upon the immediate subject of this work, I shall perhaps be excused for citing. "Through the Company's territories," remarks the bishop, "what have perhaps struck me most forcibly, are the great moderation and the general ability with which the different civil functionaries apparently perform their arduous duties, and the uniform good order and obedience to the laws which are enforced through so vast a tract of country, amid a warlike, an armed, and I do not think a very well-affected population. The unfavourable circumstances appear to be *the total want of honourable employment for the energies and ambition of the higher rank of natives*, and the extreme numerical insufficiency of the establishment allowed by the Company for the administration of justice, the collection of revenue, and, I am almost tempted to add, the permanent security and internal defence of their empire." There was at this time a restless feeling in the upper provinces of India, and a general revolt of the native army, if not the whole armed population of the country, appeared to be no improbable contingency. Circumstances, not wholly dissimilar to those of the early part of 1857, had occurred, or were still in operation.

to give some colour to this suspicion of a coming danger. The mutiny at Barrackpore seemed to indicate the temper of our troops, and the war in Burmah, occupying, as it did, the attention of the Government, and diverting to a distant point no small part of our military strength, suggested that a favourable moment had arrived for a hostile internal movement. Bishop Heber was so alive to the supposed danger, that he wrote a farewell letter to his wife, to be delivered to her in the event of his falling by the hands of the insurgents. But in November he seemed to think that the danger had subsided, and he wrote: "A general revolt was, a little time since, thought not unlikely, but the period seems now gone by; and the alarming mutiny at Barrackpore was apparently made in concert with no other regiment. But there certainly is, in all the Doab, in Oude, and Rohilcund, an immense mass of armed, idle, and disaffected population, and I am inclined to doubt whether the Hon. Company's tenure of their possessions is worth many years' purchase, unless they place their army on a more numerous establishment than it now is, and do something more for the internal improvement of the country, and the contentment of the higher ranks of the natives, than they have hitherto seemed inclined to do."— *Life of Bishop Heber, by his Widow.*

greatly pleased," he wrote to Lord Amherst, "with the church, chaplain, and congregation of Meerut, all of which are more English than anything of the kind which I have seen in India. In Mr. Fisher, the chaplain, I had, I confess, been led to expect some share of fanaticism and intemperate zeal, of both of which I am bound to acquit him. The sermon which I heard him preach was extremely plain and sensible, and with regard to his native converts, who are numerous, he has solemnly assured me, and I have not the smallest reason to disbelieve him, that he has sought after none of them, and given instruction to none, who have not voluntarily come to request it of him. Two such came, whilst I was in Meerut; and a third, during the same time, received baptism. Mr. Fisher asked me to perform this ceremony myself, but in consequence of the rule which I have laid down not to become needlessly conspicuous in the pursuit of objects which are not my immediate concern, I declined. For the same reason I have abstained from distributing tracts, or acting in any way, which might excite the jealousy of those whom it is on all accounts desirable to conciliate. The work of conversion is, I think, silently going on; but those who wish it best will be most ready to say '*festina lente.*'"

It was not improbably "the story of the sepoy," which had caused Bishop Heber to regard Mr. Fisher as an over-zealous and indiscreet man. This story was then some years old, but it was discussed by Heber on this visit to Meerut—and we may be sure, not in the same spirit in which it was commented upon, a third part of a century afterwards. The story was this: A naik or corporal of the 1st battalion of the 25th Regiment of Native Infantry, was in the year 1819 converted to Christianity by the agency, direct or indirect, of Mr. Fisher, and formally baptized.[*] He was a man of good character, much esteemed by his comrades; and his conversion created no little excitement among the Brahmins, of which his battalion was mainly composed. From the society of his comrades he necessarily became an outcast. He could not work with them; he could not eat with them; he could not join in their religious ceremonies. The excitement created in the lines by the apostacy of Purrubdeen Pandeh attracted the attention of the regimental authorities and subsequently of the Government, and there was an inquiry into the circumstances attending the conversion of the man. The result was that he was removed from the regiment. He was not dismissed; he was not, as has been said, "punished, because he became a Christian." He was offered either translation to another regiment in a higher rank, or a pension in accordance with the scale of the rank which he had attained. He chose the latter. He said that it should never be said of him that he had obtained any worldly advantage by taking up the cross. He, therefore, refused promotion. But the question

[*] A native missionary laboured at Meerut, under Mr. Fisher's auspices. See Corrie's "Memoirs." "Mr. H. Fisher at Delhi, his father at Meerut, and Mr. Tornans at Cawnpore, have each a native missionary, who labours around them, and instructs especially those natives who profess Christianity."

which has arisen does not relate to the behaviour of
the convert, but to the conduct of the Government.
The conduct of the Government, in this instance,
was in the autumn of 1857 denounced from a large
number of Protestant pulpits, in all parts of the
British isles. It was said that a sepoy at Meerut
had been dismissed from the service because he had
dared to become a Christian. And it was asked,
with a latitude of logic, which, astounding though it
was to every instructed mind, took the understandings
of large congregations by storms, whether the ways
of God to man were not justified in a very striking
manner by the fact that the great catastrophe of the
sepoy revolt in Upper India had commenced in that
very station which, nearly forty years before, had been
the scene of the unparalleled iniquity of the sepoy's
dismissal. The cause of this clerical outburst, on a
solemn day of fast and humiliation, was the extensive
distribution by the Church Missionary Society of a
circular letter signed by its secretaries, in which this
story of the sepoy was told with an inaccuracy, which
however unintentional, was most mischievous in its
results; and in which the great disasters in Upper
India, that had filled so many homes with mourning,
were attributed to the unholy conduct both of the
Christian Government and the Christian community
in India. The contents of that document were taken
upon trust by hundreds of English clergymen, who
not having previously given a thought to the subject of Christianity in India, rejoiced in the oppor-
tune arrival of an available suggestion—and I cannot

say that I am surprised at the effect of the circular, for it bore the honoured name of Mr. Henry Venn.[*]

From the North-Western Provinces of India Bishop Heber proceeded to Bombay. It was no insignificant proof of the progress that had been made in the external assertion of Christianity by a Christian Government and a Christian community, that he found there were five churches for him to consecrate, though Bishop Middleton had visited Bombay only four years before. And as a further proof of the Christian feeling both of the Government and of the community, it is to be recorded that the Bishop's efforts for the establishment, throughout the diocese, of "district committees in aid of Bishop's College and the Society's Missions in India," were warmly seconded by both. A meeting was held in furtherance of these objects, at which the Governor of Bombay, the Commander-in-Chief, and most of the principal officers of Government attended; and the Bishop was especially delighted because the Governor who had given him this support was so great and so good a man as Mountstuart Elphinstone.[†]

In the month of August 1825, Bishop Heber took ship for Ceylon. In that beautiful island there appeared to him to be "better hopes of an abundant and early harvest of Christianity than are to be found

[*] See Appendix.

[†] As the fact here stated is of some interest and importance, in connection with the much-mooted question as to the extent to which the servants of Government in India may properly take part in public meetings for the promotion of Christianity, I give the Bishop's own words :—" A sermon preached on Whit Sunday at St. Thomas's Church was succeeded the following day by a meeting of the friends of our Society, attended by the Governor, the Honourable Mr. Elphinstone, the chief and two puisne justices, the Commander-in-Chief (Sir Charles Colville), and almost all the mem-

in all India besides."   Nothing could have been more
cordial than his intercourse with the missionaries of
the island—nothing more pleasing than the impression
which it left on their minds.  His sojourn among them
was brief, but eventful.*  A missionary meeting was
held, at which the Governor not only attended but
presided ; and a committee was formed similar to that
established at Bombay.   Heber said afterwards that
he had passed a most interesting month in Ceylon, but
never in his life so laborious an one.  He had intended
to spend the ensuing Christmas at Madras and to
visit the Southern Provinces, before the setting in
of the summer heats—but this idea was afterwards
abandoned, and the cold weather of 1825 found him
again located in Calcutta.

Here one of his first labours was the establishment
of a diocesan committee of the Society for the Propagation of the Gospel, with the same objects as those

bers of Government, together with
all the clergy of the island, and a
majority of the principal civil, naval,
and military officers now within the
limits of the Presidency. . . . .
An example has thus been set to
Ceylon, Madras, and Calcutta, which
is of the greater value from Mr.
Elphinstone's high reputation for
talent, and pre-eminent knowledge
of the natives of India, their feelings,
and interests."—*Letter to the Rev. A.
Hamilton, Secretary to the Incorpo-
rated Society for the Propagation of
the Gospel in Foreign Parts.—Life of
Reginald Heber, by his Widow, vol. ii.,
pp.* 317, 318.

* Mr. Robinson, at this time the
bishop's chaplain, gives the following account of Heber's first meeting with the Ceylon missionaries :—
" At daybreak I attended his lordship six miles from Colombo to Cotta,
the principal missionary station.  He
was received, on entering, by five
missionaries, and Mr. Lambert read
an address, in the name of all, expressive of their joy at ranging
themselves under his paternal authority. . . . .  The scene was most
beautiful.  We were embowered in
the sequestered woods of Ceylon, in
the midst of a heathen population;
and here was a transaction worthy
of an apostolic age,—a Christian
bishop, his heart full of love, and full
of zeal for the cause of his Divine
Master, received in his proper character by a body of missionaries of
his own Church, who, with full confidence and affection, ranged themselves under his authority, as his
servants and fellow-labourers,—men
of devoted piety, of sober wisdom,
whose labours were at that moment
before him, and whose reward is in
heaven."

already formed at Bombay and Ceylon. It was his
earnest desire to enlist the sympathies of all the chief
members of the Anglo-Indian community in behalf of
the great cause of Christian missions in the East.
There had been meetings before this for missionary
purposes, and committees had been formed, but they
had been confined mainly to the missionaries themselves and to the local clergy; but Heber desired to
engage in the good work a far wider circle of Christians, and he appealed, therefore, boldly, in his own
name, to the Anglo-Indian community at large. He
sent a circular letter to all the chief European residents of Calcutta, in which, after adverting to what
had taken place at Bombay and Colombo, he announced his intention of preaching a sermon, on
Advent Sunday, on behalf of the Society for the
Propagation of the Gospel, and of holding a meeting,
to which he invited them, at his own house, on the
following day. The circular appears to have been
worded with great care. Nothing could have been
better calculated to catch the timid and the wavering.
It called, at the outset, the attention of the Christian
community to the proceedings of a meeting held at
Bombay, "in which the Honourable Mr. Elphinstone
and all the members of the Government took an
active and munificent part, and which has been since
followed up by collections in all the different churches
of that presidency, and by the accession of the names
of the most distinguished civil and military officers
at its principal stations." No one knew better
than Bishop Heber that, although much of the old

alarm, with which the English in India, and especially the servants of Government, had contemplated anything like interference with the religions or the religious usages of the people, had greatly subsided, there was still some of the ancient leaven remaining, especially among the higher official functionaries of the presidency. The practical support, therefore, given to the Bishop's missionary exertions at Bombay by Mr. Elphinstone, who was held in the highest estimation in all parts of India as a model of a high-minded and sagacious Indian statesman, was a great fact, which Heber knew well was worth more to the missionary cause than a phalanx of serried arguments. But still he recognised the expediency of emphatically declaring that nothing was further from his thoughts than a violent crusade against the religions of the country. He was, above all things, anxious not to irritate or to alarm the public mind. " I will only beg leave to add my hope," he proceeded to say in this remarkable appeal, " that the caution and temper displayed in all the measures and by all the functionaries of the benevolent society whose cause I plead; the inoffensive and useful nature of the institution of Bishop's College; and the countenance and support which, in consequence, both these have received from our sovereign and countrymen at home, and in this country from so many distinguished individuals in the service of her Majesty and the Honourable Company, will be regarded as sufficient grounds of assurance that, neither in the projected meeting, nor in the association consequent to it, anything will be suffered which is likely to give offence to our unconverted fellow-subjects, or which is at variance with that wise respect for their feelings and prejudices, which has been uniformly maintained and enforced by the Government of British India."

The logic of this is, that the highest servants of the Government may attend missionary meetings without offending the prejudices or alarming the minds of the natives of the country. More than thirty years have passed since this theory was insinuated by Bishop Heber—a man moderate, although zealous, and cautious without timidity— but still the extent to which it may be safely carried out in practice is one of the most difficult points within the entire range of the great missionary question. People are even now hotly discussing it, and with no nearer approach to its solution than had been attained in Bishop Heber's days. In a subsequent chapter of this work, something more may be said on this important subject. Here it is sufficient to indicate that at the beginning of the second quarter of the present century it was not conceived that the participation of Government servants, in proceedings at all events of a deliberative character, having for their object the evangelisation of Hindoos and Mussulmans, was in any way censurable or objectionable. The Bishop's appeal was responded to heartily and generously at Calcutta, as it had been at Bombay; and he was so much pleased with the support he received, that he declared that if it had not been for considerations connected with the health and the education of his children, he would have desired nothing better than to end his days in his diocese. How much his heart was with the missionaries, and what a comprehensive view he took of their labours in all parts of the country, may be gathered from an elaborate letter which he wrote at this time to the Secretary of the Christian Knowledge Society, and from another to the Propagation Society, both of which throw considerable light on the state of Christianity in India at the close of the first quarter of the present century.[*]

In the early part of 1826, accompanied by Mr. Robinson, afterwards Archdeacon of Madras, Bishop Heber took ship for the southern coast. He was about to fulfil the intention formed, but frustrated, in the preceding year, of making a visitation tour through the southern part of his gigantic diocese. He was much pleased with everything that he saw at Madras—with the Governor (Sir Thomas Munro)— with the clergy—with the churches—with the missionary establishment at Vepery—with the Christian converts and with the native schools. There was unmistakeable evidence that much had been done in that part of the country to diffuse the light of truth among the heathen. It was at Madras that the first English church had been built. It was on the Madras coast that the first Protestant mission had been planted. It was on the Madras coast that the early Syrian churches had numbered their Christian converts by thousands. The whole country was alive

* See "Life of Reginald Heber," Vol. II., pp. 344—360; and 365—368.

with historical traditions and associations which irre-
sistibly appealed to his imagination.   He was about
to traverse the scenes of the early labours of Ziegenbalg, of Schwartz, and of Schulze—he, " the chief
missionary," to tread in the footprints of the *first.*

There was one thing, however, which disquieted
him at this time.   There was sharp contention among
the Southern missionaries upon a point, which, from
the very commencement of the Christian labours of
the Protestant Church in the East, had been a subject
of more or less deliberation and discussion.   Everybody knows that Caste is the great stumbling-block
of Christianity.   Well aware of this difficulty, the
Jesuits, with their usual address, had sought rather
to enlist it into their service than to make war upon
it as an abomination.   The Brahminical cord was, in
their eyes, a serviceable institution.   Nay, indeed,
they Brahminised themselves.   " Christianity made
easy," was what they aimed at; and they achieved
considerable success.   By not being over-nice in these
matters, they made what they called " converts" by
thousands—converts to a Christianity only one degree
removed from the heathenism which they were said to
have abjured.   The early Protestant missionaries were
satisfied with no conversions that were not genuine.
But they had not grappled with the great difficulty
of Caste.   A large number of their first converts
were men of the lowest caste, or of no caste at all.
But, as time advanced and their labours extended,
they perceived the necessity of some concessions to
an institution so interwoven with the very life of

Hindoo society, and they suffered converts of different castes to sit apart from each other at church, and to communicate separately at the Lord's table. This necessity was deeply deplored by Ziegenbalg, by Schwartz, by Gerecké, and other holy men, who prayed earnestly that God would so turn the hearts of their converts as to make all this social exclusiveness a folly and an abomination in their eyes; but well considering the whole matter, and setting before them the example of the early apostles, they came to the conclusion that by insisting too rigidly upon the observance of an unappreciable equality, they would jeopardise the success of the great cause to the promotion of which they had given their lives. All through the eighteenth century this system of concession appears to have been recognised by the Protestant missionaries. But early in the nineteenth, the Baptists of Serampore set their faces strenuously against it. The utter denial of Caste was held to be an essential condition of Christianity. Carey, Marshman, and Ward would have nothing to do with men, who desired to carry with them, into their new conversion-state, any of the old garments of heathenism, which they had worn in their days of darkness.* And some of the younger missionaries, in Southern India, had now determined to carry into practice the same views of the duty of a Christian teacher, and had steadfastly arrayed themselves against the toleration which was still the rule of their elder brethren on the coast.

* See ante, page 238.

There was strife, therefore, among the missionaries, which Heber was anxious to allay. The question had been brought before him, before he quitted Bengal. He had there sought to arm himself with all the information that he could obtain, respecting not only the practice of the earlier Protestant missionaries, but the true nature of the institution of Caste. There was then in Bishop's College a Christian convert, known as Christian David. He had been a pupil of Schwartz; and was truly a remarkable man. No less distinguished for his intelligence than for his piety, he was regarded by the good Bishop as the one of all others to whom he might most expediently refer for the solution of his doubts. Heber drew up, therefore, a series of questions, which he submitted to the native Christian, and received from him a series of replies, stated not only in excellent English, but with a force and precision which could not be easily surpassed.

First, with regard to the nature of Caste, it was declared by Christian David, that it was, among the natives of Southern India, " purely a worldly idea "— " not connected in their minds with any notion of true or false religion;" that the native converts, drawn from the higher castes, were disinclined to intercourse with low-caste proselytes, not on religious or superstitious grounds, but simply for social reasons; that there were certain distinctions between high-caste and low-caste persons, not by any means ideal, and that these distinctions were not to be gilded over merely by the acquisition of worldly wealth. He especially set forth that low-caste people indulged habitually in an unseemly mode of speech—frequently using coarse or indecent expressions very revolting to the feelings of high-caste men; and that they were altogether less decorous and self-respectful in their way of life. Learning, he said, might elevate them; and if a pariah became learned he was called a pundit, and respected by the Church; and then his brother converts would associate with him, but still they would not "from worldly fear or pride" eat with him from the same dish. From the days of Ziegenbalg downwards they had been wont to sit at church in two separate divisions, and had communicated separately at the Lord's table, drinking out of the same cup, but the high-caste converts drinking first. As a proof, however, that these were regarded as merely worldly distinctions, Christian David said that high-caste and low-caste, among the Christian congregations of the South, were buried in a common burial ground, and took part promiscuously in the funeral ceremonies, "as if with the consciousness, contrary to the heathen nations, that death levelled all distinctions."

Rather by mild remonstrance and persuasion than by the enactment of any stringent rules, which might have proved great obstructions to Christianity, the elder missionaries had sought to mitigate the evil; and Christian David declared that under the ministration of Schwartz the evil had considerably diminished. But Mr. Rhenius, of the Church Missionary Society, a truly conscientious and devout Christian,

A A

had taken other views of the duties of Christian teachers, and had gained over to his opinions the younger missionaries in the South; so that they agreed, as I have said, among themselves, to make the total repudiation of Caste, even in its mere social aspect, an essential condition of admittance to the Christian Church; and they had, moreover, spoken and preached against the elder missionaries—even the most venerated of their predecessors—denouncing them as "corrupters of the Gospel" for having permitted such things to soil the purity of Christianity. Of all this Christian David spoke with profound regret. His own opinions were naturally inclined towards the doctrine and the practice of his old master Christian Schwartz. The mild interference and affectionate advice of the Bishop might, he thought, dispose the hearts of the younger missionaries towards greater toleration and forbearance.

Very earnestly and very conscientiously did Heber revolve this important subject in his mind. It is in accordance with all that we know of the character of the man, that he should have inclined towards the more conciliatory practices of the elder missionaries. But he deferred any final decision, until the opportunity should arrive for the collection of further information and the delivery of a sounder and fuller judgment on the spot. When, therefore, he visited the Southern Presidency, he wrote letters of inquiry to some of the principal missionaries, and instituted a select committee of the Christian Knowledge Society for the purpose of making further investigations into the subject. From one letter written to the Rev. D. Schreivogel, though little more than a series of questions, the bent of his opinions may be derived. It appeared to him, after much deliberate consideration, that Caste, as represented to exist among the Christian converts on the Coast, was in reality an institution differing little in its essential features from the social exclusiveness prevailing in Christian countries. Is there no such thing, he asked himself, as Caste in Europe? Is there no such thing as Caste in America? Do not the high and the low sit apart in our English churches? Do not our well-dressed high-caste folks go up first to the altar to communicate? Do high and low sit down to meat together—do their children attend the same schools? Are there no pariahs amongst us? In other civilized countries, is there not a prevailing sense of Caste, apart from all associations of worldly distinction? Does not the Spanish hidalgo wear his Caste bravely beneath his threadbare cloak? Is the wealthiest mulatto fit companion for the poorest white? It may be called Caste in one part of the world; it may be called blood, or anything else in another; but in its essential features the one thing differs but little from the other. It is an intelligible and appreciable Christian principle that all men in the sight of God are equal. But it is equally certain that all are not equal in the sight of Man; and it is a fair presumption that God never intended them to be equal. Social distinctions exist everywhere; and if, argued the Bishop, the distinctions which exist among the converts on the Southern coast

A A 2

are merely social distinctions, why should we endanger
the success of our efforts by endeavouring to enforce
a law of equality, which is maintained among no other
classes of men?

In this wise thought Bishop Heber. He had said
from the first, that if he could be of any service to
the Christian cause in India, it would be as a mode-
rator—that by a conciliatory course, smoothing down
the asperities of the over-zealous, he might hope to
do much good as the chief missionary; and now he
believed that it was his duty to cast in the weight of
his authority upon the side of those who had resolved
not to pour too much of new wine into the old bottles.
But many wise and devout Christians since that time
have believed that the "gentle Heber" was altogether
wrong; and another Bishop, at a later period of the
annals of Christianity in India, reversed his decision,
by emphatically pronouncing against all toleration for
the iniquities of Caste. He regarded the institution
altogether with other eyes. It was, in Bishop Wilson's
estimation, an ingrained part of the religion of Hindooism; and it is not to be doubted that in the
unconverted state of the Hindoo mind, Caste is much
more than a social or a civil institution. But what
Christian David affirmed, and what Bishop Heber
believed, was, that in the converted state it ceased to
be associated in men's minds with the articles of their
faith, and was regarded only as a matter of worldly
pride or social convenience. This may have been
right, or may have been wrong. But whether right
or wrong, Bishop Heber firmly believed that he was

making no compromise with any of the essential truths of Christianity. He believed, on the other hand, that he was deciding as the Apostles of old would have decided; and that such a decision would conduce to the diffusion of genuine Christianity.

Still pondering these things in his mind, the Bishop quitted Madras, and turned his face towards the South. He had been obliged, not without regret, to abandon the idea of visiting Tranquebar. Perhaps it was as well that he did so—for there could be no other than painful associations suggested by the fallen glories of the first Protestant mission; and there was little, indeed nothing, that he could do, in the face of the decrees of the Danish Government, to restore it to its former vitality. It was proposed by the authorities to absorb the remaining missionaries into the Establishment, and so to suffer the Mission to die a natural death. One of them, thus threatened, and unwilling to " apostatise to a chaplaincy," wrote to the Bishop, beseeching him to cause his translation to the Vepery Mission, where he would no longer be subject to the Danish Government. At Cuddalore, the Mission, founded by M. Schulze in 1736, was scarcely in a more flourishing condition. Mr. Rosen, who had taken charge of it only a short time before, found that the native congregation consisted of barely fifty members, though it had once numbered three hundred. Everywhere, indeed, there were signs of painful decadence in the old historic Missions of Southern India, except, perhaps, at Tanjore, where the labours of Schwartz, more reverenced by a native prince than those of Ziegenbalg by a Christian Government, were still bearing good fruit. In the Mission Church, on the evening of Easter Day, when the service was performed in Tamul, the Bishop pronouncing the blessing, there were gathered together no less than thirteen hundred Christian converts. The Bishop was touched to the heart by the spectacle of their devotion; and declared that one such day was worth years of common life.*

The Bishop spent some days at Tanjore, in the course of which he made the acquaintance of the Rajah, who, years before, had been the pupil and the friend of Schwartz, and who still held the good man in the most reverential and affectionate remembrance. The great missionary's place was still filled by Mr. Kohloff, now well stricken in years, but labouring with unabated zeal in the cause of his Master. For him also the Rajah had a profound respect—saying, at times, " Whatever John Kohloff asks of me shall

---

* See Archdeacon Robinson's "Last Days of Bishop Heber." The Archdeacon gives a pleasing account of this congregation:—"I desired," he says, "one of the native priests to ascertain how many were present, and I found they exceeded thirteen hundred. . . . . I have seen no congregation, even in Europe, by whom the responses of the liturgy are more generally or correctly made, or where the psalmody is more devotional and correct. The effect was more than electric, it was a deep and thrilling interest, in which memory, and hope, and joy mingled with the devotion of the hour, to hear so many voices, but lately rescued from the polluting services of the pagoda, joining in the fine and heavenly music of the Easter Hymn and the Hundredth Psalm, and utter-ing the loud 'Amen' at the end of every prayer. For the last ten years I have longed to witness a scene like this, but the reality exceeds all my expectations. I wish that some of those (if any of that small number still remain) who deem all missionary exertion, under any circumstances, a senseless chimera, and confound the humble and silent efforts of these devoted men with the dreams of fanaticism or the frauds of imposture, could have witnessed this sensible refutation of their cold and heartless theories. The Bishop's heart was full; and never shall I forget the energy of his manner and the heavenly expression of his countenance, when he exclaimed, as I assisted him to take off his robes, 'Gladly would I exchange years of common life for one such day as this.'"

be done." It was a great thing, indeed, for the
mission that such a man sat on the throne of Tanjore; and so deeply was Heber impressed with a
grateful sense of what the Rajah had done for Christianity, that he composed a short prayer for the
temporal and the spiritual welfare of the Prince, to
be translated into Tamul, and used in all the mission
churches throughout the province. It ended with a
supplication for his conversion to Christianity. What
would have been thought of this some years before?
Thousands of native converts were then taught by
the Lord Padre Sahib of the Feringhees to pray for
the apostasy of the ruler of the country, who had
recently been on a pilgrimage to Benares. It is easy
to imagine what an outcry this would have excited
some twenty years before—how Heber's "sanguinary"
indiscretion would have been denounced as the origin
of every subsequent disaster. Even now the incident
may be regarded by many not without some feeling of
wonder. At all events, it cannot be said that, in that
part of the country, Christianity did not openly assert
itself under the auspices of the great representative
of the hierarchy of England.

On the 1st of April, the Bishop arrived at Trichinopoly, where he found the Mission in a very decayed
state; and on the following morning, he preached at
the station church. In the afternoon he confirmed
fifty-two candidates. He appeared to be in good
health; full of animation, full of energy. But the
day was unusually hot, and in the evening, he complained of languor, and was induced to forego his

intention of attending the native congregation. But
the following morning found him again at his work.
He went at daybreak to the Mission church in the
Fort, and after listening to the service in Tamul,
confirmed several native converts, made many inquiries
about the state of the Mission, and received an
address from the native Christians praying that he
would provide them with a spiritual chief. He then
went home; and, as is the wont of Englishmen in
India after their morning labours, prepared himself
for the bath. No mortal eye ever saw him alive
from that time. The corpse of Reginald Heber was
found by his alarmed attendants; his soul had gone
to its rest.

There is no need that I should write anything
about the character of Reginald Heber; for every one
knows what were the gentleness, the amenity, the
goodness of the man—how rich he was in intellectual gifts, and yet how much richer in charity and
loving-kindness and good-will towards men, and in
lowly reverence for his God. It is enough that it
should be said in this place, that with him the Church
was not before the Gospel, and that he was more of
a missionary than an ecclesiast. It had been from
the first his ambition, not to be the head of the
Anglican Church in India, but to be " the first mis·
sionary in the East;" and although he did not go
about preaching in unknown tongues to the benighted
children of the soil, he gave up heart, head, time,
health, life itself, to the great work of diffusing the
light of truth, in the manner which he believed to be

most surely calculated to result in eventual success. It may be said that there was no grand enthusiasm— no heroic ardour in the man.　And truly there is little of fiery zeal discernible in his character and his career.　The first of living missionaries has described him as "the gentle Heber:" * and gentle he was in the best, the holiest, the most Christian sense. Gentle, too, he was on principle — gentle the system by which he hoped to turn aside the heathens from their superstitions.　But more genuine earnestness was nowhere to be found; although it was of the reasoning and reflecting kind; not impetuous or impulsive.　Equally removed from the extreme views of those who at that time contended, and do still contend, that all men in authority—all the servants of the State—should scrupulously abstain from taking part, direct or indirect, in the conversion of the people; and of those, on the other hand, who would counsel a course of unsparing iconoclasm, striking down the false Gods of the heathen with the strong hand of the Christian conqueror, were the opinions which he encouraged from the first, and which under the influence of time and ripening experience grew into settled convictions.　He was anxious that nothing should be done to alarm or to irritate the public mind; and, therefore, he always counselled prudence and forbearance, and a due regard, especially on the part of Government, for the feelings and prejudices of the unconverted.　But he believed, at the same time, that Christian men could not assert their

* Dr. Duff's "Letters on the Indian Mutiny."

Christianity too boldly; and that it was the duty of the head of the Christian Church in India to give no uncertain sound. Bishop Middleton had conceived that any open and direct episcopal connection with missionary societies was impossible. Bishop Heber thought otherwise, and two months after his arrival, he accepted the office of President of the Auxiliary Church Missionary Society at Calcutta. Bishop Middleton had conceived it to be impossible for him to ordain to the ministry a Christian convert who had been for some time employed as a catechist by the Christian Knowledge Society. Bishop Heber ordained him out of hand, and sent his examination papers to the Archbishop of Canterbury.* Bishop Middleton had talked about "silencing" the missionary clergy: Bishop Heber opened his arms to receive them, and desired that they should be allowed the freest utterance of their opinions without regard to their conventional orthodoxy. And they, in turn, were glad to submit themselves to him. "They all cheerfully," he said,—"such at least as were of the Church of England—received licenses and submitted themselves to my authority. They are, in fact, very respectable and pains-taking young men, who are doing far more in the way of converting and educating the natives than I expected, and are well pleased to find themselves recognised as regular clergymen, and treated accordingly."

* And I have no doubt that they both surprised and delighted the Archbishop, for the candidate for holy orders was that Christian David of whom I have already spoken, and whose answers to Heber's queries on the subject of Caste in the churches are distinguished by a high order of intelligence.

There is no doubt that this general toleration, this catholic sympathy, imparted strength, as it gave union to the Christian cause.* It assuredly endeared Heber to a large number of his fellow-labourers, and removed the impression that, however much the establishment of the Indian episcopate may have added dignity and stateliness to the Anglican Church, it had done little to give an impetus to vital Christianity. Some, indeed, thought that the Bishop was too regardless of form, that he did not sufficiently parade the mitre, and rustle the crinoline of his lawn sleeves. Indeed, he was guilty of the episcopal solecism of wearing a "solah topee," (or white-pith hat) and encasing his lower limbs in loose white trousers, like any subaltern or indigo-planter in that torrid clime.† But although his episcopal majesty was thus stripped of its externals, it never became a jest; and there was seldom a truer bishop—*επισκοπος*—or overseer; seldom one who overlooked his flock with a more comprehensive eye, or who did more to keep them together in the bonds of a common brotherhood.

---

* Hear what Archdeacon Corrie said about this feature of his episcopal character:—"Our Bishop is the most free from party views of any man I ever met with. In a ruler this is beautiful; and I have felt the benefit resulting from it. But a few years ago it seemed as if it was impossible to exercise such a spirit. Certainly, in those days, Bishop Heber would not have been raised to the bench, when unlimited submission was the only condition of co-operation. Some would have given up the Church Missionary Society, and resolved all the episcopal societies into the diocesan connection."

† *See* Archdeacon Robinson's "Last Days of Bishop Heber."—

"The Bishop's manner everywhere is exceedingly popular; and though there are some points, such as his wearing white trousers and a white hat, which I could wish were altered with more regard to his station, and which perhaps strike me the more after being accustomed to the particular attention of Bishop Middleton to such points, yet really I feel compelled to forgive him, when I observe his unreserved frankness, his anxious and serious wish to do all the good in his power. . . . I see the advantage which Christianity and our Church must possess in such a character to win their way, and to keep all together in India."

It was no small thing for the episcopate of Bishop Heber, it was no small thing for the cause of Christianity in India, that at that time Corrie and Thomason were at hand, to aid the Bishop alike with their wise counsel and their active ministrations. Thomason, who for some time had been the very life of all the religious and educational associations in the metropolis of British India—who was, indeed, a kind of secretary-general, unstinting of labour, and unsparing of self—betook himself to England, a few months before the close of Heber's career, to return thence only to die. There was much in his character that resembled the good Bishop's, and therefore, that endeared him to his chief.* His departure was a heavy loss to the Christian cause; but Corrie remained behind to carry on the good work. He preached Heber's funeral sermon; and, as next in ecclesiastical rank, discharged the duties of the episcopate. About the permanent succession to the office he was naturally very anxious, although he never expected, and, indeed, never desired to see the mitre on his own brows. Deeply deploring Heber's death, he had written to his friend Sherer,—" Our late beloved Bishop was so entirely a missionary, that we can

---

* The "gentleness" both of his personal character, and of the system which he had prescribed to himself as that best calculated to give effect to his efforts for the conversion of the heathen, was one of the features in which he most resembled the Bishop. Speaking of the early educational measures, consequent upon the passing of the Charter of 1813, in which he was so deeply interested, he wrote to Sir Charles (then Mr.) Metcalfe: "In the Chinsurah schools the Scripture has not been introduced. They are schools for knowledge, not for religion. *I apprehend these gentle expedients are the best.* But time will show how and when effectual good is to be accomplished. The field is vast, and the mind is bewildered in looking around it. It seems, however, time to fix on some definite spot, and say, ' Here we begin.'"— *MS. Correspondence.*

scarcely hope to see one like him;"—and as, ever
and anon, reports came from England, of this or that
expected nomination, he was disquieted by the apprehension that the choice of the Government at home
would fall upon a mere Churchman. "Rumours," he
wrote, "have reached us about a new bishop, and
men unknown to missionary fame have been named.
This seems sad: let us in patience wait the event."
He waited, and he found that the bishopric had
been conferred, not on a missionary priest, but on
a pictorial critic.

# CHAPTER X.

Government connexion with Idolatry—Juggernauth—The British Government and the Religious Endowments of the People—The Pilgrim-Tax—
Gradual extension of State-Patronage—Results of our interference.

WHAT I have written hitherto, has been chiefly of
the efforts and the endeavours—the failures and the
successes—of individual men, either wholly unconnected with the British Government, and suffering
contumely, perhaps, at its hands; or only bound to it
as the ministers of a State Church, and the recipients
of certain sums of State money. It is time now,
however, that I should speak of the Government
itself; of the position which it occupied—of the
attitude which it assumed, at this time; of the manner
in which by its tolerance it fostered, or by its intolerance it depressed the false religions of the country.
It has been incidentally shown that up to this time,
it was the almost universal opinion, even of those
who were most diligent in their endeavours for the
promotion of Christianity in India, that the Government, as such, should stand entirely aloof from all
missionary proceedings; that any direct interference
of the State for the conversion of Mahomedans or

Hindoos to the religion of the Saviour would, by exciting alarm and causing irritation, rather retard than accelerate the progress of Christianity in India. What was held to be the duty of the Government was the practice of general toleration towards all the religions professed by the people under their rule, permitting every man, without restraint and without interference, to worship his God, true or false, in his own way. Christian men sought for liberty to diffuse, without hindrance from the strong hand of authority, the religion in which they gloried; but, if at any time they had thought of seeking the direct aid of that strong hand, the idea had been abandoned, and passive rather than active encouragement was the support they looked for from the State.*

But, it was alleged that the State had not remained neutral—that whilst at one time it had suppressed, and, at a later period, had surlily permitted the diffusion of Christianity, it had actively encouraged the worst forms of idolatry. Little by little, this grave charge gathered strength and consistency. Little had been heard of it until the early part of the present century, when Claudius Buchanan set it a-going. The feeling out of which it arose may have existed before his time; but in an inert and undemonstrative shape. A conviction, indeed, of the heinousness of the idolatry, of the grossness of the

* Towards the close of the last century, before the passing of the Act of 1793, the idea of despatching a number of missionaries and schoolmasters to India, to be under the control of Government, had been conceived in England, and embodied into the resolutions submitted to Parliament. Mainly on this account, the resolutions (which are given in the Appendix) met, as already stated, with a disastrous fate.

superstitions, by which they were surrounded, seems
to have dawned but slowly upon the intelligence
of the English in India. Not very keenly alive to
the beauty and the holiness of their own blessed
religion, and considerably ignorant of the real character of Hindooism, they had been rather attracted
by the "excellent moralities of the Hindoos," than
repulsed by their abominations, and had seen in many
of the barbarities, which we now most deplore and
condemn, only the courage of the hero and the
patience of the martyr. Old Zephaniah Holwell,
who must have had a rare taste of the excellent
moralities of the Moors in the Black Hole of Calcutta, wrote, perhaps in revenge, some treatises on
the tenets of the Gentoos, in which he commended,
in the highest strain of eulogy, the simple, the
rational, the sublime religion of Brahma; declared
that the detestable rite of Suttee was based "upon
heroic, as well as rational and pious principles;" and
concluded his panegyric with the assertion that a true
Brahman is "the purest model of genuine piety that
now exists or can be found on the face of the earth."
He was by no means singular in these opinions. The
excellent moralities, both of the Gentoos and the
Moors, and the simple, rational sublimity of the
religions they professed, had their admirers, and, I
may add, their followers, at a much later period of
our history.

The European mind was first awakened to a sense
of the enormities of Hindooism by the revelations of
Claudius Buchanan, who visited Orissa in 1806, and

there first made the acquaintance of the giant-idol, known as Juggernauth. Within the influence of the salubrious sea-breezes of Pooree, he found the monster holding high carnival, and straightway noted his proceedings. The picture was a terrible but instructive one. There, on the sandy coast of Orissa, was a stately pagoda, grand against the sky; shrine of a mighty Moloch, tended by hundreds of priests, and venerated by millions of worshippers;—a hideous grotesque thing, of huge proportions, in the semblance of mutilated humanity, stuck about with pseudo-divine emblems, and endowed in the language of the priests, and in the imaginations of the people, with all kinds of miraculous gifts. Thousands and tens of thousands of people from all parts of the country flocked to this famous temple every year, to see the god go forth, amidst all kinds of manifest indecencies, upon his periodical excursions; there to prostrate themselves before him, or, may be, to die miserably upon the road. The pilgrimage in itself was a fearful thing. Hard the struggle—often bravely encountered; often all obstacles surmounted—climate, want, horrible disease; and the weary traveller arrived within the sacred precincts, to perish beneath the crushing wheels of the great idol-car, in ecstatic mockery of martyrdom. Few, perhaps, in proportion those sudden immolations; but loud the outcry about them. Greater far the number whom the pilgrimage destroyed; who died by what are called natural causes on the line of road—by fever, dysentery, and such-like grim diseases of the country; rife at all times, rifest at the season of the great carnival of the Rutt Juttra. Some said, ten thousand people, men and women, died for Juggernauth, one way or other, every year; that is, died for the priestly Brahmans—old Zephaniah's purest models of genuine piety to be found on the face of the earth; three thousands of whom were supported in connection with the imperial idol, each having, therefore, three men and one-third of a man as his annual share of human sacrifice. But others, good Dr. Carey included, computed the annual waste of life, "caused by this one idol," at 120,000 human beings, thus giving each pure model forty victims as his individual quota of the great holocaust.[*]

The accounts, indeed, published by the Baptist missionaries were even more distressing than those which emanated from the English Churchman. They spoke of "numbers" of miserable creatures prostrating themselves beneath the wheels of the great idol-car—of a hundred and fifty people killed at one time by the pressure of the crowd at the gate of the

---

[*] "Idolatry destroys more than the sword, yet in a way which is scarcely perceived. The numbers who die in these long pilgrimages, either through want or fatigue, or from dysenteries and fevers caught by lying out and want of accommodation, is incredible. I only mention one idol, the famous Juggernauth, in Orissa, to which twelve or thirteen pilgrimages are made every year. It is calculated that the numbers who go thither is, on some occasions, 600,000 persons, and scarcely ever less than 100,000 persons. I suppose that, at the lowest calculation, 1,200,000 persons attend. Now, it only one in ten died, the mortality caused by this one idol would be 120,000 in a year; but some are of opinion that not one in ten survive and return home again."— *Periodical Accounts of the Baptist Mission.*

Buchanan says that when he inquired on the spot as to the number of pilgrims, at the time of the Rutt Juttra, he was told that a lakh (100,000) "would not be missed."

temple.* But they declared at the same time, that the pilgrims were willing to listen to the Christian preacher, and received with avidity copies of the Holy Scriptures in the native tongues. Arguing upon this fact, Claudius Buchanan declared that the immense gathering of heathens from all parts of the country was a golden opportunity for Christianity; and, with greater boldness than the majority of his countrymen, propounded the "sanguinary" doctrine that Government ought to step in and turn the opportunity to account. "The Bible," he said, "is, by the inscrutable providence of God, at hand; it has been translated into the languages of Asia. Would it not, then, be worthy of the East India Company to order ten thousand copies to be distributed annually at Juggernauth, in any manner that prudence would justify and experience direct, as a sacred return for the revenue we derive, if it should be thought right that revenue should be continued. The Scriptures would thus be carried to the extremities of India and the East. Is it possible that the shadow of an objection should arise against such a

* See the statements of Messrs. Smith and Green. "You would have been astonished to see the vast number of pilgrims crossing the river at Cuttack. As far as the eye could reach, we could not see the end of the ranks: it put us in mind of an army going to battle. . . . . You can easily conceive what a multitude of men, women, and children must have been at the temple, for one hundred and fifty or thereabouts to have been killed by the crowd. They trod one upon another in approaching the temple gate. Ten sepoys per company from all the battalions from Barrackpore to this station had permission to visit the temple. A famine was produced in the country, and great numbers of the pilgrims died of hunger and thirst. We talked to some of them, but it was of no use; they said, whether we survive or not, we will see the temple of Juggernauth before our death. Numbers killed themselves by falling under the wheels of the idol's car. They laid themselves flat on their backs for the very purpose of being crushed by it."—*Periodical Accounts of the Baptist Mission.*

measure, innoxious as it is humane and heavenly in
its tendency? Are we afraid that 'the wretches,
who come to lay their bones within the precincts of
Juggernauth,' would mutiny and take away our dominion? Would not the consequence be rather that
'the blessing of him that was ready to perish' would
rest upon you?"

Thus, on the 25th of May, 1813, wrote Claudius
Buchanan to the Court of Directors of the East
India Company. Perhaps there were not many who,
in those days, looked upon the immense gathering of
people around the temple of Juggernauth, as a mighty
congregation to be preached to by Christian men;
but all these accounts of the horrors and the impieties
attending the carnival of the great Moloch of Hindooism filled the humane with compassion, and the
religious with sorrow, and raised a common cry of
indignation against the Government which tolerated
such things. In truth the whole subject was not
very clearly understood; and, as commonly happens
in these cases, the loudest noise came from the
emptiest understandings. But, at all events, there
was one broad patent truth, namely, that there
existed, not only amidst the sand-hills of Pooree, but
in many other parts of the country, that which, for
want of a better designation, was called "Government Connexion with Idolatry." And, straightway,
this idea having taken possession of the public mind,
it was declared that the Christian Government of
India, not content with their exertions to suppress
the diffusion of the saving truths of the Gospel, were

openly and authoritatively aiding and abetting the worst forms of devil-worship; that they were taking all the hideous indecencies and revolting cruelties of Hindooism under their especial patronage; sending their own masters-of-the-ceremonies to preside over the hellish orgies; and with paternal tenderness managing the property of the idol temples, pampering the priests, cherishing the dancing girls, and doing such honour to heathenism generally as was best calculated to maintain it in a high state of exultant obesity.

These grave charges set people a-thinking about the matter in all its length and breadth. There were some who then saw, or thought that they saw, things for the first time in their true light; and boasted that the scales had fallen from their eyes. Others were there, who, not less seriously pondering the question, settled themselves down in the conviction, that the existing state of things was right, not simply on the score of expediency, but on that also of inalienable justice. The idolatry which the British Government was accused of fostering was many centuries old. It had existed under the native Governments, and had been protected by them; and the English conqueror, who in a general way had pledged himself to deprive the people of none of the rights, privileges, and immunities which they had enjoyed under their former rulers, might not unreasonably believe that he was compelled to continue the State-patronage of the religions of the people which he had found in existence at the period

of conquest. Nay, indeed, the pledges given to the
natives had not always been given in a general way.
Right or wrong, it had been the policy of the British
Government to impress upon the people that under
the new rule of the Feringhee there would be no
interference with the religions of the country—that
religious freedom would be granted to them to the
fullest extent, and that the property of their temples,
and the privileges of their priesthood, would be
secured to them in the same state as they might have
been found by us on the first occupation of the territory. When, for the first time, in 1793, anything
like a regular administrative system was inaugurated,
the regulations framed by Cornwallis and Barlow
distinctly set forth that the laws of the Shastre and
the Koran would be preserved to them, and that they
would be suffered to worship in their own way, as un-
restrictedly as though there had never been a change
of Government. Nothing, indeed, could have been
more intelligible than such language as the following:—"The many valuable privileges and immunities which have been conferred upon the natives of
these provinces evince the solicitude of the British
Government to promote their welfare, and must satisfy
them that the regulations which may be adopted for
the internal government of the country will be calculated to preserve to them the laws of the Shastre and
the Koran in matters to which they have been invariably applied, to protect them in the free exercise of
their religion, and to afford security to their persons

and property."* Nor was the regard for the religions of the people confined to Indian legislators. The legislature of Great Britain took the same view of the matter. Even the protection of Caste was decreed by Act of Parliament. "And in order," it was declared, "that due regard may be had to the civil and religious usages of the natives, be it enacted that the rights and authorities of fathers of families and masters of families, according as the same may be exercised by the Gentoo or Mahomedan law, shall be preserved to them within their families respectively, nor shall the same be molested or interrupted by any of the proceedings of the said courts; nor shall any act done in consequence of the rule or law of caste, so far as respects the members of the same family only, be deemed a crime, although the same may not be justifiable by the laws of England."† The utmost toleration, indeed, for the religions and the religious and social usages of the people was held to be the duty of the British Government. All the material and moral rights and privileges, which they enjoyed before they became the subjects of that Government, were declaredly continued to them; their temples, and temple-lands, and idolatrous endowments were in no wise to be taken from them, and the lessons taught by their priests were not to be violently gainsaid. And yet it does not appear to me that at the bottom of this toleration there was any of that heathenism which is so often charged to it.

---

* See Preamble to Regulation 3 of 1793.
† 37 George III. cap. 142, sec. xii., following 21 Geo. III. cap, 70.

If there were any question at all for the solution
of the rulers of India in those days, it was a very
simple question of right or wrong. A certain tract
of country, by conquest—by cession—no matter how—
passed, from beneath the rule of the old native Government, under the yoke of the encroaching European.
The new Government declaredly took upon itself
all the duties and responsibilities of the old. Ever
as they extended their dominions, the British professed to appear upon the scene of their new triumphs
not as spoliators, but as deliverers. Life and property were to be more secure, justice was to be more
respected, under the new Christian Government, than
under that which it had supplanted. It was not our
business to inquire either how the property had come
into the hands of the existing owners, or whether,
being in such hands, it was turned to good or bad
uses. All that we rightly had to recognise was the
fact of possession. We professed to draw no distinctions; we did not tell the merchant that he might
keep his gains, but that the priest must disgorge
his possessions, because the British Government was
a trading government, and not an idolatrous one. It
was conceived to be more just to say to the priest,
or to the temple, or to the idol, or to whomsoever
the property might belong, "It is yours; you have
got it. No matter how you came by it; no matter
what you do with it. You enjoyed it undisturbedly
under the old Government, and you shall enjoy
it undisturbedly under the new."

And this was the system under which the British

ruler invariably acted. He did not lay his hands upon temple property; firstly, because he believed that he had no right to take any property at all; and secondly, because, strong in that belief, he was repeatedly telling the people that under the new rule of the Feringhee all their old rights and privileges would be respected, and most especially the ancient right of worshipping their gods in their own way. The case appeared to be a very simple one, admitting of no dispute. Moreover, there may have been in former days, as there are at the present time, some who believed that a good Hindoo (good after his kind), or a good Mahomedan, was likely to be a better subject than a bad Hindoo or a bad Mahomedan; and who, therefore, felt that they would advance the interests of the State, and promote the happiness of the people, by encouraging them in the faithful observance of their several religions, whether true or false.

It was not, in those early days, a question in any degree between Christianity and Idolatry. For, in truth, there were no means of converting the people to Christianity. We had not even the means of asserting our own Christianity—except at the great presidential towns. But it *was* a question whether the people would, in any sense, be better—better as men, or nearer Heaven—for the decadence of the ancestral faiths, to which they clung with blind veneration; worshipping, darkly as we know, but still worshipping.

It is not for me to say whether, in the sight of

God, an erring faith or an erring love is better or
worse than no faith and no love.  But I know that,
humanly speaking, there is better hope of the eventual growth of the truthful and the lovely from
a soil in which rank weeds have grown luxuriantly,
than from one hard and stubborn as a rock, in
which nothing has ever grown.  I know, too, that in
the concerns of life, I would rather trust a good
Hindoo—meaning thereby one strong in faith and
strict in observance—than one spiritually cold and
ceremonially neglectful.  The thing venerated may
be bad, but there is veneration—a desire for something beyond, a respect for something above, which
elevates, perhaps purifies, and at all events is better
than the inanition of the beasts that perish.  Moreover, although there is something sublimely ridicu-
lous in the assertion that a genuine Brahman is the
finest specimen of true piety that the world has ever
seen, it does not follow that everything connected
with Brahmanism is absolutely gross and debasing.
The sacred writings of the Hindoo are very different
from the sacred writings of the Christian, but there
are truths in them nevertheless which it is well to
cherish, and good moral rules which it is well to
observe.  It may, therefore, have been not wholly
desirable, either for the sake of the people themselves, or that of the State under which they lived,
that their temples should fall into decay and their
hierarchy into contempt.  This view of the matter
may be sound, or it may be unsound; but I do
perceive that every one who adopts it is fairly

open to the charge of encouraging and patronizing idolatry.

But the theory was sometimes pushed so far, and in so bad a spirit, that it is hardly matter of surprise that such a charge shonld have been made. There, doubtless, were men in the early part of the present century, who did not merely tolerate Hindooism as something in their estimation better than absolute infidelity, but who applauded and upheld it as something excellent itself, and to be fostered on account of its excellence. That Mr. Lionel Place, who has an unsavoury reputation as the earliest English patron of idolatry, in an extended official sense, was one of this class of persons is very generally declared. There were, doubtless, English Hindoos and Mahomedans before his time—Job Charnock, for example, who is said to have sacrificed every year a cock at the tomb of his wife, on the anniversary of her death. But this Mr. Lionel Place, "Collector of the Company's Jagheer at Madras," was the first to give authoritative exposition to his views, and practically to illustrate Government interference in his own person. Some forty miles distant from Fort St. George is the city of Conjeveram, whose temples are among the most celebrated in Southern India. There is the great Conjeveram temple and the little Conjeveram temple, and it is hard to say how many priests in their service, swarming in all the straight intersecting streets of the "City of Gold." Towards the close of the last century these famous pagodas were falling into decay; the gardens around them were uncultivated; their common ceremonies were negligently performed; their periodical festivals had lost much of their pristine grandeur; their funds had been turned to improper uses; altogether, the gods were being defrauded out of their dues,—when the benevolent eye of Mr. Place fell upon them, and his heart was stirred with compassion; and believing that any how a good Hindoo was better than a bad one, he stepped in to save the temple from wreck, and idolatry from degradation; and in a report which has greatly shocked the present generation, contended for the expediency of State interference, in a large political sense,* as tending to make better subjects, and more to conciliate the people. What he recommended to Government he did himself, as far as he could, by his own individual efforts. It is said that he even went so far as to present offerings at the shrines of the idols, and to this day the Brahmans exhibit what they describe as the votive gifts of the good collector.† His representations to

* See his Report to the Board of Revenue, in which the following passage occurs: "The management of the Church Funds has heretofore been thought independent of the control of Government; for this strange reason, that it receives no advantage from them; but inasmuch as it has an essential interest in promoting the happiness of its subjects, and as the natives of this country know none superior to the good conduct and regularity of their religious ceremonies, which are liable to neglect without the interposition of an efficient authority, such control and interference becomes indispensable. In a moral and political sense, whether to dispose them to the practice of virtue, or to promote good order and subordination by conciliating their affections, a regard to this matter is, I think, incumbent."

† Of the fact, indeed, there is no doubt. Hear what Dr. Duff, who visited Conjeveram half a century afterwards, says on the subject. "Probably no one bearing the honoured name of 'Christian,' has left behind him so distinguished a reputation for his services in the cause of idolatry as Mr. Place. When visiting Conjeveram last year (1849), I found his name still cherished with traditionary reverence by the votaries of Brahmanism. The nomenclature which he had introduced was still in vogue. The native officers spoke of the pagoda as the

Government were successful; and in 1796 the temples were placed under his charge, and he undertook, willingly enough, the due appropriation of what he called the "Church Funds."

This is commonly cited as the first instance in which the British Government took upon itself the office of dry nurse to Vishnu; but although it had not previously interfered in the internal management of the temples, it had in other ways handled the unclean thing. Indeed, such handling, more or less, was a necessity of empire. For example, the British Government found, first in one place, then in another, that its new dominion extended over certain places, long held in repute among the Hindoos as points of pilgrimage. The pilgrims, who flocked from all parts of the country to the holy place, were subject to a tax, imposed by the native Government which we had supplanted. What our predecessors had taken we thought it no iniquity to take. So the proceeds of the pilgrim-tax, or such portion thereof as had been received by the native Government, passed into our Christian coffers; and it

---

'Established Church;' of the temple revenues as the 'church funds;' of the Brahman keepers of the idol shrines as the 'churchwardens.' In the neighbourhood of one of the great temples a spacious garden was pointed out as the 'gift of Mr. Place to the god;' within was shown a gorgeous head ornament, begemmed with diamonds and other jewels, worth a thousand pounds, which Mr. Place had presented to the great idol. During his collectorate, he was wont to send for all the dancing girls, musicians, and instruments, elephants and horses attached to the different temples in the surrounding districts, in order to celebrate the Conjeveram festival with the greatest pomp. Attending in person, his habit was to distribute clothes to the dancing girls, suitable offerings to the officiating Brahmans, and a lace garment of considerable value to the god."—*India and its Evangelization:* a lecture delivered by Dr. Duff to the Young Men's Christian Association, in December, 1850, at Exeter Hall.

appeared to be, on the *non-olet* principle of the old
Roman, as good coin as any other.

There were but two courses, in such a case,
between which the choice of the British ruler lay,
on his first assuming the administration of these
pilgrim-funds. He might have continued the existing
system, established by his predecessor, or he might
have declared that he would have nothing to do with
revenue derived from an idolatrous usage. In either
case, it appears to me that he must have laid himself
open to the charge of encouraging Hindooism. What
has been said of the receipt by the British Government of the proceeds of the pilgrim-tax is well
known. It is certain, however, that the Mahomedan
Government, which imposed the tax, in the districts
where we first found it in existence, had no idea of
encouraging Hindooism. It was imposed as a puni-
tory or suppressive measure, in a spirit of hostility to
Hindooism. To abolish this tax, or to refuse to
receive the portion of it paid to Government, would
have been to confer a boon upon the pilgrims, or
more properly upon the priests, which would have
been a mighty encouragement to Hindooism. It
would, in this case, have been said that the first act
of the British Government was to exhibit its tender
regard for idolatry by removing all the restrictions
upon it—indeed, by largely endowing it. This is no
mere hypothesis. Mr. Law, the collector of Gaya,
where the British Government first became the
recipient of this tax, has been sarcastically censured
for reducing it, " as a tradesman lowers the price of

his goods to increase the number of his customers."
But if the reduction of the tax increased the number
of pilgrims, how much more would its total abolition
have increased it; and if the partial measure is
condemned, as an encouragement of Idolatry, what
amount of condemnation would be heaped by the
same writers on so complete an act of grace as the
entire removal of the impost.

The next place to which the British Government
was called upon to direct its attention, in connexion
with this matter of the pilgrim-tax, was the province
of Cuttack, taken from the Mahrattas in the early
part of the present century. There Juggernauth
held his court; and to Juggernauth, as I have already
shown, pilgrims were wont to flock by thousands. On
assuming the government of the province, the first
conception of the British ruler was that inasmuch
as that the Mahrattas had levied their collections on
the pilgrims in a very oppressive manner, it would be
an act of humanity to abolish the tax altogether.
Those were not days in which the "religious element"
was likely to enter very largely into the consideration
of the question; and it must be admitted that Lord
Wellesley, or his secretary, settled it in a manner
not very consonant with our present ideas of Christian
propriety. It was found that as it cost a considerable
sum of money to keep the temple in repair, and to
pay the salaries of the "establishment," duties which
had devolved on the former Government, it was
expedient not altogether to abandon the assets from
which the expenditure had formerly been met. The

tax was, therefore, reimposed. " His Excellency in
Council is satisfied," so went the order, " that it will
be in every point of view advisable to establish moderate rates of duty or collection on the pilgrims proceeding to perform their devotions at Juggernauth.   Inde-
pendently of the sanction afforded to this measure by
the practice of the late Hindoo Government in Cuttack,
the heavy expense attendant on the repair of the
pagoda, and on the maintenance of the establishment
attached to it, render it necessary, from considerations
connected with the public resources, that funds
should be provided for defraying this expense." So
far it appears to have been merely a money-question.
Taking upon itself certain obligations previously
borne by the native ruler, the British Government
conceived that it had a clear and undisputable right
to lighten the burden as much as it could by asserting
its right to any proceeds which had passed into the
coffers of its predecessor.   But the view taken by
Lord Wellesley was by no means bounded by these
pecuniary considerations.   He thought whether the
continuance of the tax would be grateful or not to
the Hindoos, and he came to the conclusion that they
would look with approving eyes upon its continuance,
because it would afford the best possible guarantee
for the due protection of their religion by the dominant state.   " His Excellency," so went the document
already quoted, " understands that it will be consonant
the wishes of the Brahmans attached to the pagoda,
well as of the Hindoos in general, that a revenue
would be raised by Government from the pagoda.

The establishment of this revenue will be considered both by the Brahmans and the persons desirous of performing the pilgrimage, to afford them a permanent security that the expenses of the pagoda will be regularly defrayed by Government, and that its attention will always be directed to the protection of the pilgrims resorting to it, although that protection would be afforded by the Government under any circumstances. There can be no objection to the British Government availing itself of these opinions for the purpose of relieving itself from a heavy annual expense, and of providing funds to answer the contingent charges of the religious institutions of the Hindoo faith maintained by the British Government."

Nothing can be plainer than this language. The British Government here undertakes to maintain the religious institutions of the Hindoo faith. Thus was Government connexion with Idolatry openly declared and authoritatively established. As it was held that there could be no objection to this sort of thing, the Government of the day not merely connected itself with, maintained, encouraged, protected Hindooism, but took an active part in the management of its affairs. The State, indeed, from that time, became Juggernauth's churchwarden. Regulations were framed, scales of fees were fixed, certificates were provided, and appointments were made by Government. All this is very dreadful in the eyes of Christians at the present time; but, to judge the matter rightly, we must regard it with the eyes not of the present, but of a bygone, generation. In recent days, emboldened

by success, we have dared openly to assert our
Christianity. But half a century ago, when the
question of political supremacy was yet unsettled,
our Government, in its dealings with the people of
the soil, thought it best for its own safety to be
openly of no religion. Whether upon any other
principle, and by any other practice, it would, in
that most important conjuncture, have built up our
vast Anglo-Indian empire upon a more secure or a
less secure foundation, can, in this world, only be
vaguely conjectured. But it is due to the memory
of some of the greatest statesmen who have at any
time administered the affairs of that empire, to bear
steadily in mind the experimental character of that
extension of dominion which has since become the
chronic state of our existence in India, and, as some
think, the very condition of our tenure. We must
not view the actions of our forefathers by the light
of our present enlarged experience.

As to what, rightly considered, that experience has
taught us, there may be differences of opinion; but
it is easy to understand the policy of our predecessors,
without conceiving that it necessarily indicates any
love for the unclean thing; or that the many evils
which, from time to time, necessarily grew out of
this State patronage, are proofs of the un-Christian
character either of the Government or of its executive
officers. But when account was taken of these evils,
doubtless, they were very serious. Special attention
has been directed to the idolatry of Juggernauth,
which, by reason of its gigantic proportions and its

excessive monstrosity, has always stood forth, in the sight of European nations, as the great representative of the idolatries of the Indies. But Government connexion with idolatry extended itself over the whole country; and as new provinces passed under British rule new examples of this unholy alliance arose to swell the great sum-total of our practical heathenism. Such things were then regarded as the necessities of our position. Leaping suddenly into the throne of a heathen prince—as at Poonah, or other places easily to be named—we took up, as we had done elsewhere before, the said prince's liabilities, without regard to the nature of the contract; and in the discharge of them, we doubtless entered into details of administration very repugnant to the feelings of Christian men. Not merely did the State afford protection to idolatry, by securing to it the endowments it had enjoyed under the native rulers of the country, but it entered, in a variety of ways, into the internal management of the pagodas and the regulation of their ceremonies, and actively participated in what it would have been sufficient to passively tolerate. It was done with good intentions, I do not doubt; rather, perhaps, it should be said, in furtherance of a good principle. Without some such intervention and supervision of the State, the property of the temples was in a fair way to be misappropriated by the priests; and what the Government really intended to do was simply to protect Moloch against the felonies of his own servants, and see that his business was conducted in a proper methodical way.

"If we are to do it at all," it was said, in those
days, "we may as well do it handsomely. A corrupt
heathen church is no worse than a well-ordered one.
What is Christianity to gain by ecclesiastical abuses
and hierarchical frauds in the bosom of Hindooism?"
So thought those who thought anything about the
matter. But many did not think at all. They went
about this work as about any other work. They
collected the idol tribute; saw that it was devoted
to its proper uses; that the servants of the temple
were duly paid; its ceremonies properly performed,
and the necessary repairs executed in a proper work-
manlike way.* Now this was something beyond
neutrality; something more than mere toleration.
Such as it was, too, it went on, in many parts of the
country, for years. Nor was it merely in the administration of the revenues of idolatry and the superintendence of its establishments that our tender
regard for the heathenism of the people evinced

---

* A writer in the *Oriental Christian Spectator* thus enumerates the various ways in which the servants of Government were employed in the conservation of idolatry:—"They (the Government clerks) collect the revenues derived from the *Enams* (rent-free lands) held by the temples and from the offerings which are presented: They regulate all disbursements, such as the payment of the servants of the idol, and the expenses incurred on feast-days: They make regular periodical returns relative to their proceedings to the collector's office; and their accounts find the same place in the general dufter, or record, as those connected with the regular business of Government: The Mamlutdar, or his substitute, makes a regular visitation of the temples, as the 'master of ceremonies.' The clerks, appointed by Government, have charge of the idol's property, and hire dancing girls, and engage readers of the Paranas when they are in requisition! The temples, of which we now write, are from time to time repaired by order of the European collector; and there are instances on record of orders having been issued for the European assistant collector to proceed to the temple to see that the repairs were executed! It is a well-known fact, and one observed both by natives and Europeans, that the present prosperity of the idol's estates, the real conservation of the shrines, the regularity of the attendance upon them, and the zealous performance of the heathen rites are principally to be attributed to the services of Government."

itself. We made much open display of our reverence for their institutions, by attendance at their festivals; turning out our troops to give additional effect to the show; firing salutes in honour of their high-days and holidays; and sanctioning, nay promoting, the prayers and invocations of the Brahmans to propitiate the deity for a good harvest or a good trade.* Some thought too, that in our law courts there was· more recognition of Mahomedanism and Hindooism than became a Christian Government; and even questioned the propriety of admitting any other than Christian oaths. But as the object of all judicial procedure is to elicit truth, and by eliciting truth to secure justice, it was not easy to perceive how this great end was to be attained by releasing the consciences of the people from all obligations likely to render them faithful witnesses. Moreover, there were some ugly promises on record, pledging the Government to administer the laws according to the Shastres and the Koran; and it was not, there-

---

* See the following classification of anti-Christian usages, as set forth in a memorial addressed in 1837 to the Government of Bombay :—

1. In the employment of Brahmans and others for the purpose of making heathen invocations for rain and fair weather.
2. In the inscription of "Shree" on public documents, and the dedication of the Government records to Gonesh and other false Gods.
3. In the entertainment in the courts of justice of questions of a purely idolatrous nature, when no civil right depends upon them.
4. In the degradation of certain castes, by excluding them from particular offices and benefits not connected with religion.
5. In the servants of Government, civil and military, attending in their official capacity at Hindoo and Mahomedan festivals, with a view to participate in their rites and ceremonies, or in the joining of troops and the use of regimental bands in the processions of heathen and Mahomedan festivals, or in their attendance in any other capacity than that of a police for the preservation of the peace.
6. In the firing of salutes by the troops, or by the vessels of the Indian navy, in intimation and honour of heathen festivals, Mahomedan idols, &c.

fore, clear that these deviations from pure Christian practice were as demonstrably discreditable to our Government as others noted above.

There is in all interference a principle of growth and expansion. We seldom interfere by halves. It was natural, therefore, that when once the servants of Government began to interfere in the ecclesiastical concerns of the Hindoos, they should have continually extended the sphere of their interference, and gone more and more into details of management where only a general supervision had, in the first instance, been contemplated by Government.* The mismanagement of the native officials themselves— the injustice, perhaps, which was being done to the many by the few—often roused the sympathies of the European functionary, who, looking at the case only as between man and man, did, from a pure love of justice, what he might have shrunk from doing, had he regarded the issue as one between Christianity and Idolatry. Knowing that he himself had no other thought than that of doing justice to his neighbour, irrespectively of all conflicting creeds, it did not occur

---

* See for example the following, taken from a Madras report in the Parliamentary papers :—" When we first assumed possession of the various districts of the Madras Presidency, we did not find the religious institutions of the natives enjoying that degree of support from the Government which we have since extended to them. Our connexion with the Hindoo idolatry has grown with our growth ; we found that in many districts pagodas were enriched by large landed endowments ; that the lands attached to them were cultivated by ryots, under engagements with the dharmarkastera, or the priests of the temples ; in course of time we observed that in many instances those lands were mismanaged, the ryots brought complaints of oppression, and the people pointed to the decay of their temples, as the consequence of the mismanagement and the neglect of the lands. The result was that, in numerous instances, we displaced the dharmarkaster, and ourselves took charge of the duties of the management of the temple and the cultivation of the lands."

to him that his actions might be misjudged; and that, however remote may have been his intentions from all thought of encouraging Hindooism, it was impossible to dissever the knowledge of his acts from such associations in the minds of the people. It was not the thing itself so much as the interpretation put upon it that was injurious to Christianity; for it was impossible to disabuse the native mind of the belief that the English Government, which exhibited so tender a regard for the welfare of the idolatrous institutions of the country, was really anxious to perpetuate them.

And so, little by little, the English Government came to be regarded, especially in the Southern and Western parts of the great Indian peninsula, as the firm friends and supporters of the idolatrous institutions of the country. And certainly the practical results of their patronage seemed well to entitle them to the distinction. It is not to be doubted that idolatry flourished under the superintendence of a powerful Christian Government. Wherever the British collectors administered its affairs, the temple was in a high state of prosperity.* In this we amply

---

* See the following, which is contained in the official document quoted in the preceding note :—" The reports received from the collectors of the different zillahs of the Madras Presidency show that the superintendence of no less than 7,600 Hindoo establishments, from the famous pagoda of Seringham to the common village temples, has hitherto been vested in the officers of Government. And this was something more than a nominal superintendence ; the people did not merely regard the collector as the friendly guardian of their religion, but they looked up to him as the regulator of its ceremonies and festivals—as the supervisor of the priests and servants of the pagodas—as the faithful treasurer of the pagoda-funds—and the comptroller of the daily expenses of idolatry. ' We have hitherto,' says the collector of North Arcot, ' stood to these pagodas in the obligation of sovereigns, and our interference has extended over every detail of management ; we regulate their funds, super-

redeemed our pledges to the people. Perhaps, indeed, we went beyond them. There were, however, able and enlightened statesmen who conceived that the compact, actual or constructive, between the British Government and the people, involved not merely toleration, but protection also on the part of the former; and that it was as much our duty to defend the religions of the country from internal dangers as against external assaults. The assumption in this case was, that whatever the native Government would have done in such a case we also were bound to do. But, in point of fact, we were doing not what the native Government would have done, but what it ought to have done (when the rulers and the ruled were of a common faith), for the conservation of the religions of the country and the due administration of ecclesiastical affairs. And we certainly had contracted no obligation to do *more* for the protection of the religions of the country than the native rulers, whose thrones we had usurped.

In looking back at the authoritative enunciations of the British Government, it would seem as though

intend the repairs of their temples, keep in order their cars and images, appoint the servants of the pagodas, purchase and keep in store the various commodities required for their use, investigate and adjust all disputes, and at times even those of a religious nature. There is nothing appertaining to or connected with the temples that is not made a subject of report, except the religious worship carried out daily in them.' The collector of Tinnevelly, a district never visited by the violence of Mahomedan zeal, where Hindoo idolatry has always flourished undisturbed, writes in terms very similar : ' The present control and interference of the district Government authorities extends over almost everything connected with the pagoda ; from the collection of its revenues (from whatever source derived), and the management of its lands, to the regulating of its daily usual expenses, its periodical festivals, and its repairs. Accounts in detail, including every item of receipt and expenditure, are kept and controlled, and the appointment and dismissal of its servants made, by the officers of Government.'"

it had commonly set out on a safe middle course, but had imperceptibly drifted into danger. What some of these enunciations were may expediently be shown. On assuming the government of any new territory, previously under native rule, it has been our wont to announce to the people that they should be protected in the free exercise of their religions—that neither their institutions nor their usages should be assailed. Thus, in 1801, solemn declaration was made, in the following terms, to the people of the Carnatic :—

"Although the Right Honourable the Governor in Council trusts that the experience which the inhabitants of the Carnatic have already had will have rendered it unnecessary for his Lordship to explain the general principles of moderation, justice, protection, and security, which form the characteristic features of the British Government, yet his Lordship in accepting the sacred trust transferred to the Company by the present engagements, invites the people of the Carnatic to a ready and cheerful obedience to the authority of the Company, in a confident assurance of enjoying, under the protection of public and defined laws, every just and ascertained civil right, with a free exercise of the religious institutions and domestic usages of their ancestors."

As was the language of Lord Wellesley, so also was that of Lord William Bentinck. When, more than thirty years afterwards, the Coorg territory was annexed to the British-Indian empire, there went forth (in May, 1834,) a similar promise to the people :—

"Whereas it is the unanimous wish of the inhabitants of Coorg to be taken under the protection of the British Government, his Excellency the Right Honourable the Governor-General has been pleased to resolve that the territory heretofore governed by Veer Rajunder Woodyer shall be transferred to the Honourable Company. The inhabitants are hereby assured that they shall not again be subjected to native rule; that their civil rights and religious usages will be respected, and the greatest desire will invariably be shown by the British Government to augment their security, comfort, and happiness."

And as were the pledges of Lord William Bentinck, so also were those of Lord Dalhousie, when, in 1849, the annexation of the Punjaub was proclaimed :—

"The British Government will leave to all the people, whether Mussulman, Hindoo, or Sikh, the free exercise of their own religions; but it will not permit any man to interfere with the other in the observance of such forms and customs as their respective religions may either enjoin or permit."

Other similar pledges might be cited ; but these, spread over a space of half-a-century, will suffice. It is well that the reader should bear them steadily in mind. It was equally just and politic that such pledges should be given. It would have been equally unjust and impolitic to ignore them at any subsequent time.

But such general promises of toleration as these did not bind the Government to any active interference in the ecclesiastical affairs of the people. It was no part, indeed, of the original design that we should take the administration of the mosques and pagodas into our own hands. But in the course of the first quarter of the nineteenth century, regulations were issued in both the Bengal and the Madras Presidencies, which, although originating in nothing more than a desire to do justice between man and man by the prevention of fraudulent practices, have ever since, in the minds of many Christian men, been a reproach to the British Government and to the British nation. These Regulations set forth that, " Whereas considerable endowments had been granted in money, or by assignment of

lands, or of the produce or portions of the produce of
lands, by former Governments of this country, as well
as by the British Government and by individuals, for
the support of mosques, Hindoo temples, colleges, and
choultries, and *for other pious and beneficial purposes*; and whereas there were grounds to believe
that the produce of such endowments was, in many
instances, appropriated contrary to the intentions of
the donors; and whereas it was the duty of the
Government to provide that all such endowments
be applied according to the real intent and will of
the grantor," &c. &c.; " the general superintendence of all endowments," &c. was to be thenceforth
" vested in the Board of Revenue;" and that " it
should be the duty of the Board of Revenue to take
such measures as might be necessary to ensure that
all endowments made for the maintenance of establishments of the description above mentioned were
duly appropriated to the purpose for which they
were destined by the Government, or the individual
by whom such endowments were made." " In like
manner," proceeded the Regulations, "it shall be the
duty of that Board to provide, with the sanction
of Government, for the due repair and maintenance
of all public edifices which have been erected at the
expense either of the former or the present Government, or of individuals, and which either are or can
be rendered conducive to the convenience of the community." To enable the Board the better to carry
into effect the duties entrusted to them by this
Regulation, local agents were to be appointed in each

zilah : "and," said the Regulations, "the collector of the zilah shall be ex officio one of those agents." And in order that the beneficent intention of these Acts might not be misinterpreted, it was set forth that it was "to be clearly understood that the object of the Regulation was solely to provide for the due incorporation of lands or other endowments, and not to resume any part of them." The words which I have used are those of the Madras Regulation (VII. of 1817), which follows very closely the Bengal Act XIX of 1810. The substance of the Regulations was held to be bad enough: but the words, if possible, were still worse, for they openly declared the conservancy of the false religions of the country to be a "pious and beneficial purpose." Some portions of these Regulations were subsequently modified; and, as will presently be seen, the practice which they created was disallowed by the Home Government; but substantially they remained unrepealed up to the close of the reign of the East India Company. It remained for Her Majesty's Government to sweep them out of the code.

# CHAPTER XI.

Ignorance of the people of England—Their dawning apprehensions—Mr. Charles Grant—The extension of the ecclesiastical establishment—Bishop Wilson—The despatch of 1833—Misgivings of the Court—Subsequent orders.

It was long before the state of things described in the last chapter was well understood by Christian England.   People had heard of Juggernauth, and had encouraged exaggerated ideas of the wholesale slaughter committed by the crushing wheels of the great idol-car.   Every child's book, illustrative of the manners and customs of foreign nations, had an impressive picture of Juggernauth making high holiday at the expense of hundreds of prostrate worshippers. But it was little known to what extent the great Pooree temple, or any other idol-home of the same kind, was supported and patronised by the British Government.

The history, indeed, of British administration in India was, for a long time, a sealed book.   How India was governed few people cared to inquire.   It was not until the first quarter of the present century had worn away, that the religious mind of England was in any way awakened to a sense of the extent to

which the British Government in India had linked
itself with the idolatries of the country, and of the
evils resulting from this unnatural alliance.  Then the
voice, perhaps of expostulation, perhaps of denun-
ciation, was heard at public meetings and in private
assemblies.  The religious societies addressed themselves to the consideration of the great question, and
individual men, appealing to the public mind through
the press or from the platform, gave utterance, with
no uncertain sound, to the convictions which had
forced themselves upon them.  Many, indeed, conceiving that the source of the evil lay in the indifference, if not in the impiety, of the Court of
Directors, spoke in no measured language of the
delinquencies of that body ; and even the placid
dulness of the India-House elections was for a time
disturbed by appeals to the religious sensibilities of
languid proprietors; and men who were not proprietors
"qualified" for the purpose of infusing more of the
religious element into the constituency at large.
Candidates for the Direction were compelled to put
forth manifestoes declaratory of their views on this
important question,* and long debates in the Court of

---

* Mr. Tucker has left on record
the following account of an attempt
that was made to extract a religious
pledge from him :—"I was called
upon by a proprietor to give a pledge
that I was friendly to particular views
connected with this subject, and disposed to promote particular objects.
.  .  .  .  On my declining to give
the pledge required, the proprietor
observed that it was 'high time for
him, and other proprietors who
thought as he did, to look out for
a candidate who would give such a
pledge, and that it was high time for
those, who were not proprietors, to
become such for the same purpose.'"
In a few pregnant sentences of this
paper, Mr. Tucker enunciated his
views—"I am of opinion," he wrote,
"that the Government should never
identify itself with the missionary
and other societies which have been
instituted for the propagation of the
Christian religion in the East.  In
the minds of the people of India,
Government is habitually associated
with the idea of power, of force, and

Proprietors evinced the interest that was taken in the subject. In language, temperate and respectful —more potent for its very moderation—the missionary societies addressed the Court of Directors.* But the Court meaning only toleration, slowly took up the notion that they were actively encouraging idolatry, and by such encouragement tending to make the heathen believe that the Christian Government under which they lived rejoiced in their superstitions and desired to perpetuate them.

But a great change was now impending; new counsels were about to prevail. The year 1833 was, in many respects, a great year for Christianity in India—not merely because the East India Company then ceased to be a trading company, and so

---

I am persuaded that the slightest demonstration of an intention to use force for the conversion of these people would alarm their fears in a degree to produce immediate and serious dangers. Our Government is established in the spirit of toleration, and a sort of tacit compact or understanding exists that we shall not interfere with the religion of our native subjects. Our Government stands in the situation of a powerful umpire, whose duty it is to afford equal protection to all, and to maintain in the free exercise of all civil rights (and among these liberty of conscience) its subjects of whatever description, with strict impartiality. I consider, then, that the Government could not take part in the missionary societies with the slightest prospect of advancing the interests of religion, nor without departing from those principles, upon a strict adherence to which its own existence essentially depends."

* The Christian Knowledge Society, for example, declared themselves to be " anxious to acknowledge its grateful sense of the attention and kindness invariably evinced by the Honourable Company in promoting its (the Society's) objects in that part of the world," and thus mildly expressed their sense of the evil of the " toleration" system :—" That among the causes, which appear to offer a powerful obstruction to the proceedings of the society, is the encouragement afforded, however inadvertently, by the Company and its agents, to the idolatrous worship of the East, by means of the imposts levied on the pilgrims and worshippers at the several temples, and by the revenues thence derived, the inference from which regulation of the Government is feared to have been an opinion too generally adopted by the native population, that so far from any objection being felt by the Company to the continuance of the idolatrous rites and corrupt practices of heathenism, it rather intends to afford them its patronage and support, in thus being contented to derive from them a considerable revenue."

ceasing, began at once to take a deeper and more
solemn interest in the welfare of the people of the
country, and to address themselves earnestly and
devotedly to the work of Government with an enlarged sense of their duties as the rulers of a mighty
empire; but because there were a variety of concurrent circumstances then at work, some of a personal
and accidental character, to give a new impulse to the
great cause, and to unite Christian men in England
and in India in one common effort for the assertion
of their national faith and the rescue of the British
Government from its degrading subserviency to the
idolatries and superstitions of the country.

Many predicted then that the East India Company,
ceasing altogether to be a trading company, would
not long survive the loss of its mercantile privileges.
But the excitement which the great change created
in political and commercial circles met with slight
response from the religious world. The great battle
of Christianity had been fought twenty years before.
During the period which had since elapsed, the
country had been thrown open to the Christian missionary. All obstructions and impediments to the
diffusion of Gospel truth had been removed. There
was no longer, therefore, any common ground on
which Christians of all denominations could take
their stand. The Church of England alone was interested in the provisions of the Act of Parliament
under which India was thenceforth to be governed.
It was part of the Government scheme to divide the
enormous diocese of Calcutta. Two other episcopal

sees were to be established—one including the pre-sidency of Madras, the other the presidency of Bombay. This was, at all events, great gain to the Church; in the estimation of Churchmen it was great gain to Christianity. But the interest which it excited was but limited; and it was not then said, as it had been said in 1813, that a new epoch in the history of Christianity in India would date from the passing of that new charter.

Against these episcopal arrangements the East India Company remonstrated.* They had no objection to the bishops, but bishops are costly commodities, and the Company resented the idea of the expense. Their arguments, however, were overruled. It was not the least of the favourable circumstances to which I have above alluded, that Mr. Charles Grant was then President of the Board of Control. The "Young Charles Grant" who, twenty years before, had done battle in defence of the Company, side by side with his father, the venerable director, had graduated in the school of statesmanship, and taken rank as a Cabinet Minister.† If his

* "Your petitioners," wrote the Court of Directors, in a petition to Parliament, "whilst they are sincerely desirous that adequate means should be provided for the spiritual instruction and consolation of all classes of the public servants stationed in India, must be permitted to remark that no evidence has been brought before them, which satisfies them of the necessity of adding to the establishment two suffragan bishops and two chaplains of the Church of Scotland, and that without such evidence they could not consider it just to employ the revenue of India in maintaining these officers."

From this Sir James Carnac dissented, saying, with much truth:—"The experiment has been tried; and the apprehension of any ill effects with reference to the feelings of the natives has been proved to be groundless. I can speak from experience to the highly beneficial results which have followed the increase of the episcopal establishment in India, among which its zealous and successful exertions for the encouragement of general education among the natives may be enumerated to its honour."

† The elder Charles Grant died in 1823.

D D

industry had been equal to his ability and his integrity, he might have taken the very highest rank.
The one great drawback of constitutional indolence
prevented him from doing justice to himself—it may
be said, and to the world.   For, with his high Christian principles and his pure sense of universal justice,
he might, had he gone to the front, have raised the
standard of our political ethics and given a higher
tone to the practical statesmanship of the age.   Far
short of what he might have done, still what he did,
subsiding long before his time into a tradition, has
not been without its uses.   It is for others to speak
of the genuine humanity which glowed in his colonial
despatches.   It is mine to record, in this place, that
to what he did, as Indian Minister, the cause of
Christianity is deeply indebted.   He had not forgotten the lessons of his youth.   He had not forgotten
that, many years before, his father had fought at the
head of that little band of Christian heroes which had
bravely withstood the sneers and buffets of the world,
and steered right on to what seemed, to all but the
eye of Faith, an unattainable success.   And now,
that the power was in his own hands, and it was his
to shape the measures which were to determine the
future career of Christianity in India, he was true to
the training of his early youth, and the aspirations
of his later manhood, and he bethought himself,
earnestly and reverently, of what was to be done most
effectually to promote it.   What he did will be told
presently.   It is only a small part of his doing, that
he gave increased dignity to the Church establish-

ment in India, and so promoted that outward assertion of our national faith which had once been so greatly neglected. He believed that the financial objections of the Court ought to be overruled; and although in the earlier stage of the negotiations between the Company and the Government, he did not press the point, he subsequently adhered to the original proposal for the additional bishoprics, and easily carried Parliament with him.

Whether, consistently with strict justice, a Christian Government can support its own Church out of revenues derived from Hindoo and Mahomedan tax-payers may be an open question. The arguments on either side are too well known to need repetition. It is sufficient to say here, that if it be justifiable to support any Christian Church establishment at the expense of the revenues of India, it is justifiable to support an effective one. If the English were to have a State Church at all, under episcopal superintendence, there was no reason why that episcopal superintendence should not have been in some measure proportionate to the local requirements of the country. And it was demonstrable that one bishop could by no possibility perform the duties of a diocese extending from the Himalayahs to Point de Galle, and stretching out across the great waters to Australia and the Cape of Good Hope.

The see of Calcutta was at that time vacant— vacant for the fourth time. It has been seen how Bishop Middleton was struck down by *coup de soleil* in his carriage, and how Bishop Heber had perished

D D 2

suddenly in his bath. Since the disastrous day at Trichinopoly, which had witnessed the latter event, two other bishops had made their way to Calcutta, and had died at the very outset of their episcopal careers. The first of these, Bishop James, had arrived at Calcutta in January, 1828, and died on his way to Penang in August of the same year. In so brief a space of time, much enfeebled as he was by failing health, it was not possible that he should have done much for the cause of Christianity in India. How it happened that he was selected for such an office—for his antecedent reputation was mainly that of an accomplished art-critic—is not very apparent. But he seems to have entered upon his episcopal duties with a full sense of their importance, and to have addressed himself to their performance with a mild earnestness, which, had life and health been vouchsafed to him, would have crowned his years of office with respectable rather than brilliant results. He was a tolerant Christian* and a moderate Church-man, and in many respects resembled, though with

* At the Cape of Good Hope, where Bishop James spent some three weeks on his way out to Calcutta, he was appealed to as "a man of God," by some Mahomedan (Malay) priests, to compose the differences which had arisen between them on some points of discipline. James seems to have undertaken the office of a peace-maker, without any misgivings, although the settlement of the dispute involved a question of the right interpretation of a passage in the Koran. The Bishop said afterwards that he was glad it was a point of discipline and not of doctrine. But it does not appear that if it *had* been the latter, he would have refused to interfere. The incident is a suggestive one. It will appear, doubtless, to many, that if a Christian bishop might, without offence, act as an arbitrator in the disputes, whether doctrinal or cere-monial, of the Mahomedan priest-hood, there was no great scandal in the arm of the secular government being stretched out to allay the dis-orders and correct the malpractices—often involving violations of the law, and throwing up questions of abstract justice—which were brought to the notice of the agents of the British Government in connexion with the administration of the churches of the country.

manifest dilution, the prelate whom he succeeded. After another interval, the vacant place was filled by the appointment of Dr. Turner to the episcopal office. He arrived at Calcutta in December, 1829; but Christianity had scarcely begun to rejoice in the fostering care of this truly devout prelate when he also was struck down, scarcely beyond the threshold of his career.

His loss was deeply deplored. They who were best qualified to understand his character, and had the best means of observing the zealous and conscientious manner in which he addressed himself to the performance of his duties, were of opinion that he was better fitted for the duties of his office than any one of his predecessors, and that if he had been spared, an extended career of usefulness would have lain before him largely conducive to the prosperity of the Christian Church.* But the little space of eighteen

---

* See notices of Bishop Turner's brief career in the Memoirs of Archdeacon Corrie. Shortly after the Bishop arrived, Corrie wrote :— " The Bishop seems bent on conciliation, with more decision than his predecessors. He has become patron of the Calcutta Bible Society, president of the Church Missionary Society, and is to preside this evening at a public meeting of the Bible Association in the Town Hall. He has attended the examination of schools at Mirzapore, Mrs. Wilson's school, the Female Orphan Asylum, and other institutions."—(*Jan.* 8, 1829.)

Again, in the spring of the same year, " he (the Bishop) visited lately with me at Burdwan, and takes a lively interest in missions ; preaches in Bishop's College Chapel on Sunday evenings to the few students and others, and enters much into the affairs of that institution. A chapel is commenced at the Free School, and a Mariner's Church at the Custom House is preparing, and the building of a church at Howrah is in progress. A form of an association for the better observance of the Lord's-day has been drawn up by the Bishop, and sent to the chaplains and all the dissenting ministers, and yesterday sermons were preached in all the churches and chapels here on the duty of sanctifying the Sabbath." Some months afterwards, Corrie again wrote :—" Our increased acquaintance with the Bishop renders us more at home with him, and we see more to admire in him. He is by far the best suited for this appointment of any who have occupied it. With more practical knowledge of men and of parochial matters than any of them, he has large views of usefulness ; and with perfect pro-time that was permitted to him, before he was removed from the scene, sufficed only to make him generally acquainted with his diocese, and his name is not specially associated with any measures for the advancement of Christianity in India. He died in the month of July, 1831: and when intelligence of the event reached England, the consternation of the Church was extreme. Four bishops had now been stricken down. Three had died at their posts within five years. It was said by many to be no more than the necessary result of excessive labour in an exhausting climate. The vast extent of the diocese—the immense distances to be traversed on the episcopal visitation tours—the laborious duties involved in the "care of the churches," were eagerly commented upon as so many obtrusive proofs of the necessity of dividing the great diocesan area, and sending out more episcopal workmen to share the duties between them. Others contended that neither work nor climate had destroyed the bishops—certainly not work: that it was exceedingly healthy to itinerate; and that the judges who had been stationary at Calcutta and Bombay had died off even faster than the bishops. But, whatever may have been the cause of the mortality among the prelates, there was no doubt of the fact itself; and great account was made of the space of time which, since the first establish-

priety of language states them to Government."—(June, 1830.) After his death, the Archdeacon, who mourned it deeply, lost no opportunity, public or private, of bearing testimony to the Bishop's worth. In hourly anticipation of this event, he wrote to a friend :—"To the Indian Church the loss will be greater than any yet suffered. He unites the best qualities of his predecessors with the knowledge of the business of a clergyman in the conducting of schools, management of charities," &c.

ment of the Indian episcopate, had seen the Church without a head, and the consequent embarrassment of ecclesiastical affairs. If the arguments were not all-powerful, the men were; and the Government carried the point against the opposition of the Court of Directors. Ths Crown was empowered to divide the Indian diocese into three, corresponding with the limits of the three presidencies of India: the Bishop of Calcutta being at the same time created Metropolitan of all India.*

The first Metropolitan was Daniel Wilson. He had been for many years vicar of Islington; and in that capacity had not only won for himself the reverence and the affection of a numerous flock, but had achieved also a much wider reputation as an evangelical divine. In the ranks of the Protestant ministry of England there was not a truer Christian; there was not one in whom a more childlike simplicity, a more unselfish and unworldly singleness of purpose was united with a masculine understanding, and a scholarly, cultivated mind. Many doubted whether he had sufficient tact and address to acquit

---

* The Act declared that, "whereas the present diocese of the bishopric of Calcutta is of too great an extent for the incumbent thereof to perform efficiently all the duties of his office without endangering his health and life, and it is, therefore, expedient to diminish the labours of the said diocese, and for that purpose to make provision for assigning new limits to the diocese of the said bishop, and for founding and constituting two separate and distinct bishoprics, but nevertheless the bishops thereof to be subordinate and subject to the Bishop of Calcutta for the time being, and his successors as their metropolitan; be it therefore enacted, that in case it shall please her Majesty to erect, found, and constitute two bishoprics, one to be styled the bishopric of Madras, and the other the bishopric of Bombay, and from time to time to nominate and appoint bishops to such bishoprics under the style and title of Bishops of Madras and Bombay, there shall be paid from out the revenues of the said territories to such bishops respectively the sum of 26,000 Sicca rupees by the year."

himself, with much success, as the head of the Anglo-Indian Church. Ecclesiastical domination, indeed, was held to be somewhat out of the line of one so little versed in the ordinary commerce of life. But the missionary spirit was strong within him; and the evangelical Christianity of the country rejoiced in his mission to the East. He went forth, not without painful doubts and misgivings, expecting soon to lay his bones beside those of Middleton and Turner. But at the Cape of Good Hope, where his vessel touched, he met Simon Nicolson, who had professionally attended three of the lost bishops, and who well knew not only the proximate but the predisposing causes of their several mortal diseases; and that eminent physician, after much examination, assured him that there was no reason why he should not live and work a quarter of a century in India, and enjoy as good health as at home. And happily for the Christian Church in India, the encouraging anticipation was fulfilled.

It is a noticeable fact in the history of Christianity in the East that Charles Grant, being then President of the Board of Control, appointed such a man to be Bishop of Calcutta and Metropolitan of all India. It is a noticeable fact also that under the new Act of Parliament, authorizing the appointment of two suffragan bishops, Daniel Corrie, for some time Archdeacon of Calcutta, was the first to whom letters patent were issued. That so excellent and so loveable a man should at last receive his earthly reward, all who have, from the scattered notices of his

career in this volume, if from no other and better
source, learnt how he laboured, for well nigh thirty
years, zealously and successfully in the good cause,
must instinctively rejoice.   He had fairly earned his
mitre long before, and probably, but for the delay
attendant upon the consecration of an absentee, would
have received it.   The time, however, had now come
when his claims might be regarded without prolong-
ing the episcopal destitution of the Anglo-Indian
Church; and Charles Grant was not a man to neglect
the opportunity.   So he sent out, by Bishop Wilson,
intimation to the Archdeacon of his intention to
recommend him to the King for preferment to one of
the new bishoprics.   Those bishoprics were not established until some time after the passing of the Act;
and then with a manifest timidity—first one, and then
the other.   It was not until Trinity Sunday, June 14th,
1835, that Corrie was consecrated Bishop of Madras.

It was, doubtless, a conjunction of affairs very favourable to Christianity in India that two such men
as Daniel Wilson and Daniel Corrie should be labouring together, each in high place.   It is, also, worthy of
record among the encouraging circumstances of the
times, that Lord William Bentinck was Governor-
General of India, and that Lady William was every
inch a Christian woman.   There was a devout spirit
abroad in Anglo-Indian society.   The English in
India had outlived the old reproach of irreligion and
immorality.   To be a regular attendant at Church, to
be strict in family worship, to subscribe liberally to
missionary objects and to attend missionary meetings,

was in no wise to stand out conspicuously from the
crowd.   Even the young subaltern, from his scanty
pay, rendered scantier by the spirit of retrenchment
then abroad, contributed his monthly rupee to different
Christian funds.   In some regiments, indeed, the
" new lights," as they were profanely called, were so
numerous that they ceased to be the exceptions, and
therefore were no longer objects of derision.   Churches
were springing up at all the considerable European
stations throughout the country.   In town and in
village the Christian missionary was doing his work,
and the missionary school was thronged by the heathen
children.   Of individual endeavour, indeed, there was
no lack.   But people cried out that the Government
was not doing its duty as a Christian Government
—that still heathenism was deriving more active
support and encouragement from the State than was
consistent with the absolute neutrality, which was
said to be the rule religiously observed by the dominant race.

But here, too, a great and important change was
slowly working its way into practical operation.   The
subject of Government connexion with idolatry had
been for some years exciting deep and painful interest
in the religious mind of Christian England.   Religious societies and devout individuals had eagerly
discussed it; but they had not made much impression
on men in power, until Charles Grant, in due course,
had come to be President of the Board of Control.
Then there was a new burst of hope.   Very earnestly
and solemnly he addressed himself, as a Christian

statesman, to the consideration of the whole question, in all its aspects; and the result of his reflections was a strong conviction that Government, with the best intentions, had allowed its toleration to fructify into active patronage of idolatry, and that the support given by the State might, without any breach of existing obligations, be greatly relaxed. This relaxation he determined, in conjunction with the Court of Directors, to enjoin upon the different Governments of India; and so a despatch was prepared, in which the whole question was reviewed with becoming moderation, and instructions were conveyed which, if not all that some zealots might have desired, went at least as far as justice demanded or policy could safely prescribe.

The despatch, after long incubation, finally received the signatures of the Court of Directors, on the 20th of February, 1833. Any sketch of Christianity in India would be incomplete without some detailed notice of this memorable document. It contained at the outset a definition of the toleration which it was incumbent upon the Government to observe;—"All religious rites and offices," it said, "which are in this sense harmless, that they are not flagrantly opposed to rules of common humanity or decency, ought to be tolerated, however false the creed by which they are sanctioned. But they could not properly be said to be tolerated, if those who are engaged in them did not experience that ordinary degree of protection to which every citizen not offending against the laws is entitled at the hands of his rulers. A religious festival, attended by immense crowds, cannot be said to be tolerated, if the Government does not provide a police sufficient to enforce order, and to ensure the safety of individuals during the celebration. And, on the other hand, the providing of such a police is not an act of favour or friendship to the mode of worship, but one of simple justice to the worshippers. Beyond this civil protection, however, we do not see that the maxims of toleration enjoin us to proceed. It is not necessary that we should take part in the celebration of an idolatrous festival, or that we should assist in the preparations for it, or that we should afford to it such systematic support as shall accredit it in the eyes of the people and prevent it from expiring through the effect of neglect or accident."

Having enunciated these general principles, the Court of Directors proceeded to apply them especially to the case of the Juggernauth festival, and the Pilgrim-tax:—" The application of these principles," it was declared, " to the subject before us is not very difficult. Although it is probable that the Hindoo rites, or at least those of Juggernauth, are less liable than formerly to the charges of cruelty and open indecency, their essential character is, of course, not changed. They are at variance with the precepts and practice of Christianity, and they seem opposed even to the plain injunctions of a natural religion. This, however, is not a reason for prohibiting them by law; and if they are not to be so prohibited, if they are to exist at all, they must receive from the civil power that measure of protection which it affords to any other act, the doing or the not doing of which it treats as a matter of indifference. To this extent, we entirely concur with Lord William Bentinck. On the other hand, we cannot conceive that a Government which believes those rites to be deeply founded in error, and to be productive, even in a civil view, of serious evil, is obliged, or is at liberty, to show to them any degree of positive sanction or encouragement."

It was then considered how far, the obligation on the part of Government to maintain an efficient police force for the protection of the pilgrims being admitted, it was morally competent for them to continue the Pilgrim-tax for the sake of supplying the necessary expenses of the protective establishment. Looking at the matter purely in this light, we might regard the position of the Government as simply that of the conservator of the public peace. But it was held that the sum collected was far in excess of the amount required for the payment of the police; and that a large amount of the revenue so raised was employed in keeping in repair "the shrines, idols, or other edifices, which form the local objects of the pilgrimage, or in supporting the priests and other ministers attached to them." And thus it was argued, "from being simply conservators of the public peace at certain numerous assemblages of the people, we are become the chief agents in sustaining an idol establishment." The despatch then went on to show that "the provision of the funds, which are to be employed in supporting the establishment, creates at once a right and a motive to watch over

this expenditure;" and that the Government thus
taking upon itself not only the collection, but the
administration of the revenue, appeared before the
people of the country " in such intimate connexion
with their unhappy and debasing superstitions, as
almost necessarily to inspire them with the belief
either that we admit the divine origin of those superstitions, or at least that we ascribe to them some
peculiar and venerable authority."

This would have been strong argument against the
continuance of such administration of the Pilgrim-
funds, if there had been nothing else to say against
it; but, as it happened that after paying the police,
and otherwise contributing to the support of the idol
establishment, the Government had still a considerable surplus in hand, which surplus was swept into
their own treasury, the connexion between the State
and the Pilgrim-fund was complete, and at all points
objectionable in its completeness : " It is true," said
the Court of Directors, " that the Government in
India has always professed, and we doubt not very
sincerely, to consider the amount of the revenue
which may be obtained by means of a Pilgrim-tax, as
an object of trifling importance, when compared with
that of conciliating the natives by a well-arranged
system for the support of their favourite superstitions.
This also has always been the feeling of the Government at home. But though the chief motive of the
arrangement has always been a liberal ambition to
conciliate the natives, the natural desire of procuring
financial benefit to the Company has always mixed

itself with the former sentiment; neither of these objects, indeed, could be overlooked by the Company's servants, zealous as they have ever been to promote in every way the interests of the body by whom they have been employed."

After quoting, with much detail, the opinions expressed by the local functionaries in different parts of India, with reference to the probable effects of the withdrawal of Government interference, the Court of Directors proceeded to weigh the probabilities of a favourable or of an unfavourable impression to be made on the native mind by the abolition of the Pilgrim-tax, saying:—" We have adverted to the apprehensions entertained by some persons that the abolition of the Pilgrim-tax would be regarded by the Hindoos with dread and regret, as indicating the withdrawal of the protection hitherto afforded by this Government to their religion, and as leading to further measures of the same character. From the papers before us, from the tenor of the answers to the Governor-General's circular, and also from general principles, we think it at least as probable that the impression resulting from the abolition would be of an opposite description. We mean that the Hindoos would view the abolition as a boon, and as a new proof of special toleration, and that in this view it would tend to increase the popularity of British administration. We do not wish to lay much stress on this topic, because it is not mainly by such considerations that we must regulate our Indian administration; but it is important to bear it in mind as a set-off against anticipations so often indulged in of a different effect."

It is no small proof of the difficulties with which the whole question was beset, that it was seldom discussed by the advocates either of the one side or of the other without some manifest inconsistency. It is here, for example, set forth as an argument in favour of the abolition of the Pilgrim-tax, that it would most probably be regarded by the people as "a new proof of especial toleration." But these proofs of especial toleration were the very things which were said to render the Pilgrim-tax and all other kinds of Government connexion with idolatry so peculiarly offensive to Christianity. There was no stronger argument adduced against this connexion than that the especial toleration which it evinced, was calculated to impress the people with the conviction that their English masters regarded their idolatries with favour. If then the hypothesis of the Court of Directors, or of Charles Grant, was correct, and the people were likely to regard the abolition of the tax as an act of grace, it was, with reference to their general line of argument, a reason for maintaining rather than for rescinding the impost.

If, however, there were some weak points in the logic of this memorable despatch, there was no weakness or hesitation in the enunciation of the conclusions at which, after full consideration, the Home Government arrived. These conclusions were thus summed up, and communicated to the Governor-General in Council:—"First, That the interference of British functionaries in the interior management of native temples, in the customs, habits, and religious proceedings of their priests and attendants, in the arrangement of their ceremonies, rites, and festivals, and generally in the conduct of their interior economy, shall cease.

" Secondly, That the Pilgrim-tax shall everywhere be abolished.

" Thirdly, That fines and offerings shall no longer be considered as sources of revenue by the British Government, and they shall consequently no longer be collected or received by the servants of the East India Company.

" Fourthly, That no servant of the East India Company shall hereafter be engaged in the collection, or management, or custodies of moneys in the nature of fines or offerings, under whatsoever name they may be known, or in whatever manner obtained, or whether furnished in cash or in kind.

" Fifthly, That no servant of the East India Company shall hereafter derive any emolument resulting from the above-mentioned or similar sources.

" Sixthly, That in all matters relating to their temples, their worship, their festivals, their religious practices, their ceremonial observances, our native subjects be left entirely to themselves.

" Seventhly, That in every case in which it had been found necessary to form and keep up a police force, specially with a view to the peace and security of the pilgrims or the worshippers, such police shall

E E

hereafter be maintained and made available out of the general revenues of the country."

There was no uncertain sound in this. Conclusions thus enunciated were in reality definite instructions. It was intended that they should be acted upon, not hastily and abruptly, but with all proper caution and circumspection; in a manner neither to offend nor to alarm the people. "Such explanations," it was added, "should be given to the natives as shall satisfy them that, so far from abandoning the principles of a just toleration, the British Government is resolved to apply them with more scrupulous accuracy than ever; and that this proceeding is, in truth, no more than a recurrence to that state of real neutrality from which we ought never to have departed."

But the good seed of the despatch fell upon a hard and stubborn soil. Practically, it was long disobeyed by those whose business it was to give effect to its instructions. It was dated on the 20th of February, 1833; but, for five long years, it remained all but a dead letter. The spirit of Charles Grant ceased to animate the Government of the East India Company. The Directors, with their "old Indian" prejudices and semi-native ideas, appear then to have subsided into their old state of indifference or timidity. The authorities in India were content to do nothing, and the authorities in England were content to see nothing done. Indeed, it would seem as though the magnates of Leadenhall-street contemplated with something like dismay their own temerity in affixing their signatures to such a despatch; and being relieved from the controlling authority of Charles Grant, had sought either to stifle the document altogether or to explain away its contents. Fortunately, they could not stifle it. There were those both in England and in India, who knew the advantage they had gained, and were resolute to profit by it. Such an authoritative enunciation of the principle which was henceforth to regulate the connexion of the British Government in India with the idolatries of the country was too substantial and too vital a fact to be suffered to rest quietly in the grave of forgotten things.

So the Directors, finding that they could not strangle the despatch, determined to ignore the whole spirit and purpose of it, and to take their stand upon certain passages which, read without their context, might be supposed to impart a conditional character to the instructions which it contained. The despatch had certainly called for information. Now this "calling for further information" was in India House practice, for the most part, tantamount to the indefinite shelving of a question. Questions were in this way very often shelved. The despatch of 1833 was too decided in its tone—it expressed in language too clear and unmistakeable the desire of the Home Government to sever the existing connexion between the State and the degrading superstitions of the country —to be interpreted by any intelligent and candid mind into one of those evasive documents ; but it did contain passages on which an unwilling local Government might found pretext for almost indefinite delay. " In stating to you," it said, " our distinct opinion respecting the abolition, not only of the Pilgrim-tax, but of the practices to which we have referred as either connected with or bearing a similar construction, we desire to repeat that we are rather holding up a standard to which you are ultimately to conform your policy, than prescribing a rule which you are instantly, and without respect of circumstances, to carry into accomplishment. We are sensible that this is one of those subjects respecting which it is peculiarly difficult to give from this country any other than general instructions. As to the details of any measures regarding it, the time, the degree, the manner, the gradations, the precautions, these must in a special sense rest with the local Government."

Left thus to the discretion of the local Government the "time" would probably have been *never*, the "degree" *none*. But the local Governments were not left to themselves. The contents of the despatch of February, 1833, were well known in India; and there were men with strong religious convictions who observed with shame and indignation the lethargy into which the higher authorities had fallen. In Madras, especially, this feeling waxed stronger and stronger; for in that presidency idolatry was honoured in a more open and offensive manner than in other parts of India; the consciences of Christian men were more grossly outraged by enforced professional connexion with Heathen and Mahomedan rites and ceremonies; and altogether the subject was obtruded more painfully upon the daily lives of the Christian community. It was bad enough to be compelled to attend the festivals of the unconverted, and to salute their idols or processions, under the orders of the authorities in England; but to be forced to do these things, after the authorities had expressed their desire to absolve their servants from such duties, was well nigh intolerable. So, first at one station, then at another, there was talk about remonstrance. A memorial to the Supreme Government was proposed, and soon drawn up and circulated. Hot was the discussion; many were the dissentients; much, from some quarters, the ridicule. But still the memorial made its way; for it stated plain, undeniable facts, and it put forth in temperate language very reasonable requests. "It enumerated," said Bishop Corrie, who forwarded it to the Madras Government, "instances * wherein those whose duty it is to engage in them feel themselves aggrieved by practices and orders, which seem to them contrary to the command of God, thereby subjecting them to the painful alternative of violating the dictates of their

* The instances cited in the memorial were these:—"First, that it is now required of Christian servants of the Government, both civil and military, to attend Heathen and Mahomedan religious festivals, with the view of showing them respect. Second, that in some instances they are called upon to present offerings, and to do homage to idols. Third, that the impure and degrading services of the pagodas are now carried on under the supervision and control of the principal European, and, therefore, Christian officers of the Government, and the management and regulation of the revenues and endowments, both of these pagodas and mosques, so vested in them, under the provision of regulation vii. of 1817, that no important idolatrous ceremony can be performed, no attendant of the various idols, not even the prostitutes of the temple, be entertained or discharged, nor the least expense incurred, without the official concurrence and orders of the Christian functionary. Fourth, that British officers, with the troops of the Government, are also now employed in firing salutes and in otherwise rendering homage to Mahomedan and idolatrous ceremonies, even on the Sabbath day; and Christians are thus not unfrequently compelled by the authority of Government to desecrate their own most sacred institutions and to take part in unholy and degrading superstitions."

consciences, or incurring the displeasure of the
Government; and praying that the same toleration
and exemption which have been long granted to
their Heathen and Mahomedan fellow-subjects may be
extended to the Christian members of this presidency."
"It is my duty," added the good Bishop, "to state that
I fully concur in every part of the memorial and its
prayer." But he would not have concurred in it,
had it not been very temperate—had it not expressly
disavowed all intolerance, and sought only that which
the Court of Directors had already emphatically
sanctioned. "We explicitly disclaim," said the
memorialists, "as utterly inconsistent with our principles as Christians, all desire that the liberty of
conscience so fully and justly accorded to the
Mahomedan and Heathen should be in any degree
violated. Our sole object and wish is to see the
true principles of religious toleration, declared in the
instructions of the Honourable Court of Directors,
practically and universally enforced, believing the
policy there marked out of a real neutrality to be as
safe and salutary as it is wise."

This memorial bore two hundred signatures—the
signatures of chaplains, of missionaries, of civil and
military officers of the Government, of independent
members of society. It appears to me to be a very
temperate and respectful appeal to superior authority;
but it gave great offence to the Madras Government.
It was forwarded to Calcutta, but in announcing this
to Bishop Corrie, the Chief Secretary intimated to him
that the sentiments of the Governor were not in sup-

port of the measures advocated by the memorialists; and then he proceeded, as the organ of Government, to administer a rebuke to the Bishop. "It is matter," he wrote, "of deepest pain and concern to the Right Honourable the Governor in Council that your lordship, instead of exercising the proper influence of your office, strengthened as it must be by the personal respect which is everywhere entertained for you, in moderating the zeal of over-heated minds, should have made yourself the channel of a communication fraught with danger to the peace of the country, and destructive of the harmony and goodwill which should prevail amongst all classes of the community."

Such an extraordinary commentary as this upon what appeared to the Bishop to be a very temperate and respectful manifestation of Christian feeling, surprised as much as it vexed him. He could not sit silent under the unmerited rebuke; so he appealed at once to the Governor-General. "The authority of Government," he wrote to Lord Auckland, "to dictate to me as to the performance of my duties I entirely deny. I hold myself free to act on my own judgment as to what is my duty; and differing as I do from the Right Honourable the Governor of Madras in Council, both as to the propriety of granting the toleration prayed for by the memorialists, and as to the consequence of deferring to grant the relief sought, I consider myself to have been strictly within the line of my duty in forwarding the memorial to Government." Having then stated that the memorial had in reality been not only prepared, but printed and circulated before his arrival at Madras.* Bishop Corrie proceeded to remark. "I observe that some of the Calcutta newspapers accuse the memorialists of asking for more toleration than they are willing to grant to others; and similar opinions may be held in other quarters. I therefore take the liberty, in the name of all the clerical subscribers to the memorial, expressly to deny this: and I am persuaded that I speak the sentiments also of the lay subscribers upon this point. If the firing of a salute on Christmas Day be considered a claiming from the natives of a concession in favour of our religion, let the salute be discontinued: and if there be any other ceremony of our religion in which natives are required to attend (though I know not of any), let compulsory attendance be forbidden." How very much unlike is this to the language of an over-heated zealot. He sought for all religions full liberty of conscience, and on the part of Government universal toleration. He had never entertained in his own mind, or encouraged in others, any extreme views of the duties of the dominant Christian race. He had made every wise allowance for the difficulties with which the Govern-

* The Bishop, on first becoming acquainted with the movement in progress, forwarded, privately, a copy of the memorial to the Governor of Madras, saying, "I have always abstained from taking part in such representations, being aware that Government may have good reasons for measures which the public cannot be acquainted with, and in that of interference with pagodas, I have the fullest confidence that Government will pursue the course which appears wise and proper. But with reference to the Christian military servants of the State, who are occasionally compelled to do honour to the superstitions of the country, I am persuaded that you will not take it amiss the bringing the case to your notice." To this no answer was returned.

ment had to contend, in dealing with the religious institutions of the country; and all that, in this instance, he had striven for was exemption, for his Christian brethren, from compulsory personal connexion with these institutions. The letter of the Madras Government was, indeed, an error without excuse: it was not more at variance with abstract propriety than with the tenor of the instructions received from superior authority at home.

To Corrie, however, it was but a small matter. It was not suffered long to vex his holy spirit; for he was about to appear before a Judge, who would not rebuke him for over-heated zeal in the cause of Christianity. On the 5th of February, 1837, he died, after a brief illness, at Madras. He had held the episcopal office little more than a year, when amidst a general burst of grief, he was carried off to receive his reward. For more than thirty years, he had done the work of his Master unwearyingly and ungrudgingly, and had, perhaps, achieved a larger success than any single labourer in the same vineyard. In the Christian biography of the present century there may be more shining characters, but there are no better men. Of what he was, and how he was esteemed, as chaplain and as archdeacon, I have, but with inadequate expression, spoken in many chapters of this book. "It is almost inconceivable," said Bishop Wilson, who preached his funeral sermon, "how far in the brief space of his bishopric he had won all hearts to his mild rule, and conciliated universal esteem to the Church and her offices in his new and extensive diocese." There were servants of Christ in his time, and perhaps, on the same field of labour, with higher enthusiasm, stronger energies, and more commanding intellect, but not one who accomplished more than Corrie accomplished by mere singleness of purpose, and constancy of effort. Bengal and Upper India were studded with monuments of his successful exertions.[*] And, on the whole, I am inclined to think, that next to the holy man who melted the hearts of his audience by the touching tribute to the worth of the deceased prelate which I have quoted above, there is no one of whom the Christian historian of India will take more loving account than of Daniel Corrie, Bishop of Madras, but better known as Archdeacon of Calcutta.

Whilst the Madras memorial was slowly making its way to England, through the authorised official channels, another letter respecting the great question of Government connexion with idolatry was voyaging out to India.[†] It was the visible growth of that feeling of uneasiness and alarm, which the recollection of the Christian epistle of 1833 had engendered in the breasts of the majority of the Directors. It was precisely the kind of document, which, in any view of

---

[*] "Wherever I passed," said Bishop Wilson, in the beautiful *éloge* quoted in the text, "in places he had resided, Corrie's was the name constantly repeated. Corrie built the church and founded the mission at Chunar. Corrie built the chapel and school-house at Agra. Corrie built the two churches at Benares, and founded, or caused to be founded, the schools. At Buxar it was also the same. What he did in founding the high school at Calcutta, what as respected the free school, what in Mrs. Wilson's female schools, what at Mirzapore, what in the Church Missionary and Bible Society Committees, you all know." A longer extract, illustrative of Corrie's character, taken from this discourse will find a suitable place in the Appendix.

[†] Under date Feb. 22, 1837.

the case, was least required at such a time. Had the local Government shown any disposition to enter upon a career of rash innovation, there might have been some reason for the extension of a restraining hand. But why the Court should have taken the trouble to help the local Government to do nothing, unless they were really anxious practically to cancel the instructions issued in Charles Grant's time, it is not easy to perceive. Plainly and unmistakeably the despatch sanctioned all past delays, and encouraged future inactivity. It called the especial attention of the Supreme Government to the conditions with which the Court had burdened their former instructions, and significantly said that they had no doubt that it would take long to collect the information for which they had called. I cannot help thinking the despatch a very discreditable one. Sir Peregrine Maitland, the Commander-in-Chief of the Madras Army, a Christian warrior worthy to be held by all ages in honourable remembrance, thought so badly of it that he straightway resigned.*

The excitement which the intelligence of this event created in the religious mind of Great Britain was intense. There was an outcry against what appeared to be the unchristian retrogression of those who had pledged themselves to go forward—against the violation of the promise made five years before by the voice of authority to the Christianity of Great Britain. The pledges given in the despatch of 1833

---

* Mr. Robert Nelson, a Madras civilian, resigned the service on the same grounds.

had been virtually cancelled, and one of the highest officers of the State, ashamed of his connexion with such a Government, had retired from it in disgust. An act so decided as this—an act which told upon the public mind as no words, whether of argument or remonstrance, could have done, alarmed the Home Government of India. Alike in Leadenhall-street and in Westminster was it apparent that this policy would not do. Parliament was appealed to; Parliament was roused. Sir John Hobhouse was then the responsible Indian Minister. He told the House of Commons, that he should use "the discretion vested in him by the Act of Parliament, to direct such a despatch to be sent to India as would render it impossible for any functionary there to make a mistake." He would take care, he added, and he trusted that the Court of Directors would agree with him, to have such a despatch sent out to India as would perfectly satisfy the most tender conscience. He did not state that he had been responsible for the short-comings of the Directors during the preceding years, and that the despatch of the 22nd of February, 1837, had been written under his auspices.

The promised instructions were speedily sent. The pledge was given to Parliament on the 26th of July, 1838; and on the 8th of August, the despatch was signed. Under the influence of this pressure from without, there could be no more dallying on the banks; this time the plunge was taken. The orders sent out were clear and unmistakeable. After alluding to the previous despatches, the Directors proceeded to say:

" We have again to express our anxious desire that you should accomplish, with as little delay as may be practicable, the arrangements which we believe to be already in progress for abolishing the Pilgrim-tax, and for discontinuing the connexion of the Government with the management of all funds which may be assigned for the support of the religious institutions in India. We more particularly desire that the management of all temples and other places of religious resort, together with the revenues derived therefrom, be resigned into the hands of the natives; and that the interference of the public authorities in the religious ceremonies of the people, be regulated by the instructions conveyed in our despatch of the 20th of February, 1833." " We further desire," said the Court, " that you will make such arrangements as may appear to you to be necessary for relieving all our servants, whether Christians, Mahomedans or Hindoos, from the compulsory performance of any acts, which you may consider to be justly liable to objections on the ground of religious scruples."

It is admitted even by those who have been loudest in their condemnation of the traditional policy of the East India Company, that from that time the Court of Directors never drew back again. Their orders for the severance of all connexion between the State and the idolatries of the country were explicit and imperative; and they watched with a jealous eye the measures of the local Government, stimulating the inactive and rebuking the disobedient, and never missing an opportunity of pushing on the good work by timely exhortation and instruction. Under this pressure, the local authorities were compelled—reluctantly, I am afraid, in some cases—to move forward in the right direction; and in all the presidencies of India, the work of dissolution went on, if not with a celerity to satisfy the more eager, with a steadfastness that gave plentiful assurance to the more reasonable Christian reformers. Bonds such as then existed, the growth of years, could not be hastily severed. The complications were so great; the questions involved were so numerous; the evil to be eradicated was so much a part of the general administrative system of the country, that the work to be achieved was a great and laborious one, and only to be eventually accomplished by progressive efforts extending over many years.

## CHAPTER XII.

Severance of Government connexion with Idolatry—Employment of Native agency—Administration of temple-funds—Landed endowments—Money-payments—Missionary efforts—Bishop Wilson—Connexion of Government servants with Missionary schemes—The Hindoo law of inheritance —Education.

THE work, however, was worthily commenced. The great series of Government measures for the severance of its connexion with the idolatries of the country was fitly inaugurated by the total abolition of the Pilgrim-tax. And on the 3rd of May, 1840, in pursuance of an Act passed in the preceding month, the gate of the great temple of Juggernauth was thrown open to the pilgrim, amidst a convulsion of nature which threatened to destroy even the stately pagoda itself.

The year 1841 was a year of determined and systematic action. The supreme Government issued its orders to the minor Governments, and they in turn sent forth their instructions to the departments under them. But it was an easier thing to direct absolute withdrawal from " all interference with native temples and places of religious resort," than to carry these instructions into effect. Indeed, when the work came to be done, it was found to be very difficult. The administration of the religious endowments was so mixed up with the revenue system of the country that our public officers, in many instances, found themselves perplexed in the extreme, not knowing how to carry out the orders of the Government without doing palpable injustice to a large number of people.

The first thing to be accomplished was the substitution of some other agency from that of the servants of Government, to which the executive management of the religious institutions might be entrusted. Nothing was plainer than that the administration should be vested " in those individuals who, professing the same faith, may be thought best qualified to conduct that administration with fidelity and regularity, such individuals, together with their subordinate officers, being held responsible to the courts of justice for any breach of the duties and trusts assumed by them." The theory of this was excellent, and the practice would seem to have been easy of fulfilment; but a question arose as to the appointment of these native trustees. Doubtless, the best means of securing the conduct of the administration with fidelity and regularity was by vesting the appointment of trustees and managers in the hands of the Government. But it was objected to this, that there was little real difference between Government servants and Government nominees ; and that, therefore, the disconnexion of the Christian Government from the administration of the heathen institutions of the country would, under such a system, be incomplete. On the other hand, under any other system, there was likely to be no small amount of mismanagement and malversation, no remedy for which could possibly be supplied by our courts of justice. Here, again, a difficult question was suggested, or one, rather, made difficult by the widely different opinions brought to its solution. There were some who contended that idolatry, being an unmitigated evil, could not be rendered worse by the bad administration of its affairs—that it was better to leave it to perish by the innate force of its own corruption than to endeavour to impart any respectability and security to it. Others, on the other hand, declared that to withdraw all securities against administrative corruption was simply to superadd evil upon evil, and that there was no reason why, because the religion of the people was false, there should be no check upon the evil practices of those entrusted with the management of its affairs. That a false religion well conducted is worse than the same thing ill conducted, is not very apparent. The question, however, was considered an open one, and the practice was left uncertain. Whilst the Bombay Government resolved that the choice of administrators should be left to the worshippers themselves,*

* "In carrying out the principle of entirely severing Government and its officers from any interference whatever in matters connected with the native religious institutions, the Governor in Council is of opinion that in whatever way corporate bodies of trusts may be established, it should be provided that vacancies are to be filled up without the intervention of Government, either by a kind of election in certain families, or in such other way as the Government of India may determine upon, and that the Poojárees, or officiating priests, or the heads of the castes connected with the institution should be the parties having authority to prosecute the trustees for any malversation or breach of trust."—*Resolution of Bombay Government, Feb.* 27, 1841.

F F

in Madras the nomination of trustees was left to the British collector.

The agencies to which the charge of the religious institutions of the country were now entrusted were of various kinds. In some places, the superintendence of the temples was entrusted to a single man—to some rajah or influential zemindar; Juggernauth, for example, being given over to the management of the Rajah of Koordah. In others, the trust was vested in punchayets, or native committees, the hereditary village officers being associated with the temple priests and with private individuals of high local position.* In the same manner, the mosques were given over to the charge of respectable Mahomedan gentlemen, chosen generally from among their most regular frequenters. From that time the servants of Government ceased altogether to interfere in the internal management of the mosques and pagodas;† ceased to concern themselves about the repairs of the buildings; ceased to take part in the preparation of their

---

* The agencies employed in the Madras Presidency, in which Government connexion with idolatry existed in its most varied and extensive aspects, are thus described by Mr. Daniel Eliott, in his admirable report:—" The arrangements which have been made with respect to Hindu institutions are various. The small village pagodas had not generally been under the charge of Government officers: but, where such charge had been assumed, it has been resigned to the pujari, who is looked upon in the light of one of the village functionaries, entitled to merafis, with the smith, carpenter, and the like. In the case of larger temples, with more considerable endowments, two or more of the principal inhabitants, including generally the official head of the village or the Carnum, have been conjoined with the pujari in a committee or panchayet. Temples of more importance, with a reputation and interest extending beyond the vicinity, have been placed under the charge of committees, composed of persons of weight and influence, selected from among the residents within a wider range. Endowments belonging to matums or gurus have been left to the care of the parties interested; and institutions of which the managers have been usually appointed by such matums, have been deemed to need no other superintendence."

† Perhaps this ought to be stated with some qualification, for the Regulations, under which this management was given over to Govern-

festivals; ceased to superintend the decoration of their cars and the equipments of their idols; ceased to appoint those whose business it was to tend the gods and take custody of the temples.

But there was at least one class of religious endowments the administration of which could not immediately be handed over to native trustees. The landed revenues of the pagodas, like all other funds, were made over to the native administrators; but their collection still remained with the Government revenue officers. It was not considered just or expedient that they should relinquish the management of lands (attached to religious institutions) which had been assumed for the purpose of securing the public revenue, or in order that protection and justice might be afforded to the ryots. The continuation of the management of such lands by the revenue officers, it was remarked by the Supreme Government, was " due as a measure of justice to the agriculturists, whose contracts and engagements have been made in anticipation of the continued management of the land by Government."

Plain, however, as this may have been, as a question of abstract justice, the proposal to continue the management of the pagoda-lands was not in accordance with the theory of total withdrawal from all connexion with the religious institutions of the country. It was suggested, therefore, that Government should resume the lands, and pay, in lieu of their revenue, a fixed

ment servants, were not repealed; and the total separation aimed at was not effected. Here and there some remains of the old system have survived up to the present time. But the last link of the connexion is now (1859) about to be broken.

F F 2

annual amount to the trustees. This money-payment, however, of which I shall presently say something more, was held by some to be a more objectionable, because a more direct, method of supporting the false religions of the people. The difficulty did not escape the notice of the Court of Directors; but they believed that it could be overcome. They believed that arrangements might be made of such a character as to prevent the transfer of authority over the pagoda-lands from being injurious to the ryots—that if the revenue were fixed at an equitable amount, the collection of it might be " safely transferred to agents, to be appointed by the parties in whom the management of the affairs and funds of the institutions may be vested, subject to such penalties against exactions and other abuses of their trust as the native servants similarly employed on the part of Government would be liable to;" and, accordingly, they directed that the management of the pagoda-lands should be made over to native trustees, care being taken to secure, as far as possible, the interests of the cultivators by granting them beneficial leases before effecting the transfer.

This was another most important step towards the total severance of the ties which bound the British Government to the idolatries of the country. One more has now to be mentioned. The attendance of British officers at Hindoo and Mahomedan festivals; the turning out of our troops to grace their ceremonies; and the firing of salutes in their honour—practices which had obtained to an unfortunate extent, especially in the Madras Presidency—were now to be disallowed.

In a circular letter signed by the Military Secretary to the Government of Fort St. George, and addressed to the Commander-in-Chief, under date of July 6, 1841, it is intimated, " under instructions from the Court of Directors, conveyed through the Government of India," that " the attendance of troops or of military bands at native festivals or ceremonies, and the firing of salutes on occasions of that nature," were " in future to be discontinued, with the object of separating the Government and its officers, as far as possible, from all connexion with the ceremonies of the Hindoo and Mahomedan religions." The ordinary marks of respect paid to native princes on the occasions of their going forth or returning from such festivals or religious observances were, however, to be paid ; and the change was to be effected " in a manner calculated not to alarm the minds of the natives or to offend their feelings." These orders were circulated by the Commander-in-Chief to the generals commanding divisions, and by them to the regiments under their several commands.

But it was still objected that Government had not ceased to be connected with the religious institutions of the country, for large sums of public money were paid towards their support. It ought to have been enough to answer to this, that such money-payments represented either certain property or certain endowments enjoyed by those religious institutions before the country passed under the rule of the British Government. Our Government had taken the property, and the payments made to the mosques or pagodas were simply for value received. This is admitted with respect to one class of payments—those made in lieu of the revenues of resumed lands—but not with respect to the grants made in continuance of similar contributions from the native rulers whose authority we supplanted. It was urged that those grants being voluntary gifts might be discontinued without injustice. But, in fact, they were not less payments for value received than the others whose claims were admitted. With those grants, and with promises, actual or constructive, of their continuance, the British Government, in a transition-period (and all transition-periods are more or less critical), purchased the good-will and the quiescence of the people. I do not conceive that, having gained those ends, or, in other words, having received the value for which the promise was given, we have any sort of right to withdraw from it.

I know what will be replied to this. It will be said that they were originally grants from Hindoo or Mahomedan Governments to religions believed to be true; not, as in our case, to religions known to be false. But if those religions are now known to be false, they were equally known to be false when we undertook to endow them. This, however, is not, it appears to me, the main argument by which the objection is to be overthrown. The money paid to these people, for the support of their religious institutions, is their own money: it is money which

they pay to the state as Hindoo or Mahomedan
tax-payers. Now our system is a system of declared
religious neutrality. But considerable sums of money
are paid annually, from the revenues of India—that
is, by Hindoo and Mahomedan tax-payers—towards
the support of the Christian Church. Can it be
said, then, that the British Government especially
supports Mahomedanism and Hindooism, because it
allows some portion of the revenues derived from the
labour of the people to be devoted to the endowment
of their national faiths? If the religion of the few
is to be supported from the revenues of the country,
why, on any conceivable principle of neutrality, is
not the religion of the many? And if they who do
not contribute to the revenue are to be supplied from
it with temples and with priests, why, in the name
of all that is reasonable, are not the people who
*do?*

Moreover, it is certain that when the British
Government finally determined to disconnect themselves from the management of the religious institutions of the country, it was their policy to make
the people believe that the change was intended for
their own good, and that no grants or customary
allowances made by Government would be withdrawn. In the Madras Presidency, special instructions were given to the revenue officers to impress
this on the minds of the people:—" In carrying the
instructions which may be issued into effect," wrote
the Chief Secretary to the Board of Revenue, " it
is essential that you give your most careful attention

to local circumstances and to native feelings and prejudices, and that you make it generally understood that the object of the Honourable Court of Directors is to leave to the people the management of their own religious institutions without the interference on the part of the revenue officers of Government, and that there is no intention of withholding any authorized and customary payments and allowances."

These instructions were issued on the 12th of June, 1841, and on the 5th of July they were approved by the Supreme Government of India. Nothing could be more distinct or more comprehensive than these orders. The payments here secured to the pagodas were not merely those which had the support of some distinct engagement or promise from the British Government, but those also which had obtained by prescriptive usage. The "customary allowances," whatever their origin, were to be continued.*

---

* The question of the money-payment to Juggernauth turned upon special grounds. Lord Auckland declared that there was an absolute and unconditional pledge from Government to continue it. Mr. Mills, the Commissioner of Cuttack, was of opinion that the promise was merely a constructive one, but that it was the duty of Government to continue the payment. At a later period, however, the Bengal Government, on a deliberate reconsideration of the question, involving no small amount of historical inquiry, ruled that the abolition of the pilgrim-tax had absolved Government from its previous obligation to continue the money-payment, which had virtually been made from the surplus pilgrim-funds. The case is thus stated in the letter of the Bengal secretary (Mr. Halliday):—"The object originally in view was no doubt to secure the peaceable possession of the province, by conciliating the people in general, and by removing from them all apprehension of any design on our part to interfere with their religion; but it was fully understood by all parties that we were not to be losers by the measure, and that we were to be reimbursed by the collections from the pilgrims. When, however, the means of reimbursement no longer existed, in consequence of the boon granted to the Hindoo community at large by the abolition of the tax, and the parties in charge of the temple had before

But were there no means of meeting the difficulty by a compromise? The plain fact of a direct money-payment from the Company's treasury being held, by reason of its very plainness and directness, to be objectionable in the extreme, it was suggested that the Government might evade the continually recurring necessity of feeding the revenues of Idolatry, by making over in perpetuity to the idol-trustees certain lands, yielding an income equal to the annual donation. Another proof of the difficulties with which the whole question was beset—of the inconsistencies and contradictions which started up at every turn! A little while before, nay, about the very same time, when the land-endowment question had been discussed, and the evils of handing over the administration of certain tracts of country to private individuals had been under consideration, it had been proposed to commute these landed revenues for direct money-payments; and now the very obverse of this proposal was recommended. But when this recommendation, with especial reference to Juggernauth, was considered by the Bengal Board of Revenue, they declared that they could not concur in it. "The distinction," they said, "appears to them quite illusory; and with reference to the peculiar value set by the people on landed endowments, they are of opinion that the proposed plan involves even greater evils than that now in operation. There is, in fact, no argument against the simple

them the prospect of a great influx of pilgrims, and a still greater influx of offerings, it was neither necessary nor proper, nor consistent with the object in view, that the donation should be continued."

payment of a donation in money which does not apply with greater force against a permanent endowment in land, and if it be not just and expedient to pursue the one course, it may be certainly predicated that no case can be made out for adopting the other."[*] There being, therefore, no escape, through the agency of a compromise, Government, except when there was some special justificatory plea for resumption, held to the money-payments; and I humbly conceive that they were right.

I do not assert that it would be the part of a Christian Government to initiate concessions of revenue for the support of the religious institutions of Mahomedans or Hindoos, but it is as little the part of such a Government, having obtained the sovereignty of an Indian province by substitution— or, as some would say, by usurpation—to deprive those institutions of any endowments which they possessed at the time of our assumption of the government; and, if it be unjust to deprive them of such endowments at the outset of our career of dominion, it is doubly unjust, doubly dishonourable, to do so at a later period, when we have tided over our first difficulties by reconciling the people to the change, on the plea that the British Government would withhold from them none of the privileges and immunities which they had enjoyed under their native princes. If the resumption is to take place at all, it should take place at once, so that we may

---

* Secretary to the Board of Revenue to the Secretary to the Government of Bengal.  July 29, 1845.

not add deception to injustice. To conciliate the people in a critical conjuncture by delusive promises, to be broken in a season of security, is simply to commit a fraud upon them; it is to make promise of payment for value received, and then deliberately to dishonour it.

The Christianity which ignores truth and justice is not very appreciable. But enough was done at this time to vindicate the genuine Christianity of the nation, and fortunately no heed was given, in a general sense, to these spoliatory recommendations. There are those who think that the British Government could not have done less at such a time; I am certain that it ought not to have done more. But there was nothing to restrain the energies of independent societies, and great efforts were nobly made for the diffusion of the true faith. Throughout the whole of this epoch—I mean, up to the year 1853—the activity of the missionaries was deserving of all honour. I cannot now speak in detail of the endeavours or of the successes of individual men. History takes account of the pioneers—of those who go singly into the thicket, clearing their way with axe and hatchet, and opening the road for the later crowd; but, although in that crowd there may be men with like energies, who, as precursors, had Providence so willed it, would have done the same, yet they are but of the multitude multitudinous, and are lost in the crush.

The religious societies of Great Britain had now attained to their maturity of vigour; and they were

sending forth their torch-bearers to all the dark
places of the earth.    It was no longer a reproach
to the "lordly Episcopalians" that the Church of
England could not find in its communion men willing
to abandon the ease and comfort of home, with the
prospect of ecclesiastical preferment, in exchange for
the privilege of declaring God's truth to the heathen.
Churchmen now vied with Dissenters in the great and
glorious work.    At every place of note in the country
a missionary station was established.    Churches and
schools sprung up as if by magic.    Money in abundance was forthcoming.    From every cantonment in
India, almost, it may be said, from every town and
village in England, contributions poured in, directly
or indirectly, for the sustentation of Indian missions.

Never before had the great cause enjoyed such
earnest hierarchical support.    In Bishop Wilson, the
chief priest of the Indian Church, the pure missionary
spirit glowed with intense fervour.    In Bengal, he
was worthily seconded by Thomas Dealtry, Archdeacon of Calcutta, upon whom afterwards the mitre
of Madras descended; and in the Southern and
Western presidencies by Bishops Spencer and Carr.
It would be a privilege to write in detail of the career
of such a man as Bishop Wilson.    That the privilege
is duly appreciated, and will be worthily exercised by
him who has the best right to it, there is ample assurance, and in the assurance great comfort.    For the
period of a quarter of a century that most evangelical
of bishops, and most devout of men, presided over the
Indian Church.    No warnings of failing health, of

enfeebling age, of increasing exhaustion and prostration; no thought of home and its endearing ties, of honoured old age, and lettered ease in his native country, could drive him or lure him from his post. He had resolved to die in harness; and in harness he died, bewailing the wickedness of the heathen, in the midst of the great Indian rebellion, and praying for their conversion to the saving faith.   He was a man *sui generis*.   He lived in the world, but was not of it.   I do not think that I ever saw in a man of his advanced years such childlike simplicity.   He mixed largely with society; indeed, it may be said that, in the best Christian sense, he was of a really social disposition; hospitable, courteous, of an overflowing kindliness, incapable of a malicious feeling, or an ungenerous act; and yet I have known people to writhe beneath the guileless, unconsidered words which had fallen from his lips.   His eccentricities of demeanour, conspicuous as they were to some, and frequent subjects of irreverent discourse to men unmindful of his many fine qualities, were little observed by those who came within their genial influence, and had eyes to see and faculties to understand the inner nature of the man.   His strong devotional spirit, his self-forgetfulness in his Master's cause, his unstinting love towards his fellows, his earnestness of speech, his energy of action, had something of an almost apostolic greatness about them.   Few of his contemporaries had taken so little of the form and pressure of the times in which he lived.

In the course of his long episcopal career, he

traversed all parts of India. In the progress of
Christian missions he took the deepest interest, and
he went from station to station, encouraging, animating, aiding all. He was of the high evangelical
order of Churchmen; and he would not sanction any
of those compromises and half conversions, those
clingings to the old garments of caste, which the
earlier missionaries, not altogether without episcopal
authority, had yielded to in perfect good faith, and as
some think, with full Christian warrant. On the
banner which he carried, the word " Thorough" was
emblazoned. He did everything in a large way.
Although pure Gospel truth was far dearer to him
than the dignity of the Church over which he presided, he strove mightily for the outward honour of
that Church, and he has left an enduring monument
of his resolution in the great cathedral of Calcutta.
In the face of many discouragements—discouragements even from friends, who believed that the money
expended on that magnificent structure might have
been more profitably diffused over a larger area—he
laboured onwards unceasingly, giving largely from his
own store, and seeing the completion of his work, as
he often said he should, in time to lay his bones
beneath it. If he was mistaken in this, it was a grand
mistake. Only those, who were alike ignorant and
uncharitable, ascribed it to personal vanity. The
dominant idea in his mind was that of an outward
manifestation of the glories of the Christian Church,
speaking through its visible magnificence to the
senses of the unconverted. Why should Error be

proclaimed thus triumphantly, with all that is gorgeous and beautiful in Art to symbolise its attractions, and Truth be left without a fitting monument of its greatness?  He had visions, too, of a noble army of Christian Churchmen, in association with a richly-endowed cathedral establishment, radiating thence to the uttermost parts of the Indies, and carrying the glad tidings of salvation to places where none before had breathed the name of Christ.  He may have been right, or he may have been wrong; but right or wrong, he was moved only by honest impulses and worthy desires to do God service in that way; and the most that can be said by those who differ from him is that his way was not their way, and that in all probability he had considered the subject more thoughtfully and prayerfully than themselves.

That the character and example of such a man as Bishop Wilson must have contributed largely to that progressive improvement in the religious character of the English in India, which we contemplate with so much satisfaction, is not to be doubted.  Certainly, an impulse was given to the active Christianity of our countrymen, the good fruits of which it is not easy to overvalue.  Among the principal laymen of the period—servants of the Company—there were many men of distinguished piety and benevolence; men who, like Wilberforce Bird, Frederick Millett, and John Lowis, in Bengal; Thomas Thomason (worthy son of a worthy master), in the North-Western Provinces; J. B. Thomas, in Madras; and James Farish, in Bombay,—demonstrated, by the lustre which their Christian graces shed upon their high position, how the best servants of Christ might also be the best servants of the temporal Government. Their example was largely followed by men of less elevated station. The military servants of the Government vied with the civilians. Even the ensign cheerfully contributed his rupees to church-building funds and missionary societies. The ordinances of the Church were diligently observed. The Sabbath-day was kept holy. Family prayer became a necessity of daily life. Public theatricals languished for want of aristocratic support. English gentlemen esteemed it a reproach to be seen at the nautches of the native gentry. Society ceased to tolerate public lotteries. There was an increased demand for religious books and periodicals. And, altogether, the manifestations of a vital Christianity were not less encouraging than those evinced by contemporary middle classes at home.

But the activity of the Government servants alarmed the Government. From time to time tidings reached England that a proselytizing spirit was abroad among the officers of the State—that soldiers and civilians were usurping the functions of the missionary—and so interfering with the religions of the people of the country as to awaken suspicion of the good faith of Government itself. What was the pledged neutrality of the State so long as its officers who represented it were violating that neutrality? To what extent this violation had been carried was not very clear; but there appeared to be no reason to doubt that some indiscretions had been committed; that there had been in some cases too palpable and obtrusive an identification of the Government servant with the private individual—an application, perchance, of the resources of Government itself to purposes of Gospel-diffusion.    Perhaps, Government buildings had been lent for missionary meetings; perhaps, the native servants of the Government had been employed to collect missionary subscriptions.    At all events, some notion of this kind was entertained by the Court of Directors, who, clearly perceiving that all their efforts to convince the people of the religious neutrality of Government would be frustrated, if their officers did not practically adhere to this policy—for in the eyes of the natives the Government officers are the Government—determined in some manner to check the zeal of their *employés*.    So, after due consideration of the matter, they incubated a despatch.

On the 21st of April, 1847, Mr. Tucker being then in the chair, it was signed by the Court of Directors. It called "immediate and particular attention" to the necessity of Government servants, civil and military, abstaining from all interference with the religion of the natives of India.*    The despatch is so vague and

---

* "You are aware that we have uniformly maintained the principle of abstaining from all interference with the religion of the natives of India. It is obviously essential to the due observance of that principle that it should be acted upon by our servants, civil and military. The Government is known throughout India by its officers, with whom it is identified in the eyes of the native inhabitants, and our servants should, therefore, be aware that, while invested with public authority, their acts cannot be regarded as those of private individuals. We are, however, led by circumstances of recent occurrence to conclude that a different view of this subject is taken in India, and we, therefore, deem it necessary to call your immediate and particular attention to the absolute necessity of maintaining this most important principle in its fullest extent."

G G

meaningless, that there is reason to suspect that all
pith and purpose were cut out of it, in its passage
through Committee, Court, and Cannon Row, in a
hopeless endeavour to reconcile a diversity of conflicting opinions. No wonder that it puzzled the
Government to which it was addressed. The President in Council at Calcutta could make nothing
of it; the Governor-General at Simlah could make
nothing of it. The members of Government, one
and all, Lord Hardinge, Sir Herbert Maddock,
Mr. Millett, and Sir Frederick Currie, were all
alike thrown into a state of ludicrous embarrassment.
But as there was no meaning in the despatch—at
least, none that they could discover—they virtually
determined to take no action upon it. No orders
were to be issued to the officers of the two services;
but the heads of the minor governments, and the
Commander-in-Chief of the army, were to be made
acquainted with the Court's despatch, and instructed
to communicate it to such high and confidential
officers of the State as might be able, by their
influence, to prevent any contravention of the principle laid down by the Court. But as no one clearly
knew what that principle was, these orders were
practically nothing.

The Governor-General and Mr. Millett, referring
to a previous despatch of the Court, in which it was
declared to be the duty of Government, "and not
less of its officers, to stand aloof from all missionary
labours, either as promoting or opposing them," conceived that to be the " principle " now inculcated by

the Home Government; but as the Governor-General declared his belief that the "interference alluded to by the Honourable Court is almost unknown in the Bengal army," and as the Commander-in-Chief had "reason to believe that *no officer* contravened this order of the Court, by interfering with the religion of the natives," whilst nothing was more certain than that a large number of officers of the Bengal army "promoted missionary labours," it is clear that the principle was differently understood by different authorities, and sometimes variously interpreted even by the same functionary. In their perplexity, however, they did the best thing that they could do; they wrote to the Court of Directors for an interpretation of their previous orders; and in due course another despatch was sent out to India, not quite so indefinite as its predecessor, but still giving anything but a certain sound. "The application of the rule," it was said, "should in every case be governed by the principle on which it is founded."

But the question at issue related not to the application of the principle, but to the principle itself. The principle was declared to be a principle of non-interference with the religions of the people. But what did "non-interference" mean? The later despatch, in some measure, explained the meaning of the term, as applied to the conduct of the servants of Government. "While we are unwilling," wrote the Court, to prohibit our servants from contributing their private funds towards the promotion of objects which they may feel to be connected with the interests of the religion, we would caution them against any manifestation of a disposition calculated to excite uneasiness and alarm among the people. We think also that missionary meetings ought never to be held in official buildings, or to wear the appearance of having any official sanction." In this last sentence there is a clear and definite expression of opinion, to which I was easy to give practical effect: but it did not go very far towards the settlement of the question, and the determination of the general practice to be followed by the servants of the Government. In truth, after no small quantity of despatch-writing and minute-writing, the whole matter was left very much as I was before.

In every mixed assembly like the Court of Directors, there is sure, on such a subject as this, to be a considerable diversity of opinion. The declared policy of such a body, therefore, partakes largely of the nature of a compromise. Up to a certain point there was very little difference of opinion between the several members of the Home Government of India. They were well nigh agreed, both with respect to the principle and the practice of the non-interference of Government itself, but when they went beyond this, and began to consider the extent to which the servants Government ought to be debarred, as individual from following the dictates of conscience, and avouring to diffuse the precious truths of the pel among the ignorant people of the soil, there naturally less harmony of opinion. It seemed, on hand, perfectly clear that although no servant of the Government ought in his official capacity to identify himself with missionary operations, he had an inalienable right, as an individual man, to do what he conceived to be his duty to Christianity, by promoting the diffusion of the truth. A man, as some were wont to phrase it, did not cease to be a servant of Christ when he became the servant of the Company. It seemed to be sufficient, therefore, to instruct public functionaries in India never to bring the prestige of their official position to the aid of missionary endeavours. Every Englishman knows the difference between what he does in his official and what he does in his personal capacity. It was easy, therefore, for a soldier or a civilian to divest himself, to his own entire satisfaction, of his official capacity, when attending missionary meetings, or promoting missionary subscriptions, or entertaining missionaries at his house. But it was argued, on the other hand, that however distinct might be the actions of the private individual from those of the public functionary in his own eyes, the distinction was not equally clear in the eyes of the people of the country. In their estimation, the Collector Sahib, or the Colonel Sahib, is always the Collector Sahib, or the Colonel Sahib. Let him, it is said, adopt what precautions he may to divest himself of his official character, let him go to the missionary meeting unattended by orderlies or chuprassies, and sign his name as plain John Brown, or Thomas Smith, still, in the eyes of the natives, it is the Collector or the Colonel who attends the missionary meeting, and thus declares his hostility to the

religions of the country. It was because the people
never separate the man from the officer, and draw no
distinction between the acts of the officer and the
acts of the Government which he serves, that some
questioned the propriety of permitting public servants,
civil or military, to take any ostensible part in operations designed for the conversion of Hindoos and
Mahomedans to the religion of Jesus Christ. And
it was a necessity of this conflict of opinion, that the
instructions sent out to India by the Home Government should have been of a somewhat uncertain and
undemonstrative character.

The question, it must be admitted, is a very difficult one. Subsequent efforts have been made to
settle it, but with no better result. And, indeed, I
hardly think that it ever can be settled in a satisfactory manner. To lay down general instructions,
defining the precise extent to which the inalienable
right which every man possesses to promote the interests of his religion, may be carried in practice without
coming into collision with the duties imposed upon
the public officer by the Government which he serves,
and therefore which he is bound to obey, appears to
be a hopeless task, and if not hopeless, perhaps an
unprofitable one. It is better that every man should
follow the dictates of his own conscience in such a
matter, and that Government should deal with individual cases as they arise. Though it may be very
difficult to define in written words the limits of the
permitted and harmless interference of Government
servants in efforts for the religious advancement or

social improvement of the people, I scarcely think that in a man's own mind there can be any inward conflicts, or that any one can go far wrong for want of intelligible instructions. Much has been said, and said most truly, about the higher duties imposed upon every Christian man by the mere fact of his Christianity; and it is asked what a man is to do when his conscience tells him that his duties as an officer and a Christian are in antagonism with each other? The answer may not be a convenient one; but, once given, there is an end of the matter. He is bound to be a Christian; he is not bound to be an officer. The inward conflict may be tranquillized at once by his ceasing to be the latter.

But whilst Government were thus impressing upon their servants the duty of an absolute religious neutrality, they were themselves sanctioning measures which were by no means regarded in that light by the people, and which were calculated to create a far greater tumult than the most indiscreet demonstrations of individual men. It is not my intention to write here in detail of the great humanizing efforts of the British Government as manifested in the suppression of Suttee, of Female Infanticide, of Human Sacrifices, and other kindred abominations; but there is one measure of the British Government, belonging to this period, so intimately associated with the subject of this work, that it ought not to be passed over. I speak of the change which has been introduced into the Hindoo law of inheritance. By that law, a Hindoo, on abjuring his Hindooism, *ipso* *facto* was disinherited. The Mahomedan law was equally distinct and equally intolerant. All right to the inheritance of property, ancestral or acquired, was forfeited by apostacy. The apostate was regarded as one civilly or legally dead. That such a state of the law must have been a severe hindrance to Christianity, is plain. It was an evil, indeed, which those who laboured for the conversion of Hindoos and Mahomedans were continually bewailing; and an evil to which it appeared to them a legislative remedy might be applied without violation of the neutrality of Government. The subject was brought prominently to the notice of the Court of Directors, who, as far back as the year 1832, directed an inquiry to be made and some legislative remedy to be applied. Lord William Bentinck was then Governor-General. He at once gave his attention to the subject, and in the course of that year, 1832, a regulation was passed, the effect of which was to secure to persons, whether Hindoos or Mahomedans, or converts from those religions, the property in their possession at the time of the passing of the Act.* The regulation, however, only applied to Bengal; and was even there only a partial remedy for the evil. After many years the Bishop of Bombay called the attention of Government to the painful circum-

---

* The following is the most important portion of it:—"Whenever in any civil suit the parties to such suit may be of different persuasions, when one party shall be of Hindoo and the other of Mahomedan persuasion, or when one or more of the parties to the suit shall not be either of the Hindoo or Mahomedan persuasion, the laws of these religions shall not be permitted to operate to deprive such party or parties of any property to which, but for the operation of such laws, they would have been entitled; in all such cases the decision shall be governed by the principles of justice, equity, and good conscience."

stances in which native converts to Christianity
were placed, by the existing state of the law; and he
was told in reply that an Act which would meet all
the requirements of the case was under the consideration of the Legislative Council. This was in 1845.
The draft Act was published in the *Gazette*; and it
contained a clause enacting—" that so much of the
Hindoo and Mahomedan law as inflicts forfeiture of
rights or property upon any party renouncing, or who
has been excluded from the communion of either of
these religions, shall cease to be enforced as law in
the courts of the East India Company."

The proposed Act of which this formed a part was
that known in history as the " Lex Loci " of 1845.
It struck terror into the souls of the elder generation
of Hindoos. Already were their sons apostatising
from Hindooism, if not to any other faith; already
were they eating beef, indulging in theological disputation, and writing in the newspapers about Reform.
To abolish all penal enactments against the renunciation of their ancestral faith would clearly encourage
this spirit of inquiry—this propensity of young Bengal
to revolt against the absurdities instilled into them in
their cradle. So they memorialised the Government
against the threatened innovation, urging that such a
change struck not only at their laws, but at their
religion (how, will presently be shown), and imploring
that the matter might be reconsidered, the more especially as they regarded the contemplated change only
as a prelude to others equally alarming. The result
of this protest was that Government—after expressing

their regret that at a period when public opinion among a great part of the Hindoos had become in a high degree tolerant and enlightened, a memorial founded upon doctrines of so opposite a nature should have been presented—consented to remove the obnoxious clauses from the Act, and to embody them into a separate Regulation for future consideration.

Four years passed away, and the expurgated clauses never became a substantive Regulation. So in March, 1849, the Bishop of Bombay again called the attention of his Government to the subject, and the Government supported his plaint. Lord Dalhousie was then in the Upper Provinces; but Sir John Littler, President of the Council, at Calcutta, recorded a minute, declaratory of his conviction that it was unfortunate that the measure of relief sought for by the Bombay Government for Christian converts in that Presidency, had been so long delayed, "and apparently without any sufficient cause." "Cannot we extend the provisions of our Act?" asked Sir F. Currie. "I would do so," said Mr. Lowis. And Mr. Bethune, the Legislative Member of Council, did it. I cannot but think, too, that he did it with great judgment. The toleration clauses of the Lex Loci had not been happily worded. They aimed at too much precision and specification. They were particular, instead of general, in their phraseology; and instead of declaring a principle, suggested a palpable application to a particular case. The new legislative experiment was of a totally different kind. It was simply the enunciation of a rule of universal justice, not on the face of it designed for the protection of one particular class of persons, but of people of all colours and all creeds. Mr. Bethune's first idea had been merely to extend the provisions of the Act of 1832. But upon further consideration, he suggested the expediency of passing a brief but comprehensive Act, couched in the following terms:—

" Whereas it was enacted by section 9, regulation vii. of 1832, of the Bengal code, that ' whenever in any civil suit the parties to such suit may be of different persuasions, when one party shall be of the Hindoo and the other of the Mahomedan persuasion, or when one or more of the parties to the suit shall not be either of the Mahomedan or Hindoo persuasions, the laws of those religions shall not be permitted to operate to deprive such party or parties of any property to which, but for the operation of such laws, they would have been entitled;' and whereas it is expedient to extend the principle of that enactment throughout the territories subject to the government of the East India Company;—it is enacted as follows :

" So much of any law or usage now in force within the territories subject to the government of the East India Company as inflicts on any person forfeiture of rights or property, by reason of his or her renouncing, or having been excluded from the communion of any religion, shall cease to be enforced as law in the courts of the East India Company, and in the courts established by Royal Charter within the said territories."

The principle here laid down is one of universal toleration. The Act was not so framed as to appear to have been prepared for the protection of one particular class of her Majesty's subjects. It was ostensibly framed for the protection of all. It secured to every one, not only the property actually in his possession at the time of his renunciation of his ancestral faith, but the right to inherit property as though no such renunciation had taken place. After the passing of the Act, every Christian convert had as much right

to his share of his paternal property as the most
bigoted Hindoo in all the fraternity of his co-in-
heritors.*                              *

There would seem to be, at first sight, such a
soul of justice in the proposed Regulation, that it
would be almost impossible to find anything to object
to it.   But not only was an objection, and a very
weighty one, found by the Hindoo community, but
the very framer of the Act sent it forth from the
legislative anvil with grave doubts and misgivings on
his mind as to the propriety of the proposed enactment.   The simple fact was, that the Hindoo law of
inheritance was not based upon considerations purely
of a civil or legal character; it was interwoven with
the fabric of the Hindoo religion.   The inheritance
of every Hindoo descended to him burdened with
certain obligations or conditions; nay, indeed, it was
said to be actually contingent upon the performance
of ceremonial duties only to be performed by a co-reli-
gionist of the deceased. This was certainly an awkward
fact.   For if it did not constitute a valid argument
against the enactment of a law of general toleration,
it certainly rendered the Government fairly chargeable with something very like interference with the
religions and religious usages of the country. Regarding the matter in this light, certain persons representing themselves as " the Hindoo inhabitants of

* The Judges of the Sudder Dewany of Bengal, not thinking that this was clearly enunciated, recommended that after the words " forfeiture of rights and property," there should be inserted in the Act a passage saying, " or may be held in any manner to impair or affect any claim of inheritance." But the word " rights" included all claims of inheritance.

Bengal, Behar, and Orissa," alarmed by the intended assault upon their ancestral bigotry, again rose up to resist, and, aided by some congenial Europeans, sent in an emphatic protest against the threatened innovation. And the native inhabitants of Madras followed their example.

This was a repetition of the movement which had been so successful four years before. But it was not now doomed to like good fortune. The memorials were strongly worded. They dealt in argument; in declamation; in threats scarcely disguised. They paraded, as the strong point of their case, the assertion that the performance by the heir of the funeral ceremonies above noticed was designed to secure the eternal safety of the deceased,* and that therefore to make a new law of inheritance, would be to jeopardize every Hindoo's chance of everlasting happiness; and in this view of the case nothing could be more alarming than the threatened innovation. "Your memorialists will not conceal," said the Bengalees, "that from the moment the proposed Act becomes a part of the law applicable to Hindoos, that confidence which they have hitherto felt in the paternal character of their British rulers will be most materially shaken. No

---

* The case is thus stated in the Bengal petition:—"Among Hindoos one of that faith who abandons his religion loses the property he derived from his ancestor, because he can no longer perform the duty which alone entitled him to receive it. If a Hindoo had self-acquired property from trade or otherwise, and were to turn Mahomedan or Christian, he would incur no forfeiture of his self-acquired property. . . . . The right of succession depends exclusively upon the right to present the funeral oblations. It is by virtue of such last act, which can only be performed by a Hindoo, that sons and near kinsmen take the property, because, according to the belief of the Hindoos, it is by such acts his father's spiritual bliss, and that of his ancestors to the remotest degree, is secured, and by the tenets of the Hindoo religion an apostate from that faith cannot perform the obsequies."

outbreak of course is to be dreaded; but the active
spirit of fervent loyalty to their Sovereign, and of
pride in their rulers, will be changed into sullen submission to their will, and obedience to their power."
But far stronger than this was the language which
the English lawyers of Madras put into the mouths of
the native petitioners. They denounced the proposed
Regulation as a "direct act of tyranny;" and declared
that the British Government, " treading in the path of
oppression," would well deserve, "what it will assuredly
obtain, the hatred and detestation of the oppressed."[*]

Aided by the missionaries, the Christian converts
of Bengal sent in a counter-petition. They contended that the Hindoo law, in its integrity, as set
forth in the Institutes of Menu, had long ceased to
be practically regarded; that a return to pure Hindooism was impracticable, and that the great bulk of
the people rejoiced in their emancipation from its
cruel and pernicious thraldom. They pointed out
that "a great intellectual movement, induced in a
great measure by the progress of education, had for
the last quarter of a century been steadily advancing
in Bengal;" and that there was "a growing aversion
to the popular superstitions and ceremonies of the

---

[*] One other passage from the
Madras Memorial may be quoted:—
"When a Government has become
so regardless of right and wrong,
that on attaining to independence
it can repudiate the principles and
the pledges under which it acted in
its weakness, towards those who
helped it forward to that independence, the confidence of the people
can no longer be retained!" I need
not say that I consider that there is
a great deal of force in this, for I
have urged a similar argument, in
a preceding page, in ignorance that
it had been put forth by the Hindoos
themselves: or, it rather should be
said, for them. On the part of Government it had been pleaded, by the
official mouthpiece of Mr. Bushby,
that no conservative promises or
pledges had, at any time, been given
to the people; but how a statement
so grievously erroneous could have
been made it is difficult to understand.

country, including that rite on which inheritance depends agreeably to the Hindoo law. "Whatever special pleading," they said, "a few of our Calcutta countrymen, educated in English, and confident of the tolerant character of the British Government, may bring forward in support of an antiquated system scarcely venerated by themselves, and with whatever success they may procure subscriptions to such a memorial, the quiet agricultural population of Bengal would not spontaneously raise their voice against an act, which they could not but expect under an enlightened Christian Government." This memorial was described as "the voice of 12,000 converts in Bengal, all loyal and respectable subjects of her Majesty." "It may in itself be feeble," they said, "but the voice of justice and equity is mightier than that of any human community, however large. To that voice we appeal."

And they did not appeal in vain. The Supreme Government of India could not bring themselves to believe that they were bound, in defiance of the laws of justice and of liberty, to maintain the integrity of Hindooism inviolate; and, moreover, they were of opinion that Hindooism did not declare the right of inheritance to depend upon the obligation to perform the funeral rites of the deceased transmitter of the property. The Legislative Member of Council, Mr. Bethune, wrote a minute in support of this opinion, and broadly proclaimed "the inherent and inalienable right of every Government to regulate the law of property, and to deprive any class of its subjects of the power of securing conformity to their own opinions by the infliction of penalties which it belongs to the Government only to impose." The other Members of Council took the same view; and the Governor-General, Lord Dalhousie, drew up a brief but pregnant minute, in which he expressed entire concurrence in the doctrine " that it is the duty of the State to keep in its own hands the right of regulating succession to property." And he added: " The Government of India will, doubtless, continue as heretofore to administer to Hindoos the general body of Hindoo law; but I conceive that the Government will not do its duty, if it leaves unchanged any portion of that law which inflicts personal injury on any one by reason of his religious belief. In now acting on this principle, I can see no semblance of interference with the religion of the Hindoos, nor any unauthorised interference with rights secured to them." This minute was signed on the 9th of April, 1850; and two days afterwards the Act was formally passed.

That it offended the elder generation of Hindoos I do not think that there is any reason to doubt. A bigoted, priest-ridden Hindoo of the old school was likely to be considerably disturbed in his mind, especially when he knew that his sons, or his sons' friends, were eating beef and disputing with the missionaries, and reading the Institutes of Menu by the light of young Bengal. It was bad enough in itself; but it seemed only the precursor of other startling innovations. There was a cry that Hindooism was in danger. The faith of many in the

British Government was shaken; and the priests, who found that little by little their authority was being weakened, fomented the growing discontent. But I cannot see, that consistently with its duty, an enlightened Government could have done otherwise than it did. The principle enunciated was simply this:—that no man, by his profession of a particular faith, should entail upon himself any kind of civil disabilities. It happened that, in this particular instance, the application of the principle was favourable to Christianity and adverse to Hindooism; but this was merely an accident: the reverse might have been the case. The British Government, indeed, had aforetime publicly recognised the same principle, with the intention of removing the disabilities under which persons, not being Christians, had laboured. And if they had fairly carried it out in practice, when its operation was adverse to the interests of their own people, they would have stood upon a pedestal of right from which nothing could displace them. Unfortunately, the promise made to the people of India that no man, by reason of his colour or his creed, should be excluded from any office under the State, was not practically fulfilled. Nothing was gained to Hindooism by this spasm of toleration. The failure, doubtless, weakened the effect of the subsequent declaration against all forfeitures on the score of religious faith; but the principle itself was not less sound because, in one notable instance, the practice of the Government had been inconsistent with its promises.

H H

The principle of universal toleration cannot be too emphatically declared; but if we desire to reconcile the natives of the country to the abolition of all forfeitures and disabilities on account of religious persuasion, we must first show them that Hindooism and Mahomedanism are no disqualifications in the eyes of the Christian ruler. Let us demonstrate the sincerity of our toleration by first reducing it to practice to our own detriment. Let there be nothing one-sided in the application of the great principle; and we may carry it out to the protection of Christianity without an apprehension of danger or even of discontent.

And what was the Convert Christianity which the law had now consented to protect?

It was at the end of the first half of the nineteenth century that the old Hindoo law of inheritance was virtually abolished—a landmark in the great desert of time at which both the friends and the enemies of Hindooism might well pause to ask what had been done, from the days of ,Wellesley to the days of Dalhousie, to destroy the idolatries of the country. The sovereignty of Great Britain now extended over a hundred and fifty millions of people; and the proportion of Christians to the aggregate population of the country was, doubtless, extremely small. But not on that account were the signs of the times otherwise than most encouraging to the Christian observer. If no converts had actually been made, the fact that we had established in India an immense machinery of conversion, wherewith to commence the new half century, would have been one whereat abundantly to rejoice. If we had only, in spite of immense difficulties and almost insuperable obstructions, landed an army, with all its munitions of war and abundant means of supply, in the enemy's country, we should assuredly have done a great thing, although we had not yet struck a blow. But a blow had indeed been struck, and there were large communities of Christian converts, in different parts of India, whose interests the legislature was bound to protect.

Let us see, first, what was the Christian army that had encamped itself in the enemy's country—what the material resources at its disposal, at the close of the first half of the nineteenth century. At this time, twenty-three missionary societies were employing their agents in India and Ceylon. Those agents consisted of upwards of four hundred European or American missionaries, with a staff of more than five hundred native preachers.* The resources at their command were the inestimable words of Truth translated into all the dialects of India, and large sums of money, which enabled them to diffuse the blessed messages

* Mr. Mullens thus distributes the missionary agency :—

| — | Missionaries. | Native Preachers |
|---|---|---|
| Bengal, Orissa, and Assam . . . . | 101 | 135 |
| In N. W. Provinces | 58 | 39 |
| In Madras . . . | 164 | 308 |
| In Bombay . . . | 37 | 11 |
| In Ceylon . . . | 43 | 58 |
| | 403 | 551 |

" The numerous band of missionaries here mentioned," adds Mr. Mullens, " constitutes more than one-fourth of the entire body of missionaries sent into all parts of the world; and furnishes a splendid proof of the deep interest which Indian missions have aroused in the Church of Christ."

among the people, and to establish missionary stations
with Christian churches and schools.    If nothing
else had been done but the transfusion of the Gospel
into the spoken languages of the country, the half
century which had just elapsed would have been a
memorable one in the history of Christianity.    But
great as were the preparations made, the Christian
host had done much more than prepare for the battle.
The contest, indeed, had long before commenced; and
now there were great promises of eventual victory.

More than three hundred native churches had
by this time been established in different parts of
India; and it is computed that these churches were
the centres of an aggregate Christian community,
numbering more than a hundred thousand persons.
It cannot with truth be affirmed that the whole,
or any large proportion of these were Christians of
a very high order.    They were all under Christian
instruction; and, at all events, had cast off their
ancestral faiths.    Less than eighteen thousand of
the whole number had been admitted to church-
membership; and only five thousand of these had
been approved in accordance with a high standard
of Christian excellence.*    There is nothing peculiar

* They are thus distributed by Mr. Mullens :—

|  | Churches. | Members. | Christians. |
|---|---|---|---|
| Bengal, Orissa, and Assam . | 71 | 3,416 | 14,401 |
| North-West Provinces  . . | 21 | 606 | 1,828 |
| Madras Presidency . · . . . | 162 | 10,464 | 74,512 |
| Bombay  . . . . . . . | 12 | 223 | 554 |
| Ceylon . . . . . . . . | 43 | 2,645 | 11,859 |
|  | 309 | 17,356 | 103,154 |

to India in the large proportion which the number of merely nominal Christians, in outward connexion with the Church, bears to those who are really converted and regenerate.

Such as it was, the native Christianity of India was by no means equally diffused over the country. It seems to have started up here and there in accidental patches of greenery, and to have left many places altogether barren and desolate. It was on the Madras coast that it seemed to flourish most luxuriantly, especially in Tinnevelly and Travancore, where dwelt at least one-half of the entire native Christianity of the country. Next to that great field of missionary success —success for which there was special reason in the caste and character of the population—certain districts of Bengal are to be classed. In Krishnaghur a great movement had taken place. Some five thousand of Bengalees had been brought under Christian instruction; one-half of whom regularly attended Christian worship. In these Krishnaghur Missions, Bishop Wilson and Archdeacon Dealtry, now Bishop of Madras, ever took the deepest interest; frequently visiting the Christian villages and baptizing the people by hundreds. In Moulmein, in Tavoy, and in parts of the Burmese Empire, the American missionaries had achieved splendid successes, and are worthy to be ranked with the most devoted of our own labourers. But up to the end of the first half of the last century, Christianity had made comparatively small progress in Upper and Western India. The soil appeared to be more stubborn, and for a time, the labours of the husbandman were requited only by a scanty harvest.

Looking at the aggregate result of our efforts up to this time, there was much cause for rejoicing. A good beginning had been made. The number of real converts to a living Christianity may have been small; but it was impossible to say how even those few might multiply and bring forth fruit, some twentyfold, some fiftyfold, some a hundredfold.* A few earnest-minded men, from their own ranks, with courage and independence to face all obstacles, and with moral influence and the gift of speech to persuade their brethren, might carry conviction to the hearts of thousands, and thus the truth might go on radiating and radiating until it reached the remotest corners of the great continent of India. By means of direct European agency we could never hope to convert the nation. The hope was that, in God's good time, native apostles would be raised up to carry the glad tidings of salvation to the inner heart of Hindoo society.

Meanwhile, by other than direct appeals, the English Government and the English people were

---

* How even chance-sown seed may fructify may be gathered from the following interesting and suggestive incident, recently brought to notice by the *Friend of India*:—"At the village of Malliana, about a mile from Meerut, a native convert to Christianity was compelled, when the outbreak occurred, to leave his books in the house of a man who had sheltered him. This man read the books, was struck with them, and read them to his family daily. A knot of listeners was formed, and, as soon as peace was restored, the audience sought the aid of a missionary. More than forty persons have been baptized in consequence, and the converts commenced building a church at their own expense. Government has, of course, come forward to assist. The example has had good effect. At Kaukar Kairah, a neighbouring hamlet, the villagers assembled, and besought a convert, who was about to leave with his family, not to depart, stating that, though not prepared to embrace Christianity, they regarded it with favour."

carrying on the great work. The history of Education in India demands a volume to itself. It will some day, perhaps, be written by a more experienced hand than mine. It is enough to say, in this place, that two systems were tried: one, a system of purely secular education, under the auspices of the British Government; the other, of secular and religious teaching combined, under the superintendence of the missionaries. Each in its own proper place was right. The Government could not with propriety do more; the missionaries could not do less. The object of both was so to enlighten the minds of the people as to render the absurdities of Hindooism utterly repugnant to them. The missionaries might safely go beyond this; they might show the people saving truths, to be substituted for their pernicious errors. If the Government had done this, they would have soon emptied their schools. But in excluding, as they once did, the Bible altogether from their library shelves, and forbidding their teachers to afford, even if solicited, any religious information to the students, they exercised an amount of caution, which, however pardonable at the outset, could not be grafted upon any continuing system without discredit to the State. Perfect toleration forbids the existence of an *Index Expurgatorius;* and religious neutrality excludes the idea of prohibiting inquiry into the nature of any articles of faith, or any principles of morality. The British Government, after a time, opened its eyes to this fact, and the practice of tolerating all religions but their own was abandoned.

It was not, however, until the year 1854, that distinct instructions on the subject were embodied in a despatch from the Court of Directors to the Supreme Government of India.* This was the famous educational despatch, prepared with so much thoughtful elaboration, when Sir Charles Wood was President of the Board of Control. For this despatch, whether it be good or whether it be evil, the Parliament and People of Great Britain are answerable. No one can have forgotten the cry which, during the discussions of 1853, was raised against the Company's Government for expending such immense sums on war and so little on education. It was, indeed, the standing reproach of the Company, at that time, that it had done so little for the education of the people; and that that little was of an anti-Christian tendency. Pressure from without was brought to bear upon the Indian Minister; and missionary influences powerfully prevailed. The result was that pecuniary assistance on a large scale (in the shape of grants-in-aid) was to be rendered to the educational institutions of the country, and that the missionary schools and colleges were to be permitted to participate in this boon. The aid so granted was

---

* The following is the passage in the Education Despatch of 1854, which lays down the practice to be observed:—"Considerable apprehension appears to exist as to our views with respect to religious instruction in the Government institutions. These institutions were founded for the benefit of the whole population of India; and in order to effect their object it was, and is, indispensable that the education conveyed in them should be exclusively secular. The Bible is, we understand, placed in the libraries of the colleges and schools, and the pupils are free to consult it. This is as it should be; and, moreover, we have no desire to prevent or to discourage any explanations which the pupils may of their own free-will ask from their masters on the subject, provided that such information be given out of school hours."

to be applied strictly to objects of secular education. But, nevertheless, it was aid rendered by the British Government, from the resources of India, to institutions avowedly established for the conversion of the people to Christianity; and although I do not see that so long as the same assistance was rendered to other institutions, in which Christianity was not taught, and other religions, directly or indirectly, were, there was any violation of the boasted neutrality of the Government, I am not surprised that it should have been regarded by many as an insidious attempt to bring the power and prestige of Government to bear upon the general conversion of the people. In such a case, it is better that the Government should not even be suspected of a missionary connexion, the reputation of which is not more injurious to the State than to the missionaries themselves.

But there was something which, even more than this, alarmed the elder generation of Hindoos. The subject of native female education—indeed, of the condition generally of the women of the country, had attracted the benevolent regards of the English in India, and efforts had been made to break down that system, which, in Oriental countries, consigns one half of the human family to ignorance and to slavery. Rightly considered, this was a very difficult and embarrassing question. Reason and humanity were on the one side. On the other, were inveterate prejudices, deeply ingrained in the constitution of society. Home-staying people in this country have no notion of the institution of the Purdah. In the East, even the most apathetic will fight for it, and die for it. What we did to tear down the Purdah was not much. But even the little was a source of inquietude and a weapon of offence. And when, moreover, they found us endeavouring to accomplish another great social innovation, by legalising the remarriage of Hindoo widows, the indignation of the grey-beards waxed stronger, and in anger and astonishment they asked, What next? It was very right that the Hindoo widow, often a child-widow, should not be condemned to a life of solitude, perhaps of sin; but the old-school Hindoos looked upon such condemnation as one of their most venerable social usages, and to legislate against it was in their estimation to invade the sanctity of the Zenana, and to obtrude ourselves into the most delicate concerns of their domestic life. We were talking, too, of some day prohibiting infantine marriages, polygamy, especially in its worst form of Kulinism, and other kindred institutions; when suddenly the Great Rebellion of 1857 burst upon us and calamitously arrested our progress.

# CONCLUSION.

Retrospect—Recapitulation—Success the result of caution—The question as affected by the Rebellion of 1857—Our future policy—Proposed demonstrations—Duty of the Government—Duty of individuals—Conclusion.

LOOKING back at what I have written, I think I have made it clear that the progress of Christianity in India has been such as any reasonable person, viewing it with due regard to the exigencies of time and circumstance, would be inclined to predicate from his knowledge of predisposing causes. That this progress has been slow is admitted; but it would be a mistake to assume that, therefore, any great national sin is to be laid at the door of the English in India, either as a state or as a people. It is not strange that Christianity advanced so slowly in India. It would have been strange if it had not advanced slowly. Nay, I do not see how, without a special interposition of Providence, it could possibly have advanced in any other way.

We have seen how, at the commencement of their career in India, the English in India were licentious and irreligious; and that the un-Christian lives of those early settlers wrought mightily to the prejudice of Christianity, by blackening its face in the eyes of the natives of the country. But the lax habits and coarse manners of those exiles were importations from the mother country; and if they cared nothing about the souls of the heathen, they were in that respect only on a level with their brethren at home.

The missionary spirit infused itself but slowly into the British nation; and if we wonder that, at any particular time in the seventeenth or eighteenth centuries, there were no English missionaries in India, we shall in all probability find that there were no English missionaries anywhere. The progress of Christian missions in India, during the present century, has been only one of many practical emanations of the general revival of evangelical religion in Great Britain. The English in India have always kept pace with their brethren in the parent country. It is only within very recent times that the aggregate contributions of the English nation towards missionary objects has been otherwise than most contemptible in proportion to the general wealth of the country; and within these times the contributions of the English in India, considering their numbers and their means, have borne an honourable proportion to the aggregate national amount. It can be no special reproach to the English in India that they were not better than their countrymen at home. I have no hesitation in saying that they have never at any time been worse.

But, if the people who have gone from our shores to the Eastern Indies be not deserving of rebuke

for their active sins, or their scarcely less sinful
negligences, is not, many have asked, the Anglo-
Indian Government to be rebuked for its impiety,
or for its remissness? The answer to this question
is, I hope, to be found in the foregoing pages. It
has been seen that, at the outset of the career of the
East India Company, they had no thought of empire,
no system of policy, and no intercourse with the
people, except of a purely mercantile character. Of
the Moors, and of the Gentoos, they took no account,
except as buyers and as sellers. If they bought and
sold honestly, which, as a Company, they desired to
do, whatever may have been the overreachings of
individual merchants, they did their duty as a society
of Christian men. When time and circumstance
compelled them, in spite of themselves, to possess
territory, and, therefore, as the rulers of a people,
to inaugurate a political system, it appeared to them
that justice and expediency alike demanded that they
should govern, as their predecessors had governed
before them, and that, above all things, they should
abstain from asserting their national faith in such a
manner as to offend the prejudices of the people. As
time advanced, and their empire extended, it appeared
to them to be more and more necessary to adhere to
that system. The English in India were so few in
numbers, their means of defence were altogether so
feeble, that it seemed absolutely necessary by every
means to conciliate the people of the country, lest
they should suddenly be swept into the sea. It is
possible that they may have over-estimated the

importance of this non-assertion of the national
faith as a means of conciliation, but it was, at least,
a reasonable hypothesis that the less they obtruded
their Christianity upon the Hindoos and Mahomedans,
the less likely they were to offend the prejudices of
the people of the soil.

Indian government was, in those days, merely an
experiment, and the continuance of our empire a
problem of very uncertain solution. Political power
had been thrust upon the Company, and very
unwillingly accepted; and it was, perhaps, because
they never thought of theorising, but accommodated
themselves to surrounding circumstances, that they
were enabled to hold possession of the territory
which, province by province, had been committed
to their care. We know now that with perfect
safety our Christian Government may assert its
national faith without offence either to Mahomedan
or to Hindoo. But we do not know how far this
happy state of things has resulted from the discretion
which we exhibited at the outset of our career. We
do not know how greatly we are indebted to the
confidence established by that very forbearance which
is often branded as unseemly timidity, if not as
un-Christian indifference. We have no right to
assume, because we can now demonstrably adopt a
particular course with safety, that we might have
safely adopted it fifty years before. Everybody
knows, in the daily concerns of life, what liberties
he may take with his neighbours, so long as he
does not take them too soon. Moreover, if it were

a demonstrated fact, instead of a vague conjecture, that we might, at a much earlier period—nay, from the very commencement—have boldly asserted our national Christianity, it can hardly be a reproach to our Government, that they were not, in the very earliest stage of the great experiment of Indian Government, cognisant of that fact—a fact, indeed, which could only be ascertained by a progressive series of small attempts upon the forbearance or indifference of the people.

My own impression is—nay, indeed, it is a profound conviction in my mind—that the cause of Christianity in India is indebted, humanly speaking, to nothing so much as the often-condemned " backwardness" of our forefathers. The protection which the British Government afforded to the religious institutions of the country, and the unwillingness which for a long time it exhibited to encourage, or even to permit, any efforts for the conversion of the people to the Christian faith, seem to have disarmed them of the jealousy and suspicion with which otherwise they might have regarded the more ostentatious assertion of our national faith, as evidenced by the construction of churches, the multiplication of Christian priests, and the appearance on the scene of hierarchical dignities unknown in the earlier years of our residence in India. I do not dwell upon the effect which this confidence must have had upon the establishment, the extension, and the consolidation of our dominion; although it is obvious that upon our political success the diffusion of our Christianity wholly depended. It is too much the fashion with some writers and speakers to consider those two conditions as distinct from, nay, indeed, antagonistic with each other; as though anything which tended to the downfall of our temporal kingdom in India could have contributed to the extension of Christ's kingdom on earth. It is hardly worth while to enlarge upon this. What I am now contending for is, that if the people of India had not felt that *their* religions were secure against the assaults of the British Government, the British Government could not have asserted, as it has done, *its own* religion, without obstruction from the conflicting faiths by which it was surrounded. When the whole subject was sifted and examined, in 1812–1813, there was no more potent argument advanced in favour of the safety with which the British Government in India might, in the most open and demonstrative manner, assert its Christianity, than that derived from the fact that the people had learnt from the experience of years that their own institutions were secure from the assaults of the British ruler, and that the pledges made to them at the outset would not be broken.[*]

Up to this period, indeed—that is, up to the Charter renewal of 1813—the British Government in India, by the policy it adopted, had sown broadcast seeds of confidence in the minds of the people. "Confidence is a plant of slow growth;" but when it

---

[*] See the arguments of Lord Teignmouth and others. — *Ante*, Chapter VIII.

once takes root in the soil, it is not easily destroyed. Such confidence as our Government had generated by the unstinting toleration of years, was not to be disturbed by any manifestations, purely unaggressive in their character, of a respect for the ordinances of its own religion. The extension of the Anglican Church in India, therefore, excited no irritation or alarm in the public mind. Christian high-priests itinerated from one end of the country to another, consecrating churches, ordaining ministers, confirming native converts, visiting Christian schools, and otherwise contributing to the dignity and prosperity of our national faith. But all this the natives regarded with indifference, because their own institutions were safe. Nay, more; the toleration with which they reciprocated ours went even beyond this. It was held, and rightly held, that so long as the people thoroughly trusted the Government itself, the private efforts of individuals or of religious associations to convert the people to Christianity might, if prosecuted with prudence, be prosecuted with safety. And from that time the Christian missionary went about his holy work unobstructed by the Government, and without injury to the State. All this was great progress in the right direction; and why was it so successful? Because the Government not only stood aloof from all proselytizing efforts, but tolerated and protected the religious institutions of the country. Up to the year 1813, the natives of India may have believed that not only the English Government, but the English people, were wholly indifferent to the glory of their national

I I

faith—nay, some may have questioned whether the
Feringhee had any national faith.    But between
the years 1813 and 1833 no such doubts can ever
have entered into their minds.    They saw Christian
churches springing up everywhere; they saw the
servants of Government punctually attending public
worship on the Christian Sabbath; they saw that, on
that one day of the seven, business and pleasure were
laid aside; they saw that more Christian priests, and
some of the highest dignity, were arriving to minister
to the Christian congregations; and they saw that,
supported by the English people, though not by the
English Government, the Christian missionary was
itinerating through all parts of the country.    This
was the first experimental epoch—the epoch of vigorous self-assertion.    It was plainly demonstrated to
the people that Christianity was a living fact; and
having succeeded so far, we began to consider how
much further we might proceed without danger to
the State.

There were two directions along which the next
stage of progress might have run, but one incomparably more hazardous than the other.    There were
few persons of sound intelligence, indeed, who counselled the assumption by Government of an aggressive
attitude—or, in other words, the direct interference of
the State in measures for the evangelization of the
people.    From the adoption of such a course, nothing
better could have been looked for than disastrous
failure.    The other, though apparently not altogether
without danger, indicated a far better prospect of

success. It was clear that it was *not* the duty of the State to assail the religions of the country; but it was not equally clear that it *was* the duty of the State to protect them to an extent indicative of a desire, on the part of Government, to secure their permanence and prosperity. A question then arose as to whether the connexion of the State with the idolatries of the country might not be severed in whole or in part, without creating any popular disaffection injurious to British rule; and the question was answered in the affirmative. Then began the second experimental epoch—the epoch of self-emancipation. From 1833 to 1853, the duration of the next Charter or Act, under which India was governed, the British Government, whilst continuing to assert, and with increased vigour, its own Christianity, gradually emancipated itself from that intimate connexion with the idolatrous institutions of the country, which many had long regarded as its standing reproach. At the same time, it struck boldly at the inhuman rites and cruel practices which it had so long permitted and, although still in no wise identifying itself with Christian Missions, gave large protection and encouragement to Christian converts, by removing the disabilities which the Hindoo law had imposed upon them, and giving them equal rights of inheritance with their unconverted brethren. In doing this, the British Government did all that it could do with safety; and it was enabled to do so much, only because it abstained from taking part in any direct efforts for the conversion of the people, and prohi-

bited its own servants from taking any active part in, or otherwise officially identifying themselves with, such efforts. It will be found, indeed, at every stage of the inquiry, that the policy of the British Government in India, which has so often been said to be antagonistic to Christianity, has been conservative of its true interests; and that, however tardy the progress of evangelization may have been in proportion to the yearning desires of all true Christians, such progress could only have been attained under a system of wise precaution and prudent restraint.

The new epoch which commenced after the passing of the Act of 1853, was distinguished at the outset by new manifestations of experimental boldness on the part of the British Government. If it had not been disastrously interrupted by the great Sepoy rebellion, the epoch embracing the twenty years from 1853 to 1873 would not improbably have been mainly distinguished by State patronage of Christian education. The British Government, though still unprepared to identify itself in any way with direct efforts for the conversion of the people, had begun to manifest its interest in such undertakings by affording grants-in-aid to missionary educational institutions, and by the admission of the Bible to the libraries of the Government schools. This was held to be no departure from the principle of "religious neutrality," but it was a further experiment upon the toleration of the people, and its success would in all probability have induced other movements in the same direction. There were signs, too, of an increased inclination to interfere with the social usages of the Hindoos, when at variance with reason and humanity; and as the *alumni* of our schools and colleges grew into heads of families, taking the places of the old bigoted, uneducated Hindoos, it is probable that great progress would have been made in the improvement of the manners and customs of the people. The great rebellion of 1857 has, however, brought all this good work to a fearful stand-still, and it now only remains for us to consider how far the great question of the diffusion of the Gospel in India is affected by recent calamitous events.

The first point that suggests itself for inquiry is, to what extent, if to any, have those calamities resulted from the measures, related or glanced at in the preceding chapters, for the religious enlightenment or the social improvement of the people. To the solution of this, and of almost every other question connected with the great subject of Christianity in India, the most extreme opinions have been brought. On one side it has been declared that the mutiny has resulted from the religious apprehensions of the people, excited by the continued innovations of the English, threatening their ancestral faiths and their time-honoured social usages; and on the other side, it has been asserted with equal confidence that God has visited us with this affliction as a signal mark of His displeasure on account of our national remissness in the great work of upholding His kingdom and diffusing His word. The truth will be found somewhere at a considerable distance from either of these extremes; but the latter hypothesis is infinitely more unreasonable than the former. Whatever our national remissness—how little soever may have been the *all* that we have done to establish Christ's kingdom among the Gentiles of the Eastern world, we were never striving more earnestly or more successfully to build up that kingdom, than at the very moment when the great chastisement overtook us.

And, on that account, *did* it overtake us? Not wholly on that account; but partly on that account. It would be as uncandid to deny that the religious and social innovations of the English in India had anything to do with the outbreak, as it would be unjust to assert that they were the sole causes of it. There is nothing more difficult than to determine the extent to which the feeling of insecurity engendered by these innovations found its way to the inner heart of society. It has been said, in language of exultation, that " the whole land has been shaken by Missions to its innermost centre;"* and that Hindoos and Mahomedans

---

* See the recent work of the Rev. M. A. Sherring (formerly missionary in Benares), entitled " The Indian Church during the Great Rebellion." " The influence of missions has been felt everywhere. There is scarcely a Hindoo or a Mahomedan who has not heard of Christ. Not a few are well acquainted with the tenets of our religion and can reason upon them intelligently. The whole land has been shaken by missions to its innermost centre. The Hindoo trembles for his religion—the Mahomedan for his. Both religions seem to be crumbling away from beneath them. The jeopardy of idolatry before the mysterious power of the Gospel is palpable to every thoughtful Hindoo. He acknowledges the fact, and predicts the downfall of his own religion and the triumph of Christianity—predicts the time when there will be but one religion in all India—the Christian ; predicts the destruction of idolatry and the extinction of caste, and the universal prevalence of a creed which in his heart he now recognises, and with his lips often avows, to be infinitely superior to his own." This writer, it need scarcely be added, is not one of those who look upon the rebellion as a judgment upon us for our supineness. "God," he says, "has put great honour on his servants in India in permitting them to be the instruments of such stupendous results. * * * * I think it is manifest that God approves the work that is being done in India, and I fain hope and trust, approves also the men performing the work."

alike are trembling for their religions. This language may be exaggerated; but, although the effect produced upon the great mass of the people may have been far more superficial than is here supposed, I cannot doubt that the fears of the priesthood have been largely excited. They have trembled for their offices; trembled for their gains; trembled for the exclusiveness, which made them sovereigns among the people. And we may be sure that they did their best, in a conjuncture of circumstances favourable in the extreme to their designs, to alarm and to irritate the public mind by propagating reports of the intention of the British Government forcibly to convert the people to Christianity. Preposterous as is this idea of forcible conversion, it has often taken possession of the minds even of the more educated classes; and in the astute hands of Pundits and Moulavees no more formidable weapon can be conceived. The delusion once propagated, the hostile chiefs knew how to turn it to account; and they invariably charged their proclamations with appeals to the religious feelings of the people, who were incited to make common cause against the encroaching Feringhee.

That this apprehension of the destruction of the ancient religions of the people was *but* one of many concurrent sources of irritation is certain; but it is equally certain that it was one. I have endeavoured, in the most impartial spirit, to ascertain whether any special animosity against missionaries and missionary establishments has been exhibited by the insurgents, but there has been too much inconsistency in their conduct to admit of any general inferences being fairly deduced from it. It is certain, however, that native Christians were assailed with as much bitterness as Europeans; but this may have been, not so much on account of their faith, as because of their steadfast adherence to the British. In many cases, English scholars—that is, Hindoo or Mahomedan readers and writers of the English language—were especial objects of popular indignation. It is true that, in some places, the Christian Sabbath was fixed upon as the appointed day of insurrection, and the first attack was made upon the Christian church. But this seems rather to have been a point of convenience than of fanaticism; the great aim of the mutineers, an indiscriminate massacre of the Europeans, being greatly facilitated by their assemblage under a common roof, and the absorption of their minds by a common object. All symptoms, indeed, fairly considered, it does not appear that the anger of the insurgents was especially directed against the Christianity of their victims. The apostacy of all the Christians in the country would not have stayed the insurrection, nor do I believe that it would have even mitigated its fury.

I cannot perceive anything, therefore, in these recent calamitous events to induce us to retrace any of the steps which we have taken; but, assuredly, greater caution during the next few years is rather to be counselled than less. The religious neutrality of the British Government in India has been proclaimed by the Queen in Council, and must ever be a substantive article of our political faith. One of the prime objects—nay, the prime object (for we can do nothing without it) of all our efforts, as a Government and as individuals, during the first years succeeding the suppression of the mutiny, is the tranquillization of the public mind. Such a conflict must necessarily leave behind it an irritable condition of the whole frame of society, demanding from us the application of the most soothing remedies. Until we have restored the national confidence in the non-aggressive spirit of the British Government, all that we do will be regarded with suspicion, and, perhaps, repelled with aversion. I cannot think, therefore, that the present time is one either for the verbal enunciation, or for the practical demonstration, of what is called "a bolder Christian policy." I cannot think, as many excellent people think, that this is the time to "strike." Let the State proclaim its own religion as manfully as it will; but in all that relates to the religions of others, it cannot be too quiescent.

It is not, perhaps, sufficient to speak out on such a subject in mere generalities. An appeal has been made to the public mind on certain specific points of practice, and it may not be unprofitable briefly to consider them. One leading feature of the Christian scheme of some religious reformers is the abolition of all endowments granted by the State to the religions of the country. This question has already been discussed. To advocate such a measure is to advocate a discreditable breach of faith; and so long as Christianity is endowed from the revenues of India, such a proposal strikes at the very root of the neutrality

which is professedly the principle and the prac
of the British Government. It is not necessar
repeat what has been said on this subject in a
ceding chapter.

Then it is recommended, by some able and ex
lent men, that Christianity should be openly tau
in our Government schools; that "the formatio
Bible classes of an improved character in as n
schools as possible should be a recognised branc
the educational department," and that "inspec
should endeavour to establish them in the same
as they originate improvements of any other ki
This doctrine is supported by the high authorit
Sir John Lawrence and Colonel Herbert Edwar
The objection is of a kindred character to that w
applies to the proposal for the abolition of relig
endowments. How can we, in accordance with
system of religious neutrality, apply the reve
of India to the instruction of the people in the te
of Christianity, without, at the same time, instruc
them in their own national religions? If Christia
is to be taught in the schools, supported by the pu
purse—or, in other words, by the labour of the pe
—Hindooism and Mahomedanism must also be tau
or there can be no such thing as neutrality. B
we were to set out from a new starting-point an
ignore the neutrality principle altogether, what th
The evangelization of the people is the great obje
be attained; and I have a profound conviction
that object will not be promoted by a measure,
effect of which, in all probability, would be to er

the Government schools. It is no answer to this, that the missionary schools in which Christianity is openly taught, are well attended by heathen children. The people of India associate the idea of missionary teaching with that of argument and persuasion; but all Government measures are identified in their minds with authority and coercion. However repugnant to reason may be the idea of forcible conversion to Christianity, it is a disturbing fact in the minds of the people. Send, as is proposed, chaplains, or missionaries, or ordained schoolmasters, or other competent religious instructors, into the Government schools, and a notion, however preposterous, of this forcible conversion will immediately take possession of the public mind. In the neutrality of the Government lies the hope of the missionaries. It is the basis of all evangelical success. To depart from it will not be to promote, but to obstruct the progress of Christianity; and, therefore, I devoutly hope that the principle will be maintained.

Moreover, it is proposed that whilst we are doing everything that we can do to demonstrate the vitality of the Christian religion, the British Government should check the demonstrativeness of the religions of the country. Hindoo and Mahomedan processions are abominations in the eyes of Christian men; and, therefore, it is said that a Christian Government should not be satisfied with withdrawing from all constructive sanction and support of these obtrusive ceremonials, but should actively suppress them by the strong hand of the law. All religious processions, it is said, might be abolished, " not on religious grounds "—that is, not professedly on religious grounds, " but simply as a police measure." How would this affect the question of religious neutrality? By prohibiting all religious processions, it is said, we should prohibit those of the Christian religion. Now Romanism, it is true, delights in these processions, and in India fairly competes with Mahomedanism or Hindooism in its external displays. But Protestantism does not delight in processions, and Protestantism is the religion of the State. An Act, therefore, prohibiting religious processions in the public streets, would affect all creeds but that of the Government passing the Act. It is not, therefore, very apparent that, give it what gloss you may, such a measure would be in conformity with our avowed principles of neutrality and toleration.

If the total suppression of all religious processions in the public ways could be successfully carried out, it would be an authoritative interference with the religions of the country in no way removed from persecution. Christianity does not enjoin or permit persecution; and " truth," it has been well said,[*] " is always strongest when it is left to contend with error

---

[*] By Mr. Baptist Noel, in his recent work on " England and India." The entire passage is worthy of consideration. The Christian rulers of India, he says, " are not called to persecute Mahomedans or Hindoos, because it is the will of Christ that his religion should be extended by instruction, reasoning, and persuasion; and because man is answerable for his belief to God alone; so that no man may interfere with another man's creed as long as he does not violate his neighbour's rights or offend against public decency. They must not, as Christians, prohibit heathen worship, nor interfere with its advocates when they preach or write in its behalf, because truth is always the strongest when it is left to contend with error by itself. If error is silenced by authority, its advocates may always say that it would have conquered by fair play; but when truth prevails by argument alone, its victory is complete."

by itself." It has been asserted that these public processions are not an essential part of the religions of the country. It may be said, in the same way, that church-building is no essential part of the religion of Christ. Primitive Christianity had little or nothing to do with pulpits and pews. But to prohibit the erection of Christian churches would be to persecute Christianity; and, to prohibit those other forms of religious demonstrativeness in which Hindoos and Mahomedans rejoice, would be to persecute those creeds, and, I firmly believe, to strengthen rather than to weaken their power.

But the ability of the British Government to suppress these religious processions may be fairly doubted. It is difficult to imagine anything more fatally calculated to exasperate both Hindoos and Mahomedans, and to incite them to violent resistance. The prohibition of religious processions (including, I presume, marriage processions—events of daily occurrence,) can only be enforced at the bayonet's point; and at a time when every effort should be directed to the tranquillization of the public mind, I can imagine nothing more pernicious—but for the high character of those from whom the proposal emanates, I should say anything more insane—than to provoke desperate collisions between Fanaticism and Authority. The natives of India would, not unreasonably, regard the suppression of their external ceremonies as an act of religious persecution to be speedily followed by the demolition of their mosques and pagodas; and we should soon be in the midst of all the horrors of

another rebellion not to be trodden out as speed
the last.

The disallowance of native holidays is an
measure of reform which has recently been advoc
At the period of certain native festivals there
suspension of public business.  Government r
nises these festivals by the temporary closing
offices; and private establishments, dependent
native agency, follow the example.  Now, it is
fectly clear that we have no more right to co
the official attendance of Hindoos at the time o
Doorgah Poojah, than of Christian underlin
Good Friday or Christmas-day.  But it is not ec
plain that, therefore, the State is bound to reco
these festivals by closing the public offices.  It
be sufficient, for all purposes of toleration, to
leave of absence to every public servant applyir
permission to absent himself, in order that he
perform the services of his religion.  There a
every Government-office men of various creeds,
there will, at the time of any particular festival,
sufficient number of servants not called away to
part in it, to perform the current duties of the de
ment.  The middle course here recommended
answer all purposes; it will continue to the nati
the country the privilege which they have here
enjoyed, and which, indeed, they have a rig
expect; and it will release the Government fro
necessity of a general observance of the native
days in a manner calculated to impress the peopl
the belief that their festivals are approved by the

Another suggestion is, that Christianity should be encouraged and supported by a more liberal extension of State patronage to Christian converts.    There would seem to be an impression on the public mind in England that native Christians are, somehow or other, excluded from public employment.    There can be no greater mistake.    There is no law or regulation prohibiting their appointment to any office under the State, and if practically there is any exclusion, it must be of a local and accidental character. I never heard that Government, as a Government, had any objection to the employment of native Christians.    If, however, the number of these converts employed throughout India in the public service does not bear a just proportion to the number of Hindoos and Mahomedans so employed, and if they be equally well qualified for office, there is a reasonable presumption that personal prejudices have operated to the disadvantage of the class.    The only way to remedy the evil is to remove those prejudices. Any open and systematic encouragement to Christian converts of the nature proposed, is to be deprecated. Firstly, because we cannot, without offence to Christianity itself, bribe people to embrace it.*    And, secondly, because any especial indulgence to Christians, on the score of their religion, would be an injustice to the people of other religious persuasions, and a departure from our avowed principles of neu-

---

* " The Christian rulers of India," says Mr. Baptist Noel, "are not permitted to bribe heathens to profess faith in Christ, by the offer of office, or by attaching any honours or emoluments to that profession; for this may create hypocrites, but cannot make men Christians."

trality and toleration. Any exclusion from office or
any disproportionate preferment, on the score of
religion, would be equally unjust.

Such are the special questions of a purely religious
character which have recently been brought to the
notice of the English people, in connexion with the
momentous subject of the future career of Christianity in India. So far, then, as by "a bolder
Christian policy," it is meant to signify increased
aggressiveness against the religions of the country,
the recommendation, from whatsoever quarter it may
proceed, must be rejected by the Imperial Government. Nay, indeed, it has already been rejected.
Th eproclamation of Queen Victoria, which, on the
1st of November, 1858, was promulgated by the
Indian Viceroy to the princes and the people of the
country, contained these significant words:—"Firmly
relying ourselves on the truth of Christianity, and
acknowledging with gratitude the solace of religion,
we disclaim alike the right and the desire to impose
our convictions on any of our subjects. We declare
it to be our Royal will and pleasure, that none be in
any wise favoured, none molested or disquieted, by
reason of their religious faith and observances, but
that all shall alike enjoy the equal and impartial
protection of the law; and we do strictly charge
and enjoin all those who may be in authority under
us that they abstain from all interference with the
religious belief or worship of any of our subjects,
on pain of our highest displeasure." In these words
the Christianity of the British Government and the

British nation is worthily asserted, and the toleration of the State distinctly proclaimed. These principles are now to be wrought out in practice. In doing so, the Government is not called upon to commit itself to any further innovations, or to resort to a course of cowardly retrogression. Whatever may have been its ancient short-comings, the State had already done as much as it behoved it to do, in vindication of its own religion, before the rebellion of 1857 burst over our heads. And I think it had done all that it prudently could do in the present state of the Hindoo mind, to divest, by authoritative interference, Hindooism of its most revolting attributes. More at some future period may be done, when we see that the harvest is ready; but at present it is wiser, I do not say to leave, but to aid, the Hindoo mind to work out its own regeneration, than to force on from without the desired changes, which, to be effectual, must take growth from within.

Let the State exalt, by all possible means, the blessed religion which it professes; but, earnestly desiring to hasten the extension of Christ's kingdom upon earth, let it leave the work of religious instruction to the missionaries. Let it rebuild all the churches which have been destroyed; let it construct others wheresoever there is a Christian flock without a fold; let it increase the number of its gospel-ministers, taking especial care that the men who fight its battles are not without the means of spiritual solace and instruction; let it do all honour to the Sabbath, and observe all the ordinances of our faith, and neglect no special occasion of humiliation or thanksgiving for chastisements or mercies received. Let it, by these and other means, demonstrate to the people that the English have a religion of which they are proud, and that of the external observances of that religion they are never unmindful; and let it prove, by its unerring justice, by its respect for the rights of others, by its mercy, its toleration, its beneficence, in a word, by its *love*, that the religion thus outwardly manifested is a living principle, not a pageant and a sham.

Moved by boundless compassion for the ignorance of the people, by which their degrading superstitions are kept alive, let the State provide largely the means of secular instruction for its Hindoo and Mahomedan subjects; but let, in no sense, its educational institutions be missionary colleges in disguise.* Let knowledge of all kinds be open to the people; let there be no sealed book; no *Index Expurgatorius*. If a Hindoo or Mahomedan student desire to be instructed in the doctrines of Christianity, let the knowledge he seeks be imparted to him; but let it on no account be forced upon, or even offered to him. Let the missionaries, however, declare boldly their object; let them multiply their schools; invite all who will to enter

---

* It may, I know, be contended that strict neutrality in matters of education is impossible—the mere physical truths taught in our schools being of a nature to upset the Hindoo cosmogony, which is a part of the religion of the great bulk of the people. But although these truths are subversive of some of the doctrines of Hindooism, they are no part of our religion. They are believed by thousands who are not Christians; and being demonstrable facts, not speculative doctrines, I cannot see that Government is bound to take account of the accident of their being antagonistic to Hindooism, or that in simply enunciating them as a part of general scientific education common to the whole world, it can be charged with a violation of the principle of neutrality.

them; and unreservedly declare the truths of Christianity. This is the concern of the people of England. The business is in their own hands. Labourers will not be wanting, if they who do not labour will supply the hire. That they are prepared to do so—nay, that they are already doing so, we have ample demonstrations; and we cannot doubt that Providence in its own good time will recompense the national zeal. That more will eventually be done by teaching than by preaching, I believe. Our best hope is that large bodies of the people will drift into Christianity; not that, by a sudden plunge, diving from one shore, they will emerge into the clear light of the opposite coast of Truth. The drifting away from Hindooism is certain; for, indeed, it has long ago commenced. It has been apprehended* that the period after this drifting out of Hindooism would not be without its attendant dangers, as the people would be released from all religious restraints. But it has been argued, on the other hand, that even this transition-state is better than the old condition of superstitious darkness; and that the Hindoos are not a people to remain long without a faith to which they may cling.† In all the

---

* By Sir John Malcolm and others. Malcolm (Political History) says:— "Perhaps the greatest of all dangers will occur when our subjects, taught by us, shall cast off those excellent moral restraints with which their religion, with all its error and superstition, abounds, and yet not adopt that sincerity of faith in the divine precepts which would fill and elevate their minds."

† See Sir Charles Trevelyan's admirable "Indophilus" letters :— "Even supposing them to remain in the middle state, they are better than they were, but they cannot remain in that state. Human nature cannot do without the comforts and hopes of religion; and least of all Hindoo nature, which is not made of such stern, self-relying stuff as our Anglo-Saxon character. These natives must have some religion; they cannot go back to Hindooism. They show no disposition to turn aside to Mahomedanism; they must, therefore, go on to Christianity, towards which they are carried by the irresistible progress of events."

large towns, in which European education has made
any great progress, Idolatry has ceased to be the
religion of the younger generation; and that will
be—indeed, is fast becoming—an important epoch in
the history of Christianity in India, when the old
bigoted race of Hindoos shall disappear from the
scene, and the alumni of our English colleges
become heads of families in their place.   If they
themselves repose neither on Hindooism nor on Christianity, but take refuge in a middle state of what
they call theo-philanthropism, there is good hope for
their sons—ay, and I may add, for their daughters.
In a country where parental authority is powerful,
the bigotry of the elder generation must naturally
have been an obstacle to religious and social progress; but the children of the young men who in
their hot youth delighted to insult their idols with
mocking words and irreverent gestures, are little
likely to be deterred by any domestic influences from
advancing onward along the path of reformation.
Not cradled in Idolatry, like their fathers, they will
have a fair start from the beginning.   There will be
nothing for them to unlearn.   They may go at once
in quest of the Truth.

As for ourselves, for the small handful of Christian
men whose mission I firmly believe it is, in God's
good time, to evangelize the great Indian races, what
we have now to do is to possess ourselves in faith,
and with faith to have patience; doing nothing
rashly, nothing precipitately, lest our own folly should
mar the good work, and retard the ripening of the

harvest. But greater even than Faith and Hope is Charity; for amidst much that is doubtful in the extreme, and of most difficult solution, there is one truth most nearly concerning us all, that engenders no conflict of opinion, no inner or outer strife—one truth which every man, without the shadow of a misgiving, may take to his heart confidently and courageously—and that truth is, that we have now reached an epoch in the history of our Anglo-Indian empire in which every Christian man who is brought face to face with the natives of the country may demonstrate his Christianity as never yet he has had chance of doing it before. Be he in the service, or be he out of the service—be he old or young—be he high in rank or of humble station—he may assert his national faith by vindicating that great cardinal principle of Christianity, the forgiveness of enemies— praying for them who have persecuted and despite-fully used his race.

Increased kindness and consideration towards the natives of the country should now be the rule and the practice of every Englishman whose lot is cast among them. The amnesty which has been pro-claimed by the Queen of England should be echoed by every Christian heart. Terrible things truly have been done, and the Lord God of Recompences has suffered a terrible retribution to overtake the wrong-doers. For every Christian man, woman, or child, who has fallen in this great struggle, how many Hindoos and Mahomedans have perished at the bayonet's point, at the cannon's mouth, or in the

noose of the gibbet! Does not such great nati
punishment wipe out the national offence? and o
we not to be so satisfied with such a measur
retribution that boundless compassion may righteo
take the place of anger and revenge in every Cl
tian heart?

Such assertion of the best part of practical Cl
tianity cannot speak in vain to the people. E
Englishman so demonstrating that the religion
professes is a living principle within him is a
sionary of the best kind. His language canno
misunderstood; his doctrines cannot be gainsa
Such potent influence is there, indeed, in this
grandest of all human lessons—the forgivenes
enemies—that the bare enunciation of it has ere
converted heathens to a living Christianity. "Su
this is truth—surely this is truth!" has been
spontaneous exclamation, the irresistible belief of
hearing it for the first time.* And if there has
such power in the mere spoken words, what

* This striking fact is mentioned
by Dr. Duff in his work on "India
and Indian Missions." The Sermon
on the Mount was read by him to a
number of inquiring Hindoo youths.
The profound impression produced
on their minds by the passage, "*I
say unto you, love your enemies; bless
them that curse you; do good to them
that hate you; and pray for them who
despitefully use you and persecute you,*"
is thus described:—"So deep indeed
and intense was the impression produced, that in reference to one individual, at least, from the simple
reading of these verses might be
dated his conversion—his turning
from dumb idols to serve the living
and the true God. There was something in them of such an overwhelming moral loveliness—
thing that contrasted so lumin
with all that he had been previ
taught to regard as reveale
God, that he could not help c
out in ecstasy, 'Oh! how beaut
how divine; surely, this is the
this is the truth, this is the tr
It seemed to be a feeling, thou
a higher and holier nature,
thing akin to that experienc
the discoverer of a famous geor
cal theorem, when, in a deliri
joy, he rushed along exclaimi
have found it, I have found it!
did not rest satisfied till his th
givings went forth in a hecato
burnt victims on the altar
gods. In the other case, for
and for weeks the young H

there be in the living lesson! It is well that we should think of this, and in all humility of heart; for if we have much to forgive, may not there also be much for which we need forgiveness? The progressive improvement in the lives of the English in India is a fact which has been illustrated in these pages. We have not, in recent times, practically disgraced our Christianity, as our forefathers were once wont to disgrace it. But I am afraid that, in one important respect, we have not done all that we might have done to adorn it. We have not regarded the natives of the country as we have regarded our own people. We have not, in our daily lives, treated them with the gentleness, the respect, the consideration which they would have won from us, had they been of the same colour and the same creed. I am afraid that we have rarely, in our intercourse with them, forgotten the difference between the couqueror and the conquered, and that when we have not treated them with cruelty, we have treated them with contempt. The tone of the dominant race continually asserts itself in a manner which, if ever applied to ourselves, we should feel to be galling in the extreme. There are some who vehemently assert that this tone should now become louder and more imperious; that we should never suffer the natives of the country to forget for a moment that we are there by virtue of our superior prowess; that having now got the heel of the con-

could not cease repeating the expression, 'Love your enemies, bless them that curse you,' &c., constantly exclaiming, 'How beautiful!' 'surely this is the truth!' Nor was he allowed to rest satisfied till his grati-

tude for the discovery ended in renouncing all his sacrifices, hecatombs, and false gods, for the one sacrifice by which the true God for ever perfected them, who have come to knowledge of the truth as it is

queror upon them, we should sternly and remorsel
keep it there.   But God will never suffer us
hold these Eastern races in subjection.   If ther
one thing which more than another He has taugl
speaking terribly to us through these late calam
it is that the natives of India—abject, down-tro
as we have long supposed them to be—are capal
rising against their conquerors, and that we c
permanently hold them in subjection by their
It is by our practical Christianity, by lessons of
ness and love, by doing never to them what we
not have done to ourselves, that we must nov
deavour to perpetuate the connexion between th
countries, and to diffuse our Christianity amon
people, by showing them how holy a thing it is
how blessed its results.   To the missionary ai
the schoolmaster may well be left the direct
of preaching and of teaching.   There is no wa
appointed labourers, and there is no need, ther
that the servants of Government should trea
those especial vineyards.   But no man need com
therefore, that he is prohibited from doing the
of his heavenly Master.   By the blamelessness
life, by the gentleness of his demeanour, by his
dant charity, by his deeds of mercy, by his stea
assertion of his holy religion, proving that he i
only ready, if need be, to die for his faith, but wl
better still, to live for it, he may make the p
by whom he is surrounded, so enamoured of (
tianity, that they will exclaim, "Surely the rel
which bears such fruits is not a delusion an
imposture."

And the people of England, too—the home-staying people—they also have a duty to perform. Earnestness is a great thing, but patience is a better ; and what should be now preached to the people of England, in respect of this great matter of Christianity in India, is, that they should possess themselves in patience.   That all who appreciate the inestimable blessings of Christianity should eagerly desire to impart to others the glad tidings of salvation, is the necessary result of their own sincerity of faith. If I have said anything to encourage this desire, I shall not have written in vain.   But, as one earnestly desiring to hasten the coming of Christ's kingdom, I cannot refrain from counselling moderation in language and forbearance in action.  The Devil himself could not, in such a crisis as this, desire anything better for his own interests than a display of ignorant, unreflecting Christian zeal on the part of his enemies.   Pure as may be the source from which it springs, such zeal is not in accordance with those blessed lessons of practical wisdom taught by Him who lifted up His voice against the folly of putting new wine into old bottles, and upon whose lips ever hung the lowly exhortation to give no offence.   The people of England may be assured that the question which many would rashly attempt to solve—at any time, and under any circumstances, a very difficult and a very delicate one—is surrounded with peculiar perplexities and embarrassments, the growth of recent events, and that any arrogant rushings-in, regardless of the warning voices of those whose zeal tal

another direction, will assuredly retard the co[
which they seek to accelerate. It is vain for us
to endeavour to anticipate God's good time : we
fear nothing if we wait patiently and prayerf[
" What bright hope there is," recently said on[
the best of our new-school prelates, " that, in G
good time, India shall become, in reality, a Chri
country ! We may not, indeed, be too sanguin[
our expectation of immediate results. But the m[
is in God's hands, and we cannot doubt that He
the intention of christianizing India in the dist[
God is evidently dealing with us, and working
us, and out of all this apparent evil He will, eve
ally, bring good. Those clouds that have settle
thickly over the horizon will soon disperse, and
brightness of the Gospel of Christ will shine
more and more unto the perfect day." True, ind
And the clouds are now well nigh dispersed : the
is dawning : there is glorious promise of meri[
brightness. Let us then have Faith ; let us [
Hope ; let us have Charity. With these great g
we may " learn for the result to wait Heaven's t[
and to have confidence in Heaven's means," for
extension of Christ's kingdom upon earth.

# APPENDICES.

---

## APPENDIX I.

[Chapter II.—Page 60.]

### THE FIRST PROTESTANT CHURCH IN INDIA.

AN interesting account of Streynsham Masters' Church, and of the charities connected with it, is given by one Charles Lockyer, who visited the Madras coast at the beginning of the eighteenth century. It conveys, on the whole, rather a favourable impression of the settlement:—" The church is a large pile of arched building, adorned with curious carved work, a stately altar, organs, a white copper candlestick, very large windows, &c., which render it inferior to the churches of London in nothing but bells; there being only one to mind sinners of their devotion; though I've heard a contribution for a set was formerly remitted the Company. Church stock, anno 1703, was 6,705 pagodas in houses, plate, cash, &c., which, with orphans' money, makes their account current 13,753 pagodas. Orphans' money is when wealthy parents dying bequeath their estates to children incapable of managing them, and make the Church trustees; to provide a good education, and prevent the abuses their minority might render them incident to from a single guardian, who often prefers his own private ends to the trust reposed in him. Above three quarters of this stock not being at use, and that one might not gain all, while another's cash lying dead can increase nothing, the advance on what is let out is distributed yearly among them, in proportion to their estates in money, and makes about seven per cent. per annum round. Church stock became so considerable from the free gifts of pious persons, and monthly collections in time of divine service, for maintenance of the poor, which, one year with another, amounts to above 350

pagodas; but they wanted not near that sum, the rema
is passed to this account. Prayers are read twice a
but on Sundays, religious worship is most strictly obse
Betwixt eight and nine the bell tells us the hour of dev
draws near, a whole company of above 200 soldiers is d
out from the inner fort to the church-door, for a guard t
passing president, ladies throng to their pews, and g
men take a serious walk in the yard, if not too hot. O
governor's approach, the organs strike up, and contin
welcome till he is seated, when the minister discharge
duty of his function, according to the forms appointed b
prudent ancestors for the Church of England. The
sacraments of communion and baptism are received
England; nor is there a Sunday, but the country Prote
are examined in the catechism. They likewise keep a
school, in a large room under the library, appointed fo
purpose, where children may learn to read and write, wi
charge to their parents. Books of divinity in the librar
valued at 438*l.* 6*s.*"

## APPENDIX II.

[Chapter V.—Page 146.]

### OBSERVANCE OF THE SABBATH IN INE

[*From a Despatch of the Court of Directors, dated May 25th, 179* 

" Conceiving it a duty incumbent upon us to afford our
and military servants, and all Christians living under
protection, professing the Protestant religion, the mea
attending Divine service, in which we trust those in sup
stations will set the example, we most cheerfully acquie
your proposal for erecting chapels in the progressive m
pointed out in the 63rd paragraph of the letter to whic
are now replying, such edifices to be as plain and simp
possible, that all unnecessary expense may be avoided.

" Having thus, as far as depends upon us, provided f
due observance of public worship on the Sabbath-day
cannot avoid mentioning the information we have rece
that at the military stations it is no uncommon thing fo
solemnity of the day to be broke in upon by horse-ra
whilst Divine worship (for which the Sabbath is espe
enjoined to be set apart) is never performed at any of

stations, though chaplains are allotted to them. And we have now before us a printed horse-racing account, by which it appears that not less than eight matches were run at Chinsurah in one day, and that on a Sunday. We are astonished and shocked at this wide deviation from one of the most distinguishing and universal institutions of Christianity. We must suppose it to have been so gradual, that transitions from one step to another have been little observed; but the stage at which it is now arrived, if our information be true, must appear to every reasonable man, highly discreditable to our Government, and totally incompatible with the religion we profess.

" To preserve the ascendancy which our national character has acquired over the minds of the natives of India, must ever be of importance to the maintenance of the political power we possess in the East, and we are well persuaded that this end is not to be served either by a disregard of the external observances of religion, or by any assimilation to Eastern manners and opinions, but rather by retaining all the distinctions of our national principles, character, and usages. The events which have recently passed in Europe, point out that the present is least of all the time in which irreligion should be promoted or encouraged; for, with an attachment to the religion which we profess, is found to be intimately connected an attachment to our laws and constitution; besides which, it is calculated to produce the most beneficial effects in society; to maintain in it the peace, the subordination, all the principles and practices on which its stability and happiness depend.

" We therefore enjoin that all such profanations of the Sabbath, as have been mentioned, be forbidden and prevented; and that Divine service be regularly performed, as in England, every Sunday, at all the military stations; and all European officers and soldiers, unless hindered by sickness or actual duty, are to be required punctually to attend, for which such an hour is to be fixed as shall be most suitable to the climate. The chaplains are to be positively ordered to be regular and correct in the performance of their duty, and if any one of them neglect it, or by his conduct bring discredit on his profession, we direct that he be dismissed from our service.

" It is on the qualities of our servants that the safety of the British possessions in India essentially depends; on their virtue, their intelligence, their laborious application, their vigilance and public spirit. We have seen, and do still with pleasure see, honourable examples of all these; we are anxious to preserve and increase such examples, and therefore

cannot contemplate without alarm the excessive grov
fashionable amusement and show, the tendency of whicl
enervate the mind, and impair its nobler qualities, to intr
a hurtful emulation in expense, to set up false standa
merit, to confound the different orders in society, a
beget an aversion to serious occupations."

## APPENDIX III.

[Chapter V.—Page 147.]

### CHARLES GRANT'S FIRST MANIFESTO.

The following is an extract from a paper drawn 1
Mr. Charles Grant, in 1792, and given to Mr. Dunda
is supposed to have laid the foundation of the Resoluti
1793, given in a subsequent appendix:—

" He will not allow himself to believe, that when so
noble and beneficial ends may be served by our possessi
an empire in the East, we shall content ourselves wit
meanest and the least, and for the sake of this, frustr
the rest. He trusts we shall dare to do justice, liberal j
and be persuaded, that this principle will carry us to g
heights of prosperity, than the precautions of a selfish p
Future events are inscrutable to the keenest speculation
the path of duty is open, the time present is ours.
planting our language, our knowledge, our opinions, an
religion, in our Asiatic territories, we shall put a great
beyond the reach of contingencies; we shall probably
wedded the inhabitants of these territories to this cou
but at any rate, we shall have done an act of strict di
them, and a lasting service to mankind.

" In considering the affairs of the world as under the c
of the Supreme Disposer, and those distant territories,
strange events, providentially put into our hands, is
reasonable, is it not necessary that we might diffuse a
their inhabitants, long sunk in darkness, vice, and m
the light and the benign influences of truth, the blessi
well-regulated society, the improvements and the con
of active industry? And that in prudently and sin
endeavouring to answer these ends, we may not only hu
hope for some measure of the same success which u
attended serious and rational attempts, for the propagat

that pure and sublime religion which comes from God, but best secure the protection of his providential government, of which we now see such awful marks in the events of the world.

" In every progressive step of this work, we shall also serve the original design with which we visited India, that design still so important to this country;—the extension of our commerce. Why is it that so few of our manufactures and commodities are vended there? Not merely because the taste of the people is not generally formed to the use of them, but because they have not the means of purchasing them. The proposed improvements would introduce both. As it is, our woollens, our manufactures in iron, copper, and steel, our clocks, watches, and toys of different kinds, our glassware, and various other articles, are admired there, and would sell in great quantities if the people were rich enough to buy them. Let invention be once awakened among them, let them be roused to improvements at home, let them be led by industry to multiply, as they may exceedingly, the exchangeable productions of their country, let them acquire relish for the ingenious exertions of the human mind in Europe, for the beauties and refinements, endlessly diversified, of European art and science, and we shall hence obtain for ourselves the supply of four and twenty millions of distant subjects. How greatly will our country be thus aided in rising still superior to all her difficulties; and how stable, as well as unrivalled, may we hope our commerce will be, when we thus rear it on right principles and make it the means of their extension! It might be too sanguine to form into a wish an idea most pleasing and desirable in itself, that our religion and our knowledge might be diffused over other dark portions of the globe, where nature has been more kind than human institutions.—This is the noblest species of conquest; and wherever, we may venture to say, our principles and language are introduced, our commerce will follow.

" To rest in the present state of things, or to determine that the situation of our Asiatic subjects, and our connexion with them, are such as they ought to be for all time to come, seems too daring a conclusion: and if a change, a great change be necessary, no reason can be assigned for its commencement at any future period, which will not equally, nay, more strongly recommend its commencement now. To say, that things may be left to their own course, or that our European settlements may prove a sufficient nursery of moral and religious instruction for the natives, will be, in effect, to declare, that there shall be no alteration, at least, no effectual and safe one.

"The Muhammadans, living for centuries intermixed in great numbers with the Hindus, produced no radical change in their character, not merely because they rendered themselves disagreeable to their subjects, but because they left those subjects, during that whole period, as uninstructed in effectual points as they found them. We are called rather to imitate the Roman conquerors, who civilized and improved the nations whom they subdued, and we are called to this, not only by the obvious wisdom which directed their policy, but by local circumstances, as well as by sounder principles and higher motives than they possessed.

"The examples also of modern European nations pass in review before us. We are the fourth of those who have possessed an Indian empire. That of the Portuguese, though acquired by romantic bravery, was unsystematic and rapacious; the short one of the French was the meteor of a vain ambition; the Dutch acted upon the principle of a selfish commercial policy; and these, under which they apparently flourished for a time, have been the cause of their decline and fall. None of these nations sought to establish themselves in the affections of their acquired subjects, or to assimilate them to their manners; and those subjects, far from supporting them, rejoiced in their defeat. Some attempts they made to instruct the natives, which had their use; but sordid views overwhelmed their effects. It remains for us to show how we shall be distinguished from these nations in the history of mankind; whether conquest shall have been in our hands, the means, not merely of displaying a government, unequalled in India for administrative justice, kindness, and moderation; not merely of increasing the security of the subject and prosperity of the country, but of advancing social happiness, of meliorating the moral state of men, and of extending a superior light, farther than the Roman eagle ever flew.

"If the novelty, the impracticability, the danger of the proposed scheme be urged against it, these objections cannot all be consistent; and the last, which is the only one that could have weight, presupposes success. In success would be our safety, not our danger. Our danger must lie in pursuing, from ungenerous ends, a course contracted and illiberal; but in following an opposite course, in communicating light, knowledge, and improvement, we shall obey the dictates of duty, of philanthropy, and of policy. We shall take the most rational means to remove inherent great disorders, to attach the Hindu people to ourselves, to ensure the safety of our possessions, to enhance continually their value to us, to raise a fair and durable monument to the glory of this country, and to increase the happiness of the human race."

---

## Appendix IV.

[Chapter VII.—Page 205.]

## THE TRADITIONARY POLICY OF THE EAST INDIA COMPANY.

*[A Despatch from the Court of Directors to the Governor-General in Council.]*

"We have received, by the *General Stuart*, your letter of the 2nd November last, addressed to the Secret Committee, on the subject of certain publications which had issued from the missionary press at Serampore, and detailing the proceedings which you had thought it advisable to adopt with regard to them.

"Whatever is connected with an attempt to introduce Christianity among the natives of British India cannot but be felt as a subject of the greatest importance, and of the greatest delicacy, and we lament that circumstances should have occurred in any part of our territories, to call for the interference of our Government in matters of that description. We are anxious that it should be distinctly understood that we are very far from being averse to the introduction of Christianity into India, or indifferent to the benefits which would result from the general diffusion of its doctrines; but we have a fixed and settled opinion that nothing could be more unwise and impolitic, nothing even more likely to frustrate the hopes and endeavours of those who aim at the very object—the introduction of Christianity among the native inhabitants—than any imprudent or injudicious attempt to introduce it by means which should irritate and alarm their religious prejudices.   That the publication which first excited your attention, as well as the paper which you transmitted to us, marked C, entitled "The Use of Wisdom," is calculated to produce those effects, we conceive can admit of no doubt, and we entirely approve of your endeavours to interrupt the circulation of them.   Indeed the missionaries themselves seem to regret, and to condemn their publication.   Perhaps some doubt might be fairly entertained whether a considerable part

L L

of the paper marked B, was of a nature to have e
similar feelings, if the other publications did not prepar
mind to receive with some jealousy any works which
from the same press. In suggesting the possibility o
doubt, we by no means intend to convey any disappro
of that prudent precaution which led you to preven
further publication of this last, together with those
appear to us to be more unquestionably exceptionable.
a matter of great difficulty to draw the line which sho
once describe and characterize the publications which
be permitted to be considered as inoffensive; and a
same time distinguish them from those which a proper
caution would suppress; and at this distance from the
of Government, we can only state to you those g
principles which we are desirous should direct your co
upon this point. For this purpose we would refer you
passage in our political letter to Fort St. George of the
May, 1807, in which we briefly intimated in the foll
terms, our sentiments of what the character and condu
Christian missionaries in India, and the carriage of
Company's Government towards them ought to be:—'
we afforded our countenance and sanction to the missio
who have from time to time proceeded to India fo
purpose of propagating the Christian religion, it was far
being in our contemplation to add the influence of
authority to any attempts they might make; for, o
contrary, we were perfectly aware that the progress o
conversion would be gradual and slow, arising more f
conviction of the purity of the principles of our re
itself, and from the pious example of its teachers, than
any undue influence, or from the exertions of authority
are never to be resorted to in such cases.' In the same
we would still wish to affirm as a principle, the desirab
of imparting the knowledge of Christianity to the nati
India; but we must also contend that the means to be
for that end shall be only such as shall be free from
political danger or alarm.

" With these two positions, which appear to us to be f
mental on the subject in question, the 39th paragraph of
despatch now before us in substance corresponds, for you
after acknowledging 'your entire conviction of the co
ness of the statement which the memorial of the missio
contains relative to the motives and objects of their ze
the propagation of the sacred doctrines of Christi
observe: 'Our duty as guardians of the public welfar

even a consentaneous solicitude for the diffusion of the blessings of Christianity, merely require us to restrain the efforts of that commendable zeal within those limits, the transgression of which would, in our decided judgment, expose to hazard the public safety and tranquillity, without promoting its intended object.' Agreeing then with you in general views on this question, and impressed with the necessity of leaving the application of these principles to the discretion of the Government upon the spot, we feel that we have but little further to suggest to you upon that part of the subject.

" We observe with great satisfaction the temperate and respectful conduct of the Society of Missionaries in the discussions which took place on the subject of the publications to which your attention was directed, and of the measures which you felt yourselves called upon to adopt, and we entirely approve of the permission which you granted to them of continuing their press at Serampore. Their residence at that place would probably be attended with little additional inconvenience to your Government, and we conclude, moreover, that the British authority has long ago been established at the different Danish settlements in India. We are well aware that the progress of the missionaries, both Catholic and Protestant, for a long period of years has not been attended with injurious consequences; their numbers have not been sufficient to excite alarm, and their general conduct has been prudent and conciliating, and we have no reason to suppose that the mere circulation, in a peaceable and unobtrusive manner, of translations of the Scriptures, is likely to be attended with consequences dangerous to the public safety.

" The paramount power which we now possess in India undoubtedly demands from us additional caution upon this subject; it imposes upon us the necessity, as well as strengthens our obligation, to protect the native inhabitants in the free and undisturbed profession of their religious opinions, and to take care that they are neither harassed nor irritated by any premature or over-zealous attempts to convert them to Christianity.

" In conveying to you our approbation of the control which you had determined to exercise with regard to such publications as might issue from the press of the missionaries, we trust that it will be found not only salutary to the interests of Government, but even satisfactory to the considerate part of the missionaries themselves. They must be aware that it is quite consistent with doing all justice to the excellency of

the motives on which they act, to apprehend that thei
may sometimes require a check, and that it may be
and necessary to introduce the control or superintende
Government, whose responsibility for the public tranq
will force it to direct its views to those political consider
which the zeal of the missionaries might overlook.

" If, indeed, you had foreseen that the missionaries
have shown that entire and ready submissiveness to G
ment which their conduct has manifested, we think you
have doubted of the expediency of holding, under the ci
stances you have described, a public proceeding upor
transactions, and we would only suggest that if on any
occasion any fresh precautionary measures should b
indispensable, and the interference of Government be
required, it would be desirable, in the first instance at
to see whether a private communication from the Gov
General might not effect all that is desired, without br
into view the instrumentality of Government; its aut
cannot be seen actively to control any of their proce
without exposing it to the inference of specially sanct
and countenancing such publications, and such condu
does not prevent, and thereby making the Governm
some degree a party to the acts of the missionarie
making the missionaries appear in the character of the
of Government.

" In adverting to your prohibition of the public preacl
Calcutta to the Hindoos and Mahomedans, at the time
we approve of this measure of precaution, we do not
stand you to object to the missionaries decently perforn
their usual places of residence the duties of their reli
chapels or rooms at which admittance may be given t
converts, or to other Christians. We presume th
number of chaplains which we have appropriated 1
performance of religious duties at Calcutta is sufficient
the British, or other inhabitants of that place who comp
the English language; but we do not collect it to hav
your intention to preclude other Christians there from l
Divine service performed in a language which they
stand.

" Having thus explained to you as briefly as possil
principles on which we wish you to act with regard to t
sionaries, it remains for us only to advert to your sug
that we should 'discourage any accession to the nun
missionaries actually employed under the protection
British Government in India in the work of conversion

are, of course, aware that many of the meritorious individuals who have devoted themselves to those labours were not British subjects, or living under our authority, and that none of the missionaries have proceeded to Bengal with our licence.

" Entertaining the sentiments which we have expressed in the preceding parts of this despatch, we are very far from disapproving of your having refrained from resorting to the authority vested in you by law, and enforcing its provisions in all their strictness against the missionaries, and we rely on your discretion that you will abstain from all unnecessary or ostentatious interference with their proceedings. On the other hand, it will be your bounden duty vigilantly to guard the public tranquillity from interruption, and to impress upon the minds of all the inhabitants of India, that the British faith on which they rely for the free exercise of their religion will be inviolably maintained.

" Although the subject treated on in your letter to the Secret Committee, dated the 2nd November, 1807, does not fall strictly within the description of those to which you have informed us, in your political letter of the 16th February, 1807, you should thenceforward confine your correspondence with the Secret Committee, we nevertheless think it of a nature sufficiently important to justify a departure from the general rule, and therefore approve of your having transmitted that despatch to the Secret Committee; and we direct that this letter now written in reply to it be also kept in the Secret Department.

" Since the preceding paragraphs were written, your letter of the 7th December, 1807, to the Secret Committee has been received, with copies of the letter and memorial addressed to the Governor-General by the Rev. Dr. Claudius Buchanan.

" We desire to express our entire satisfaction at the explanation which you have thought it necessary to give of your proceedings, and as most of the observations which would naturally have occurred to us on the perusal of those documents have already been stated in this letter, we deem it unnecessary to enlarge further on the subject.

" With every disposition to make due allowance in favour of ardent zeal in the cause of religion, it would have been impossible for us to avoid noticing the improper style of Dr. Buchanan's address to the supreme authority in India, if his subsequent departure from thence had not in some degree relieved us from that necessity. We shall content ourselves at present with remarking that Dr. Buchanan, as well as other ecclesiastics who promulgate the doctrines of Christianity in

India, and who bestow such just and merited encomi
the conduct of the missionary Schwartz, would do
adopt it as the model of their own, and would always r
that discretion and moderation in their language and
are more consistent with the mild spirit of our religio
are indispensably requisite for those who are emplo
prosecuting the laborious work of conversion.

    " We are,

       Your affectionate friends,

| R. C. PLOWDEN, | CHAS. GRANT, |
| JOHN ROBERTS, | JACOB BOSANQ |
| C. MARJORIBANKS, | GEORGE SMITH |
| T. REID, | JOHN INGLIS, |
| JOHN TRAVERS, | JOSEPH COTTO |
| JAS. PATTERSON, | W. BENTLEY, |
| JOHN BEBB, | G. A. ROBINS( |
| EDW. PARRY, | |

*"East India House, London,*
   *September 7th,* 1808."

## APPENDIX V.

[Chapter VIII.—Pages 258–259.]

### THE RESOLUTIONS OF 1793.

" And whereas such measures ought to be adopted f
interest and happiness of the native inhabitants of the I
dominions in India, as may gradually tend to their ad
ment in useful knowledge, and to their religious and
improvement:

" Be it therefore further enacted, that the said Co
Directors shall be and are hereby empowered and re
to appoint and send out, from time to time, a sufficient n
of fit and proper persons for carrying into effect the pu
aforesaid, by acting as schoolmasters, missionaries, or
wise: every such person, before he is so appointed o
out, having produced to the said Court of Directors a
factory testimonial or certificate from the Archbish
Canterbury, or the Bishop of London for the time bei
from the Society in London for the promotion of Ch
Knowledge, or from the Society in Scotland for propa
Christian Knowledge, of his sufficiency for these purpos

" And be it further enacted, that the said Court of Directors are hereby empowered and required to give directions to the governments of the respective presidencies in India, to settle the destination and to provide for the necessary and decent maintenance of the persons so to be sent out as aforesaid; and also to direct the said governments to consider of and adopt such other measures according to their discretion, as may appear to them most conducive to the ends aforesaid.

" Provided always, and be it further enacted, that if any person so sent out as aforesaid shall at any time prove to be of immoral life and conversation, or shall be grossly negligent or remiss in the discharge of the duties of the station to which he shall have been so appointed, or shall engage, directly or indirectly, in any trade whatsoever, or shall accept of and hold any office or employment, public or private, other than that to which he shall have been so appointed, the governments of the respective presidencies shall be and they are hereby required to remove him from his employment, and send him back to Great Britain; and the act of government in so doing shall be final and conclusive, and shall not be examinable in any court of law whatsoever.

" And that due means of religious worship and instruction may also be provided for all persons of the Protestant communion in the service or under the protection of the said company, be it enacted that the said Court of Directors shall be and are hereby empowered and required, from time to time, to send out and maintain in their several principal garrisons and factories, a sufficient number and supply of fit and proper ministers: and also to take and maintain a chaplain on board every ship in the service or employment of the said Company, being of the burden of 700 tons or upwards: and that every charter-party to be entered into by the said Company for any ship of the burden aforesaid, or any greater burden, shall contain an express stipulation for the said Company to nominate and send on·board such ship a chaplain for the purposes aforesaid, at their nomination and expense. Provided always, that no such minister or chaplain shall be so appointed or sent out until he shall first have been approved of by the Archbishop of Canterbury or the Bishop of London for the time being."

## APPENDIX VI.

[Chapter XL—Page 426.]

### BISHOP WILSON ON BISHOP CORRIE

[*From a Funeral Sermon preached on the* 17th *March*, 1837.]

"He had been thirty years in India, a period whic few Europeans reach. Still fewer have had so lo honourable a course of service. As chaplain at ( Cawnpore, Agra, Benares, and the cathedral at Calcu was long a blessing to his various flocks. As Archdea nine years, he fulfilled the duties of that difficult offic thrice was he called to the episcopal residence to sup far as he was able, for considerable intervals, the funct the vacant See.*

"We are to remember, also, with gratitude, that this long period *he exhibited that peculiar cast of ch which India most wanted.* With all the sweetness of Heber, he had all the enlightened hold of Christian fixed simplicity of heart of Brainerd and Schwartz and Martyn. His cast of mind was humility, meekness, ness. To this he added such generosity as kept hi tinually poor, from the unlimited munificence of his b tions. There was nothing he was not ready to attem to execute, if possible, from his own funds. Whe passed during the visitation in the places where resided, Corrie's was the name constantly repeated. built the church and founded the mission at Chunar. built the chapel and school-house at Agra. Corrie b two churches at Benares, and founded, or caused founded, the schools. At Buxar also it was the same. he did in founding the High School at Calcutta,—w respected the Free Church,—what in Mrs. Wilson's schools,—what at Mirzapore,—what in the Church Mis and Bible Society Committees,—you all know.

"His accessibility, also, his kindness to the you gentleness in reproof, his charitable judgment of oth forgiveness of injuries, shed a soft brightness on this rosity of heart, which attached both natives and Eur to him with an indescribable attachment. Every on that he has lost a father, a brother, a friend. I am no ing a poetical picture of imagined perfection. No do

* After the deaths of Bishops Heber, James, and Turner.

had his infirmities; but they arose so entirely on the side of softness of nature as to deduct little from the general weight of his character. He might often be imposed upon—he might be wanting in habits of despatch in business—he might be irresolute and forgetful—he might be susceptible sometimes of prejudices which sunk the deeper into his feelings, because he said little. But all this is nothing. Had his particular errors of judgment been a thousand times more numerous than they were, they would have been lost in the just admiration and love which a constant, simple, benevolent, gentle spirit had excited during a life of thirty years in India. Such a character is more precious than gold. The bold, the vigorous, the unbending, if adorned with piety, are deserving of admiration, and are at certain periods of essential service; but the meek, the amiable, the silent, are more rare and more blessed.

"We are again to remember with gratitude that he *united in an eminent degree the missionary and the chaplain.* He was the last of that fine series of men with whom India was blessed in the last age. He stands on the same list with Brown, Buchanan, Martyn, Thomason, who were the ornaments of the Anglican Episcopal Church in India before the creation of the See. He gave himself so early and so assiduously to the cultivation of the native languages, that in Hindostanee he was a very superior scholar—wrote it with elegance, and spoke it with ease. He had a missionary's heart. Wherever he resided as a chaplain, he founded and sustained missions. The first eminent Bishop of Calcutta mentions his labours at Agra, where Abdool Messeeh was his distinguished convert, with commendation. He was the parent of the Church Missionary Society in India, the centre of union, the soul of all its operations. And when he went home for his health in 1814, I well remember the affection with which he was everywhere welcomed. There is no one who filled at the period of his death so large a space in the public mind, both here and at home, as Corrie, from the juncture when he lived, the length of his services, the cast of his character, and his union of the missionary's and chaplain's spirit. Confidence had gathered round him gradually, and from all quarters and all classes of persons, and was rapidly increasing.

"Nor must we forget the great goodness of God in *raising him to the See of the newly-founded Diocese of Madras.* Never did India feel a warmer joy than when she knew that her beloved Corrie was distinguished with this just mark of

favour by the Home Government. He was sent out
*first* Charles Grant; he was nominated Bishop by the
He would indeed have been appointed Bishop of Cal
1832, had not his distance from England and the unce
of life prevented. When at length he ascended the e
chair of Madras, it was with the warm approbation
classes. Nor did he disappoint the high expectation
of him. Never was a ruler in the house of God so l
Never did any one more successfully unite firmness i
ciple with suavity of spirit. The burst of grief thro
the diocese at his early death is indescribable. His s
his addresses at confirmation, his activity in foun
grammar-school, and a society for building churches,
respondence with his clergy, his settlement of doubtfu
his zeal in missionary and benevolent institutions—h
plicity in all he did, had won every heart."

\* When President of the India Board—now Lord Glenelg.

THE END.

London: Printed by Smith, Elder and Co., Little Green Arbour Court.

# BIOGRAPHIES OF INDIAN STATESMEN.

## BY THE SAME AUTHOR.

---

## The Life and Correspondence of Sir John Malcolm, G.C.B. By JOHN WILLIAM KAYE.

### Two Volumes, 8vo. With Portrait. Price 36s. cloth.

"The biography is replete with interest and information, deserving to be perused by the student of Indian history, and sure to recommend itself to the general reader."—*Athenæum.*

"Mr. Kaye has used his materials well, and has written an interesting narrative, copiously illustrated with invaluable documents; many unpublished letters of the Duke of Wellington are to be found among their number."—*Examiner.*

"A very valuable contribution to our Indian literature. We recommend it strongly to all who desire to learn something of the History of British India, or of the character and labours of a man who, by work, zeal, and integrity, raised himself from a Cadet to be Governor of Bombay."—*New Quarterly Review.*

"Mr. Kaye's biography is at once a contribution to the history of our policy and dominion in the East, and a worthy memorial of one of those wise and large-hearted men, whose energy and principle have made England great."—*British Quarterly Review.*

"The public are indebted to Mr. Kaye for a contribution to our biographical literature, which is not only a pleasing and instructive record of Sir John Malcolm's career, but which portrays the growth of a manly, self-relying character, and throws some additional light on the history of British Policy in India."—*Edinburgh Review.*

"One of the most interesting of the recent biographies of our great Indian statesmen."—*National Review.*

"Thoroughly agreeable, instructive reading."—*Westminster Review.*

"An important contribution to Anglo-Indian history."—*Tait's Magazine.*

# Life and Correspondence of Lord Metcalfe.
## By John William Kaye.

### New and Cheap Edition, in 2 Vols., Small Post 8vo, with Portrait, price 12s. cloth.

" Lord Metcalfe possessed extraordinary opportunities of making himself acquainted with the native character, and of estimating at its correct value the nature of the tenure by which our Indian possessions were held ; and at the present time we can value more highly the great practical discernment of one whose fortune it was to be laughed at by the superficial, because he believed in the insecurity of our Indian empire. Some additions which have been made to the present volumes, place in a strong light the sagacity and good sense of Lord Metcalfe. . . . The present demand for a new edition is a sufficient commendation of a work which has already occupied the highest rank among biographies of the great men of modern times."—*Observer*.

" A new and revised edition of the life of one of the greatest and purest men that ever aided in governing India. The new edition not only places a very instructive book within the reach of a greater number of persons, but contains new matter of the utmost value and interest."—*Critic*.

" This is a neat and timely reprint of one of the most valuable biographies of the present day. Lord Metcalfe's career is full of interest in all its phases. For firmness of purpose, purity of principle, and that stubborn courage, and nerve, which has gained England her ascendancy in the East, Lord Metcalfe was even more remarkable than the greatest of his contemporaries."—*Economist*.

" A much improved edition of one of the most interesting political biographies in English literature."—*National Review*.

" Mr. Kaye's life of Lord Metcalfe is a work too well known to need an extended notice ; but there is something to be said for this republication. It is an edition revised with care and judgment. Mr. Kaye has judiciously condensed that portion of his original work which relates to the earlier career of the great Indian statesman. Another improvement in the work will be found in the augmentation of that part setting forth Lord Metcalfe's views of the insecurity of our Indian empire. The insecurity which cast a gloom over Metcalfe's predictions has been fearfully verified by the events of 1857."—*Globe*.

" We heartily thank Mr. Kaye for this timely republication : it will do much to dispel the wide-spread ignorance that has obtained concerning the government of India."—*Eclectic Review*.

" An instructive volume of biographical history."—*Morning Herald*.

---

# Papers of the late Lord Metcalfe. Selected and Edited by J. W. Kaye.
### Demy 8vo, price 16s. cloth.

" We commend this volume to all persons who like to study State papers, in which the practical sense of a man of the world is joined to the speculative sagacity of a philosophical statesman. No Indian library should be without it."—*Press*.

---

LONDON : SMITH, ELDER AND CO., 65, CORNHILL.

65, *Cornhill, London, March,* 1859.

# NEW AND STANDARD WORKS

### PUBLISHED BY

## SMITH, ELDER AND CO.

---

## WORKS IN THE PRESS.

*Shelley Memorials.*   Edited by Lady SHELLEY.
Post 8vo.                                    (*Shortly.*)

*Life and Liberty in America.*   By CHARLES
MACKAY, L.L.D.
With *Illustrations,* 2 vols., Post 8vo.        (*Shortly.*)

*Life in Tuscany.*   By Miss MABEL SHARMAN CRAWFORD.
Post 8vo.                              (*Now ready.*)

*Hong Kong to Manilla.*   By H. T. ELLIS, Esq., R.N.
Post 8vo, with *Illustrations.*           (*Now ready.*)

*The Food Grains of India.* By Dr. J. FORBES WATSON.
8vo.                                   (*Nearly ready.*)

*The Vital Statistics of the European and*
Native Armies in India.   By JOSEPH EWART, M.D.,
Bengal Medical Service.
8vo.                                  (*Nearly ready.*)

*The Oxford Museum.*   By HENRY W. ACLAND, M.D.,
and JOHN RUSKIN, A.M.
Post 8vo, with *Three Illustrations, price* 2s. 6d. cloth.
                                         (*Just ready.*)

*Expositions of St. Paul's Epistles to the*
Corinthians.   By the late Rev. FRED. W. ROBERTSON.
1 vol., Post 8vo.

# NEW PUBLICATIONS.

*Dedicated by permission to the Right Hon. Lord Stanley, Secretary of State for India.*

## Indian Scenes and Characters, Sketched from Life. By Prince ALEXIS SOLTYKOFF.

*Sixteen Plates in Tinted Lithography, with Descriptions. Edited by Edw. B. Eastwick, Esq., F.R.S. Colombier Folio.*

*Half-bound in Morocco, Prints, 3l. 3s.; Proofs (only 50 copies printed), 4l. 4s.*

### LIST OF ILLUSTRATIONS:—

GARDENS OF AMBER, NEAR JAYPORE.
FISHERS ON THE COAST OF COROMANDEL.
FESTIVAL OF THE GODDESS DURGA, AT CALCUTTA.
HAREM CARRIAGE OF THE KING OF DELHI.
MAHARAJA HINDU RAO BAHADUR.
MOUNTAINEERS OF THE HIMALAYA.
HUNTING-LEOPARDS READY FOR THE CHASE.
CAVALCADE OF SIKH CHIEFTAINS.
SIKH CHIEFTAINS.
H. H. THE MAHARAJA OF GWALIOR AND ATTENDANTS.
THE PALACE AT JAYPORE.
A FAKEER OF RAJPUTANA.
FAKEERS.
NEGRO AND ARAB IN THE SERVICE OF THE GAIKWAR.
THE GARDENS OF BOMBAY.
DANCE OF NACH GIRLS AT BOMBAY.

## Christianity in India. By JOHN WILLIAM KAYE, Author of "Life of Lord Metcalfe," &c.

*8vo, price 16s., cloth.*

## A Lady's Escape from Gwalior, during the Mutinies of 1857. By Mrs. COOPLAND.

*Post 8vo, price 10s. 6d.*

## Speech of Lord Stanley on the Financial Resources of India. *8vo, price 1s.*

## Social Innovators and their Schemes. By WILLIAM LUCAS SARGANT, Author of "The Science of Social Opulence," &c.

*Post 8vo, price 10s 6d. cloth.*

"A work which will be read with considerable interest."—*Morning Post.*  |  "As a text-book, it will take high rank."—*Morning Chronicle.*

## New Zealand and its Colonization. By WILLIAM SWAINSON, Esq.

*Demy 8vo, price 14s., cloth.*

## The Life of J. Deacon Hume, Esq., late Secretary to the Board of Trade. By the Rev. CHARLES BADHAM. *Post 8vo, price 9s., cloth.*

2

## NEW PUBLICATIONS—continued.

### The Life of Charlotte Brontë. (CURRER BELL.)
#### Author of "JANE EYRE," "SHIRLEY," "VILLETTE," &c.
#### By MRS. GASKELL, Author of "North and South," &c.

*Fourth Edition, Revised, One Volume, with a Portrait of Miss Brontë and a View of Haworth Parsonage. Price 7s. 6d.; morocco elegant, 14s.*

"All the secrets of the literary workmanship of the authoress of 'Jane Eyre' are unfolded in the course of this extraordinary narrative."—*Times.*

"Its moral is, the unconquerable strength of genius and goodness. Mrs. Gaskell's account of Charlotte Brontë and her family is one of the profoundest tragedies of modern life."—*Spectator.*

"Let those who would know all that can be told, and ought to be told, hasten to read this history, which a woman of kindred genius has fearlessly and truthfully written of Charlotte Brontë."—*Daily News.*

"By all this book will be read with interest. As a work of art, we do not recollect a life of a woman by a woman so well executed. . . . With Mrs. Gaskell the task has been a labour of love; and, we repeat, she has produced one of the best biographies of a woman by a woman which we can recall to mind."—*Athenæum.*

"Mrs. Gaskell's life of Charlotte Brontë has placed her on a level with the best biographers of any country. It is a truthful and beautiful work, unusually bold and honest, and telling all that the reader ought to know of Miss Brontë, and all

that can be in Miss Brontë's own words."—*Globe.*

"If any one wishes to see how a woman possessed of the highest intellectual power can disregard every temptation which intellect throws in the way of women—how generously and nobly a human being can live under the pressure of accumulated misfortune—the record is at hand in 'The Life of Charlotte Brontë.'"—*Saturday Review.*

"Mrs. Gaskell has done her work well. Her narrative is simple, direct, intelligible, unaffected. No one else could have paid so tender and discerning a tribute to the memory of Charlotte Brontë."—*Fraser's Magazine.*

"We can be sincere in our praise of this book, and must not part from it without saying how often we have been touched by the tone of loving sympathy in which it is written."—*Examiner.*

"The life possesses a fearful interest that deepens in its climax as it advances towards its melancholy close."—*Literary Gazette.*

"The whole strange and pathetic story of the Brontë family is faithfully told in Mrs. Gaskell's memoir."—*Critic.*

### Sermons. By the late REV. FRED. W. ROBERTSON, A.M., Incumbent of Trinity Chapel, Brighton.

FIRST SERIES—*Sixth Edition, Post 8vo, price 9s. cloth.*

SECOND SERIES—*Fifth Edition, price 9s. cloth.*

THIRD SERIES—*Fourth Edition, Post 8vo, with Portrait, price 9s. cloth.*

"There are many persons, and their number increases every year, to whom Robertson's writings are the most stable, exhaustless, and satisfactory form of religious teaching which the nineteenth century has given—the most wise, suggestive, and practical."—*Saturday Review.*

"There must be a great and true heart, where there is a great and true preacher. And in that, beyond everything else, lay the secret of Mr. Robertson's influence. His sermons show evidence enough of acute logical power. His analysis is exquisite in its subtleness and delicacy. He has a clear, penetrative intellect, which carries light with it into the thickest darkness. But what we feel most in him is not this. It is that a brother man is speaking to us as brother men; that we are listening, not to the measured words of a calm, cool thinker, but to the passionate deep-toned voice of an earnest human soul."—*Edinburgh Christian Magazine.*

"These sermons are full of thought and beauty. There is not a sermon in the series that does not furnish evidence of originality without extrava-

gance, of discrimination without tediousness, and of piety without cant or conventionalism."—*British Quarterly.*

"We recommend the whole of the volumes to the perusal of our readers. They will find in them thought of a rare and beautiful description, an earnestness of mind steadfast in the search of truth, and a charity pure and all-embracing."—*Economist.*

"We should be glad if all preachers more united with ourselves, preached such sermons as these."—*Christian Remembrancer.*

"The Sermons are altogether out of the common style. They are strong, free, and beautiful utterances of a gifted and cultivated mind."—*Eclectic Review.*

"The Sermons are rich in evidence of his pious, manly, and soaring faith, and of his power not only to point to heaven, but to lead the way."—*Globe.*

"They are very remarkable compositions. The thoughts are often very striking, and entirely out of the track of ordinary sermonising."—*Guardian.*

### Lectures and Addresses on Literary and Social Topics. By the late Rev. FRED. W. ROBERTSON, of Brighton. Post 8vo, price 7s. 6d. cloth.

"These lectures and addresses are marked by the same qualities that made the author's sermons so justly and so widely popular. They manifest the same earnest, liberal spirit, the ardent love of truth, the lucid eloquence, the wide sympathy, and singleness of purpose."—*Literary Gazette.*

"We value this volume for its frankness and earnestness."—*Critic.*

"They throw some new light on the constitution of Robertson's mind, and on the direction in which it was unfolding itself."—*Saturday Review.*

"It is in papers such as these that Frederick Robertson makes the world his debtor."—*Constitutional Press.*

"In these addresses we are gladdened by rare liberality of view and range of sympathy boldly expressed."—*Daily Telegraph.*

3

# NEW WORKS ON INDIA AND THE EAST.

## *Personal Adventures during the Indian Rebellion, in Rohilcund, Futteghur, and Oude.* By W. EDWARDS, Esq., B.C.S.

*Fourth Edition. Post 8vo, price 6s. cloth.*

"For touching incidents, hair-breadth 'scapes, and the pathos of suffering almost incredible, there has appeared nothing like this little book of personal adventures. For the first time we seem to realize the magnitude of the afflictions which have befallen our unhappy countrymen in the East. The terrible drama comes before us, and we are by turns bewildered with horror, stung to fierce indignation, and melted to tears. We have here a tale of suffering such as may have been equalled, but never surpassed. These real adventures, which no effort of the imagination can surpass, will find a sympathising public."—*Athenæum.*

"Mr. Edwards's narrative is one of the most deeply interesting episodes of a story of which the least striking portions cannot be read without emotion. He tells his story with simplicity and manliness, and it bears the impress of that earnest and unaffected reverence to the will and hand of God, which was the stay and comfort of many other brave hearts."—*Guardian.*

"The narrative of Mr. Edwards's suffering and escapes is full of interest; it tells many a painful tale, but it also exhibits a man patient under adversity, and looking to the God and Father of us all for guidance and support."—*Eclectic Review.*

"Among the stories of hair-breadth escapes in India this is one of the most interesting and touching."—*Examiner.*

"A fascinating little book."—*National Review.*

"A very touching narrative."—*Lit. Gazette.*

"No account of it can do it justice."—*Globe.*

## *The Chaplain's Narrative of the Siege of Delhi.* By the Rev. J. E. W. ROTTON, Chaplain to the Delhi Field Force.

*Post 8vo, with a Plan of the City and Siege Works, price 10s. 6d. cloth.*

"Mr. Rotton's work commends itself to us as a clear, succinct, and most instructive narrative of the siege of Delhi. It brings vividly before us the scenes and dread realities of military life in the encampment before the beleaguered city, and makes us familiar with many interesting events which find no place in the usual military despatches."—*Observer.*

"We shall rejoice if the 'Chaplain's Narrative' re-wakens attention to the incomparable merits of the army of Delhi; and we think it is well calculated to do so, being a simple and touching statement, which bears the impress of truth in every word. It has this advantage over the accounts which have yet been published, that it supplies some of those personal anecdotes and minute details which bring the events home to the understanding."—*Athenæum.*

"'The Chaplain's Narrative' is remarkable for its pictures of men in a moral and religious aspect, during the progress of a harassing siege and when suddenly stricken down by the enemy or disease. The book contains many anecdotes exhibiting human nature under trying circumstances, and not unfavourably standing the test; it presents a picture of the social and physical evils the gallant army of Delhi had to encounter, and it well exhibits the incessant nature of the attacks made upon the key to its position."—*Spectator.*

"A plain unvarnished record of what came under a Field Chaplain's daily observation. Our author is a sincere, hardworking, and generous minded man, and his work will be most acceptable to the friends and relations of the many Christian heroes whose fate it tells, and to whose later hours it alludes."—*Leader.*

"A book which has value as a careful narrative by an eye witness of one of the most stirring episodes of the Indian campaign, and interest as an earnest record by a Christian minister of some of the most touching scenes which can come under observation."—*Literary Gazette.*

"The speciality of Mr. Rotton's narrative consists in his testimony, not to the reckless valour of our men when actually under fire: of that we hardly require to be reminded; but in his commemoration of their steady constancy and endurance under privation, and the spirit of religious earnestness which alike inspired effort in the field, and resignation on the deathbed."—*Press.*

"A close record of the events of the siege, by an eye witness."—*Examiner.*

"The military operations are detailed with clearness, and the most conspicuous deeds of heroism are fully described. We have several deathbed scenes."—*Economist.*

"These pages are full of matter which cannot fail to interest a large number of readers of all classes."—*Globe.*

"Perhaps the most complete account of that great military operation which has yet appeared."—*Critic.*

## *The Crisis in the Punjab.* By FREDERICK H. COOPER, Esq., C.S., Umritsir.

*Post 8vo, with Map, price 7s. 6d. cloth.*

"The book is full of terrible interest. The narrative is written with vigour and earnestness, and is full of the most tragic interest."—*Economist.*

"One of the most interesting and spirited books which have sprung out of the sepoy mutiny."—*Globe.*

6

## NEW WORKS ON INDIA AND THE EAST—
### *Continued.*

## Life and Correspondence of Lord Metcalfe.
### BY JOHN WILLIAM KAYE.

*New and Cheap Edition, in 2 Vols., Small Post 8vo, with Portrait, price 12s. cloth.*

" Lord Metcalfe possessed extraordinary opportunities of making himself acquainted with the native character, and of estimating at its correct value the nature of the tenure by which our Indian possessions were held; and at the present time we can value more highly the great practical discernment of one whose fortune it was to be laughed at by the superficial, because he believed in the insecurity of our Indian empire. Some additions which have been made to the present volumes, place in a strong light the sagacity and good sense of Lord Metcalfe. . . . The present demand for a new edition is a sufficient commendation of a work which has already occupied the highest rank among biographies of the great men of modern times."—*Observer.*

" A new and revised edition of the life of one of the greatest and purest men that ever aided in governing India. The new edition not only places a very instructive book within the reach of a greater number of persons, but contains new matter of the utmost value and interest."—*Critic.*

" One of the most valuable biographies of the present day. This revised edition has several fresh passages of high interest, now first inserted from among Lord Metcalfe's papers, in which his clear prescience of the dangers that threatened our Indian empire is remarkably shown. Both in price and price the new edition is a great improvement on the original work."—*Economist.*

" Mr. Kaye's life of Lord Metcalfe is a work too well known to need an extended notice; but there is something to be said for this republication. It is an edition revised with care and judgment. Mr. Kaye has judiciously condensed that portion of his original work which relates to the earlier career of the great Indian statesman. Another improvement in the work will be found in the augmentation of that part setting forth Lord Metcalfe's views of the insecurity of our Indian empire. The insecurity which cast a gloom over Metcalfe's predictions has been fearfully verified by the events of 1857."—*Globe.*

" A much improved edition of one of the most interesting political biographies in English literature."—*National Review.*

## The Life and Correspondence of Sir John
### Malcolm, G.C.B. BY JOHN WILLIAM KAYE.
### *Two Volumes, 8vo. With Portrait. Price 36s. cloth.*

"The biography is replete with interest and information, deserving to be perused by the student of Indian history, and sure to recommend itself to the general reader."—*Athenæum.*

" One of the most interesting of the recent biographies of our great Indian statesmen."—*National Review.*

"This book deserves to participate in the popularity which it was the good fortune of Sir John Malcolm to enjoy."—*Edinburgh Review.*

" Mr. Kaye has used his materials well, and has written an interesting narrative, copiously illustrated with valuable documents."—*Examiner.*

"There are a great many matters of general interest in these volumes. Not a little of the spirit of Arthur Wellesley runs through the book."—*Globe.*

" Thoroughly agreeable, instructive reading."—*Westminster Review.*

" A very valuable contribution to our Indian literature. We recommend it strongly to all who desire to learn something of the history of British India."—*New Quarterly Review.*

" Mr. Kaye's biography is at once a contribution to the history of our policy and dominion in the East, and a worthy memorial of one of those wise and large hearted men whose energy and principle have made England great."—*British Quarterly Review.*

## The Parsees : their History, Religion, Manners,
### and Customs. BY DOSABHOY FRAMJEE.
### *Post 8vo, price 10s. cloth.*

"Our author's account of the inner life of the Parsees will be read with interest."—*Daily News.*

" A very curious and well written book, by a young Parsee, on the manners and customs of his own race."—*National Review.*

"An acceptable addition to our literature. It gives information which many will be glad to have carefully gathered together, and formed into a shapely whole."—*Economist.*

## Suggestions Towards the Future Government
### of India. BY HARRIET MARTINEAU.
### *Second Edition. Demy 8vo, price 5s. cloth.*

"As the work of an honest able writer, these Suggestions are well worthy of attention, and no doubt they will generally be duly appreciated."—*Observer.*

"Genuine honest utterances of a clear, sound understanding, neither obscured nor enfeebled by party prejudice or personal selfishness. We cordially recommend all who are in search of the truth to peruse and reperuse these pages."—*Daily News.*

## British Rule in India. BY HARRIET MARTINEAU.
### *Sixth Thousand. Price 2s. 6d. cloth.*

" A good compendium of a great subject."—*National Review.*

" A succinct and comprehensive volume."—*Leader.*

.•. A reliable class-book for examination in the history of British India.

# NEW WORKS ON INDIA AND THE EAST—
## *Continued.*

## *The Defence of Lucknow:* A STAFF-OFFICER'S DIARY. By Capt. THOS. F. WILSON, 13th Bengal N. I., Assistant-Adjutant-General.

### *Sixth Thousand. With Plan of the Residency. Small post 8vo., price 2s. 6d.*

"Unadorned and simple, the story is, nevertheless, an eloquent one. This is a narrative not to be laid down until the last line has been read."—*Leader.*

"The Staff-Officer's Diary is simple and brief, and has a special interest, inasmuch as it gives a fuller account than we have elsewhere seen of those operations which were the chief human means of salvation to our friends in Lucknow. The Staff-Officer brings home to us, by his details,

the nature of that underground contest, upon the result of which the fate of the beleaguered garrison especially depended."—*Examiner.*

"We commend the Staff-Officer's Diary for its unostentatious relation of facts, recorded with a degree of distinctness that vouches for the authenticity of the writer's statement."—*Press.*

"The Staff-Officer supplies exact military information with brevity and distinctness."—*Globe.*

## *Tiger-Shooting in India.* By LIEUTENANT WILLIAM RICE, 25th Bombay N. I.

### *Super Royal 8vo. With Twelve Plates in Chroma-lithography. 21s. cloth.*

"These adventures, told in handsome large print, with spirited chromo-lithographs to illustrate them, make the volume before us as pleasant reading as any record of sporting achievements we have ever taken in hand."—*Athenæum.*

"A remarkably pleasant book of adventures during several seasons of 'large game' hunting in Rajpootana. The twelve chromo-lithographs

are very valuable accessories to the narrative; they have wonderful spirit and freshness."—*Globe.*

"A good volume of wild sport, abounding in adventure, and handsomely illustrated with coloured plates from spirited designs by the author."—*Examiner.*

## *The Commerce of India with Europe, and its Political Effects.* By B. A. IRVING, Esq.

### *Post 8vo, price 7s. 6d. cloth.*

"Mr. Irving's work is that of a man thoroughly versed in his subject. It is a historical handbook of the progress and vicissitudes of European trade with India."—*Economist.*

## *Views and Opinions of Brigadier-General Jacob, C.B.* Edited by Captain LEWIS PELLY.

### *Demy 8vo, price 12s. cloth.*

"The statesmanlike views and broad opinions enunciated in this work would command attention under any circumstances, but coming from one of such experience and authority they are doubly valuable, and merit the consideration of legislators and politicians."—*Sun.*

"The facts in this book are worth looking at. If the reader desires to take a peep into the interior of the mind of a great man, let him make

acquaintance with the 'Views and Opinions of General Jacob.'"—*Globe.*

"This is truly a gallant and soldierly book; very Napierish in its self-confidence, in its capital sense, and in its devotedness to professional honour and the public good. The book should be studied by all who are interested in the choice of a new government for India."—*Daily News.*

## *Papers of the late Lord Metcalfe.* Selected and Edited by J. W. KAYE. *Demy 8vo, price 16s. cloth.*

"We commend this volume to all persons who like to study State papers, in which the practical sense of a man of the world is joined to the

speculative sagacity of a philosophical statesman. No Indian library should be without it."—*Press.*

## *The Life of Mahomet and History of Islam to the Era of the Hegira.* By WILLIAM MUIR, Esq., Bengal Civil Service. *Two volumes 8vo, price 32s. cloth.*

"The most perfect life of Mahomet in the English language, or perhaps in any other. . . . The work is at once learned and interesting, and

it cannot fail to be eagerly perused by all persons having any pretensions to historical knowledge."—*Observer.*

9

# MR. RUSKIN'S WORKS ON ART.

## The Elements of Drawing.

*Second Edition. Crown 8vo. With Illustrations drawn by the Author. Price 7s. 6d., cloth.*

"The rules are clearly and fully laid down; and the earlier exercises always conducive to the end by simple and unembarrassing means. The whole volume is full of liveliness."—*Spectator.*

"We close this book with a feeling that, though nothing supersedes a master, yet that no student of art should launch forth without this work as a compass."—*Athenæum.*

"It will be found not only an invaluable acquisition to the student, but agreeable and instructive reading for any one who wishes to refine his perceptions of natural scenery, and of its worthiest artistic representations."—*Economist.*

"Original as this treatise is, it cannot fail to be at once instructive and suggestive."—*Literary Gazette.*

"The most useful and practical book on the subject which has ever come under our notice."—*Press.*

## Modern Painters, Vol. IV. On Mountain Beauty.

*Imperial 8vo, with Thirty-five Illustrations engraved on Steel, and 116 Woodcuts, drawn by the Author. Price 2l. 10s. cloth.*

"The present volume of Mr. Ruskin's elaborate work treats chiefly of mountain scenery, and discusses at length the principles involved in the pleasure we derive from mountains and their pictorial representation. The singular beauty of his style, the hearty sympathy with all forms of natural loveliness, the profusion of his illustrations form irresistible attractions."—*Daily News.*

"Considered as an illustrated volume, this is the most remarkable which Mr. Ruskin has yet issued. The plates and woodcuts are profuse, and include numerous drawings of mountain form by the author, which prove Mr. Ruskin to be essentially an artist. He is an unique man, both among artists and writers."—*Spectator.*

"The fourth volume brings fresh stores of wondrous eloquence, close and patient observation, and subtle disquisition. Such a writer is a national possession. He adds to our store of knowledge and enjoyment."—*Leader.*

"Mr. Ruskin is the most eloquent and thought-awakening writer on nature in its relation with art, and the most potent influence by the pen, of young artists, whom this country can boast."—*National Review.*

## Modern Painters, Vol. III. Of Many Things.

*With Eighteen Illustrations drawn by the Author, and engraved on Steel. Price 38s. cloth.*

"Every one who cares about nature, or poetry, or the story of human development—every one who has a tinge of literature or philosophy, will find something that is for him in this volume."—*Westminster Review.*

"Mr. Ruskin is in possession of a clear and penetrating mind; he is undeniably practical in his fundamental ideas; full of the deepest reverence for all that appears to him beautiful and holy. His style is, as usual, clear, bold, racy. Mr. Ruskin is one of the first writers of the day."—*Economist.*

"The present volume, viewed as a literary achievement, is the highest and most striking evidence of the author's abilities that has yet been published."—*Leader.*

"All, it is to be hoped, will read the book for themselves. They will find it well worth a careful perusal."—*Saturday Review.*

"This work is eminently suggestive, full of new thoughts, of brilliant descriptions of scenery, and eloquent moral application of them."—*New Quarterly Review.*

"Mr. Ruskin has deservedly won for himself a place in the first rank of modern writers upon the theory of the fine arts."—*Eclectic Review.*

## Modern Painters. Vols. I. and II.

*Imperial 8vo. Vol. I., 5th Edition, 18s. cloth. Vol. II., 4th Edition. Price 10s. 6d. cloth.*

"A generous and impassioned review of the works of living painters. A hearty and earnest work, full of deep thought, and developing great and striking truths in art."—*British Quarterly Review.*

"A very extraordinary and delightful book, full of truth and goodness, of power and beauty."—*North British Review.*

"Mr. Ruskin's work will send the painter more than ever to the study of nature; will train men who have always been delighted spectators of nature, to be also attentive observers. Our critics will learn to admire, and mere admirers will learn how to criticise: thus a public will be educated."—*Blackwood's Magazine.*

10

SMITH, ELDER AND CO.

## WORKS OF MR. RUSKIN—*continued.*

### *The Stones of Venice.*

*Complete in Three Volumes, Imperial 8vo, with Fifty-three Plates and numerous Woodcuts, drawn by the Author. Price 5l. 15s. 6d., cloth.*

**EACH VOLUME MAY BE HAD SEPARATELY.**

Vol. I. THE FOUNDATIONS, with 21 Plates, price 2l. 2s. 2nd Edition.

Vol. II. THE SEA STORIES, with 20 Plates, price 2l. 2s.

Vol. III. THE FALL, with 12 Plates, price 1l. 11s. 6d.

"The 'Stones of Venice' is the production of an earnest, religious, progressive, and informed mind. The author of this essay on architecture has condensed it into a poetic apprehension, the fruit of awe of God, and delight in nature; a knowledge, love, and just estimate of art; a holding fast to fact and repudiation of hearsay; an historic breadth, and a fearless challenge of existing social problems, whose union we know not where to find paralleled."—*Spectator.*

"This book is one which, perhaps, no other man could have written, and one for which the world ought to be and will be thankful. It is in the highest degree eloquent, acute, stimulating to thought, and fertile in suggestion. It will, we are convinced, elevate taste and intellect, raise the tone of moral feeling, kindle benevolence towards men, and increase the love and fear of God."—*Times.*

### *The Seven Lamps of Architecture.*

*Second Edition, with Fourteen Plates drawn by the Author. Imperial 8vo. Price 1l. 1s. cloth.*

"By 'The Seven Lamps of Architecture,' we understand Mr. Ruskin to mean the Seven fundamental and cardinal laws, the observance of and obedience to which are indispensable to the architect, who would deserve the name. The moralist, the theologist, the divine, will find in it ample store of instructive matter, as well as the artist. The author of this work belongs to a class of thinkers of whom we have too few amongst us."—*Examiner.*

"Mr. Ruskin's book bears so unmistakeably the marks of keen and accurate observation, of a true and subtle judgment and refined sense of beauty, joined with so much earnestness, so noble a sense of the purposes and business of art, and such a command of rich and glowing language, that it cannot but tell powerfully in producing a more religious view of the uses of architecture, and a deeper insight into its artistic principles."—*Guardian.*

### *Lectures on Architecture and Painting.*

*With Fourteen Cuts, drawn by the Author. Second Edition. Crown 8vo. Price 8s. 6d. cloth.*

"Mr. Ruskin's lectures—eloquent, graphic, and impassioned—exposing and ridiculing some of the vices of our present system of building, and exciting his hearers by strong motives of duty and pleasure to attend to architecture—are very successful."—*Economist.*

"We conceive it to be impossible that any intelligent persons could listen to the lectures, however they might differ from the judgments asserted, and from the general propositions laid down, without an elevating influence and an aroused enthusiasm."—*Spectator.*

### *The Political Economy of Art.* Price 2s. 6d. cloth.

"A most able, eloquent, and well-timed work. We hail it with satisfaction, thinking it calculated to do much practical good, and we cordially recommend it to our readers."—*Witness.*

"Mr. Ruskin's chief purpose is to treat the artist's power, and the art itself, as items of the world's wealth, and to show how these may be best evolved, produced, accumulated, and distributed."—*Athenæum.*

"We never quit Mr. Ruskin without being the better for what he has told us, and therefore we recommend this little volume, like all his other works, to the perusal of our readers."—*Economist.*

"This book, daring, as it is, glances keenly at principles, of which some are among the articles of ancient codes, while others are evolving slowly to the light."—*Leader.*

### *Notes on the Pictures in the Exhibition of the Royal Academy, &c., for* 1858. By JOHN RUSKIN.

*Fifth Thousand. 8vo, price One Shilling.*

### *A Portrait of John Ruskin, Esq., Engraved by* F. HOLL, *from a Drawing by* GEORGE RICHMOND.

*Prints, One Guinea; India Proofs, Two Guineas.*

11

## MISCELLANEOUS.

**ANNALS OF BRITISH LEGIS-LATION,** A CLASSIFIED SUMMARY OF PARLIAMENTARY PAPERS. Ed. by Professor LEONE LEVI. The yearly issue consists of 1,000 pages, super royal 8vo, and the Subscription is Two Guineas, payable in advance. The Twenty-eighth Part is just issued.

"A series that will, if it be always managed as it now is by Professor Levi, last as long as there remains a Legislature in Great Britain. These Annals are to give the essence of work done and information garnered for the State during each legislative year, a summary description of every Act passed, a digest of the vital facts contained in every Blue Book issued, and of all documents relating to the public business of the country. The series will live, while generations of men die, if it be maintained in its old age as ably and as conscientiously as it is now in its youth."—*Examiner.*

"The idea was admirable, nor does the execution fall short of the plan. To accomplish this effectively, and at the same time briefly, was not an easy task; but Professor Levi has undertaken it with great success. The work is essentially a guide. It will satisfy those persons who refer to it merely for general purposes, while it will direct the research of others whose investigations take a wider range."—*Athenæum.*

**ANTIQUITIES OF KERTCH,** AND RESEARCHES IN THE CIM-MERIAN BOSPHORUS. By DUNCAN McPHERSON, M.D., of the Madras Army, F.R.G.S., M.A.I. Imp. 4to, with Fourteen Plates and numerous Illustrations, including Eight Coloured Fac-Similes of Relics of Antique Art, price Two Guineas.

"It is a volume which deserves the careful attention of every student of classical antiquity. No one can fail to be pleased with a work which has so much to attract the eye and to gratify the love of beauty and elegance in design. . . . The book is got up with great care and taste, and forms one of the handsomest works that have recently issued from the English press."—*Saturday Review.*

**WESTGARTH'S VICTORIA,** AND THE AUSTRALIAN GOLD MINES IN 1857. Post 8vo, with Maps, price 10s. 6d. cloth.

"Mr. Westgarth has produced a reliable and readable book well stocked with information, and pleasantly interspersed with incidents of travel and views of colonial life. It is clear, sensible, and suggestive."—*Athenæum.*

"A lively account of the most wonderful bit of colonial experience that the world's history has furnished."—*Examiner.*

"We think Mr. Westgarth's book much the best which has appeared on Australia since the great crisis in its history."—*Saturday Review.*

"A rational, vigorous, illustrative report upon the progress of the greatest colony in Australia."—*Leader.*

"The volume contains a large amount of statistical and practical information relating to Victoria."—*Spectator.*

"To those who refer to these pages for solid and guiding information, they will prove most valuable."—*Globe.*

"The best book on the subject."—*Critic.*

12

**TAULER'S LIFE AND SERMONS.** Translated by Miss SUSANNA WINK-WORTH. With a Preface by the Rev. CHARLES KINGSLEY. Small 4to, printed on Tinted Paper, and bound in Antique Style, with red edges, suitable for a Present. Price 7s. 6d.

"Miss Winkworth has done a service, not only to church history and to literature, but to those who seek simple and true-hearted devotional reading, or who desire to kindle their own piety through the example of saintly men, by producing a very instructive, complete, and deeply interesting life of Tauler, and by giving to us also a sample of Tauler's sermons tastefully and vigorously translated."—*Guardian.*

"No difference of opinion can be felt as to the intrinsic value of these sermons, or the general interest attaching to this book. The Sermons are well selected, and the translation excellent."—*Athenæum.*

"The sermons are chiefly remarkable for their simple earnestness and directness. The translation is easy and good."—*National Review.*

"The sermons of Dr. John Tauler have merit, and of the highest kind."—*New Quarterly.*

**CHANDLESS'S VISIT TO SALT LAKE:** BEING A JOURNEY ACROSS THE PLAINS TO THE MORMON SETTLEMENTS AT UTAH. Post 8vo, with a Map, price 2s. 6d. cloth.

"Mr. Chandless is an impartial observer of the Mormons. He gives a full account of the nature of the country, the religion of the Mormons, their government, institutions, morality, and the singular relationship of the sexes, with its consequences."—*Critic.*

"Those who would understand what Mormonism is can do no better than read this authentic, though light and lively volume."—*Leader.*

"It impresses the reader as faithful."—*National Review.*

**DOUBLEDAY'S LIFE OF SIR ROBERT PEEL.** Two volumes, 8vo, price 18s. cloth.

"It is a good book of its kind. . . . It is well worth reading, and very pleasantly and sensibly written."—*Saturday Review.*

"This biography is a work of great merit, conscientiously prepared, plain, clear, and practically interesting."—*Leader.*

"It is a production of great merit, and we hail it as a most valuable contribution to economical and statistical science."—*British Quarterly.*

**CAYLEY'S EUROPEAN REVOLU-TIONS OF 1848.** Crown 8vo, price 6s. cloth.

"Mr. Cayley has evidently studied his subject thoroughly, he has consequently produced an interesting and philosophical, though unpretending history of an important epoch."—*New Quarterly.*

"Two instructive volumes."—*Observer.*

## MISCELLANEOUS—*continued.*

### BUNSEN'S (CHEVALIER) SIGNS OF THE TIMES; OR, THE DANGERS TO RELIGIOUS LIBERTY IN THE PRESENT DAY. Translated by Miss SUSANNA WINKWORTH. One volume, 8vo, price 5s. cloth.

"A valuable work by a man of consummate intellect, and on a subject second to none in interest and importance."—*Economist.*

"Dr. Bunsen is doing good service, not only to his country but to Christendom, by sounding an alarm touching the dangers to religious liberty in the present state of the world."—*British Quarterly.*

### THE COURT OF HENRY VIII.: BEING A SELECTION OF THE DESPATCHES OF SEBASTIAN GIUSTINIAN, VENETIAN AMBASSADOR, 1515-1519. Translated by RAWDON BROWN. Two vols., crown 8vo, price 21s. cloth.

"It is seldom that a page of genuine old history is reproduced for us with as much evidence of painstaking and real love of the subject as in the selection of despatches made and edited by Mr. Rawdon Brown."—*Times.*

"The despatches of Giustinian furnish valuable illustrations of English politics at a critical epoch."—*Globe.*

"Very interesting and suggestive volumes."—*British Quarterly Review.*

"Most ably edited."—*Fraser's Magazine.*

### PAYN'S STORIES AND SKETCHES. Post 8vo, price 2s. 6d. cloth.;

"A volume of pleasant reading. Some of the papers have true attic salt in them."—*Literary Gazette.*

"Mr. Payn is gay, spirited, observant, and shows no little knowledge of men and books."—*Leader.*

"A most amusing volume, full of humorous adventure and pleasant satire."—*Press.*

### STONEY'S RESIDENCE IN TASMANIA. Demy 8vo, with Plates, Cuts, and a Map, price 14s. cloth.

"A plain and clear account of the colonies in Van Diemen's Land."—*Athenæum.*

"A perfect guide-book to Van Diemen's Land."—*Examiner.*

"One of the most accurately descriptive books upon Van Diemen's Land that we remember to have read."—*New Quarterly.*

### THE PRINCIPLES OF AGRICULTURE; ESPECIALLY TROPICAL. By P. LOVELL PHILLIPS, M.D. Demy 8vo, price 7s. 6d. cloth.

"This volume should be in every farm-house, and it would pay a landlord to present it to his tenants."—*Critic.*

"This treatise contains nearly all that is known of the science of agriculture."—*Observer.*

### FORBES' (SIR JOHN) SIGHT-SEEING IN GERMANY AND THE TYROL. Post 8vo, with Map and View, price 10s. 6d. cloth.

"Sir John Forbes's volume fully justifies its title. Wherever he went he visited sights, and has rendered a faithful and extremely interesting account of them."—*Literary Gazette.*

### CONOLLY ON THE TREATMENT OF THE INSANE. Demy 8vo, price 14s. cloth.

"Dr. Conolly has embodied in this work his experiences of the new system of treating patients at Hanwell Asylum."—*Economist.*

"We most earnestly commend Dr. Conolly's treatise to all who are interested in the subject."—*Westminster Review.*

### ROSS'S ACCOUNT OF RED RIVER SETTLEMENT. One vol., post 8vo, price 10s. 6d. cloth.

"The subject is novel, curious, and not without interest, while a strong sense of the real obtains throughout."—*Spectator.*

"The history of the Red River Settlement is remarkable, if not unique, among colonial records."—*Literary Gazette.*

"One of the most interesting of the romances of civilization."—*Observer.*

### ROSS'S FUR HUNTERS OF THE FAR WEST. Two vols., post 8vo, with Map and Plate, 21s. cloth.

"A well written narrative of most exciting adventures."—*Guardian.*

"A narrative full of incident and dangerous adventure."—*Literary Gazette.*

"Mr. Ross's volumes have an historical value and present interest."—*Globe.*

"Mr. Ross's volumes supply many particulars not to be found in Lewis and Clarke or Hearne and Richardson."—*British Quarterly.*

### RUSSO-TURKISH CAMPAIGNS OF 1828-9. By Colonel CHESNEY, R.A., D.C.L., F.R.S. Third edition. Post 8vo, with Maps, price 12s. cloth.

"The only work on the subject suited to the military reader."—*United Service Gazette.*

"In a strategic point of view this work is very valuable."—*New Quarterly.*

### THE MILITIAMAN AT HOME AND ABROAD. With Two Etchings, by JOHN LEECH. Post 8vo, price 9s. cloth.

"Very amusing, and conveying an impression of faithfulness."—*National Review.*

"The author is humorous without being wilfully smart, sarcastic without bitterness, and shrewd without parading his knowledge and power of observation."—*Express.*

"A very lively, entertaining companion."—*Critic.*

"Quietly, but humorously, written."—*Athenæum.*

13

## MISCELLANEOUS—continued.

**THOMSON'S MILITARY FORCES AND INSTITUTIONS OF GREAT BRITAIN.** 8vo, price 5s. cloth.

"A well arranged and carefully digested compilation, giving a clear insight into the economy of the army, and the working of our military system."—Spectator.

**LEVI'S MANUAL OF THE MERCANTILE LAW OF GREAT BRITAIN AND IRELAND.** 8vo, price 12s. cloth.

"It is sound, clear, and practical. . . . Its contents are strictly those of a manual—a handbook for law chambers, offices, and counting-houses; requisite in most of such places, and superfluous in none."—Athenæum.

"Its simplicity and faithfulness make it an extremely serviceable book."—Examiner.

"An admirable work of the kind."—Law Times.

"It presents a fair summary of the law on the great subject of which it treats."—Law Magazine.

**THOMSON'S LAWS OF WAR AFFECTING COMMERCE AND SHIPPING.** Second edit., greatly enlarged. 8vo, price 4s. 6d. boards.

"Mr. Thomson treats of the immediate effects of war; of enemies and hostile property; of prizes and privateers; of license, ransoms, re-capture, and salvage of neutrality, contraband of war, blockade, right of search, armed neutralities, &c., &c."—Economist.

**UNDINE.** From the German of "De la Motte Fouqué." Price 1s. 6d.

**HOPKINS'S HANDBOOK OF AVERAGE.** 8vo, price 12s. 6d. cl.

**MORICE'S HAND-BOOK OF BRITISH MARITIME LAW.** 8vo, price 5s., cloth.

**WARING'S MANUAL OF THERAPEUTICS.** Fcap. 8vo, price 12s. 6d. cloth.

**VOGEL ON DISORDERS OF THE BLOOD.** Translated by CHUNDER COOMAL DEY. 8vo, price 7s. 6d. cloth.

**DUNCAN'S CAMPAIGN WITH THE TURKS IN ASIA.** Post 8vo, price 2s. 6d., cloth.

**SIR JOHN HERSCHEL'S ASTRONOMICAL OBSERVATIONS** MADE AT THE CAPE OF GOOD HOPE. 4to, with plates, price 4l. 4s. cloth.

**DARWIN'S GEOLOGICAL OBSERVATIONS** ON CORAL REEFS, VOLCANIC ISLANDS, AND ON SOUTH AMERICA. With Maps, Plates, and Woodcuts, 10s. 6d. cloth.

**SMITH'S ZOOLOGY OF SOUTH OF AFRICA.** Royal 4to, cloth, with Coloured Plates.

| | |
|---|---|
| MAMMALIA | 12 |
| AVES | 7 |
| REPTILIA | 5 |
| PISCES | 2 |
| INVERTEBRATA | 1 |

**THE BOTANY OF THE HIMALAYA.** Two vols., royal 4to, cloth, with Coloured Plates, reduced to 5l. 5s.

**LEVI'S COMMERCIAL LAW OF THE WORLD.** Two vols., royal 4to, price 6l. cloth.

**TRACK CHART OF THE COAST OF WESTERN INDIA.** Two sheets, price 15s.

**CENTRAL AMERICA.—A RESIDENCE ON THE MOSQUITO SHORE, ETC.** By THOMAS YOUNG. Second edition, post 8vo, price 2s.

**GOËTHE'S CONVERSATIONS WITH ECKERMANN.** Translated by JOHN OXENFORD. Two vols., post 8vo, 5s. cloth.

**M'CANN'S ARGENTINE PROVINCES, &c.** Two vols., post 8vo, with Illustrations, price 24s. cloth.

**ROSS'S ADVENTURES ON THE COLUMBIA RIVER.** Post 8vo, 2s. 6d. cloth.

**DOUBLEDAY'S TRUE LAW OF POPULATION.** Third edition, 8vo, 6s. cloth.

**SIR JOHN FORBES'S MEMORANDUMS IN IRELAND.** Two vols., post 8vo, price 1l. 1s. cloth.

**POETICS: AN ESSAY ON POETRY.** By E. S. DALLAS. Post 8vo, price 2s. 6d. cloth.

14

## MISCELLANEOUS—*continued.*

WOMEN OF CHRISTIANITY EXEMPLARY FOR PIETY AND CHARITY. By JULIA KAVANAGH. Post 8vo, with Portraits, price 5s., in embossed cloth.

WOMAN IN FRANCE. By JULIA KAVANAGH. Two vols., post 8vo, with Portraits, price 5s., cloth.

STEINMETZ'S NOVITIATE ; OR, THE JESUIT IN TRAINING. Third Edition, post 8vo, 2s. 6d. cloth.

A CONVERTED ATHEIST'S TESTIMONY TO THE TRUTH OF CHRISTIANITY. Fourth edition, fcap. 8vo, 3s. cloth.

SWAINSON'S LECTURES ON NEW ZEALAND. Crown 8vo, price 2s. 6d. cloth.

PLAYFORD'S HINTS FOR INVESTING MONEY. Second edition, post 8vo, price 2s. 6d. cloth.

LEIGH HUNT'S MEN, WOMEN, AND BOOKS. Two vols., price 10s. cloth.

LEIGH HUNT'S TABLE TALK. 3s. 6d. cloth.

LEIGH HUNT'S WIT AND HUMOUR. 5s. cloth.

LEIGH HUNT'S JAR OF HONEY FROM MOUNT HYBLA. Price 5s. cloth.

NATIONAL SONGS AND LEGENDS OF ROUMANIA. Translated by E. C. GRENVILLE MURRAY, Esq. With Music, crown 8vo, price 2s. 6d.

JUVENILE DELINQUENCY. The Prize Essays. By M. HILL and C. F. CORNWALLIS. Post 8vo, price 6s. cloth.

EVANS'S (REV. R. W.) SERMONS ON THE CHURCH OF GOD. 8vo, price 10s. 6d.

EVANS'S (REV. R. W.) RECTORY OF VALEHEAD. Fcap. cloth, price 3s.

THOMPSON'S AUSTRIA. Post 8vo, price 12s.

INDIAN MEAL BOOK : RECIPES FOR USING INDIAN CORN-FLOUR. By Miss LESLIE. Price 1s. 6d. sewed.

PAPER LANTERN FOR PUSEYITES. Price 1s.

TAYLER'S (REV. C. B.) SERMONS. 12mo, price 1s. 6d. By the Author of "Records of a Good Man's Life."

TAYLER'S (REV. C. B.) SOCIAL EVILS. In numbers, each complete, price 6d. each.

I.—THE MECHANIC.
II.—THE LADY AND THE LADY'S MAID.
III.—THE PASTOR OF DRONFELLS.
V.—THE COUNTRY TOWN.
VI.—LIVE AND LET LIVE; OR, THE MANCHESTER WEAVERS.
VII.—THE SEASIDE FARM.

EPITAPHS IN THE WORDS OF SCRIPTURE. Fcap., price 1s. 6d.

FUR PREDESTINATUS, DIALOGISMUS INTER CALVINISTAM ET FUREM. Post 8vo, price 1s. 6d.

OBLIGATIONS OF LITERATURE TO THE MOTHERS OF ENGLAND. By Miss HALSTED. Price 2s. 6d.

BOOK OF ENGLISH EPITHETS. Super royal 8vo, price 9s.

ELEMENTARY WORKS ON SOCIAL ECONOMY. Uniform in foolscap 8vo, half-bound.

I.—OUTLINES OF SOCIAL ECONOMY. 1s. 6d.
II.—PROGRESSIVE LESSONS IN SOCIAL SCIENCE.
III.—INTRODUCTION TO THE SOCIAL SCIENCES. 2s.
IV.—OUTLINES OF THE UNDERSTANDING. 2s.
V.—WHAT AM I? WHERE AM I? WHAT OUGHT I TO DO? &c. 1s. sewed.

*•* These works are recommended by the Committee of Council on Education.

15

# WORKS ON INDIA AND THE EAST.

**THE ENGLISH IN WESTERN INDIA:** BEING THE EARLY HISTORY OF THE FACTORY AT SURAT, OF BOMBAY. By PHILIP ANDERSON, A.M. 2nd edition, 8vo, price 14s. cloth.

"Quaint, curious, and amusing, this volume describes, from old manuscripts and obscure books, the life of English merchants in an Indian Factory. It contains fresh and amusing gossip, all bearing on events and characters of historical importance."—*Athenæum.*

"A book of permanent value."—*Guardian.*

**LIFE IN ANCIENT INDIA.** By Mrs. SPEIR. With Sixty Illustrations by G. SCHARF. 8vo, price 15s., elegantly bound in cloth, gilt edges.

"We should in vain seek for any other treatise which, in so short a space, gives so well-connected an account of the early period of Indian history."—*Daily News.*

"Whoever desires to have the best, the completest, and the most popular view of what Oriental scholars have made known to us respecting Ancient India must peruse the work of Mrs. Speir; in which he will find the story told in clear, correct, and unaffected English. The book is admirably got up."—*Examiner.*

**THE CAUVERY, KISTNAH, AND GODAVERY:** BEING A REPORT ON THE WORKS CONSTRUCTED ON THOSE RIVERS, FOR THE IRRIGATION OF PROVINCES IN THE PRESIDENCY OF MADRAS. By R. BAIRD SMITH, F.G.S., Lt.-Col. Bengal Engineers, &c., &c. In demy 8vo, with 19 Plans, price 28s. cloth.

"A most curious and interesting work."—*Economist.*

**THE BHILSA TOPES;** OR, BUDDHIST MONUMENTS OF CENTRAL INDIA. By Major CUNNINGHAM. One vol., 8vo, with Thirty-three Plates, price 30s. cloth.

"Of the Topes opened in various parts of India none have yielded so rich a harvest of important information as those of Bhilsa, opened by Major Cunningham and Lieut. Maisey; and which are described, with an abundance of highly curious graphic illustrations, in this most interesting book."—*Examiner.*

**THE CHINESE AND THEIR REBELLIONS.** By THOMAS TAYLOR MEADOWS. One thick volume, 8vo, with Maps, price 18s. cloth.

"Mr. Meadows' book is the work of a learned, conscientious, and observant person, and really important in many respects."—*Times.*

"Mr. Meadows has produced a work which deserves to be studied by all who would gain a true appreciation of Chinese character. Information is sown broad-cast through every page."—*Athenæum.*

**RIFLE PRACTICE.** By the late Brig.-Gen. JACOB, C.B. 4th edition, 8vo, 2s.

16

**TRACTS ON THE NATIVE ARMY OF INDIA.** By Brigadier-General JACOB, C.B. 8vo, price 2s. 6d.

**ADDISON'S TRAITS AND STORIES OF ANGLO-INDIAN LIFE.** With Eight Illustrations, price 5s. cloth.

"An entertaining and instructive volume of Indian anecdotes."—*Military Spectator.*

"Anecdotes and stories well calculated to illustrate Anglo-Indian life and the domestic manners and habits of Hindostan."—*Observer.*

"A pleasant collection of amusing anecdotes."—*Critic.*

**ON THE CULTURE AND COMMERCE OF COTTON IN INDIA.** By Dr. FORBES ROYLE. 8vo, price 18s. cloth.

**THE FIBROUS PLANTS OF INDIA** FITTED FOR CORDAGE, CLOTHING, AND PAPER. By Dr. FORBES ROYLE. 8vo, price 12s. cloth.

**THE PRODUCTIVE RESOURCES OF INDIA.** By Dr. FORBES ROYLE. Super royal 8vo, price 14s. cloth.

**ROYLE'S REVIEW OF THE MEASURES ADOPTED IN INDIA FOR THE IMPROVED CULTURE OF COTTON.** 8vo, 2s. 6d. cloth.

**A SKETCH OF ASSAM:** WITH SOME ACCOUNT OF THE HILL TRIBES. Coloured Plates, 8vo, price 14s. cloth.

**BUTLER'S TRAVELS AND ADVENTURES IN ASSAM.** One vol. 8vo, with Plates, price 12s. cloth.

**DR. WILSON ON INFANTICIDE IN WESTERN INDIA.** Demy 8vo, price 12s.

**CRAWFURD'S GRAMMAR AND DICTIONARY OF THE MALAY LANGUAGE.** 2 vols. 8vo, price 36s. cloth.

**ROBERTS'S INDIAN EXCHANGE TABLES.** 8vo, second edition, enlarged, price 10s. 6d. cloth.

**WARING ON ABSCESS IN THE LIVER.** 8vo, price 3s. 6d.

**LAURIE'S SECOND BURMESE WAR — RANGOON.** Post 8vo. with Plates, price 2s. 6d. cloth.

**LAURIE'S PEGU.** Post 8vo, price 14s. cloth.

# CHEAP SERIES OF POPULAR FICTIONS.

Well printed, in large Type, on good Paper, and strongly bound in cloth.

## JANE EYRE. By CURRER BELL. Price 2s. 6d. cloth.

"'Jane Eyre' is a remarkable production. Freshness and originality, truth and passion, singular felicity in the description of natural scenery and in the analysation of human thought, enable this tale to stand boldly out from the mass, and to assume its own place in the bright field of romantic literature."—*Times.*

"'Jane Eyre' is a book of decided power. The thoughts are true, sound, and original; and the style is resolute, straightforward, and to the purpose. The object and moral of the work are excellent."—*Examiner.*

"A very pathetic tale; very singular, and so like truth that it is difficult to avoid believing that much of the characters and incidents are taken from life. It is an episode in this work-a-day world, most interesting, and touched at once with a daring and delicate hand. It is a book for the enjoyment of a feeling heart and vigorous understanding."—*Blackwood's Magazine.*

"For many years there has been no work of such power, piquancy, and originality. Its very faults are on the side of vigour, and its beauties are all original. It is a book of singular fascination."—*Edinburgh Review.*

"Almost all that we require in a novelist the writer has; perception of character and power of delineating it; picturesqueness, passion, and knowledge of life. Reality—deep, significant reality—is the characteristic of this book."—*Fraser's Magazine.*

## SHIRLEY. By CURRER BELL. Price 2s. 6d. cloth.

"The peculiar power which was so greatly admired in 'Jane Eyre' is not absent from this book. It possesses deep interest, and an irresistible grasp of reality. There is a vividness and distinctness of conception in it quite marvellous. The power of graphic delineation and expression is intense. There are scenes which, for strength and delicacy of emotion, are not transcended in the range of English fiction."—*Examiner.*

"'Shirley' is an admirable book; totally free from cant, affectation, or conventional tinsel of any kind; genuine English in the independence and uprightness of the tone of thought, in the purity of heart and feeling which pervade it; genuine English in the masculine vigour or rough originality of its conception of character; and genuine English in style and diction."—*Morning Chronicle.*

"The same piercing and loving eye, and the same bold and poetic imagery, are exhibited here as in 'Jane Eyre.' Similar power is manifested in the delineation of character. With a few brief vigorous touches, the picture starts into distinctness."—*Edinburgh Review.*

"'Shirley' is very clever. It could not be otherwise. The faculty of graphic description, strong imagination, fervid and masculine diction, analytic skill, all are visible. . . . Gems of rare thought and glorious passion shine here and there."—*Times.*

"'Shirley' is a book demanding close perusal and careful consideration."—*Athenæum.*

"'Shirley' is a novel of remarkable power and brilliancy; it is calculated to rouse attention, excite the imagination, and keep the faculties in eager and impatient suspense."—*Morning Post.*

"'Shirley' is the anatomy of the female heart. It is a book which indicates exquisite feeling, and very great power of mind in the writer. The women are all divine."—*Daily News.*

18

## VILLETTE. By CURRER BELL. Price 2s. 6d. cloth.

"'Villette' is a most remarkable work—a production altogether *sui generis.* Fulness and vigour of thought mark almost every sentence, and there is a sort of easy power pervading the whole narrative such as we have rarely met."—*Edinburgh Review.*

"This novel amply sustains the fame of the author of 'Jane Eyre' and 'Shirley' as an original and powerful writer. 'Villette' is a most admirably written novel, everywhere original, everywhere shrewd."—*Examiner.*

"There is throughout a charm of freshness which is infinitely delightful: freshness in observation, freshness in feeling, freshness in expression."—*Literary Gazette.*

"The tale is one of the affections, and remarkable as a picture of manners. A burning heart glows throughout it, and one brilliantly distinct character keeps it alive."—*Athenæum.*

"'Villette' is crowded with beauties, for which we look to the clear sight, deep feeling, and singular though not extensive experience of life, which we associate with the name of Currer Bell."—*Daily News.*

"'Villette' is entitled to take a very high place in the literature of fiction. The reader will find character nicely conceived and powerfully depicted: he will discover much quiet humour, a lively wit, brilliant dialogue, vivid descriptions, reflections both new and true, sentiment free from cant and conventionality, and bursts of eloquence and poetry, flashing here and there."—*Critic.*

"The fascination of genius dwells in this book, which is, in our judgment, superior to any of Currer Bell's previous efforts. For originality of conception, grasp of character, elaboration and consistency of detail, and picturesque force of expression, few works in the English language can stand the test of comparison with it."—*Morning Post.*

## WUTHERING HEIGHTS AND AGNES GREY. By ELLIS and ACTON BELL. With Memoir by Currer Bell. Price 2s. 6d. cloth.

"There are passages in this book of 'Wuthering Heights' of which any novelist, past or present, might be proud. It has been said of Shakespeare that he drew cases which the physician might study; Ellis Bell has done no less."—*Palladium.*

"There is, at all events, keeping in the book; the groups of figures and the scenery are in harmony with each other. There is a touch of Salvator Rosa in all."—*Atlas.*

"'Wuthering Heights' bears the stamp of a profoundly individual, strong, and passionate mind. The memoir is one of the most touching chapters in literary biography."—*Nonconformist.*

## A LOST LOVE. By ASHFORD OWEN. Price 2s. cloth.

"'A Lost Love' is a story full of grace and genius. No outline of the story would give any idea of its beauty."—*Athenæum.*

"A tale at once moving and winning, natural and romantic, and certain to raise all the finer sympathies of the reader's nature."—*Press.*

"A real picture of woman's life."—*Westminster Review.*

"A very beautiful and touching story. It is true to nature, and appeals to all who have not forgotten love and youth."—*Globe.*

"A novel of great genius; beautiful and true as life itself."—*New Quarterly Review.*

"A striking and original story; a work of genius and sensibility."—*Saturday Review.*

"This volume displays unquestionable genius, and that of a high order."—*Lady's Newspaper.*

# NEW NOVELS.

### (TO BE HAD AT ALL LIBRARIES.)

**ELLEN RAYMOND; OR, UPS AND DOWNS.** By Mrs. VIDAL, Author of "Tales for the Bush," &c. 3 vols. *(Now ready)*

**LOST AND WON.** By GEORGIANA M. CRAIK, Author of "Riverston." 1 vol. 2nd Edition.

**AN OLD DEBT.** By FLORENCE DAWSON. 2 vols.

"A powerfully written novel; one of the best which has recently proceeded from a female hand. . . . The dialogue is vigorous and spirited."—*Morning Post.*

"The author possesses great and varied powers: her originality is unquestionable. Over the whole work is spread the delicate and indefinable charm of feminine taste and purity."—*Illustrated News of the World.*

**SYLVAN HOLT'S DAUGHTER.** By HOLME LEE, Author of "Kathie Brande," &c. 2nd edition. 3 vols.

"The well-established reputation of Holme Lee, as a novel writer, will receive an additional glory from the publication of 'Sylvan Holt's Daughter.' It is a charming tale of country life and character."—*Globe.*

"There is much that is attractive in 'Sylvan Holt's Daughter,' much that is graceful and refined, much that is fresh, healthy, and natural."—*Press.*

**MY LADY: A TALE OF MODERN LIFE.** 2 vols.

"'My Lady' is a fine specimen of an English matron, exhibiting that union of strength and gentleness, of common sense and romance, of energy and grace, which nearly approaches our ideal of womanhood."—*Press.*

"The story is told throughout with great strength of feeling, is well written, and has a plot that is by no means commonplace."—*Examiner.*

"A novel which may be read from beginning to end without skipping or fatigue, and with an interest that never flags."—*Literary Gazette.*

"A novel written by an author of distinction, who for the nonce assumes the anonymous."—*Illustrated News of the World.*

"'My Lady' evinces charming feeling and delicacy of touch. It is a novel that will be read with interest."—*Athenæum.*

**EVA DESMOND; OR, MUTATION.** 3 vols.

"A more beautiful creation than Eva it would be difficult to imagine. The novel is undoubtedly full of interest."—*Morning Post.*

"There is power, pathos, and originality in conception and catastrophe."—*Leader.*

"This interesting novel reminds us more of Mrs. Marsh than of any other writer of the day."—*Press.*

**THE CRUELEST WRONG OF ALL.** By the Author of "Margaret; or, Prejudice at Home." 1 vol.

"The author has a pathetic vein, and there is a tender sweetness in the tone of her narration."—*Leader.*

"It has the first requisite of a work meant to amuse: it is amusing."—*Globe.*

"This novel is written with considerable power: its tone is high, and the moral sound."—*Morning Herald.*

20

**THE MOORS AND THE FENS.** By F. G. TRAFFORD. 3 vols.

"This novel stands out much in the same way that 'Jane Eyre' did. . . . The characters are drawn by a mind which can realize fictitious characters with minute intensity."—*Saturday Review.*

"It is seldom that a first fiction is entitled to such applause as is 'The Moors and the Fens,' and we shall look anxiously for the writer's next essay."—*Critic.*

"The author has the gift of telling a story, and 'The Moors and the Fens' will be read."—*Athenæum.*

"This is one of the most original novels we have lately met with. . . . The characters really show a great deal of power."—*Press.*

**GASTON BLIGH.** By L. S. LAVENU, Author of "Erlesmere." 2 vols.

"'Gaston Bligh' is a good story, admirably told, full of stirring incident, sustaining to the close the interest of a very ingenious plot, and abounding in clever sketches of character. It sparkles with wit, and will reward perusal."—*Critic.*

"The story is told with great power; the whole book sparkles with esprit; and the characters talk like gentlemen and ladies. It is very enjoyable reading."—*Press.*

"A charming work of fiction."—*Morning Chronicle.*

**THE THREE CHANCES.** By the Author of "The Fair Carew." 3 vols.

"This novel is of a more solid texture than most of its contemporaries. It is full of good sense, good thought, and good writing."—*Statesman.*

"Some of the characters and romantic situations are strongly marked and peculiarly original. . . . It is the great merit of the authoress that the personages of her tale are human and real."—*Leader.*

"The authoress has a mind that thoroughly appreciates the humorous in life and character."—*Globe.*

**THE WHITE HOUSE BY THE SEA:** A LOVE STORY. By M. BETHAM-EDWARDS. 2 vols.

"A tale of English domestic life. The writing is very good, graceful, and unaffected; it pleases without startling. In the dialogue, people do not harangue, but talk, and talk naturally."—*Critic.*

"The narrative and scenes exhibit feminine spirit and quiet truth of delineation."—*Spectator.*

"A novel made up of love, pure and simple, in the form of an autobiography."—*Leader.*

**MAUD SKILLICORNE'S PENANCE.** By MARY C. JACKSON, Author of "The Story of My Wardship." 2 vols.

"The style is natural, and displays considerable dramatic power."—*Critic.*

"It is a well concocted tale, and will be very palatable to novel readers."—*Morning Post.*

# NEW NOVELS—*continued.*

## THE PROFESSOR. By CURRER BELL. 2 vols.

"We think the author's friends have shown sound judgment in publishing the 'Professor,' now that she is gone. . . . It shows the first germs of conception, which afterwards expanded and ripened into the great creations of her imagination. At the same time her advisers were equally right when they counselled her not to publish it in her lifetime. . . . But it abounds in merits."—*Saturday Review.*

"The idea is original, and we every here and there detect germs of that power which took the world by storm in 'Jane Eyre.' The rejection of the 'Professor' was, in our opinion, no less advantageous to the young authoress than creditable to the discernment of the booksellers."—*Press.*

"Any thing which throws light upon the growth and composition of such a mind cannot be otherwise than interesting. In the 'Professor' we may discover the germs of many trains of thinking, which afterwards came to be enlarged and illustrated in subsequent and more perfect works."—*Critic.*

"There is much new insight in it, much extremely characteristic genius, and one character, moreover, of fresher, lighter, and more airy grace."—*Economist.*

"We have read it with the deepest interest; and confidently predict that this legacy of Charlotte Brontë's genius will renew and confirm the general admiration of her extraordinary powers."—*Eclectic.*

## RIVERSTON. By GEORGIANA M. CRAIK. 3 vols.

"It is highly moral in its tone and character, as well as deeply interesting, and written in an excellent style."—*Morning Herald.*

"A decidedly good novel. The book is a very clever one, containing much good writing, well discriminated sketches of character, and a story told so as to bind the reader pretty closely to the text."—*Examiner.*

"Miss Craik is a very lively writer: she has wit, and she has sense, and she has made in the beautiful young governess, with her strong will, saucy independence, and promptness of repartee, an interesting picture."—*Press.*

"Miss Craik writes well; she can paint character, passions, manners, with considerable effect; her dialogue flows easily and expressively."—*Daily News.*

"A production of no little mark, and qualified to interest old as well as young."—*Leader.*

"Decidedly a clever book; giving hopes of a capacity in the writer for better things in the future."—*Economist.*

"The author shows great command of language, a force and clearness of expression not often met with. . . . We offer a welcome to Miss Craik, and we shall look with interest for her next work."—*Athenæum.*

## FARINA. By GEORGE MEREDITH. 1 vol.

"A masque of ravishers in steel, of robber knights; of water-women, more ravishing than lovely. It has also a brave and tender deliverer, and a heroine proper for a romance of Cologne. Those who love a real, lively, audacious piece of extravagance, by way of a change, will enjoy 'Farina.'"—*Athenæum.*

"An original and entertaining book."—*Westminster Review.*

"We cordially recommend it for general purchase and perusal."—*Daily News.*

"'Farina' cannot fail to amuse the most sober minded reader."—*Critic.*

"It has a true Rhenish flavour."—*Press.*

## BELOW THE SURFACE. 3 vols.

"The book is unquestionably clever and entertaining. The writer develops from first to last his double view of human life, as coloured by the manners of our age. . . . It is a tale superior to ordinary novels, in its practical application to the phases of actual life."—*Athenæum.*

"There is a great deal of cleverness in this story; a much greater knowledge of country life and character in its various aspects and conditions than is possessed by nine-tenths of the novelists who undertake to describe it."—*Spectator.*

"The novel is one that keeps the attention fixed, and it is written in a genial, often playful tone. The temper is throughout excellent."—*Examiner.*

"This is a book which possesses the rare merit of being exactly what it claims to be, a story of English country life; and, moreover, a very well told story."—*Daily News.*

"'Below the Surface' merits high praise. It is full of good things; good taste—good feeling—good writing—good notions, and high morality.'—*Globe.*

"Temperate, sensible, kindly, and pleasant."—*Saturday Review.*

"A more pleasant story we have not read for many a day."—*British Quarterly.*

## THE ROUA PASS. By ERICK MACKENZIE. 3 vols.

"It is seldom that we have to notice so good a novel as the 'Roua Pass.' The story is well contrived and well told; the incidents are natural and varied; several of the characters are skilfully drawn, and that of the heroine is fresh, powerful, and original. The Highland scenery, in which the plot is laid, is described with truth and feeling—with a command of language which leaves a vivid impression."—*Saturday Review.*

"The attractions of the story are so numerous and varied, that it would be difficult to single out any one point of it for attention. It is a brilliant social picture of sterling scenes and striking adventures."—*Sun.*

"'The Roua Pass' is a work of very great promise. It is beautifully written. The romance is ingenious and interesting; the story never flags."—*Critic.*

"The peculiar charm of the novel is its skilful painting of the Highlands, and of life among the Highlanders. Quick observation and a true sense of the poetry in nature and human life, the author has."—*Examiner.*

"A capital fiction. As a landscape novel, it is altogether delightful."—*Globe.*

"'The Roua Pass' is a good novel—the best of the season."—*Westminster Review.*

"This is a very good novel."—*Guardian.*

## THE NOBLE TRAYTOUR. A CHRONICLE. 3 vols.

"The 'Noble Traytour' is a chronicle, interesting for its facts, interesting for its association, and, above all, interesting and important for the clear views which it gives of the modes of life in 'merry England,' at the eventful period to which it refers."—*Observer.*

"It is an Elizabethan masquerade. Shakespeare, the Queen, Essex, Raleigh, and a hundred nobles, ladies, and knights of the land, appear on the stage. The author has imbued himself with the spirit of the times."—*Leader.*

"The story is told with a graphic and graceful pen, and the chronicler has produced a romance not only of great value in a historical point of view, but possessing many claims upon the attention of the scholar, the antiquary, and the general reader."—*Post.*

"The book has great merit. The portraits of Elizabeth and Essex are well and finely drawn."—*Critic.*

## POETRY.

**POEMS.** By Lieut.-Col. WILLIAM READ. (*In the Press.*)

**POEMS.** By FRED. W. WYON. Fcap. 8vo. Price 5s. cloth.

**IONICA.** Fcap. 8vo, 4s. cloth.

"The themes, mostly classical, are grappled with boldness, and toned with a lively imagination. The style is rich and firm, and cannot be said to be an imitation of any known author. We cordially recommend it to our readers as a book of real poetry."—*Critic.*

"The author is in his mood, quizzical, satirical, humorous, and didactic by turns, and in each mood he displays extraordinary power."—*Illustrated News of the World.*

**THE SIX LEGENDS OF KING GOLDENSTAR.** By the late ANNA BRADSTREET. Fcap. 8vo, price 5s.

"The author evinces more than ordinary power, a vivid imagination, guided by a mind of lofty aim."—*Globe.*

"The poetry is tasteful, and above the average."—*National Review.*

"This is a posthumous poem by an unknown authoress, of higher scope and more finish than the crowd of poems which come before us. The fancy throughout the poem is quick and light, and musical."—*Athenæum.*

**POEMS.** By ADA TREVANION. 5s. cl.

"There really is a value in such poems as those of Ada Trevanion. They give an image of what many women are on their best side. Perhaps nowhere can we point to a more satisfactory fruit of Christian civilisation than in a volume like this."—*Saturday Review.*

"There are many passages in Miss Trevanion's poems full of grace and tenderness, and as sweet as music on the water."—*Press.*

**POEMS.** By HENRY CECIL. 5s. cloth.

"He shows power in his sonnets, while in his lighter and less restrictive measures the lyric element is dominant. . . . . If Mr. Cecil does not make his name famous, it is not that he does not deserve to do so."—*Critic.*

"There is an unmistakeable stamp of genuine poetry in most of these pages."—*Economist.*

"Mr. Cecil's poems display qualities which stamp them the productions of a fine imagination and a cultivated taste."—*Morning Herald.*

**ENGLAND IN TIME OF WAR.** By SYDNEY DOBELL, Author of "Balder," "The Roman," &c. Crown 8vo, 5s. cloth.

"That Mr. Dobell is a poet, 'England in time of War' bears witness."—*Athenæum.*

**THE CRUEL SISTER,** AND OTHER POEMS. Fcap. 8vo, 4s. cloth.

"There are traces of power, and the versification displays freedom and skill."—*Guardian.*

**POEMS OF PAST YEARS.** By Sir ARTHUR HALLAM ELTON, Bart., M.P. Fcap. 8vo, 3s. cloth.

"A refined, scholarly, and gentlemanly mind is apparent all through this volume."—*Leader.*

**POEMS.** By Mrs. FRANK P. FELLOWS. Fcap. 8vo, 3s. cloth.

"There is easy simplicity in the diction, and elegant naturalness in the thought."—*Spectator.*

**POETRY FROM LIFE.** By C. M. K. Fcap. 8vo, cloth gilt, 5s.

"Elegant verses. The author has a pleasing fancy and a refined mind."—*Economist.*

**POEMS.** By WALTER R. CASSELS. Fcap. 8vo. 3s. 6d., cloth.

"Mr. Cassels has deep poetical feeling, and gives promise of real excellence. His poems are written sometimes with a strength of expression by no means common."—*Guardian.*

**GARLANDS OF VERSE.** By THOMAS LEIGH. 5s. cloth.

"One of the best things in the 'Garlands of Verse' is an Ode to Toil. There, as elsewhere, there is excellent feeling."—*Examiner.*

**BALDER.** By SYDNEY DOBELL. Crown 8vo, 7s. 6d., cloth.

"The writer has fine qualities; his level of thought is lofty, and his passion for the beautiful has the truth of instinct."—*Athenæum.*

**POEMS.** By WILLIAM BELL SCOTT. Fcap. 8vo, 5s., cloth.

"Mr. Scott has poetical feeling, keen observation, deep thought, and command of language."—*Spectator.*

**POEMS.** By MARY MAYNARD. Fcap. 8vo, 4s., cloth.

"We have rarely met with a volume of poems displaying so large an amount of power, blended with so much delicacy of feeling and grace of expression."—*Church of England Quarterly.*

**POEMS.** By CURRER, ELLIS, and ACTON BELL. 4s., cloth.

**SELECT ODES OF HORACE.** In English Lyrics. By J. T. BLACK. Fcap. 8vo, price 4s., cloth.

"Rendered into English Lyrics with a vigour and heartiness rarely, if ever, surpassed."—*Critic.*

**RHYMES AND RECOLLECTIONS OF A HAND-LOOM WEAVER.** By WILLIAM THOM. With Memoir. Post 8vo, cloth, price 3s.

**KING RENE'S DAUGHTER.** Fcap. 8vo, price 2s. 6d. cloth.

**MAID OF ORLEANS,** AND OTHER POEMS. Translated from SCHILLER. Fcap. 8vo, price 2s. 6d.

---

London: Printed by SMITH, ELDER and Co., Little Green Arbour Court.

CPSIA information can be obtained at www.ICGtesting.com
Printed in the USA
LVOW112006170613

338961LV00012B/396/P